Alternative Credit Institutions and Poverty Alleviation

About the Author

Dr. Birendra Suna, Post-Doctoral Fellow, Indian Council of Social Science Research, New Delhi attached with Centre for the Study of Social Systems, JNU, New Delhi. He obtained M.A. M.Phil & Ph.D.(Sociology)from Jawaharlal Nehru University, New Delhi, India and Post-Doctorate in Sociology from Albert-Ludwigs- University Freiburg, Germany. Teaching research interests are Economic Sociology, Social Capital, Sociology of Development, Globalisation and Global Governance, Cybernetic World & Multiculturalism, Labour Migration, Social Inequality and Social Stratification. He has presented research papers in national and international seminars/conferences. He contributes research papers to different journals and periodicals, edited books. His second book is on "health for all: Micro health insurance schemes in India".

Alternative Credit Institutions and Poverty Alleviation

A Sociological Interpretation of SHG's

Birendra Suna

CONCEPT PUBLISHING COMPANY PVT. LTD.
NEW DELHI-110059

ISBN-13 : 978-81-8069-934-4

First Published 2013

Concept Since 1974

Concept Publishing Company Pvt. Ltd.
A/15-16, Commercial Block, Mohan Garden
New Delhi-110059 (India)
: 25351460, 25351794, : 091-11-25357109
E: publishing@conceptpub.com, W: www.conceptpub.com
H-13, Bali Nagar, New Delhi-110 015, India.

Cataloging in Publication Data--*Courtesy:* D.K. Agencies (P) Ltd. <docinfo@dkagencies.com>

Suna, Birendra.
Alternative credit institutions and poverty alleviation : a sociological interpretation of SHGs / Birendra Suna.
p. cm.
Includes bibliographical references (p.) and index.
ISBN 9788180699344

1. Self-help groups—India—Umerkote (Block) 2. Microfinance—India—Umerkote (Block) 3. Women in development—India—Umerkote (Block) 4. Poverty—India Umerkote (Block)—Prevention. I. Title.

DDC 361.430954133 23

Dedicated
to
My Niece
Puchu, Ambi & Lichu

Foreword

Poverty is a situation of insufficiency of resources to meet the basic needs of an individual, household, community, region or nation for a life with dignity and satisfaction. It is cumulative consequence of economic, socio-cultural, political spatial and historical events, processes institutions, norms and systems. Poverty alleviation is one of the most significant imperatives for any person, household, community and country. For successful implementation of any poverty eradication programme, it requires togetherness of the forces of the state, market and society at local, regional, national and global levels as per as possible.

India has been aware of the problem of poverty and need poverty alleviation since its inception. It was the basis of rise of economic nationalism which provided very strong incentive for the Indian freedom movement. Putting an end to mass poverty in rural and urban areas through planned development programmes was the promise of the era of democratic India under the leadership of Jawaharlal Nehru between 1947-64. The limits of Nehruvian approach created the need of free thinking and more effective initiative during the Indira Gandhi regime which was propelled to power with massive mandate in response to her call for "Garibi Hatao". But in 1980s, it has been witness to incremental shift in the developmental paradigm in India with more and more role and space for micro-group initiatives through the institutions of credit and market. Micro-credit schemes and self-help groups have become the two pillars of the new architecture of poverty alleviation schemes in the age of liberalisation. In this context, the present study is extremely relevant as it is based upon the sociological realities of one of the most deprived States of our country-Odisha.

Dr. Birendra Suna has begun with a brief overview of conventional approaches to describing and explaining forms of poverty. He criticises the main approaches and programmes adop. .d for poverty alleviation. Then he argues about such initiatives which focus on 'collective action' and social capital as a way of better understanding of how structural inequalities work their way out in people's everyday life. In this research, Dr. Suna has explored the role of social capital as well as self- help groups in mediating the relationship between structural inequalities and collective action for poverty alleviation. In doing so, he has focused upon two correlated discourses—firstly, social formation rooted in the time and space that creates people's context for lives; and secondly, the economic growth and development related a 'privileged' form of expertise about the patterns of inequalities in income and livelihood systems. After illustrating the recent developments in social theory and theoretical significance of understanding of sociology of poverty, the study has been organised around the theory "social capital" as an alternative sociological method that has provided useful insights about the interlinks across the classes, castes, gender, and ethnicity and the dynamics of poverty alleviation. In order to demonstrate the base theory, Dr. Suna has conducted an empirical survey in the State of Odisha with reference to the proposed objectives and hypotheses. The major findings of the study are presented here in a systematic and elaborate manner to the roles of the micro-credit mechanisms as alternative institution that may be more effective for the poverty ridden people to move out of the chronic poverty situation and get freed from the clutches of village moneylenders. The 'income-bond-syndrome' between the individual member and the self-help group is an important finding of this study which deserves further study in a composite way.

I am confident that this particular work of Dr. Birendra Suna will be attracting the attention of scholars, policy makers, voluntary organisations, along with other concerned individuals and groups, who are engaged in promoting poverty alleviation processes, programmes and projects.

Prof. Anand Kumar
Co-ordinator
Global Studies Programme
Centre for the Study of Social Systems
School of Social Sciences
Jawaharlal Nehru University
New Delhi-1100067

Acknowledgements

Firstly, I would like to thank my supervisor Prof. M.N. Panini for providing me creative, constructive and substantial ideas throughout my nine years of JNU academic life which I have started with MA course work in 1999. Most importantly, it is my pleasure to work with him, this work could not have been formulated in a profound structure, nor could I reach to this stage had I not received his innovative thoughts and productive comments and criticisms. I am also thankful to Prof. Anand Kumar for his thought-provoke guidance during the process of writing this thesis.

I would like to thank Bishnu *dada,* who deposited my JNU MA entrance examination application form at the eleventh hour of last date of March in 1999.

I have also had a great luck to be connected with JNU that has an extraordinary libraries, viz., Central Library, DSA , EXIM bank and so have had available a wide range of books and journals. Special thanks to Assistant Librarian, Dr. Gopal Krishna. With regard to the communication age, I am greatly indebted to CSSS/SSS computer centre network.

For nine years I have been blessed to be part of the Centre for the Study of Social Systems, popularly known as "Social Systems" JNU and have had colleagues from across the corner of India and world. I have depended upon countless acts of support, generosity, and guidance from my teachers Prof. C.N. Venugopal, Prof. R.K. Jain, Prof. J.S. Gandhi, Prof. T.K. Oommen, Prof. K.L. Sharma, Prof. Dipankar Gupta, Prof. Nandu Ram, Prof. Ehsanul Haq, Prof. Avijit Pathak, Prof. Susan Visvanathan with whom I did my course work in M.A. and M.Phil. in 1999-2002. In general, I have had nurture my academic career by attending seminars and lectures of different Centres of JNU and particularly "Sociology Centre" teachers lectures by Prof. Tiplut Nongbri, Associate Prof. Vivek Kumar, Associate Prof. Renuka Singh, Prof. Maitrayee Chaudhuri, Associate Prof. Nilika Merhotra, Associate Prof. Amit Sharma, Prof. S.S. Jodhka, Assistant Prof. V. Sujatha, Associate Prof. Harish Narayandas and Assistant Prof. G. Srinivas. I express my sincere thanks to them. Of course it was a great opportunity for me to have an incredible academic boost up from Prof. Emeritus Yogendra Singh. I am greatly obliged to him. I would also like to thank the office staff of CSSS and SSS especially Satishji (SO), A.K.Talwar sir, Negi sir, and Jangiani sir, Bharat Bhaiya, and Bhupinder Bhaiya for always helping me out whenever I landed in any trouble.

I would like to thank JNU Health Centre staff and Dr. Aggarawal, Dr. Patra, Dr. Rath for taking care of my health during my stay at JNU.

Words cannot express my gratitude for my Maa and Baba and Badi Maa and Babu, Aunt and Uncle, whose unconditional support and inspirations provoke me to higher education. Naturally, this has been a family members love and affection which cannot be conveyed with words, of them—Sona Uncle, Cheena Uncle, Sidhartah, Kakali Kaki and Mona uncle, Kishor uncle and Marta aunt, Sabita aunt, Junathan, Kamalachan, Makrand, brother Dharmendra, sister-in-law Sunamani, nephew Aditya; cousins Popu, Guddun, Bebu, Sonu, Viva, Rekha, Shika, Eva, Rupa, late Iti, Sankhu, Siva, Nanda Bhaina, Sada Bhaina, Shyam, Rajendra, Surendra, Narendra, Rina, Putu, Turshar, Chintu, Bimal, Mini, Soraj, Muna, Kuna, Runa, Lique, Lima, Bablu, Hemant and Ulumpa, Rajkumar, who believed in my potential and encouraged me. My profound thanks to brother-in-laws Lakhan, Udya *dada*, and Haldhar.

I am grateful to my family-doctor, Dr. B.B. Sahu who takes care of my family members even in my absence.

Trilachan Mamu, and Papu the 'blood donor' for Das, Sahu and Sona family, who stand by whenever anybody required blood. I am greatly obliged to them.

I would also like to thank Narayan uncle, Dilip uncle, Sundarlal uncle, Dr. Gabinda *dada*, Dr. Santash Panda, Dr. Monaj Panda, Dr. Lachhu, Dr. Das, Uttam *dada* and Sapan *dada*, and Rabi *dada* for their constant inspirations of value of higher education.

I would also like to thank my School and college teachers Rath sir, Natha sir, Ray sir, Maharana sir, Santra Sir, Prakash Patnaik (General Science specialist), S. Mishra (NCC, coordinator), Khirda Patnaik (sports coach), Dr. Pradip Chaudhary (Western Orissa Historian), Dr. Anil sir, Pankaj sir, Sasank, Soraj sir, Deebakar sir, Rath sir, Smt. Anita Majhi (Principal), Suren Parida (Gandhian) who build up my academic base and constant inspirations and sources of knowledge for me.

My heartiest thanks to all my school and college friends—Santunu, Avaya, Anil, Buni, Krushna, Hari, Gupta, Ruby, Sanjukta, Sabita, Madushumita, Ashit, Gyanendra, Bishawjit, Phiraj, Babula, Dasarath, Gopal, Tapan, Dipti, Tukuni,Usha, Rebati, , Sarala, Minoti, Linga, Papu Gilani, Nihar, Martin, Rita Bairagi, Rita Das, Aslam, Ashok, Gandhi Padhi, Panda sir, Sukant, Nagesh, Amal, Sikin, Nabin, Naresh, Subrat, Prakash and Nilakontho.

I would like to mention the ever lasting all types of support of Undivided KBK JUNites Dr. Ramanath Nayak , Dr. Sartik Bag, Dr. Rajkumar Khosla, Dr. Niranjan Chichuan, Dr. Kapil Khemundu, Dr. Sadanand Bag, Dr. Pradyun Bag, and Iswar, Sarbewar, Sankar, Sitaram, Luna, Munna, Krushna, Sankar, Bulu, Sindu *da*, Jaga, Viveka, Sidharth, Sunil, Nata, Bona Bhai, Mahesh, Sambhu, Jasbant, Xeeloo, James, Tushar, Prabhakar Bhai, Robin Bhai, whose contributions in making me sane is immense.

I also thank to all my JNU friends and classmates for their positive criticisms and supports—Tinu, Vir, Lobo,

Ashutash, Kanak Suman, Pankaj, Sachin, Amit, Inder, Satish, Dhiraj, Phakir Bhai, Rati Bhai, Bhisnu Bhai, Subir, Sumit, Devi, Tushar Bhai, Manoranjan, Neeraja, Swati, Sumit, Labyna, Lakesh, Sudhir, Rakha, Sujit, Uma, Lila, Manjeer, Urna, Indrani, Ishani, Swasati, Alok, Samya, Niharika, Ritika, Dr. Niranjan Sarangi (economists UNDP, Sri Lanka), Bibhu, Pradeep, Subhas, Chandan, Godadhar, Sarada, Rajiv, Netaji, Ajay *dada*, (statistician, Planning Commission, GoI), Sauma Bag (Cartographer, CSRD, JNU), Soraj, Pradip, Dr. Tapas *dada*, Dr. Aurobinda Bhai and Dr. Sheema Bhabi, Dr. Samir Bhai, Sumanta, Dr. Pancha *da*, Monaj Nag, Dr. Susanta Bhai, Sagar Satapathy (Editor-in-Chief, Breaking News Online), late Pritam Bhai, Grishu, and many more.

Dr. Pankaj Deep, whom I called Dada (brother) who arrived at the verge of my thesis and supported me. Dada, I thank you from core of my heart.

I would like to thank Mathew Titus, the Executive Director Sa-Dhan (The Association of Community Development Finance Institutions) New Delhi, and staff HR. Nilesh, Programme executives, Amulya and Hari and Librarian for helping to use their library which is the store house collection on Microfinance and SHG and also I extend my thanks to NABARD Bhubaneswar Branch for providing me necessary documents on SHG and Loans disbursement. I thank the Branch Manager and the Staff.

My field work in Nabarangpur has been blessed by help and document supports from a large number of office staff of ITDA, Block Office Umerkote, NGOs-SEDP and SAHARA, Bank Official and news reporters. I am grateful to Narayan *dada*, Ashok Bhaina, Monaj Dhala, Animators Samaru and Geeta *nani* and others those who helped during the field study—master Guddun (camera man), Miltan, Santu, Krishna, Prakash and especially I am thankful to the respondents who spare their valuable time and share their views about SHG.

I would like to thank third batch GSPian (2004) for their constants on-line discussion with me about the SHG, Grameen and Nobel Prize specially I would like to thank Sabrina, Bianca, Sebastian, Ali, and Mike.

I would like to thank the Ministry of Social Justice and Empowerment, Government of India for providing me Rajiv Gandhi Fellowship which helped me to manage financial burdens at the rear end of my thesis work.

I thank to Basant Patnuru (Sr. Lecturer, Invertis, Institute of Management Studies, Bareilly, UP) for editing my work.

I am fortunate enough for having a brotherly childhood friends Soraj, Tukuna, Ratan, Sailen and Bijay. I thank them for their confidence and encouragement on me and my study.

I would like to thank Lenka Bhai and Nirmal Mamu, who stand by me whenever I was in trouble both morally and financially.

I am lucky to have my cousin Sujit (Bintu) and I thank him, for his incredible typing skills.

I owe my deepest gratitude to Sanjay uncle and Srabani aunt for their love, affection, moral and financial support.

I am deeply grateful to Concept Publishing Company Pvt. Ltd. and editorial board, who edited the final manuscript and have provided necessary feedback. I have tried my best to avoid mistakes, eventhough these unavoidably slide into any Manuscript. It has perhaps been even more challenging to write about this topic without felonious one side or another. Still I felt that this scholarly approach might enhance the sense of the question and will drop light on the problems and thus to a future explanation.

Birendra Suna

Contents

List of Abbreviations

ARF	–	Automatic Refinance Facility
ARDB	–	Agriculture and Rural Development Bank
ASA	–	Association for Social Advancement
BAAC	–	Bank for Agriculture and Agricultural Cooperatives
BASIX	–	Bharatiya Samrudhi Investment and Consulting Services
BC	–	Banking Correspondent
BPL	–	Below Poverty Line
BPPY	–	Biju Pani Panchayat Yojana
BRAC	–	Bangladesh Rural Advancement Committee
BS	–	Balance Sheet
CAPART	–	Council for Advancement of Peoples' Action and Rural Technology
CARE	–	Cooperative for American Relief Everywhere
CASHE	–	Credit and Savings for Household Enterprise
CB	–	Community Bank
CBO	–	Community Based Organization
CCD	–	Covenant Centre for Development
CD	–	Community Development
CDR	–	Credit Deposit Ratio

CDFI	–	Community Development Financial Institution
CEAD	–	Centre for Education and Agriculture Development NGO. AP
CEFI	–	Community Enterprise Forum International
COVA	–	Confederation of Voluntary Association
CRISIL	–	Credit Rating Information Service of India Ltd.
DA	–	Democratic Association
DCB	–	District Cooperative Bank
DCCB	–	District Central Cooperative Bank
DDM	–	District Development Manager
DFID	–	Department for International Development (UK)
DHAN	–	Development of Human Action
DP	–	Dandakaranya Project
DRDA	–	District Rural Development Authority
DWCRA	–	Development of Women and Children in Rural Area
EAS	–	Employment Assurance Scheme
ECB	–	External Commercial Borrowings
EGS	–	Employment Generation Scheme
FARR	–	Friends Association for Rural Reconstruction
FC	–	Farmer Club
FEO	–	Field Extension Officer
FI	–	Financial Institution
FO	–	Field Officer
FWWB	–	Friends of Women's World Banking
GA	–	Group Account
GB	–	Grameen Bank

GAD	–	Gender and Development
GIDE	–	Global Unit for Integrated Development Education
GoI	–	Government of India
HADP	–	Hill Area Development Programme
HCR	–	Head Count Ratio
ICDS	–	Integrated Child Development Services
IFAD	–	International Fund for Agricultural Development
IRDP	–	Integrated Rural Development Programme
IRMA	–	Institute of Rural Management, Anand
IWDS	–	Indian Women Development Society
KCCB	–	Koraput Central Cooperative Bank
KPGB	–	Kalahandi Panchabati Gramya Bank
KPGB	–	Koraput Panchabati Gramya Bank
IRV	–	Individual Rural Volunteer
LFI	–	Local Financial Institution
LIC	–	Life Insurance Corporation of India
LMS	–	Liquidity Management Support
LRTS	–	Local Resources and Traditional Skills
MCRIL	–	Microcredit Ratings International Limited
MAPP	–	Massive Agriculture Production Programme
MCID	–	Microcredit Innovation Department, NABARD
MFALDA	–	Marginal Farmers and Agricultural Labour Development Agency
MIFDEF	–	Microfinance Development and Equity Fund
MFDF	–	Microfinance Development Fund
MIS	–	Management Information System
MNP	–	Minimum Needs Programmes

MRCP	–	Maharashtra Rural Credit Project
MYRADA	–	Mysore Resettlement and Development Agency
NABARD	–	National Bank for Agriculture and Rural Development
NBFC	–	Non-Banking Financial Companies
NCT	–	National Capital Territories
NEED	–	Network of Entrepreneurship and Economic Development
NGO	–	Non-Governmental Organization
NPA	–	Non-performing Assets
NSAP	–	National Social Assistance Programme
NSSO	–	National Simplex Survey Organisation
PACS	–	Primary Agricultural Cooperative Societies
PANI	–	People Action for National Integration
MGNREGA	–	Mahatma Gandhi National Rural Employment Guarantee Act
PCARDB	–	Primary Credit Agriculture and Rural Development Bank
PLR	–	Prime Lending Rate
PPP	–	Purchasing Power Parity
PRA	–	Participatory Rapid Appraisal
PRADAN	–	Professional Assistance for Development Action
PRI	–	Panchayat Raj Institutions
RBI	–	Reserve Bank of India
RDD	–	Rural Development Department
REDP	–	Rural Entrepreneurship Development Programme
RFAS	–	Rural Financial Access Survey
RGVN	–	Rashtriya Gram Vikas Nidhi
RLEGP	–	Rural Landless Employment Guarantee Programme

RMK	–	Rashtriya Mahila Kosh
RMTS	–	Regular Meeting Transaction Statement
RRB	–	Regional Rural Bank
SAA	–	Service Area Approach
SARD	–	Social Action for Rural Development
SAG	–	Self Help Affinity Group
SAHARA	–	Society for Agriculture, Health & Education, Animal Husbandry and Rural Development Action
SC	–	Social Capital
SBI	–	State Bank of India
SEDP	–	Socio-Economic Development Programme
SEWA	–	Self Employed Women's Association
SFMC	–	SIDBI Foundation for Micro Credit
SGRY	–	Swarnajayanti Gram Rozgar Yojana
SGSY	–	Swarnajayanti Grameen Swarozgar Yojana
SHG	–	Self Help Group
BLP	–	Bank Linkage Programme
SHIPI	–	Self Help Promoting Institution
SIDBI	–	Small Industries Development Bank of India
SME	–	Small and Medium Enterprises
SRO	–	Self Regulatory Organization
TRYSEM	–	Training of Rural Youth for Self Employment
TrW	–	Tribal Welfare
UNDP	–	United Nations Development Programme
UGB	–	Utkal Gramya Bank
VDP	–	Village Development Programme
WAD	–	Women and Development
WID	–	Women in Development
WWF	–	Working Women's Forum
ZP	–	Zilla Panchayat

List of Tables

List of Charts and Figures

1

Introduction

"I shall consider India really independent when nobody in this country will go to bed in empty stomach and no village of this country would reel under poverty........ "

— ***Mahatma Gandhi***

In general, in the present world, Self-Help Group (SHG) technique occupies an important place in the strategies for poverty alleviation, rural development and women empowerment particular. Cooperation and conflict have been twin features of human societies. Self-Help, mutual aid and joint action for collective self-reliance constitute the basic values of cooperation. Therefore, cooperation as a form of economic organisation has ingrained in it two value systems which may be identified in an enterprise values and institutional values. Self-Help is one of the attributes of cooperation. As a form of economic organisation, besides economic efficiency it also envisages propagation of a value system.

1.1. The Concept of Self-Help Group

The decade of nineties witnessed a growth of various

people's organisations. The SHG programme is a supportive, a formal solidarity institution, usually change-oriented mutual aid group that addresses a life problem or condition commonly shared by all members. Its purpose may be personal or social change or both. Significance of social movement is power to the people, which has born out of the realisation that society's traditional arrangements for solving their problems are inadequate. The Self-Help refers to provision of aid to self and it emphasises self-determination, self-reliance, self-production and self-empowerment by mobilising internal resources of persons, the group or the community. In traditional rural and urban societies, Self-help takes various forms.

The fundamental nature of the Self-Help is a form of cooperation. It is mainly concerned with the poor, vulnerable and economically backward women and men. The SHG underlines "by the people, of the people and for the people" and in other words it strongly underlines that SHG "by the poor, of the poor and for the poor" for sustaining livelihood. The indispensable characteristics of a SHG are most felt need, homogeneity, solidarity, self-enforcement of rules, participative in democracy way, leadership, benefits from collective action *vis-á-vis* individual action and transparency in operations. The SHGs mechanism is a substitute for the rural people, by which they generate their own fund. The SHG as an informal group or association of like minded individuals with common economic need who undertake a systematic economic activity pertaining directly in decision making and sharing benefits on an equitable basis.

The SHG as a homogeneous group of rural poor voluntarily formed to save small amount out of their earnings, which is convenient to all the members and agreed upon by all to form a common fund corpus for the group and to its members meeting their productive and emergent credit need. Barish (1971)[1] while describing about historical background of the SHG, pointed out that the earliest group organised especially as a self-help group was formed in the early 1800s. It was very interesting to note that six drunkards pledged to abstain from drinking and also tried to involve other drunkards in order to reform them. Towards the end of the nineteenth century, the settlement house movement began whereby a member of neighbourhood helped newcomers to adjust to their environment. Later parents' associations date back to a public education Association started by a citizen's organization in 1896 and they were sponsoring problem solving lectures for the parents and trying to foster cooperation with teachers. Small citizens' groups during 1931 as a result of cooperative self-movement in California were emerged to combat unemployment. These were the cooperative self help associations. It helped them a lot to exchange labour of the members for fuel, fish, vegetables and other necessities. These associations worked on the philosophy of "rehabilitation through self help". These cooperatives grew and helped their members to maintain self-respect, independence and morale.

In 1995, the National Bank for Agriculture and Rural Development (NABARD) defines a self-help group as "which denotes an institutional framework for individual or households who have agreed to cooperate on a continuing basis of pursuing one or more objectives. A self-help group is a membership organisation, which implies that its risks, costs and benefits are shared among its members on an equitable basis and that its leadership and for manager for their deed". In this context the role of Self-help group (SHGs), especially of women has assumed a critical challenge. Self-help group approach is the key element of social mobilisation. Being self-supporting, self-governing organisation, they are devoid of bureaucratisation and politicisation.

It is now going to be two decades since the NABARD pilot project which began in 1992 to provide SHG-bank linkage programme to the poor, especially in rural households and become and successful nodal formal financial institutions. While Non Governmental Organisations (NGOs) have taken the leading role in order to forming SHGs, a number of financial service promoters and intermediaries, official and non-official are currently associated with the programme. Further, several central government ministries and State governments have launched potential projects and schemes involving the organisation of savings and credit groups, usually of poor women. Indeed, SHGs are currently seen as an essential and integral part not only of non-financial services delivery, but also as a channel for the delivery of non-financial services within larger objectives of livelihood promotion, community development and women's empowerment. The NABARD (1995), while documenting the best practices of banking with the poor, commented on the characteristics of the SHGs. It was stated that the SHG members should be residents of same area, homogeneous and numbering at least five persons, should hold regular meetings and the leaders should be elected by the members with group functionaries or positions being rotated among the members. Regarding banks, it stated that the economically backward are capable of meeting commercial loan obligations without seeing any concession or subsidies. Hence, banks should take significant initiatives to reach the poor. They could do this by providing credit in quantities both significant and sitting overtime for productive and income generating activities of the poor.

The Self-help groups are potential 'micro-banks' either on their own, or through higher levels of association, capable of using their own resources, grants and borrowed funds for financial intermediation. Apart from accessing, funds from the formal financial sector, self-help group also a forum for propagating development ideas and information, an association for community mobilisation or an organisational unit for linking up with other economic, social and political interventions. The self-help group movement has now been accepted as an effective intervention strategy for poverty alleviation. The self-help groups linked micro finance includes such credits which are provided to the rural poor on easy terms and conditions and give access to several income generation activities. Considering this the future strategy of rural credit institutions would have to include strengthening the credit delivery system for increases employment opportunities in rural non-farm sector.

Almost all major donor agencies support the SHGs in India as well as in Odisha in way or another. Many success stories are available, describing how memberships in the SHGs changed the life of a particular individual or group for the better. Many NGOs in India are promoting the SHG mechanism and linking it to various other developmental interventions. There is ample evidence that the SHG approach is a very effective, efficient and relevant for organising and empowering the economically backward. However, problems do arise with design; development and introduction within the role of the SHGs, and a range of approaches have emerged in representing different methods of ensuring effectiveness and sustainability of this community institution. These models envisage solely financial intermediation or include other non-financial elements as well. Given the diversity of approaches being practised, it is desirable to examine costs and benefits emerging SHG federations, particularly those promoted by leading in SHG development towards wider replication of the SHG model. It is also expected to help in directly funds from donors and other finance providers into the future development of effective institutions and activities in the micro finance sector. It is, however, noticed that the Self-help group movement has achieved partial success in various parts of the country.

1.2. Definition of Microcredit[2]

The dependence of the rural poor on the non-institutional

sources of credit like that of the moneylenders is one of the causes, which perpetuates poverty. The philosophy behind microcredit has been to make use of the enormous talent among the poor people that needed a portion of financial resources and a lot of trust. Microcredit as an alternative source of credit for the poor has received wide attention in recent years. Rabinson (2001) for many observers, microcredit or microfinance is a collection of banking practices built around providing small loans and accepting tiny savings deposits is a short arrangement for poverty reduction. To others, microcredit is still to be fully developed and tested by time. Few will disagree, though, that microcredit has already shaken up the world of international development. One of the most of striking elements that the pioneering models grew out of experiments in low-income countries like Bangladesh and India rather than from adaptations of standard banking models in developed nations. Microcredit is one of those small ideas that turn out to have enormous implications. When the Nobel laureate Muhammad Yunus, a Professor of Economics at a Bangladesh University, started making small loans to local villagers in the 1970s, it was unclear where it would go. Around the world, scores of state-run banks had already tried to provide loans to poor households, and they left a legacy of inefficiency, corruption, and millions of dollars of squandered subsidies. Economic theory also provided ample cautions against lending to low-income households that lack collateral to secure their loans. But Yunus vowed to one day make profits and he argued that his poor clients would pay back the loans reliably. Today, Yunus is recognised as a visionary in a movement that has spread globally, claiming over 80 million customers at the end of 2007.[3] They are served by microcredit institutions that are providing small loans without collateral, collecting deposits, and, increasingly, selling insurance, all to customers who had been written off by commercial banks as being unprofitable. Advocates see the changes as a revolution in thinking about poverty alleviation and social change and not just a banking movement.

The movement has grown through cross-pollination. Muhammad Yunus's Grameen Bank has now been replicated on five continents. Approaches started in Latin America have found their way to the streets of El Paso and New York city; experiments in Bolivia have given birth to institutions in Uganda and Azerbaijan, and policymakers in the world's two most populous countries, India and China are now developing their own homegrown microcredit versions. Recognising the energy and activity, the United Nations designated 2005 as the International Year of Microcredit.

The World Bank (1997) defined microcredit as a programme that provides credit for self-employment and other financial and business services to poorest of the poor. There is resurgence of interest on the approach of microcredit instructions in delivering various credit services to poor women and other marginalise sections of the society to enable them to create self-employment based on their skill and upliftment of their socio-economic living standard (Datta and Raman 2001).

Morduch (1999) demonstrated that the microcredit institutions evolved their own design features such as class eligibility for membership in the group ranging from landless to minimum landholdings[4]. Yaron and Besley (1994) mentioned that these institutions remain most successful one in terms of :

- Outreach and performance in delivering credit services to the poorest of the poor women and small artisans in the rural and urban areas.
- Reduction in adverse selection of borrowers.
- Development of collateral substitutions.
- Offering cost effective approaches to the formal institutions.

Zeller (1994) and Wenner (1995) observed that, "the success of group lending is attributed to various factors such as the ability of the group to mitigate asymmetric information problems in the credit makers through active screening of members". Social cohesion and heterogeneity of asset holdings (Zeller, 1998), social ties between borrowing group members (Floro and Yotopoulos, 1991) self-selection or assortative matching of members (Ghatak and Guinnane 1999), group pressure to repay the loans (Besley and Coate 1995 and Paxton *et al.*, 2000) and peer monitoring through intra-group insurance (Wydick 1999). Datta and Raman (2001) illustrated the group formation under microcredit institutions are based on a growing institution concept in terms of resources and management skills of the women members to reduce the gender inequality and to increase their confidence to get involved in issues and programmes in the public and private spheres.

The Microcredit or microfinance mobilisation as a programme to help out the poorest of the poor and vulnerable groups has gained wide acceptance since last three decades. Indira Misra (2003:11) described that "poverty is an increasingly feminine face. Lack of basic resources hits a woman directly and through her present and future offspring". Credit is essential for the poor, particularly in times of crisis. The terms of credit can be transparent only under a well-laid system. Generally, poor people have to depend in credit from the informal sources, because formal financial institutions require collateral proper written documents, which are not at all easy for the economically backward people. Availability of credit depends, moreover, on credit worthiness which is determined by possession of assets, and poor people have no assets except their physical labour.

In this century, the option to work towards poverty alleviation through microcredit or microfinance is gaining increasing recognition not only in the developing countries but developed countries also. Poverty subsist both the developed and developing countries—only difference is composition, i.e., it is "relative" in developed countries and "absolute" in developing countries[5]. Financing to the poor for enhancing income and ensuring livelihood has now become a major task for industrialised and non-industrialised countries. The policy for financing the poor may differ from country to country but the aims and objectives remain alike in the world—promoting sustainable livelihood and alleviating poverty. Willingness to take risk and borrowed credit gives courage, responsibility and helps the poor to generate income which leads them to live with dignity and self-respect.

The founder of Grameen Bank[6] in Bangladesh, Noble Peace Prize winner Muhammad Yunus, happened to observe that "the poor in rural areas remained poor not because they did not work hard, but because they did not possess the initial capital to invest in their economic activity. The terms on which they obtained the initial capital were iniquitous and did not leave any surpluses with them except to keep their bodies and souls together. It was in this state that the people were surviving". In fact, the success of Grameen Bank had ripple affects in many developed and developing countries, including India. It has brought microcredit to the forefront of discussion on the future role of development finance. Obviously, self-employment as visualised by Yunus has been able to provide sustainable livelihoods for the poorest of the poor and vulnerable people than merely subsisting on low wages.

The existence of traditional saving groups has been well documented and has a long and successful history in India. Desai and Namboodiri (2001) quoted that, informal Self-Help Groups (SHGs) oriented to saving and credit functions are not new phenomenon. Some forms of credit instruments were in operation even before 1904 when Co-operative Credit Societies Acts was passed.

Credit instruments such as Nidhis and Chit Funds were popular in India. They had several distinguishing features such as to encourage thrift, mobilise small savings and inculcate in the members the habits of punctuality and planning for future. The useful role played by these instruments in the rural areas as an important source of credit to people with moderate needs was well recognised (Namboodiri and Shiani, 2001:402).

Devasia and Antony (2004) discover that the social development is a plea for integrated view of the scope of development, which would embrace development in all aspects. This can be ensured with self-help group. It should mean growth and development in all aspects, which encompasses equality, status, security and complete physical, mental and social well-being of the group. The social status of women is a reliable indicator of the social development of a society. Women's development is possible only if they are given opportunity to develop freedom and participation in decision making.

Smith and Philheimer (1983) defined the SHG as a voluntary group valuing personal interactions and mutual aid as a means of altering or ameliorating the problems perceived as alterable pressing and personal by most of its participates. These groups are voluntary associations of people formed to attain collective goals—social and economic. Bouman (1984) the policy and development planners cherish the myth that poor people do not have the spirit to thrift, but recent reports from different parts of the globe deconstructed the myth.

The microcredit schemes using self-help group were designed against the background of the failure of the earlier schemes—anti-poverty programmes. The major factor behind the satisfactory development of SHGs is the role of Non Government Organisations (NGOs) and Self-help Promoting Institutions (SHPIs). These SHGs have not cropped up overnight. Whatever gain the SHG members have not or the benefits banks have received is because of hard work of field workers (FWs) who are generally women. According to Dasgupta (200:383) the Animator (person who helps SHG member to maintain their record and bank transaction) faces lot of problems from different quarters while promoting SHG. The first problem while entering the village is the resistance they generally face. The second problem is related to work risk which includes :

- Inadequacy of training.
- Attracting unhealthy attention from male world.
- Need to work late into the night.
- Travelling through isolated areas in infrastructural backward places.

The NGOs which can support their FWs under these hazards can succeed in linking their SHGs to banks. Banks too are gradually realising the significance of the SHG credit in terms of :

- Credit according to the need of the clients, also according to the affordable framework for bank.
- Gradual improvement of credit handling capacity by the poor.
- Credit-discipline.
- Lower transaction cost.

The approach between the Bank and the SHG stresses the importance of links between commercial banks on the one hand and non government organisations (NGOs) on the other. As it is a mechanism for channelising credit to the poor on a sustainable basis. In this model, rural women are expected to form groups and borrow credit from the banks as a group. The default of the bank loan by any one member is the responsibility of concerned group members. The second change that is striking in the microcredit scheme as against earlier schemes is that the bank does not question the purpose for which the loan is given. In the area of microcredit, NGOs play a very critical role. For instance, in Bangladesh, NGOs are able to benefit a much larger number of women with microcredit. The number of NGOs in India is also quite insufficient and whosoever is operating in the rural areas are not giving total attention towards the beneficiaries.

The narrative of microcredit has indeed greatly successful in Bangladesh where output created by this sector accounts for more than one per cent of the country's national income. It is interesting to note that in 2002, part of national income accruing to the poorest 20 per cent of the population was 9 per cent in Bangladesh. This compares with 8.9 per cent in India and only 4.7 per cent in China (Mukherjee 2007:31). Microcredit schemes are being implemented in several States in India. Starting with a significant upward movement since the mid-1990s, microfinance through independent microfinance institutions (MFIs) and through linking the self-help group have played a commendable role. Thus, since 1996, the SHGs method has become a regular component of the Indian financial system and also tool for the poor to get loan from the formal financial institutions.

The global and regional networks are active in formal financial sector are mainly Women World Banking (WWB) which is a global network affiliating 50 organisations in 42 countries of Africa, Asia, Europe, Latin America and North America. WWB has attracted funds from the local commercial banks to make them available to low income women either directly or through her affiliated group.

The global microcredit and poverty alleviation agenda is significant to the receiver as well as to the donors. Weber (2002) observed that, the potential of microcredit applied at the level of individuals within local communities can be seen to reflect what Gill has identified and referred to conceptually as disciplinary neoliberalism at the global level. The disciplinary component of microcredit might be essential to the objective of extending the social disembedding logic of the global unification movement to the level of local communities.

The microcredit agenda is significant in that it is conducive to facilitating policy changes at the local level according to the logic of the globalisation agenda while at the same time advancing its potential to discipline locally in the logic of the global governance programme. Thus, from the perspective of the architects of global development the harmonisation of local social policy at the global level along the rules and norms of the unification movement provides for a coherent set of tools that may facilitate as well as govern the global agenda.

According to Deacon (2000:213), an exposition of the global socio-economic of microcredit and poverty alleviation elucidates how the "poverty alleviation" programmes is implicated in strategies of global governance. Microcredit, although implemented at the level of local communities, is policy initiated not at the national level but at the level of global institutions. For Deacon it is the "supernationalisation of local social policy". The normative discourses of "poverty alleviation" appropriated in the public transcripts may be instrumental to efforts to manage or offset what Sinclair has identified as the contest between global governance and local governance.

The root of the savings and credits, however, is success of economic activities started by the poor. There are "credit plus" inputs. If the poors do not have the enterprise as individuals, it has to be realised at group level of the delivering system has to fill the gap. Linking thrift self-help group and formal credit institutions is mutual useful. Self help promotion institutions, i.e., voluntary agencies can play a temporary role where available. Generally, the linkage has to be direct for it is imperative that there is an organic relationship between credit agencies barriers have to be overcome. Credit is a major factor in boosting economic development if it is effectively utilised. The government's recent initiative to streamline credit operations and delivery system through micro credit movement and strengthening and expansion of credit institutions can definitely help in the revival of rural economy.

1.3. The Literature

Since the initiation of the SHG, thrift and credit transactions and development of microcredit or microfinance institutions (MFIs) and Non-Banking Financial Companies (NBFCs), and engagement of large number of poor people in the SHG and microcredit method for enhancing income and sustaining livelihood, there are several studies have been done both by practitioners and academic social scientists. Interestingly, several studies have been conducted by social scientists, financial institutions and agencies, which highlight the positive trends and impact of SHG on empowerment, credit accessibility and the social change. It is very difficult to review all the relevant studies since proper documentation of such studies is still to be ensured. Therefore, available relevant studies, particularly case studies, workshops, seminars and symposia, have been critically reviewed.

Following literatures has been dealt on different aspects of SHG and microcredit. These literatures contain and present valuable insights, and have their limitations. Therefore, my objectives for this work are to connect the various findings of the practitioners and academician, to synthesise and put together those findings and test my own hypotheses. In this way, this work is both a demonstrative and a prospective one for the field of SHG and microcredit.

Shylendra (1996) examined the role of the Regional Rural Banks (RRBs, 1975) in achieving institutional reforms in rural credit in terms of loan diversification in Andhra Pradesh, India. A random sample of 197 borrowers from Tungabhadra Gramin Bank (TGB) was drawn from Bank records of the 1989 household survey. The study revealed that RRBs had benefited the better-off rather than the poorest, due to individual and security based lending policies. On the other hand, there was a larger coverage of the poor households under poverty alleviation schemes which were household-based. This has paved way for the current innovative self-help group based lending, to supplement the formal credit agencies in reaching the rural poor more effectively.

Ramesh (1997), while comparing the six principles of cooperating between primary agricultural credit societies (PACs) (1) To raise capital for the purpose of giving loans and supporting the essential activities of the members, (2) To collect deposits from members with the objective of improving their savings habit, (3) To supply agricultural inputs and services to members at remunerative prices, (4) To arrange for supply and development of improved breeds of livestock for the members, (5) To make all necessary arrangements for improving irrigation on land owned by members, and (6) To encourage various income-augmenting activities such as horticulture, animal husbandry, poultry, bee-keeping, pisciculture and cottage industries among the members through supply of necessary inputs and services and the SHGs (1.viability, 2.management, 3.resource mobilization, 4.loan operation, 5.overdues, and 6. loan recovery) stated that these principles were overtly seen in the functioning of the SHGs rather than in primary agricultural cooperative societies (PACS). The distinctiveness of the SHGs lies in the fact that they are fully democratic, autonomous and thrift based and is functioning in the same socio-economic and political environment in which PACS are functioning. While exhibiting basic characteristics of cooperatives in letter and spirit, SHGs continue to be functionally effective and flexible and deserve to be known as "new-wave cooperatives".

Katz (1965) observed that in the fields on physical handicap, mental illness, mental retardation and drug addiction, the self-help organisations formed by parents, ex-patients and their relatives assumed prominent roles in providing social services, education, group aid and support to research and have significantly influenced public awareness and policy in these fields. These practical developments often occurred without much professional aid or understanding. The assisting principle, i.e., the use of people with a problem to help other people who have the same problem in severe form, has universal therapeutic application.

Mukherji (1977) reiterated that social movement is a prolonged action of deprived homogeneous group to strengthen the roots of the group in the society to which the group belongs. The collective mobilization for action directed explicitly towards an alteration or transformation of the structure of a system can be understood as a social movement, which is essential for social change. By social movement, reciprocal relationships become stronger and people come forward to help each other.

Nagayya (2000) maintains that an informal arrangement for credit supply to the poor through the SHG's is fast emerging as a promising tool for promoting income-generating enterprises. He has reviewed the initiatives taken at the national level with a view of institutional arrangements to support this programme for alleviation of poverty among the poor, with focus on women. He maintained that NABARD and SIDBI are playing a prominent role at various stages of implementation of this programme. There are other national level bodies also supporting, viz., Rastriya Mahila Kosh (RMK), Rashtriya Gramin Vikas Nidhi (RGVN), etc.

He called for an imperative need to enlarge the coverage of the SHGs in advance portfolio of banks as part of their corporate strategy, to recognize perceived benefits of the SHG's financing in terms of reduced default risk and transaction costs.

Chawla and Patel (1987) had stated that, the SHG, an informal organisation, which is set up and run by local people. People, those who participate are also the beneficiaries of the programme. Though, it is a loose organisational structure, but strong commitment, mutual bondage and sense of purpose. Carr and Chen (1996) visualised that the SHG concept is common in the context of both rural and urban development. In the rural agriculture scenario, it is often considered as a group of farmers coming together to achieve any specific objective, which will lead to better livelihood condition and a higher income. It serves as an effective mechanism for mobilising and organising farmers and villagers to achieve livelihood. The objectives are self-supporting and enhancement of income and participating in rural development, which benefits to a substantial number of poor farmers, landless labourers and economically backward urban and rural communities.

Ommen (1977) while emphasising the women's movement and groups highlighted to recognise the importance of empowering women. Also, he defines "social movement as an institutionalised collective action, guided by an ideology and supported by an organisational structure". This social movement can aim at reforms and revolutionary change in every sphere of life and in basic values.

Fernandez (1995) observed that the basis of the self help group exist prior to any interventions. A common bond like caste, sub-caste, blood kinship, community and place links the members. Governments or banks must have the experience to identify these natural groups which are commonly called "Affinity Groups" — what links together the group members. Therefore, it is not primarily the need for credit, but a capital stock or relationships built on mutual trust and confidence, degree for social and economic homogèneity and on the gut feeling of its members that the group offers the best opportunity to realize their taken and often supposed aspirations to develop economically and socially without creating social tension locally, with which they cannot cope.

Ahmad (1999) through a case study on Thrift Groups in Assam highlighted that women are coming to the administration directly for their just rights and to address their grievances boldly. It proved that the SHGs are successful in North East States of India even in the midst of insurgency. Similarly, Gurumoorthy (2000) maintained that the SHG is a viable alternative to achieve the objectives of rural development and to get community participation in all rural development programmes. The SHG is a viable organisational set-up to disburse micro credit to the rural women for the purpose of making them entrepreneur and encouraging them to enter into entrepreneurial activities. Credit needs of the rural women can be fulfilled wholesomely through the SHG's. The women led the SHG's have successfully demonstrated how to mobilise and manage thrift, appraise credit needs, maintain linkages with the banks and enforce financial self discipline. SHGs enhance the equality of status of women as participants, decision-makers and beneficiaries in the democratic, economic and social and cultural spheres of life. They encourage women to take active part in the socio-economic progress of the society.

Tyagi (1999) quoting the concept of self help promotion explained that promotion as a development approach believes that even poor people have the inherent capacity to organise themselves and fulfil their requirements. It tries to build upon this existing self help potential of the poor and assist them as producers and in the identification of occupations and activities, which provides a higher net return on invested labour and capital. Thus, it attempts to raise the level of voice of majority of the poor in the economic system by the building up of an institutional framework that is tuned to their capacities of self-administration and better geared towards serving their needs. People organise themselves into the SHGs and through these groups, people with few resources start to change their conditions of production and consumption at a micro level. It may steer the development of a village economy in a different direction by enlarging the scope for village level enterprises. Usually, it starts with economic activities, but need not necessarily be limited to that and it may well be extended to social, political and cultural activities.

Bhatia and Bhatia (2000) through few case studies highlighted that recovery of the SHG's is higher than other credit extended to borrowers. Moreover, involvement of the SHG's had helped the bank branches in recovery of old dues. They observed that there have been perceptible changes in the living standards of the SHG members, in terms of ownership of assets, increase in savings and borrowing capacity, income generating activities and income levels as well.

Rao (2002) maintain that a review of the genesis and development of the SHGs in India reveals that the existing formal financial institutions have failed to provide finances to landless, marginalized and disadvantaged groups. The origin of the SHG's could be treated to mutual aid in Indian village community. The SHG encourages savings and promote income generating activities through small loans. The experience available in the country and elsewhere suggests that the SHGs are sustainable to have replicability, stimulate savings, and in the process help borrower to come out of vicious circle of poverty.

Malhotra (2000) in his study of 174 women beneficiaries, in Rae Bareilly of the State of Uttar Pradesh, drawn and covered randomly from four formal financial agencies of credit, i.e., the Community Banks (CBs), the Regional Rural Bank (RRBs), Primary Agricultural Cooperative Societies (PACS), and the Agricultural and Rural Development Bank (ARDBs) revealed that less than half a per cent of female population against 3.5 per cent of male population in the study area were clients of the banks. Furthermore, only 7.64 per cent of the total number of cases financed and only 6.96 per cent of the total quantum of credit extended by RBI have gone to women. It was observed that 83 per cent of loan cases availed by women; male members were primarily responsible for the end use of credit.

Puhazhendhi and Jayaraman (1999) analysed the functioning of SHGs, in performance, sustainability, empowerment of women, economic impact on the members, future potentials, etc. They observed that SHGs in Tamil Nadu are performing well towards social change and transformation. The emerging trends are leading to positive direction of empowerment of members and promotion of micro finance. Dasgupta (2000) in his paper on *'informal journey through self-help group'* observed that micro-financing through informal group approach has effected quite a few benefits, viz., (i) savings mobilised by the poor; (ii) access to the required amount of appropriate credit by the poor; (iii) matching the demand and supply of credit structure and opening new market for financial institutions; (iv) reduction in transaction cost for both lenders and borrowers; (v) tremendous improvement in recovery; (vi) heralding a new realisation of subsidyless and corruptionless credit, and (vii) remarkable empowerment of poor women. He stressed that the SHGs should be considered as one of the best means to counter social and financial citizenship not as an end in itself.

Datta and Raman (2000) highlighted that the SHGs are characterised by heterogeneity in terms of social and economic indicators. The success of the SHGs in terms of high repayment is mostly related to the exploitation of prevailing social ties and cohesion found among women members. Social cohesiveness among members spring not only from their diverse background of knowledge base, skills occupations and income levels, but also due to the dynamic incentive system of progressive lending to the groups on the successful completion of loan repayment. However, the SHGs are heavily dependent on external financial agencies for their lending operations.

Satish (2001), in his paper raised certain issues related to the functioning of SHGs. Adequate care should be taken to ensure homogeneity of socio-economic status of the members, while forming SHGs. The process of the SHG formation has to be systematic whether a Bank or an NGO forms it. He emphasised that the SHGs experiment has to be spread throughout rural India rather than being concentrated in a few pockets of the country. The NGOs are more suited for forming and nurturing the SHGs because of their flexible nature of work procedure, and they do not stick to bureaucratic procedure of functioning. It is meant for the people especially the vulnerable and where the state is unable to reach the unreached. Hence, it is quite essential to strengthen the NGOs and their resources so that they can work increasingly and closely associate with the nation development.

Barbara and Mahanta (2001) in their study maintained that the SHGs have helped to set up a number of micro-enterprises for income generation. Rashtriya Gramin Vikas Nidhi's (RGVN) credit and saving programme in Assam has been found successful as its focus is exclusively on the rural poor. It adopted a credit delivery system designed specially for them with the support of a specially trained staff and a supportive policy with no political intervention at any stage in the implementation of the programme.

Puhazhendhi, and Satyasai (2001) attempted to evaluate the performance of the SHGs with special reference to social and economic empowerment. The findings of their study revealed that the SHGs as institutional arrangement could positively contribute to the economic and social empowerment of rural poor and the impact on the latter was more pronounced than on the former. Though there was no specific pattern in the performance of the SHGs among different regions, the southern region could edge out other regions. The SHGs programme has been found more popular in the southern region of India and its progress in other regions is quite low, thus signifying an uneven achievement among the regions. Older groups had relatively more positive features like better performance than younger groups.

Manimekalai and Rajeshwari (2001) in their paper highlighted that the provision of micro-finance by the NGOs to women SHGs has helped the groups to achieve a measure of economic and social empowerment. It has developed a sense of leadership, organizational skill, management of various activities of a business, right from acquiring finance, identifying raw material, market and suitable diversification and modernization.

Sharma (2001) maintained that through the SHGs, women's empowerment is taking place. Their participation in the economic activities and decision-making at the household and society level is increasing and making the process of rural development participatory, democratic, sustainable and independent of subsidy, thus, macro-financing through SHG's is contributing to the development of rural people in a meaningful manner. Interestingly, Singh (2001) in his study in Uttar Pradesh highlighted that the SHG is now functioning in the place of moneylenders because loan could be taken at any time as and when needed for any purpose. There are no formalities involved and the transaction cost is low. He also studied the size, composition, characteristics of rural self-help groups, to examine their functions and the impact on generation of income and employment, to identify the major constraints and problems of the group and suggest measures for overcoming these problems. He suggested that the banks and other financial institutions and the State government should come forward to help the rural poor through the SHGs and provide liberalised credit facilities at cheaper rates of interest.

Nirmala (2003) in her study indicates the SHG programme is making a favourable impact on the living standards of its beneficiaries. It holds better promises for poverty alleviation and employment generation than the earlier programmes due to its structure of easy credit, savings and peer monitoring. However, for its greater success, imparting activity-oriented training appropriate to the present activities and future needs SHG. It enhances capacity-building and enable them to participate in decision making. Empowerment requires the development of consciousness among the members to use credit effectively and ensure sustainability of the activity in the future. Further, it also requires constant monitoring and supervision by the implementing agencies as well. Paul (2002) states that empowerment of women is one of the important indicators of growth and development of the nation. Therefore, the paramount importance for the women organisations such as the SHG is that, it needs effective management and developed skills and interests by the SHPIs. It could be well ascertained that women's development could be achieved by empowerment, which thereby enables women to be the agent of social change. Organisational behaviour like, capacity building, and monitoring are the key to women's empowerment. Women's organisations in group provide them a platform to discuss help senses in their own society. In this process, the women will not only identify their problems, but also become aware of their natural capacities in order to raise their position in the family and in the society.

Mohindra (2003) states that, the SHG is not only a tool for raising income and eliminating poverty but also achieving good health. For Wagstaff (2002), poverty remains the main cause of ill-health and thus comprehensive strategies are required to improve the well-being of poor communities. Exploring interventions aimed at poverty alleviation in terms of their health production potential could increase the effectiveness and efficiency of outcomes in well-being, and overall equity impacts of interventions involving social change. Such understanding may also help to clarify the causal pathways between poverty and health. The research aims was to evaluate the SHGs in terms of health and equity, with a special focus on women's well-being, in a particular context. The framework will integrate Amartya Sen's theory of capabilities[7]. The conception of capabilities refers to:

> "The alternative combinations of functionings from which a person can choose. Thus, this notion of capability is essential one of freedom that is the range of options a person has in deciding what kind of life to lead. Poverty of live in this view, lies not merely in the impoverished state in which the person actually lives, but also in the lack of real opportunity-given by social constraint as well as personal circumstance-to choose other types of living. Even the relevance of low income, meagre possession, and other aspects of what are standardly seen as economic poverty relates ultimately to their role in curtailing capabilities. Poverty is thus, ultimately a matter of capability deprivation."

Fisher *et al.* (2002) focus on geography of India that provides background on India and its microfinance experience. The clear definition of what microcredit is expected to do is very helpful. The introduction parts explain the debate between two schools of thought, viz., the finance school and the poverty school. The finance school tends to focus on the service of providing for the financial needs of those who can qualify, whereas the poverty school focuses on the need to reach poor people. They then acquaint the reader with a variety of developmental needs that could be impacted through micro-finance, including livelihood promotion, developing the local economy, empowerment, and building democratic people's organizations. It focuses on self-help group in urban settings with their non-traditional community and kinship ties. They highlighted that the operating cost for SHG transactions has to bear by the SHG promoting institutions. The study also found that the development stages of the SHG, highlights the wide range of diversity in the performance of individual self-help group. The author discusses on formation of leader for the group, its coordination, costs, and rewards with respect to the SHG. They focus on formal and informal financial industry and measurement issues, proposing a rating mechanism for microfinance and issues related to the measurement of wide developmental impacts in India. The text sets out how micro-finance can be designed in practice to contribute to a wide range of development objectives. It included that the SHG is not only guided for social and economic security, promoting livelihoods but also provided insights for building democratic people's organisations and empowering women. This text has provided an extensive analysis on the great diversity of microfinance practice in India, and its many innovative ideas and organisational features. It also accumulated detail about the fast expanding movement of poor people's nature on saving of money and borrowing credit from formal financial institutions (Banks) and using that amount in income generating activities for livelihood.

Joshi (2006) describes in her *'Social Banking'* about the Indian banking scenario from both a historical and a theoretical perspective. She discusses the development of social banking, its working and its relevance for the present and the future. The book presents, contribution of banking institutions in promoting savings and investments and extending the reach of banking services. The author argues the case for large-scale social banking and microfinance for the alleviation of poverty. She also provides an extensive analysis of the remarkable traits that have made social banking a success in India and enabled the Indian banking system to reach millions of low-income savers and borrowers. It clearly demonstrates the tremendous potential embedded in well-designed institutional interventions towards self-help group. Rural poor women and men have succeeded in evolving an innovative alternative banking practice, i.e., first saving than credit by the assistance of microfinance institutions. Self-help promoting institutions provided credits on low rate of interest at the door step of the clients (SHG member), which in turn brought high repayment rate. This simple method between client and microcredit institutions is called as a social banking process that caters especially to the development needs of the poor in sharp contrast with conventional commercial banking, which has marginalised the poor from availing loan.

Guerin and Palier (2005) observed that, microfinance is often presented not only as an efficient tool to poverty alleviation, but also a means of promoting empowerment of the most marginalised sections of the society especially women. Though the reality has shown the fundamental relation between microfinance and empowerment of vulnerable women is neither linear nor unequivocal and that it is even less systematic. Their observations put an attempt to nourish the debate on theoretical reflections and case studies, and also engaged practitioners and researchers from various backgrounds. The link between microcredit and empowerment is all the more insignificant and sometimes unforeseeable as microfinance projects take place within an economic, socio-cultural, ability to repay the loan and political context.

Present work's key concepts, i.e., microcredit as an alternative credit for the poor, poverty alleviation, self-help group, empowerment of marginalised in general and women in particular, bank linkages, sustainability of SHG and sustaining of livelihoods are the important terms are used from sociology and economy. The fundamental importance of the study is a socio-economic one so, some theories have been critically analysed - Modernisation, Marxists and neo-Marxists, Women in Development, Gender and Development. The theory applied for this study is "social capital". Microcredit projects are as a developmental project so one should need to analyse and understand with reference to the endogenous perceptions. The diversity of various studies and the results are different. Some studies shown very positive results and some are very much mixed or confused. Microfinance, for the poor is a tool for sustaining livelihood but not a panacea for completely staying away from the trap of poverty because when "absolute poverty" is removed, "relative poverty" will take place.

Poverty, vulnerability, marginalisation, malnutrition, unhealthy environment and unhygienic drinking water and illiteracy are part and parcel of the estimated 26 per cent Indians who live in distress, cheerless, and compunction life. The rural scenario is more vulnerable with 74 per cent poverty stricken people of which majority are marginal farmers and landless labourers[8]. Nearly 73 per cent people are living in the remote corner of India where they do not avail the presence of banks and government machinery. The bank facilitates loan and assistance to them, those who are creditworthiness but not to the poor. Though the State mechanisms are present in the rural areas, but it is only serving to those people who are influential and dominant in the locality.

1.4. Objectives of the Study

The principal objectives of the study is to contribute a

consistent and relevant approaches to various Self Help Promoting Institutions (NGOs, Banks, Village Committee, government agencies and Self-employed individual) which are engaged for promoting SHGs as a vehicle for alleviating poverty. The objectives of the study are as follows:

(i) To analyse the thrift (saving) behaviour of the groups in the light of members' perception, ability and constraints.
(ii) To analyse the credit behaviour across the self help groups and location in terms of structural differences and the difference in the economic status of the members.
(iii) To study the possible bias in the credit disbursement and allocation in the light of socio-economic status of members.
(iv) To provide a current perspective on the functioning of the SHGs in financial intermediation, and their support institutions.
(v) To undertake a historical origin of SHGs, microfinance institutions and its impact on poverty alleviation.
(vi) To assess the existing capacities and training needs for the groups' for capacity building.

1.5. Hypotheses

Following hypotheses has been empirically tested :

(i) Microcredit oriented SHGs are the appropriate alternative institutional arrangement for the poor and poverty alleviation.
(ii) Self-help group are an effective way of promoting socio-economic empowerment of poor women.

(iii) The usefulness of SHG's is not up to the desired satisfaction level due to various socio-cultural factors.

1.6. Statement of the Problems

'Poverty' in general, is widespread social evil in India, particularly Orissa is a epicentre with 43 per cent below poverty line people, so Nabarangpur district and its Block Umerkote is not exempted from the cruelty of poverty. Odisha as a whole, it is not only lacking potential human resources and inadequate State government's plan policy and promise in implementation level but also time and again it is experiencing natural calamities, such as draught in western part of the State and heavy flood, cyclone and super-cyclone in the eastern part of State, affecting to health of the people and causing unfertile to the cultivable land by which food-grain production is decreasing day-by-day. The State is having plenty of amount of natural resources but it is lacking to use the resources in sustainable manner (detailed has discussed in third chapter with data). Above causes are prohibiting to the people from full participation in social, economic and political life and whose experiences, contributions, concerns and dreams are rarely considered in planning for the future. SHG programme holds the promise of a series of motivating option for reducing poverty and promoting rural development in India. Alleviation of poverty is not just about the quantity of borrowers reached but also recognising the quality and range of financial services that meets the needs and desires of the poor.

As per government plan and policy developmental methods are being taken place in the Block for uplifting the poverty ridden marginalise, vulnerable and economically backward people. Apart from government's SHG promoting agencies (IRDP, ICDS and PRIs), in this Block number of Non-governmental organisations (NGOs) are active, which are providing assistance to the poor people on education, different type of training for enhancing income, and awareness for forest protection. The NGOs which are more active in this Block, namely, Socio-Economic Development Programme (SEDP) and Society for Agriculture, Health & Education, Animal Husbandry and Rural Developmental Action (SAHARA) promoting the SHG for sustainable livelihood by different means, such as, group formation, pertaining training for savings and credit behaviour which aims to alleviate poverty, especially focusing on women. The SHPIs takes more interests to involve in SHG programme because, woman is the home maker, who knows everything about her family and her feeling towards her children and her household economic status. Therefore, SHPIs choose woman as the main participant for savings and credit entity in the SHG and the Bank linkage programme. The role of women in alleviating poverty is one of the most profound lessons of development experience since 1970s with the initiation of SHG movement in India and also in the world. This study examines the ways in which SHG programme has become an alternative means to access of the rural poor women to formal sources of finance, which excluded them from formal financial markets in 1970s.

1.7. Methodology of the Study

Normally, methods are classified as either qualitative or quantitative, the latter corresponding to a positivist orientation and the former often related to more inductive strategies (Patton, 1990). In general, qualitative methods are extremely useful in defining the social process by which problems emerge and for suggesting strategic points of programmatic intervention to deal with particular problems (Brewer and Hunter, 1989). Quantitative techniques "are most often useful in understanding the extent and scope of specific problems" and "for defining the parameters within which various potential solutions may be debated. Patton

(1990) notes that quantitative methods facilitate comparison and statistical aggregation of data producing a broad, generalisable set of findings presented succinctly and parsimoniously.

Primary data were collected through personal interviews and observations and through indirect means as well, such as informal talks with the Government employee (BDO, WEO, and CDPO), the NGOs functionaries, the Bank officials, the news reporters, the social workers and friends of the respondents. These later sources were also useful in cross-checking the accuracy of the information given by the respondents about the nature and degree of their involvement, operations and performance of the SHG.

For the convenience and empirically justifying the objectives and hypotheses, data has collected from both secondary and primary sources. In the secondary sources, there are literatures (books, journals, research papers, working papers, demographic data, BPL lists, etc.). The literatures produced by sociologists, economists, Self-help group promoting institutions (SHPIs), social activists, anthropologists, political scientists, and policy planners, are used for the present work.

The tools used for primary data is "semi-structured" interview schedule. Apart from interview schedule, "Focus Group Discussion" (FGD) was taken place and by the help of video camera whole discussion process has been documented (a documentary film has developed). Before collecting primary data, pilot study was done twice in the year 2004 and in the year 2005. On the base of pilot study and by the help of secondary sources, a set of semi-structured interview schedule has been developed. In order to validate of the interview schedule, it was tested in the year 2006 (May) in the Block itself. Some modifications were made to the earlier interview schedule for the final filed survey. With the final sets of interview schedule field survey has done in the months of December-February (2006-07). The schedule was carried out the base line information of the respondent's factors (psychological, physical, and socio-economic) influenced her to join the SHG and her participation in decisions making, planning and its implementations and outcome after joining the SHG (socio-economic status and poverty level). The field survey has made easier for the author as he is familiar with the local tribal dialects and languages of the respondents (Santhali, Ho, Gondi, Bhatri, Bengali). The data collected from the field has processed (codified) into the Statistical Package for Social Science (SPSS) programme to bring into being and presented with absolute number and percentage in the tables and finally it was analysed on the discourse of social and economic perspectives.

1.8. Sample Size of the Study

To carry out systematic study of the socio-economic matrix of self-help group, microfinance institutions and as concepts are taken as alternative mechanism for poverty alleviation, purposefully Odisha State has selected as the author is well acquainted with its social settings (tradition, culture, costumes, norms, etc.) and socio-economic situations (persistence of poverty). The State contains 30 districts. Out of 30 districts, one district has taken, e.g., Nabarangpur. This district is in-built with 10 revenue Blocks. Of the 10 Blocks, one Block has selected, e.g., Umerkote. Umerkote Block contains 18 Panchayats. Out of 18 Panchayats, four Panchayats have been selected, viz., Badakumari, Badabharandi, Burja and Chikalpadar. From four Panchayats, twenty self-help groups (209 respondents) have been selected. To examine and explore the cross-cultural and socio-economic condition of the respondents[9] and their involvement with the SHG movement for poverty alleviation, three communities have been selected, namely,

Scheduled Tribes and Scheduled Castes and Bengali SCs including Bengali general castes.

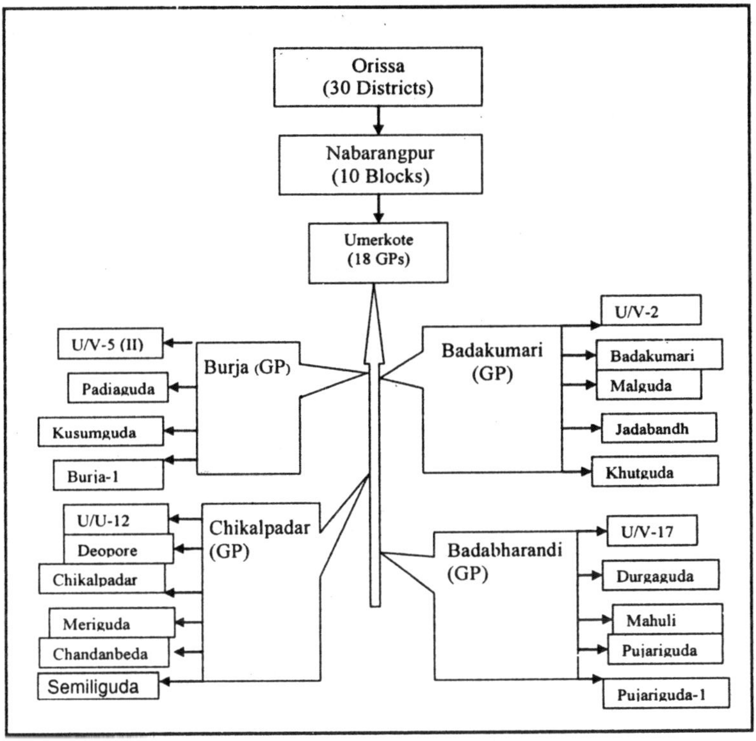

Fig. 1.1: Field Sample Figure

Note : GP-Gram Panchayat

REFERENCES

1. Barish, H. (1971): *'Self-help Groups: Encyclopedia of Social Work'*, 16th Issue, Vol.II, New York, pp.1163-1169.
2. Microcredit focuses primarily on credit; on the other hand microfinance encompasses both credit and savings. In Asia, still the concept microfinance has not got maturity. So the two concepts have been used interchangeably in this work.

3. http://www.grameen-info.org (acceded on 5/12/2007)
4. No need of prior entrepreneurial experience for holding entrepreneurships, monthly repayments to weekly repayments; individual lending to group based lending; requirement of collateral to no-requirement and group lending contracts to no-group lending contracts. See Morduch, 1999 for variations on design features of different microcredit institutions in the world.
5. Detail on relative and absolute poverty has been described in the third chapter of the work.
6. Detail has been discussed in the third chapter of this study.
7. Sen, A.K (1999· Development as Freedom OUP, Oxford, pp.86-88, also see P ınkaj Deep, 2007: "Implementation of Tribal Development Policies: A Study of Tribal Sub-Plan in G. Udayagiri and Kashipur Blocks in Orissa", Ph.D. Thesis submitted to Jawaharlal Nehru University, New Delhi, Unpublished thesis.
8. Karmkar (ed.) (2008): Microfinance in India, Sage Publications, New Delhi, p.20.
9. Throughout the study, the terms "respondent", "Member" and "household" have been used interchangeably as per the requirement of the analysis.

2

Development, Poverty Eradication and Women's Empowerment : An Appraisal

"The value of the living standard lies in the living, and not in the possessing of commodities which has derivative and varying relevance".

—*A. Sen, 1987:25*

This chapter outlines some of the theoretical issues and debates arising from critiques of the concept of development. Attempts have been made to highlight the complex and often paradoxical assumptions behind policies and programmes of development. The central theme of discussion entitled "social capital and the SHG" provides a practical introduction to the task of applying Women in Development (WID) and Gender and Development (GAD) frameworks followed by microcredit strategies. Since 1950s, throughout the World in general and the third world particularly, there has been a proliferation of developmental policy, programmes and projects designed to uplift low-income groups, especially for low-income women, and vulnerable section of society. In the last two decades the attention of development experts, NGOs, governments and policy makers has turned to the institution known as the SHG that is seen as playing a critical role in effectively combating poverty. Development through the SHG became an innovation in meeting the credit needs of the poor in order to enable them to cross the threshold of poverty by exploiting economic opportunities that they can perceive. Development theorists hold that the SHG represents the process by which "social capital" as distinct from financial assets, machinery, land and other resources has now become critical for development. However, it requires a basic theoretical knowledge to understand the significant process of critique and discussion.

2.1. Definition of Development

The concept, "development" has been characterised by multiple definitions and a great deal of vagueness and impression. The literary meaning of development points out that, it is an act of developing or the process of being developed, proceeding one stage to new stage (*Chambers Twentyfirst Century English Dictionary, p.366*). It is a process in which something passes by degrees (both quantitative and qualitative) to a different stage, especially a more advanced or matured stage. Such definitions could include those based on modernisation, which focus on standards of living as evidenced through any number of variables. Development has now come to mean catching up with the standard of living and life styles of advanced countries, but development may also mean that economies increase their potential for growth and realise that potential. As such even the developed countries can be "developed". In these days of globalisation even the development of developed countries cannot be taken for granted. Earlier it was thought that developed countries cannot slide down the path of development. These days even developed countries can face acute problems and crises. According to Asante (1991) "development is a collective responsibility in which all have to share in the labour as well as the fruits and people become the 'end' and the 'means' of development. People's interests, values and aspirations necessarily determine the content, strategies and modalities of development"[1].

"Development", is a process by which the members of a society increase their personal and institutional capacities to mobilise and manage resources to produce sustainable and justly distributed improvements in their quality of life consistent with their own aspirations Karten (1990)[2]. Economic growth is treated mainly as a function of investment, a simple formula links appropriate levels of investment with the incremental capital output ratio and desired growth rates. The process of economic growth is characteristically followed to a series of stages which would ultimately spread benefits to all, thereby alleviating poverty and inequality.

However, the unit of "development" is not constant. The dynamic aspect is that, development discourse takes different shape accordingly to time and space. Dreze and Sen (1989)[3] criticise the narrow definition of development. According to them development is about "pursuit of freedoms". These freedoms as economic opportunities, social opportunities, political freedom, transparency and trust in the community and security which takes place with the time. They opine that development as freedom takes note of political and social aspects because an individual is "free" when she or he has a wide range of choice.

By the end of the 1990s, many analysts began to notice that economic growth was not necessarily correlated with other development objectives, such as rapid employment creation, the reduction of poverty and inequalities, and the provision of basic needs. Particularly, the third world countries such as Brazil, Iran, Kenya, Mexico, Pakistan, and South Africa and the like, in which rapid economic growth had been attained but severe mal-development problems were appearing. Economic growth was not eradicating poverty or creating employment opportunities at the speed anticipated and in many cases, the income inequalities were increasing. By 1970s, some 944 million people, 52 per cent of the total population of the South, were still living in absolute poverty (UN 1989: 39), despite the development efforts of the previous decades. Indeed, by the early 1970s, it had become commonplace to argue that throughout much of the Third World growth was accompanied by increased inequality (Gariffin 1989:165).

The United Nations Development Programme (UNDP) has identified poverty alleviation as a part of its quest for a new paradigm of sustainable human development. The established financial institution view is that large sections of the poor in the developing world have experienced economic progress and that without development assistance the situation of the poor would have been worse. Poverty alleviation, however, is difficult to define. Even more difficult is measuring whether and to what degree poverty alleviation has occurred. What unites most definitions of poverty alleviation is broad agreement that "participation" and "empowerment" of poor people are essential to poverty alleviation.

2.2. Modernisation Theory

Modernisation has been analysed mainly by two approaches. First is the evolutionary approach in which modernisation is an evolutionary stage in the human society. While the Marxian evolutionist believe that the stage of modernisation can only be brought by the scrapping the existing order. The developing countries of the world are termed "traditional" and their counterpart at higher stage of economic and technologically developed countries known as "modern". The phenomenal growth of knowledge, sciences and technology has created modern state.

Modernisation theory took shape in the 1950s in the

United States and bears an American stamp. Modernisation theory is usually referred as a paradigm. The assumptions of the modernisation theorists, who had in some sense a global perspective, are particularly important to an understanding of the effects of development on poverty. They saw one road along which all nations travelled, regardless of where they started. Since all aspects of a society were synergistically modernized, the end was universally desirable, and the process was inevitable, there was little reason for them to consider differential impact.

Rostow, *The Stages of Economic Growth: A Non-Communist Manifesto* (1960) put forward a five-stage theory of development, was influential because of its simplicity. He distinguished five stages through which all countries have to pass. These are: (i) the traditional society; (ii) the preconditions for take-off; (iii) the take-off; (iv) the drive to maturity (self-sustained growth); and (v) the age of high mass consumption. The preconditions for take-off and the drive to maturity stages were considered to be the two most important, with the former removing obstacles to growth through the development of entrepreneurial ambition and reinvestment, and the latter consolidating these key features of development process. Rastow was criticized because he never mentioned about the dependency concept, the world market, terms of trade or colonialism. He liked assistance from outside such as the World Bank, International Monetary Fund (IMF), Foreign Direct Investment (FDI), Multinationals Companies (MNCs), and military advisors.

From the late 1960s, modernisation theory increasingly went out of fashion in development practice and in academic discourse. Perhaps above all, modernisation theory lacked a convincing account of the causes of modernisation. Entrepreneurship and innovation may be important factors in modernising processes but the question remains as to whether such individual behaviour reflects a process of wider social transformation. Moreover, it was also increasingly criticised by Marxists and Neo-Marxists from the late 1960s that modernisation theory failed to see any coherence between advanced and third world countries.

2.3. Marxist and neo-Marxist Development Theory

Marxism, the Eurocentric approach regards socio-economic and political relations as determined by the relations of production. It examines imperialism from the perspective of the capitalist countries in the centre of the world system and looks for reasons for existence of imperialism. Marxists emphasise the historical progressive role of capitalism. Marx and Lenin describe the role of the spread of capitalism in Eastern despotic or absolute societies as historically progressive. Economic development was stimulated as major feudal landholders transformed themselves into capitalist entrepreneurs. Simultaneously the feudal oppression was lifted from the shoulders of the peasants, who would in due course form a working class, which could be recruited for a socialist revolution. Lenin (1917) pointed out the dangers of exorbitant profits being transferred from the periphery to the core countries, retarding capitalistic development potential. Further, the relationships between the local bourgeoisie in the periphery and the bourgeoisie in the core, preventing the genesis of a progressive bourgeoisie. Marxists still adhere to nineteenth century development optimism. For example, they view the concept of scarcity as an invention of the bourgeoisie to legitimise economic inequality.

One of the best-known Neo-Marxist development theories is the "dependency theory". Advocates of this school are Celso Furtado (1963), Fernando Cardoso and Enzo Falleto (1979), and Teontonio Dos Santos (1970), and popularised in the third world countries such as Latin America, Asia and Africa through the writings of Ander Gunder Frank (1969a, 1969b, 1979).

Frank was a leading critic of development economics and

modernisation theory. He mounted a detailed criticism of the "dual society" thesis, which maintained that underdevelopment societies had a dual structure of traditional and modern, each with its own dynamic. In his *Latin America: Underdevelopment or Revolution* (1969a) attributed that world capitalism transformed earlier social systems even as it came into existence, converting them into sources of its own further development. For Frank, the economic, political, social and cultural institutions of the underdeveloped countries resulted from the penetration of capitalism, rather than being original or traditional. Frank focused on the metropolis-satellite or centre-periphery relations in Latin America. He said, the underdevelopment of peripheral-capitalist regions of people was characterised by three contradictions. Firstly, the monopolistic expropriation of economic surplus; secondly, metropolis-satellite polarisation, and finally, the contradiction of continuity in change.

According to Brazilian geographer Teontonio Dos Santos (1970), the relationship between centre and periphery, a spatial form of dependence, in which some countries (the dominant) have achieved their self-sustaining economic growth, while others (the dominated and dependent) have grown only as a reflection of changes in the dominant countries. The incorporation of Latin America into the capitalist world economy directly through colonial administration, but more subtly through foreign trade, geared the region's economies toward demands for the centre, even when the export economy was locally owned. Dependence skewed the region's social structure so that local power was held by small ruling class that used the gains from exporting for luxury consumption rather than investment[4]. This process has led to a growing social, political and economic marginalisation of many Latin Americans. Poverty and stagnation stemmed in underdeveloped countries because of external exploitation[5].

World systems theory has obvious affinities with the dependency school. This theory was developed in the mid-1970s, when East Asian countries were experiencing swift growth that could no longer be described as dependent development, particularly as they had begun to challenge the economic superiority of the USA in a number of areas. Another factor conducive to the rise of world systems theories was the oncoming crisis on socialist countries. Wallerstein was the most outspoken figure in this new discourse of world systems. Wallerstein (1974) argued that a capitalist world economy had existed since the sixteenth century, that is, since the beginning of the colonial era. He pointed out that within the world system there are three main economic zones. These are (i) core, (ii) semi-periphery, and (iii) periphery. The core consists of countries with efficient, complex production systems and high levels of capital accumulation. Core states are administratively well organised and militarily powerful. Peripheral countries have the opposite characteristics, while the semi-periphery combined elements of both. World systems theory saw spatial relations as exploitative, that is, involving the flow of surplus from periphery to core[6].

Another world systems thinker is Samir Amin, who began publishing on this topic in 1976. He did agree with the existence of a non-capitalist mode of production which saw its surplus appropriated through unequal trade. This unequal trade led to a stagnation in the expansion of the national market and thus to a disarticulated economic system. Amin (1977) explains underdevelopment as an outcome of three factors. First, unevenness of productivity between spheres or sector unevenness of the productivity between centre and periphery; second, the disarticulation or distortion of the underdevelopment economies of the periphery made up of non-integrated sectors, with less flow of internal exchanges in the bid to satisfy the external demands imposed on them by the economies of the centre;

and finally, the centre that dominates economically, socially and politically over the periphery. The central premise is that while economic growth characterises the economic sectors at the centre. It contributes to the development of underdevelopment and the disarticulation of the social formations of the periphery[7].

Palma (1978) a sociologist, criticized to Frank's dependency theory. He viewed that dependency theory is static and unhistorical. Bienefeld (1981) changes in the global capitalist system, such as industrialisation and economic growth in Latin America and East Asia, supposedly disagree with dependency theory's notion of blocked development in the periphery. As James (1997) proclaimed dependency theory is all but dead and it is now a theoretical-political memory.

However, the outstanding critique of dependency and world systems theories came from Brenner's *"The Origins of Capitalist Development: A Critique of Neo-Smithian Marxism"* (1977). For Brenner, an entire line of Marxists and neo-Marxists intending to negate the optimistic model of economic advance derived from Adam Smith (i.e. widening trade and a deeper division of labour bringing economic development) ended up with a theory that was the mirror image of Smith's model. Wallerstein carried this idea to its logical conclusion by defining capitalism as production for profit *via* exchange and focusing on the expansion of the world market. With this market came a world division of labour, the development of different methods of labour control in the various specialised zones, and the creation of strong and weak states in core and periphery. For Brenner, both kinds of analyses erred by displacing class relations from the main body of development theory. Brenner argued that the incorporation of more productive resources into the world system did not determine the economic development process, nor did the transfer of surplus and build-up of wealth in the core, nor even specialisation of labour control systems.

2.4. Gandhian Model

The Gandhian idea of development is based on the foundational ethics of *ahimsa* (non-violence). In Gandhian era, the concept of development was not so highlighted, there for he used the term progress rather than development, more with respect of ethics and cosmic integrity. According to Gandhi, "by economic progress means moral progress and it leads to social development". As such he never made an academic contribution to "development". However, he pleaded for an organised effort to change the ruling paradigm and move towards a superhuman stage. According to him, "the cosmic-moral organisation, faith is the path of spirituality and spirituality in its true sense is the motive force behind development". Gandhian development of society is with the human only that "every human being has a right to live and, therefore, to find the wherewithal to feed himself and where necessary to clothe and house himself"[8]. He said, "there is enough in the world to meet the needs of everyone but there is not enough to meet the greed of everyone". If every small village became self-sufficient then one would have an ideal setting for life. Therefore, he did not talk about macro-economic model. All villages should become self-sufficient and it must work from the bottom up approach and not the top down method.

Sarvodaya (the uplifting of all) was a main *mantra* of Gandhian development. Society most strives for the economic, social, spiritual and physical well-being of all not just the minority capitalists. He favoured a holistic approach to well-being and a total upliftment of the community. For him, "the well-being of every individual was an important concern"[9]. He believed that there should be an equitable distribution of resources and that community must become self-sustaining through reliance on local products instead of large-scale imports from outside. Gandhi was opposed to large-scale industrialisation, and favoured small scale industries that promote local self-sufficiency, which called *Swadeshi*.

On "self-sufficiency" Gandhi said, the unit of society should be a village or a manageable small group of people who would in the ideal be self-sufficient (in matter of their vital requirements) as a unit. Every village's first concern will be to grow its own food crops and cotton for its cloth. Every village has to be self-sustained and capable of managing its affairs even to the extent of defending itself against the whole world[10]. According to Gandhi, the system of co-operation was far more necessary for the agriculturists than for the mat weavers. The land belonged to the State, therefore, it yielded the largest return when it was worked co-operatively. Let it be remembered that co-operation should be based on strict non-violence[11]. Gandhi's theory of "trusteeship" is no make-shift, certainly no camouflage. Trusteeship doctrine will survive like all other theories. It has the sanction of philosophy and religion behind it. That possessors of wealth have not acted up to the theory does not prove its falsity; it proves the weakness of the wealthy. No other theory is compatible with non-violence[12]. The secret of successful cooperative effort is that the members must be honest and know the great merit of cooperation and it must have a definite progressive goal. Self- Employed Women's Association (SEWA) is such a kind of cooperative which follow the Gandhian doctrine of cooperation, trusteeship which is leading to self-sufficiency for the poor women.

2.5. Women in Development Theory

In the discourse of development practice, the development initiatives had preoccupied with economists and colonial administrators in the 1930s and largely ignored the women issues. These approaches identified development with modernisation and assumed the wholesale adoption of Western technology, institutions, and beliefs. During the

1940s and 1950s, development planners designed projects aimed to modernise colonies all over the world. Many of these projects failed, but this did little to undermine most development experts' faith in modernisation.

Boserup's *Women's Role in Economic Development* (1970) investigated the impact of development projects on Third World women. She discovered that most of these projects ignored women and that many technologically sophisticated projects undermined women's economic opportunities and autonomy. Training in new technologies was usually offered to men, which meant that most "modern" projects improved male opportunities and technological knowledge but reduced women's access to both technology and employment which automatically "trickle down" to women and other disadvantaged groups in Third World nations.

Moser (1993) the WID approach, with its determination to integrate women into development, slowly became a concern of many governments and donor agencies. The United Nations Decade for Women was launched in 1975 with the Mexico City conference on the theme "Equality, Development and Peace". The World Plan of Action that emerged from the conference and set the agenda for the Decade for Women established the goal of integrating women into the development process. However, the WID approach has important limitations that have tended to restrict its transformative capacity on many levels. Because this approach relies heavily on modernisation theory, it generally assumes that Western institutions hold most of the answers and it often ignores the possible contribution of indigenous knowledge. It also tends to see development as an activity of a government-to-government nature and consequently refrains from criticising third world governments. It sees the state as a solution, rather than a potential problem for the advancement of women.

During the 1970s, this approach influenced the thinking and practice of some academics and activists for example,

NGOs that called for women's projects that were completely separate from men's[13]. They argued for a development approach to women that recognised the dangers of integrating women into a patriarchal world, and they sought instead to create "women-only" projects, carefully constructed to protect women's interests from patriarchal domination. This approach has sometimes been referred to as Women and Development (WAD)[14] .

The WAD paradigm emphasises the distinctiveness of women's knowledge, women's work, and women's goals and responsibilities in overall social development. It argues for recognition of this distinctiveness and for acknowledgement of the special roles that women have always played in the development process. For example, the WAD perspective gave rise to a persistent call to recognise that women are the mainstay of agricultural production in many areas of Africa, although their contribution has been systematically overlooked and marginalised in national and donor development plans. This concern was captured in the slogan "Give credit where credit is due." Campaigns designed to change policies and place women's issues and concerns on national and international agendas have been a key area of activity for people working within this development paradigm, and disseminating information has been an important strategy. Efforts to organise have been oriented both to making mainstream bureaucracies more responsive to women's needs and to strengthening bonds among women through active, autonomous local groups and networks[15]. Then onwards recognition to women issues become a focal point in development discourse.

During the 1970s, in the context of ongoing social movements challenging authority, the arguments of the dependency school and the growing concern for women issues with the third world poverty have influenced liberal development thinking. Officials at the International Monetary Fund (IMF) and the World Bank committed their institutions to waging a war on poverty and providing basic human needs for all. WID specialists also adopted this approach, targeting poor women and their basic human needs as the primary goals of WID policies. As Moser (1989) pointed out, this anti-poverty approach recognised, and tried to serve, women's practical anti-gender needs by focusing on improving women's access to income through such efforts as small-scale, income-generating projects. Thus, in the 1970s, radical and orthodox development thinkers and planners agreed on the centrality of poverty alleviation, although they differed on how to bring it about (Jaquette, 1982).

Where dependency theorists saw debt as a component of the long-term capital flows draining wealth from poorer to richer countries, the international development agencies, particularly the IMF and World Bank, drew a conclusion consistent with the modernisation approach. The third world economies required structural adjustment to revive themselves and flourish. Structural-adjustment programmes (SAPs) were designed to reduce government expenditure and increase the power of market forces in third world economies, thereby increasing their productivity and efficiency. Once again, the assumptions of liberal development thinking has dominated the SAPs, including the assumption that economic prosperity would benefit women as well as men. In this context, the emphasis has been on increasing women's economic contribution to increase overall economic efficiency and bring about equity for women (Moser, 1989). A few development specialists working on women's issues in the official agencies have begun to question the underlying assumption that structural adjustment would, in the long run, benefit everyone. Some have recognized that women and children have suffered from the short-run dislocations caused by the SAPs, a recognition that has resulted in the implementation of special programmes to alleviate the short-term effects of the SAPs on vulnerable groups (women, children, the aged, and the disabled). Elson (1991) argues that many of these policies have an inherent male bias.

Standing (1989) argued that there was a feminisation of the labour force throughout the 1980s in industrialising countries. With the SAPs comes pressure on governments to deregulate. With employers seeking to improve their competitive position through flexible labour practices, more jobs have become "feminised": they have taken on the characteristics of insecure, low-paying jobs with few prospects for advancement. This accounts, in part, for the increase in female labour-force participation, as men are less willing to take these jobs. In many countries, female unemployment rates in the 1980s declined relative to male unemployment rates. Standing blamed this trend on the feminisation of labour and the employers' desire to have a cheaper, more disposable or flexible labour supply[16].

Some feminists and development theorists have remained unconvinced by both the WID and the WAD approaches, arguing that neither addresses the fundamental factors that structure and maintain gender inequalities. These scholars and activists have turned to the Gender and Development (GAD) perspective which emerged in the 1980s as an alternative to WID and WAD. This framework is also referred to as the "empowerment approach" or "gender-aware planning".

Drawing on the socialist-feminist perspective, the GAD approach argues that women's status in society is deeply affected by their material conditions of life and by their position in the national, regional, and global economies. GAD also recognises that women are deeply affected by the nature of patriarchal power in their societies at the national, community, and household levels. Moreover, women's material conditions and patriarchal authority are both defined and maintained by the accepted norms and values that define women's and men's roles and duties in a particular society (Sen and Grown, 1987).

The GAD adopts a two-pronged approach to the study of women and development, investigating women's material conditions and class position, as well as the patriarchal structures and ideas that define and maintain women's subordination. The focus is on relationships between women and men in the society, not on women alone. Gender relations are seen as the key determinant of women's position in society, not as immutable reflections of the natural order but as socially constructed patterns of behaviour that is the social construction of "gender" which can be changed if this is desired. The GAD approach focuses on the interconnection of gender, class, and race and the social construction of their defining characteristics. Women experience oppression differently, according to their race, class, colonial history, culture, and position in the international economic order (Moser 1993). These points are key in the approaches of black and Third World feminism. GAD recognises the differential impacts of development policies and practices on women and men and sees women as agents, not simply as recipients, of development. This perspective thus calls into question both gender relations and the development process.

Molyneux (1985) argued that within the GAD perspective, a distinction is drawn between women's interests (a biological category that assumes homogeneity) and gender interests (a socially constructed set of relations and material practices). As suggested above, gender interests can be either practical or strategic. Practical gender needs arise out of concrete conditions; these are immediate perceived needs, such as the need to provide food, shelter, education, and health care. Strategic gender interests arise out of an analysis of women's subordination and require changes in the structures of gender, class, and race that define women's position in any given culture. Strategic interests include the goal of gender equality[17].

The politicisation of practical needs and their transformation into strategic interests constitute central aspects of the GAD approach, as does the empowerment of women to achieve this goal. The GAD approach provides a way to analyse policies and organisational efforts to determine which one will both meet short-term practical needs and help to change the structures of subordination. In the 1980s, donor agencies and state machineries consolidated their WID activities, but the GAD perspective increasingly shaped the interests and activities by feminist NGOs, for instance Grameen Bank and SEWA.

The WAD approach remained particularly strong, as women continued to organize at the grass-roots level and through broader networks to increase recognition and support for women's special contributions to national development. The continuous pressure applied by organised women's groups remained significant, forcing governments and other agencies to take women seriously and address their concerns. Activists also challenged feminist scholars and academics to strengthen the links between theory and practice and to revise theories to accommodate new forms of analysis arising from experience.

In some cases, policies and programmes that clearly continued to work within the WID paradigm (as defined in this chapter) adopted GAD as their newer, perhaps more fashionable, label. Ironically, although the GAD framework actually goes farther than WID in challenging patriarchal structures, some agencies adopted the term *gender* or GAD to reassure men that their interests and concerns were not being overlooked or undermined by an excessive focus on women. Some agencies that still use the language of WID have moved toward making more far-reaching critiques of the structure of gender relations and toward promoting policies and programmes that challenge fundamental inequalities. Labels, therefore, no longer provide a clear guide to identifying the theoretical paradigm underlying policies and programmes; one also needs to examine their content more closely.

Scott (1995) has pointed out modernisation and dependency theories conceptualising themes like modernity, development, self-reliance, and revolution within a vision informed by gendered preoccupations and conceptions; these extended to the dominant policies and practices of international agencies and revolutionary government alike. In modernisation theory, Scott argued, modernity and rational, forward-looking, male dominated public sphere were contrasted with a feminized backward traditional society, while the achievement of modernity was seen as a power struggle with the feminine on the way to maturity[18].

Kabeer (1994) has distinguished between two groups within the WAD school. Firstly, dependency used the traditional Marxist feminist framework and saw inequalities between man and woman for the larger global economy; this analysis extended the WID critique of mainstream development theory. Secondly, a group focusing on "global capitalist patriarchy and male violence" was aligned more with radical feminism, which saw gender having precedence over class. The international network of third world women researcher DAWN mainly adhered to the WAD perspective[19].

In one of the main research document produced by DAWN, Sen and Grown (1987) have argued that the perspective of poor oppressed women provide a powerful vantage point or examining the effects of development programmes and strategies. This was so because oppressed women knew poverty, yet women's undervalued work was nevertheless all social reproduction. Such experiences with economic growth were determined by gender and class. Often, the effects of these policies have been devastating to the poor, have greatly affect the middle class, and have had little or no positive impact on the wealthy. They revealed some common and difficult problems that women's organisations must struggle with. Many groups have been wary of viewing large public policy issues as within their domain. They have not developed enduring and effective channels for acquiring representation. They avoid clear assignment of responsibilities or delegation of authority for fear of mirroring existing hierarchies or established power structures. They tend to look with suspicion upon and political force or body that is not of their own making based on experiences of attempted and successful cooperation. They have not worked out ways of power-sharing within organisations. Organisations must be broadened and democratised, must explicitly reject personal aggrandisements, and must show respect for the many voices of our movement. Their recipe for resolving such problems includes "resources" (finance, knowledge, technology, etc.), skills training and leadership formation on the one side, and democratic processes, dialogue, participation in policy and decision making and techniques for conflict resolution on the other[20].

It remains problematic to group together men and women or different ethnic groups or races, when one is analysing either the level of development or the effects of development strategies. Differential effects are thereby masked, much as average income levels mask groups living in absolute poverty. Women are often treated as subsidiary members of male-headed households in measures of development. This ignores their own major contributions to the family, the variety of complicated family structures that exist in both first and third worlds, and the frequently inequitable distribution of resources within the family.

However, women have generally been disregarded in development practice, as they have in theory. The litany of the underdevelopment of women and the adverse effects of development on women is now central to the field of household's development. Women are disproportionately represented among the poor and are disproportionately responsible for family survival, particularly that of young children. While it is not easy to distinguish between the specific effects of development on women and the long-term effects of poverty and patriarchy, the lives either of non-poor women are often incredibly difficult compared to the lives either of non-poor women or of men. This not to say that men's lives are easy or that many men do not suffer as a result of some development practices and from devastating poverty. However, many of the problems that women face are directly and undeniably related to the fact that they are women.

According to Buvinic and Lycette (1988) specifically, women are disadvantaged or disproportionately responsible in the areas of education, family, health, work, exposure to poverty, displacement, and environmental hazards[21]. Ferguson (1990) describes that, it has become commonplace to note that development hurts women, that it cuts women off from access to the land, creates more work for women to do, and increases women dependency on men. In rural areas, where women often do most of the subsistence farming, only men are provided with machinery, training, land ownership, and credit. Women lose power and resources at the same time as their workload increases they assist their husbands and do their own subsistence farming on land that is farther from home and of poorer quality. Men both earn and control the disposition of cash. Men follow jobs and leave rural areas. They often establish new families in the cities, provide little financial support to the rural family, and on their rare return visits impregnate their wives. Rural women also suffer disproportionately from environmental degradation, going farther and farther to get water and fuel. Urban women receive less education and training than men, and are usually forced intc the informal economy-increasing their work-load, providing them with jobs that are often dangerous, and giving them no job security or possibility for advancement.

They are also frequently denied credit and property rights. Women in urban areas are often isolated and apart from family and kinship networks[22].

According to Moser (1993), the welfare approach is based on three assumptions. First, those women are passive recipients of development, rather than participants in the development processes. Secondly, that motherhood is the most important role for women in society, and thirdly, that child-rearing is the most effective role for women in all aspects of economic development. While this approach itself sees as "family-centred" in orientation, it focuses on women entirely in terms of their reproductive role. It assumes men's role to be productive and it identifies the mother-child dyad as the unit of concern. The main method of implementation is through the top-down handouts of free goods and services and, therefore, it does not include women in local organisations in participatory planning processes, where training is included it is for those skills deemed appropriate for non-working housewives and mothers. In their mothering roles low-income women have been the primary targets for improving family welfare, particularly of children, through an increasing diversity of programmes reflecting a broadening of the mandate of welfare over the past three decades[23].

By 1970s, dissatisfaction with the welfare approach was widespread in the world. The criticism was initiated in three levels. First in United States, a group of female professionals and researchers who were concerned with the increasing evidence that Third World development projects were negatively affecting women; secondly, development economists and planners who were concerned with the failure of modernisation theory in the Third World; and thirdly, the United Nations that concerned both these concerns. The voicing of these concerns led to the UN 1975 International Women's Year Conference (IWY). This finally, put women on the agenda and provided legitimacy for the proliferation of a wide diversity of Third World women's organisations, in turn leading to the UN designating 1976-85 as the Women's Decade. During this decade the critique of the welfare approach resulted in the development of a number of alternative approaches to women. Moser (1993:69) sees the efficiency approach as the predominant policy approach to women. Its purpose being to ensure that development is made more efficient and effective through women's economic contribution, what she is referring to here are the adjustment measures implemented by numerous governments, under aegis of multinational financial institutions.

Today, although much of this sentiment has changed, much has remained the same. The dominant thinking in the late 1980s and early 1990s has been that the state has a leading, but only facilitating, role in the economy. Development is now seen as the responsibility of private companies and, increasingly, non government organizations (NGOs). In addition, the market is seen as the main intermediary of decision-making.

2.6. The Anti-Poverty Approach

In the development paradigm, mainly poor people are classified as targets because of their identification as a 'vulnerable group' outside of the economy. Rothenberg (1953) noted on parameters of welfare approach. According to him any welfare model formally requires (1) specification of the agents (individual, groups, and systems of groups); (2) specification of the concept of welfare; (3) specification for the alternative situations for which welfare comparisons are to be made; and (4) formulation of a rule whereby welfare comparisons can be made for particular alternative situations[24]. They are given assistance because they are low-income group and they only recognised during the work hours, and whatever they are earning is not sufficient for their daily basic requirement. Poor sections of society are the passive recipients of welfare and they are seen as the problem and not the solution.

In India, to eradicate poverty, the anti-poverty approach methods were introduced from the 1970s onwards. Its purpose is to ensure that poor women increase their productivity. Women's poverty is seen as the problem of underdevelopment. It recognises the productive role of the women and seeks to meet practical gender needs to earn an income. Buvinic, *et al.* (1983) has argued that this is a toned-down version of the equity approach, arising out of the reluctance of development agencies to interface with the manner in which relations between men and women are constructed in a given society. The anti-poverty policy approach to women focuses mainly on their productive role, on the basis that poverty alleviation and the promotion of balanced economic growth requires the increased productivity of women in low-income households[25].

Holcombe (1995) describes that, there is a broad consensus in the development community about the priority of poverty alleviation and also about the importance of participation and empowerment. In the search of models or even magic solution to poverty, the significance of participation and empowerment to the implementation of models is often overlooked. Participation and empowerment are essentially functions of process, not models. They occur only because of process set in motion by the staff of organisations implementing poverty alleviation. To make participation and empowerment of the poor possible—whatever we think those concepts mean—we need to enable the participation and empowerment of those staff working directly with poor people. For how can staff that feel disempowered and excluded from participation be expected to encourage the participation[26].

2.7. The Empowerment Approach

In many respects empowerment approach has arose from dissatisfaction with the original Women in Development as equity approach, because of its perceived co-option into the anti-poverty and efficiency approaches. However, the empowerment approach differs from the equity approach. This relates not only its origins but also in the causes, dynamics and structures of women's oppression which it identifies and in terms of the strategies it proposes to change the position of third world women. Moser (1993) has pointed out that, the origins of the empowerment approach are derived less from the research of First World women and more from the emergent feminist writings and grassroots organisational experience of Third World women[27]. As Jayawardena (1986) has argued that, the women's movement was not imposed on women by the United Nations or Western feminists, but has an independent history. The empowerment approach acknowledges inequalities between men and women and the origins of women's subordination in the family. It also emphasises the fact that women experience oppression differently according to their race, class, colonial history and current position in the international economic order. This approach recognises the triple role of women and seeks through bottom-up women's organisations to raise women's consciousness to challenge their subordination[28]. The main features of empowerment approach are:

1. The "welfare approach" prior to 1970 focused on women's reproductive roles and related population issues, with programmes initiated on birth control.
2. The "equity approach" reflected calls for equality coming from the UN decade for women. This met with considerable resistance from men.

3. The "anti-poverty approach" focused on women entering the workforce, or having access to income-generating activities.
4. The "efficiency approach" was aligned with IMF structural adjustment programmes and stressed women's participation in newly restructured economies.
5. The "empowerment approach" reflected third world feminist writings, grassroots organizing and women's need to transform laws and structures through a bottom-up approach.

2.8. Alternative Development Model

In response to such criticism, feminists and development activists made a series of attempts at reformulating development theory. Alternative development has been concerned with introducing alternative practices and redefining the goals of development. This has been successful in the sense that key elements of both have been adopted in mainstream development. Even if not consistently practised it is now generally accepted that development efforts are more successful if the community participates. NGOs now play key roles on the ground and in development cooperation. This success reflects not simply the strength of NGOs and grassroots politics but also the 1980s rollback of the state, the advance of market forces and the breakdown of regulation. All the same, the goals of development have been generally redefined. It is now widely accepted that development is not simply a matter of GDP growth and human development is a more appropriate goal and measure of development. This also means that alternative development has become less distinct from conventional development discourse and practice since alternatives have been absorbed in mainstream development. In the context of alternative development several pertinent positions and methodologies have been developed[29]. According to Pieterse, "alternative" generally refers to three spheres-agents, methods and objectives or value of development. The hallmark of alternative development is participation of the local and use of their knowledge or the implementing knowledge in development from bottom-up.

Chambers (1983) has popularised the notions of "farmer first" and "putting the last first" as an alternative methods for rural development and poverty alleviation. His central argument is that, "doing development" typically falls to outsiders—people who, however well-intentioned are neither from the target areas nor have directly experienced the problems of poverty, deprivation, insecurity, vulnerability and exploitation. Their visions, interpretations and actions are thus built upon preconceptions and misperceptions about the rural poor. He pointed out that "the last should be given first position in rural development— the targeted one" who is marginalised and the "rural development tourism" or the rural development "tourists" should be given second position[30].

As the practice of poor people's development was evolving, mainly through information and by growing social activism of literate people and their consciences. A base of knowledge was accreting that led to the design of "alternative visions" of development. This model is away from concepts of linear, universal progress principally defined by economic growth and towards peace, equity and social justice. Generally, these visions are not discussed in the context of traditional development. The new visions of development model are not just for women nor have only women contributed to their definitions. However, they do derive much their power from their insistence, that development does not benefit women as well as men, that does not delight in diversity, and that does not work to reduce oppression is not in fact development. A social transformation is called for bringing stability, peace, equality, the satisfactions of basic needs for all, and harmony with nature. According to Goulet (1985:155) above all, alternative development has led to "self-determination and increased human capacity—a process by which a populace acquires a greater mastery over its own destiny".

'Alternative' generally refers to three aspects—agents, methods and objectives or values of development. According to Nerfin (1977), alternative development is the "landscape of 'Third System' or *'Decentralisation of Power'* the importance of which is apparent in view of the failed development efforts of government and economic power. Often this seems to be the key point: alternative development is development from below or base"[31]. In this context, 'below' refers both to 'community' and to NGOs. In several respects alternative development revisits Community Development (CD) of the 1950s and 1960s. Carmen (1996) describes that, community development goes back to American social work, which *via* British colonialism entered colonial development, and in the 1950s supplemented modernisation efforts. This genealogy accounts for the ambiguity of some of the key terms in alternative development, such as 'participation' or social capital.

Alternative development is frequently identified with development by NGOs. But given the wide variety of NGOs and NGO practices, the equation "alternative development is what NGOs do" would obviously be inadequate. NGO ideology is organisation led and too limited to account for alternative development. Alternative development involves further distinguishing elements with respect to development methodology (participatory, endogenous, self-reliant) and objectives (geared to basic needs). The alternative referred to alternative in relation to state and market, but not necessarily in relation to the general discourse of developmentalism.

Alternative development has been concerned with introducing alternative practices and redefining the goals of development. This has been successful in the sense that key elements of both have been adopted in mainstream development. Even if not consistently practised it is now generally accepted that development efforts are more successful if the community participates. NGOs now play key roles on the ground and in development cooperation.

However, alternative development has failed to develop a clear perspective on micro-macro relations, an alternative macro approach, and a coherent theoretical position, although, it is often claimed that there is an alternative development paradigm. These reflections on alternative development are followed by queries on poverty alleviation, which increasingly caught on the horns of a dilemma between the aims of human and social development and the constraints of structural adjustment and global monetarism represented by the international financial institutions (e.g., World Bank and International Monetary Fund).

Alternative development can be viewed as a roving critique of mainstream development, shifting in position as mainstream development shifts, as a series of alternative proposals and methodologies that interconnected. It can be viewed as concerned with local development, with alternative practices on the ground or as an overall challenge to the mainstream and part of a global alternative. For example, the big gap of centre and periphery of before 1970s has been fulfilled by the Grameen and SHG model by the support of local, national and international microfinance sectors.

According to Pieterse (2001) alternative development has been changing over the years. It presents a loose profile of critical sensibilities and alternative practices that leave so many areas open that its claim to present an alternative model to mainstream development thinking is exaggerated and misplaced. A basic question is whether alternative development is an alternative way of achieving development, sharing the same goals as mainstream development but using different means, participatory and people-centred. It would seem this way if we consider the enormous increase of development funds being channelled or re-channelled through NGOs during the past two decades. This suggests ample peaceful coexistence between mainstream and alternative development.

Historical evidence suggests that, although ultimately development should make it possible to reduce poverty, during the period of transitional growth to an industrial society the welfare of significant minorities of the population may not increase at all and may even decline. Development and more specifically, and industrial revolution may be a rather unpleasant process. For example, soup kitchens, food distribution programmes, health promoters, water and sewer projects and the bourn one Self-Help Group Programme.

Of course, this is not the whole picture. There have been positive changes taken place after the invention of Grameen Bank and SHG models. Not only the middle-class women benefited from the employment opportunities but rural women (low-income women) also involve herself for self-employment jobs in the home itself. Home based employment opportunities are created by the help of self-help group funds. Moghadam (1990:21) noted that, as development increases, and as women are drawn in greater numbers into paid employment and public life, their subjugation as women is undermined and gender roles and constructs change. Thus development has long-term emancipatory effects.

2.9. Social Capital : The Concept

However, the subsequent discrediting of modernisation, social welfare, theories and approaches in its sociological and economic pretext and its replacement, respectively by the world-systems and neo-classical growth theories has led to the new situation, where the units of analysis in contemporary studies of development are either nation-states and transnational corporations or rational individuals and firms. The contribution of civil society and other institutional arrangements that mediating the space between states and markets has been lost, incorporating themselves neither into a coherent body of knowledge nor sensitive and sensible policy prescriptions. The idea of social capital is both appealing and promising. Precisely, because it offers a potential strategy for obviating these concerns while bridging theoretical and disciplinary parts. Therefore, an attempt has been made to put a logical structure for integrating social capital into development theory and policy by observing and explaining the empirical studies conducted at the micro and macro level. Under the empirical study facts and figures has been collected and explored the conditions on which social capital is a method for poverty alleviation through Self-Help Group model. The model suggests on explanation of mobility processes as the outcome of strategic action of social groups trying to improve or defend their life-chances.

According to Hanifan (1916) the concept of social capital describes "those touchable substances that count for most in the daily lives of people". He was particularly concerned with the nurturing of goodwill, fellowship, sympathy and social intercourse among those that make up a "social unit"[32]. The contemporary appearance of social capital was first identified by Jacobs, Bourdieu and Passeron, and Loury in 1960s. Since then, the theory have been used extensively and developed by James Coleman, Ronald Burt, Robert Putnam and Alejandro Portes. Presently, it has widely been using by vast number of social, political and economy theorists. Rational choice theorist considers, social capital as an informational resource emerging as a result of interaction between rational agents needs to coordinate for mutual benefit.

The most extensive empirical research and coherent

theoretical advances have come in late 1980s and 1990s from two distinct literatures within the so-called "new sociology of economic development", namely ethnic entrepreneurship studies (at the micro level) and comparative institutionalist studies of state-society relations (at the macro level). The main advocates of micro level studies are, Light, Portes, and Waldinger. The macro level studies are attributed with the scholars like Bates, Amsden, Evans and Wade. The basis for attempting such a synthesis rests on the centrality of two key concepts shared by these literatures, concepts referring to two distinct but complementary forms of social capital. These concepts are respectively, "embeddedness" and "autonomy". The idea of embeddedness comes originally from Karl Polanyi but was introduced to contemporary sociologists by Granovetter.

According to Granovetter (1985), "all economic action was inherently enmeshed in social relations of one configuration of other, and that development essentially brought about a change in the kind of embeddedness, not degree"[33]. In his discussion of embeddedness, Granovetter dismissed the distinction between "markets and hierarchies" employed by the new institutional economists. In his view, "order and disorder, honesty and malfeasance have more to do with different type of social relations (personal ties, networks). Social mechanisms needed to be in place to protect the social ties among powerful institutional actors—especially those transcending the public and private realm—from becoming vehicles for corruption, nepotism, or exploitation.

The theoretical appreciation of social capital of Bourdieu (1986) was broadly dominated within a Marxist framework. He began by distinguishing between three forms of capital: economic, cultural and social (the aggregate of the actual or potential resources which are linked to possession of a durable network of more or less institutionalised relationships of mutual acquaintance and recognition). A basic concern was to explore the processes making for unequal access to resources and differentials in power — the ways in which these fed into class formation and the creation of elites. The possession of social capital did not necessarily run alongside that of economic capital, but it still was, in his view, an attribute of elites, a means by particular networks held onto power and advantage. In Field's (2003:19) word, he "presumed that social capital generally functions to mask the naked profit-seeking of its holders, and is, therefore, inimical with the open democratic society that Bourdieu espoused in his journalism and political activism". According to Burt (1992), social capital refers to "friends, colleagues, and more general contacts through which we receive opportunities to use, relations within and between firms and the final arbiter of competitive success"[34].

Loury (1992) stated that, social capital refers to "naturally occurring social relationships among persons which promote or assist acquisition of skills and traits valued in the marketplace. It is an asset which may be as significant as financial bequests in accounting for the maintenance of inequality in our society"[35]. According to Ports (1995) social capital refers to the "capacity of individuals to command scare resources by virtue of their membership in networks or broader social structures"[36].

Coleman (1994) cited that social capital is defined by its function. It is not a single entity, but a variety of different entities, having two characteristics in common: they all consist of some aspect of a social structure, and they facilitate certain actions of individuals who are within the structure. Like other forms of capital, social capital is productive, making possible the achievement of certain ends that would not be attainable in its absence[37].

Putnam (2000) defined, "whereas physical capital refers to physical objects and human capital refers to the properties of individuals, social capital refers to connections among individuals—social networks and the norms of reciprocity and trustworthiness that arise from them"[38].

Drawing upon a base of rational choice theory Coleman (1994) looked to social capital as part of a wider exploration of the nature of social structures. He argued that social capital was defined by its function. "It is not a single entity, but a variety of different entities, having two characteristics in common: they all consist of some aspect of a social structure, and they facilitate certain actions of individuals who are within the structure"[39]. However, as Portes (1998), Foley and Edwards (1999) have pointed out, a number of problems flow from defining social capital by its function. In particular, the same "outcome" could flow from very different processes. However, Coleman's explorations were to highlight the possibility that different institutions and social structures were better suited to the cultivation of reciprocity, trust and individual action than others. Like other social investigators he highlighted the role of the family and kinship networks, and religious institutions in the creation of social capital. He believed that changes in both spheres were problematic. They were less able to socialise in appropriate ways; ties appeared to be looser and weaker[40]. Beem (1999:19-20) argues that, therefore, trust between individuals becomes trust between strangers and trust of a broad fabric of social institutions. Ultimately, it becomes a shared set of values, virtues, and expectations within society as a whole.

Putnam in his *Bowling Alone: The Collapse and Revival of American Community* (2000) gave importance to three types of social capital. First, social capital allows people to resolve collective problems more easily. People often might be better off if there is social interaction and cooperation. Second, in social transactions, social capital greases the wheels that allow communities to advance smoothly. Where people are trusting and trustworthy and where they are subject to repeated interactions with fellow members. A third way is which social capital improves people's lot is by widening their awareness of the many ways in which their fates are linked. People who have active and trusting connections to others develop characters which are good for the rest of society. The networks that constitute social capital also serve as conduits for the flow of helpful information that facilitates achieving people's goal. Social capital also operates through psychological and biological processes to improve individual's lives[41].

Woolcock (2001) criticizing Putnam's *Bowling Alone*, advocated three different types of social capital. These are: First, *"Bonding"* social capital which denotes binds between people in similar situations in society, such as immediate family, close friends and neighbours. Second, *"Bridging"* social capital, which encompasses more distant ties of like persons, such as loose friendships and workmates; and third, *"Linking"* social capital, which reaches out to unlike people in dissimilar situations, such as those who are entirely outside of the community, thus enabling members to influence a far wider range of resources than are available in the community[42]. Bonding capital is good for undergirding specific reciprocity and mobilising solidarity. Bridging networks, by contrast, are better for linkage to external assets and for information diffusion. Moreover, bridging social capital can generate broader identities and reciprocity, whereas bonding social capital bolsters our narrower selves. Bonding social capital constitutes kind of sociological superglue, whereas bridging social capital provides a sociological[43].

According to Field (2003), the thrust of social capital is that "relationships matter" and "social networks are a priceless asset" for positive feature social development. Social interaction, trust, tolerance and cooperation assist people to build communities, to commit themselves to each other, and to "knit the social fabric"[44].

Individuals' choices are shaped by their social settings, which social scientists often call "structure". Structure varies from the factors that produce the consequences of decisions, such as Self-Help Group or otherwise called as "solidarity Group" which has capable for sustaining human livelihoods and alleviating poverty. Social capital theory provides a way to formalise social structures and examine the effects of structure on self-help group's decisions. To specify the structure of "microcredit", we most specify what choices the groups face, how those choices lead to outcomes and how the members evaluate those results. Those choices of microfinance structure capture different social theories. Social theory explains what behaviour we should expect as a consequence of those theories.

In general, social capital theory can be a model for social situations and a model for self-help groups and microfinance. Social situations cover the range of group interactions in different settings. We assume that people have certain goals and that they attempt to realise those goals through their actions. The focus of the study is on how individuals' attempts to achieve their goals by the one another's actions and that by the help microfinance institutions. Therefore, in this study special attention has been given to the social capital theory. Therefore, sociologically we must analyse the social capital because it represent social facts. Social capital represents the functional aspects of society. It involves reciprocal obligations, statuses and ends and means as between two or more actors in mutual contact. Social capital is the foundation for sorting out any social problems. A sense of belonging and the concrete experience of social networks can, bring great benefits to people. Social interaction is the basic condition for social existence. It is the most inclusive group process. Groups develop through interaction with other groups.

The "top-down" (macro level) and "bottom-up"(micro level) organisational dilemmas of development, and the weakness identified earlier with social capital as it is currently employed in the literature, suggest that providing a precise definition and measures of social capital is an inherently difficult assignment[45]. Nevertheless, some important lessons emerge from a review of embeddedness and autonomy, two of the key forms of social capital identified by economic sociologists of development. First, the general idea of social capital is on the strongest theoretical grounds when it draws on and extends the combined insights of Durkheim, Weber, and Simmel in the roles that different types of social relationships play in effecting institutional outcomes. Rather that trying to prove or refute assertions that social relations are always and everywhere the construction of "rational" agents, or instead the result of primordial norms or "culture" a more fruitful approach invokes a social-structural explanation of economic life and seeks to identify the types of and combinations of social relations involved, the institutional environments shaping them, and their historical emergence and continuity.

There are both costs and benefits associated with a given "source" of social capital. Social capital always relies on long-term benefits. Top-down resources and bottom-up capacity building need to be in a dynamic and cooperative relationship in order to assemble the range of people and materials capable of overcoming problems or to take advantage of opportunities. Similarly, trust and norms of reciprocity, fairness, and cooperation are 'benefits' that are nurtured in and by particular combinations of social relationships, they are undeniably important for facilitating and reinforcing efficient institutional performance, but they do not exist independently of social relationships. Precisely, "consequences" may be one indicator of the types and combinations of social capital that are present, but they are not be confused with social capital itself.

Strategic combinations of difficult types social capital are required to sustain economic life provides a firm rebuttal of arguments that state-society relations are inherently a zero-sum game. Whether states perform well or poorly is an empirical issue, and which of these outcomes prevails turns on the coherence, credibility, and capacity of the state, the nature and extent of its engagement with civil society, and importantly, the organisational features of civil society itself. Under-governed societies are as hostile to equitable development as over-governed economies. What is true of the state holds also for other large institutions, especially those with a developmental agenda without a capacity to give in a responsive and accountable manner while simultaneously cultivating with receivers a more just, participatory and equitable social environment, development initiatives will struggle to achieve their goals. In the post cold war ear, these basic sources of social capital have been largely overlooked in our celebration for liberalisation (free markets), privatisation and globalisation.

Social capital has a number of distinctive properties, among them being the possibility that it can be deployed for both developmental and destructive purposes, and that a given form of social capital confers costs as well as benefits. It is the specific combinations of different types of social capital at the micro and macro level that determines whether the calculus of costs and benefits favour the former or the latter. Furthermore, the calculus of these costs and benefits changes over time, as development itself alters the underlying conditions shaping the prevailing combinations of social relationships. Social capital is thus a crucial but enigmatic component of the development equation, precisely because it can enhance, maintain or destroy physical and human capital. The challenge for development theorists and policy-makers alike is to identify the mechanisms that will create, nurture and sustain the types and combinations of social relationships conducive to building dynamic participatory societies, sustainable equitable economies, and accountable developmental states[46].

2.10. Social Capital, Microcredit and Poverty Alleviation

Social ties facilitate the poor's access to credit and lowers its cost, they do so on a more diverse and complex manner than the mainstream literature on development finance indicates (Bastelaer, 1998:1). In addition to the horizontal networks of borrowers that are largely credited for the success of financial institutions, like Grameen Bank, SEWA, etc. Credit delivery systems also rely heavily on vertical relationships between lenders and borrowers. This perspective helps situating the relatively recent and innovative concept of microcredit or microfinance within a continuum of institutional arrangements of credit for the poor for alleviating poverty.

The group meets each day and allocates the commons for the day there is flow of social interaction producing a flow of externalities. This would more sensibly be termed "social labour" than social capital. The persistence of social interaction can be defined either in terms of its composition or its structure. For example, Self-help group is designed to have persistence in terms of its composition, the same group of men or women meet and discusses their problems and constraints. Putnam (2000) would confine the concept of social capital to forms of social interaction which have compositional persistence. This is because he has focuses upon the benefit of trust-building. There are other economic benefits of social interaction which gain from at least some composition rotation. The other term in sociology is social network which is a spontaneous free association of members whereas a SHG is an organisation and has a defined membership.

However, social capital is not only the sum of the institutions which underpin society; it is also the glue that holds them together. But now it is quite fastened as SHG which is not only glue, but it is a "quick fix" which is bonding people very quickly to alleviate poverty. It includes the shared values and rules and problems for social conduct expressed in personal relationship, trust and common sense of civic responsibility that makes society more than a collection of individuals. Without degree of common identification with forms of governance, cultural norms, and social rules, it is difficult to imagine a functioning society. In developed and industrial economies, households generally acquire credit, against individual guarantees, from commercial sources that reach loan decisions on the basis of readily available information of borrowers' credit risk. In most developing economies, however, poor household usually do not have access to these guarantee mechanisms, such as non-real estate-based collateral[47]. This situation, combined with the overall lack of information about these potential borrowers' creditworthiness, contributes to a virtual exclusion of this group of borrowers from formal credit institutions.

Stiglitz and Weiss (1981) suggested that, however, several classes of institutional arrangements offer to these borrowers' valid substitutes for individual collateral and to the lenders low-cost alternatives to imperfect creditworthiness information[48]. According to Stiglitz (1990), unless, new institutions find substitutes for the mechanisms used by the moneylenders to overcome the problems of screening incentives and enforcement, the moneylanders' power is unlikely to be broken by the entry of institutional credit. An increasing number of finance institutions provide credit to the poor on the basis of "social collateral", through which borrowers' reputation, or the social networks to which they belong, take the place of traditional physical or financial collateral. Since these arrangements are built, to various degrees, on the extent and strength of personal relationships, they provide a fertile ground for the analysis of the role of social capital in the provision of credit. In addition credit arrangements rely on several classes of social capital identified in the conceptual literature, such as horizontal, vertical and ethnic-based relationships. Finally, the role of social connections in obtaining credit is also greatest for poor borrowers— as the financial needs of the borrowers increase, their reliance on immediate social networks for credit decreases.

Traditionally, membership in a credit union was the result of some common bond among the members: employment or membership in the same community. Closed bond credit unions are usually organized at the workplace and membership is open only to employees. Open bond credit unions operate in a given community and membership is open to any member of the community, where available, financial cooperatives often choose to become affiliated with a national apex institution which will provide training and technical assistance and channel resources from external donors to the national financial cooperative system[49]. One of the oldest modalities of microfinance delivery is the credit union, or financial cooperative. In the informal sector, ROSCAs (Rotating Savings and Credit Associations) have always been an important way for poor households to fill the gap left by formal financial institutions. The concept ROSCA is also known in various names in various countries. For example, *Chit Fund* in India, *Kye* in Korea, *Partners* in Jamaica, *Susu* in Ghana, *Njangeh* in Cameroon, *Tontine* in Senegal, *Cheetu* in Sri Lanka, *Arisan* in Indonesia, and *Pasanaku* in Bolivia (Bastelaer 1998:2). These methods were applied by socially connected group to credit market exclusion and a widespread way to crystallise social relations in an informal system of internal credit delivery. Besson (1995) claims that the oldest identified ROSCAs are more than 400 years old, but Izumida (1992) describes the *Kou* system, introduced in Japan in the twelfth or thirteenth century, which features are strikingly similar to that of the contemporary ROSCA (quoted in Bastelaer, 1998).

According to Montgomery and Weiss (2004) "Credit unions are probably best characterized as 'semi-formal': unlike informal ROSCAs, they are registered entities subject to commercial law, but are not usually regulated or supervised under banking law". Although in some countries specific regulations for credit unions are being developed. These institutions are member owned and provide financial services—usually savings and credit services, in some cases insurance to members. They are non-profit institutions and there are no external shareholders. These national institutions may in turn associate with one of the international credit union apex agencies the World Council of Credit Unions (WOCCU).

Theoretical framework has precisely anaylsed about the social worth of the productivity of micro-credit institutions. The framework puts the standard theory of project analysis in terms of the terminology of microcredit. By defining precisely the social worth of service to the poorest, the framework helps to judge the trade oust between service to the poorest and service to others.

2.11. Social Capital as an Alternative Credit Institution : An Argument

Social capital itself monitor the group, or other way we can say the peer monitoring or "solidarity group" approach to credit delivery is based on the assumption that the poor represent a much lower credit risk than the formal financial sector generally assumes and that, under specific circumstances, they can be trusted to repay small uncollateralized loans, using a lending methodology that relies on traditional and personal interactions among borrowers. Group lending is the most visible. But by no means collectively labelled microfinance. Like the *Chit Fund*, the group-lending mechanism has attracted the interest of practitioners as well as theoreticians.

Though, the solidarity group approach to lending to the poor saw a rapid expansion from the early 1970s, through the work of UNO in Brazil and the Grameen Bank in Bangladesh, the concept is more than a century old. Woolcock (1998:95) describes the conditions that led to the first deliberate attempt to establish financial institutions with the poor in developing countries on the basis of theu social, rather than their material resource. He is referring to the "people's Banks" as were collectively called the credit cooperatives that Frederick Raiffeisen created in mid-nineteenth century in Germany. These cooperatives present intriguing parallels with the goals, methods, and results of present day group lending programmes, as exemplified in some of the eligibility requirements for membership set forth by Raiffeisen: Residence in small rural communities, trustworthiness as gauged by current members, and unlimited liability for loans of fellow members (Bastelaer, 1998:6).

Ghatak and Guinnane (1998) listed two important differences between the People's Banks and Grameen Bank models, both of which affect the role of solidarity groups in explaining performance. The first difference is the source of funds—while some German cooperatives relied on external sources of funds for their on-lending operations, they mobilised a large part of their capital from local funds, cooperative assets and deposits. The second difference relates to the duration of the group, which in the German model was a direct result from the long-term participation of members in the cooperative. In Grameen approach, groups exist only for the duration of the extended loans, although in practice groups that are constituted for new loans often share the same memberships[50].

In a holistic perspective micro-finance is a process of social intermediation and building social capital. Process of social intermediation is an investment that is made for development of both human resources and institutional capital to make marginalized groups self-reliant in preparing them to engage in formal financial intermediation. According to Elaine & Barton (1998), social intermediation is a financial intermediation with a capacity building component, aimed at those sectors of society that lack access to credit and savings facilities. It can be understood by transformation of beneficiaries into clients or customers and formal financial institutions and marginalized groups. The concept of social capital is the key of theoretical element in social intermediation, derived from the anthropological element and sociological literature. According to Pischke (1991) micro-finance is primarily social as the Latin root of credit (*credere*) is to believe or entrust.

The social development approach of micro-finance is based on the premise that people should earn money by investing in viable micro-enterprises. They should earn profit from their enterprises. Major share of the profit should be reinvested in enterprises for their growth. The other share of the profit should be spent on social development, i.e., health, education, housing, sanitation, etc., by earning profit from the viable micro-enterprises, people will increase their paying ability for services delivered to them under different social development projects run by NGO and governments.

It can be argued that development projects can never expect to achieve participatory and empowering poverty alleviation unless the management of those projects is itself participatory and empowering. Intervening organisations must model the participatory and empowering behaviours that they expect clients to adopt. Development practitioners who call for participation and empowerment need to practice what they preach.

2.12. Microfinance Institutions and Impact in Alleviating Poverty

Theoretically it is clear from the above discussion that, microfinance has been seen as an important tool for alleviating poverty though it is not panacea. In terms of understanding poverty, a simple distinction can be drawn within the group "the poor" between the long-term or "chronic poor" and those who temporarily fall into poverty as a result of adverse shocks, the "transitory poor". Within the chronic poor one can further distinguish between those who are either so physically or socially disadvantaged that without welfare support they will always remain in poverty (then 'destitute') and the larger group who are poor because of their lack of assets and opportunities. Furthermore within the non-destitute category one may distinguish by the depth of poverty (that is how far households are below the poverty line) with those significantly below it representing the 'core poor', sometimes categorised by the irregularity of their income. In some Latin American cases for example the core poor or destitute are taken to be those below 50 per cent of the poverty line (although Latin American poverty lines are generally higher than in Asia)

In principle, microfinance can relate to the chronic (non-destitute) poor and to the transitory poor in different ways. The condition of poverty has been interpreted conventionally as one of lack of access by poor households to the assets necessary for a higher standard of income or welfare, whether assets are thought of as human (access to education), natural (access to land), physical (access to infrastructure), social (access to networks of obligations) or financial (access to credit) (World Bank 2000:34). Lack of access to credit is readily understandable in terms of the absence of collateral that the poor can offer conventional financial institutions, in addition to the various complexities and high costs involved in dealing with large number of small, often illiterate, borrowers.

The poor have thus to rely on loans from either moneylenders at high interest rates or friends and family, whose supply of funds will be limited. MFIs initially attempted to overcome these barriers through innovative measures such as group lending and regular savings schemes, as well as the establishment of close links between poor clients and staff of the institutions concerned. As we have seen in more recent years a more strictly commercial approach has been applied in some MFIs and countries. The case for microfinance as a mechanism for poverty reduction is simple. If access to credit can be improved, it is argued, the poor can finance productive activities that will allow income growth, provided there are no other binding constraints. This is a route out of poverty for the non-destitute chronic poor. For the transitory poor, who are vulnerable to fluctuations in income that bring them close to or below the poverty line, microfinance provides the possibility of credit at times of need and in some schemes the opportunity of regular savings by a household itself that can be drawn on. The avoidance of sharp declines in family expenditures by drawing on such credit or savings allows "consumption smoothing".

It is one of the most interesting generalizations to emerge from the microfinance and poverty literature that the poorest of the chronic poor (the core poor) will borrow essentially for protectional purposes given both the low and irregular nature of their income. This group, it is suggested, will be too risk averse to borrow for promotional measures (that is for investment in the future) and will, therefore, be only a very limited beneficiary of microfinance schemes (Hulme and Mosley, 1996: 132). The view that it is the less badly-off poor who benefit principally from microfinance has become highly influential and, for example, was repeated in the World Development Report on poverty (World Bank, 2000:75).

The poorest of the poor may be missed by microfinance for many of the reasons that the poor as a whole are excluded from the formal financial sector: higher transaction costs and default rates usually result in higher interest rates than the formal financial sector, and in the absence of collateral lenders may ration credit even at these higher rates. If the investment projects undertaken by the poorest of the poor have lower marginal returns, perhaps because this group suffers from a lack of other capital inputs, they will not be able to bear these higher rates of interest anyway. And even if relatively high return projects are available to them, the poorest of the poor may not be willing to undertake such projects if they incur greater risks.

This successful interaction within and between bottom-up and top-down initiatives is the cumulative product of an on-going process that entails getting the social relation right. Entrenched poverty, inequality, discrimination, under-employment, and lawlessness all serve to undermine the particular combinations of social relations required for sustainable, equitable and participatory development. At the macro level, external development assistance should be conditional on these objectives being seriously addressed; at the micro level internal projects should seek to nurture participatory organisations that are empowered to assume increasing levels of responsibility for their own well-being while also building linkages between local communities and formal institutions[51].

Social capital provides sociologists in particular with a fruitful conceptual and policy device by which to get beyond exhausted modernisation and world-systems theories. It makes potentially important contributions to questions of economic development, contributions that complement orthodox economic approaches in some respects and challenge them in others. Social capital's greatest merit, however, is comprehensive multi-and inter-disciplinary approach to some of the most pressing issues of our times. Social capital is open debate for historians, political scientists, anthropologists, economists, sociologists and policy makers.

REFERENCES

1. Asante, M. K. (1991) : *The Book of Africa Names*, Africa World Press, Trenton, N.J.
2. Korten, D.C. (1990) : *Getting to the 21st Century*: Voluntary action and the global agenda, West Harttord, CT: Kumarian Press.
3. Dreze, J. and Sen, A (1989) : *Hunger and Public Action*, Oxford, Clarendon Press.

4. Santos, T.D. (1970): "The Structure of Dependence", Vol.60, No.2, *American Economic Review*, pp.231-236.
5 Pretes, Michel (1988): "Underdevelopment in Two Norths: The Brazilian Amazon and the Canadian Arctic", Arctic, Vol. 41, No.2 (June) pp. 109-116.
6. Wallerstein, I. (1974) : *The Modern World System*, Academic Press, New York.
7. Amin, S. (1977) : *Imperialism and Unequal Development*, Harvester Press, Brighton.
8. *The Collected Works of Mahatma Gandhi*, Vol.87.
9. Quoted in David Simon, (Ed.) (2006) : *Fifty Key Thinkers on Development*, Routledge.
10. Gandhi, M.K. (1962) : *Village Swaraj*, compiled by H.M. Vyas, Navajivan Publishing House, Ahmedabad, India, pp.40-41.
11. *Ibid.*, 41.
12. *Ibid.*, 53.
13. Parpart, J. (ed.) (1989) : *Women and Development in Africa: Comparative Perspectives*, University Press of America, Lanham, MD, USA, p. 32.
14. Rathgeber, E. (1990) : "WID, WAD, GAD: Trends in Research and Practice", *Journal of Developing Areas*, Vol. 24, No.4,. pp.489-502.
15. *Ibid.*, pp. 495-97.
16. Standing, G. (1989): "Global Feminization through Flexible Labour, *World Development*, Vol. 17, No. 7, pp. 1077-1095.
17. Molyneux, M. (1985): "Mobilisation without Emancipation: Women's Interests, *State and Revolution in Nicaragua, Feminist Studies*, Vol. 11, No. 2, pp. 227-254.
18. Scott, C.V. (1995) : *Gender and Development: Rethinking Modernisation and Dependency Theory*, CO: Lynne Reiner, Boulder.
19. Kabeer, N. (1994) : *Reversed Realities: Gender Hierarchies in Developing Thought*, Verso, London.
20. Sen. G. and C. Grown (1987) : *Development, Crisis and Alternative Visions: Third World Women's Perspectives*, Monthly Review Press, New York.
21. Buvinic, M. and M.A. Lycette (1988) : "*Women, Poverty, and Development in the Third World*", in J.P. Lewis (ed.) *Strengthening the Poor: What have We Learned*? Overseas Development Council, Washington, DC. pp.149-62.

22. Ferguson, K.E. (1990) : "Women, Feminism, and Development", in K. Staudt (ed.) *Women, International Development, and Politics*: The Bureaucratic Mire, Temple University Press, Philadelaphia, PA. pp. 291-303.
23. Moser, C. (1993) : *Gender Planning and Development: Theory, Practice and Training,* London, Routledge.
24. *Rothenberg*, J. (1953) : "Conditions for a Social Welfare Function", *The Journal of Political Economy*, Vol. 61, No.5, pp. 389-405.
25 Buvinic, M., Lycette, M.A. and McGreevey, W.P. (eds.) (1983): *Women and Poverty in the Third World,* The Johns Hopkins University Press, Baltimore, Md Durnin, JVGA.
26. Holcombe, S. (1995) : *Managing to Empower: The Grameen Bank's Experience to Poverty Alleviation*, Zed Books, London. pp. 1-12.
27. *Ibid.*, p.23.
28. Quoted in Neluka Silva (2004) : *The Gender Nation: Contemporary Writings from South Asia,* Sage Publications, pp. 132-33.
29. Pieterse, Jan Nederveen (2001) : *Development Theory: Deconstruction/Reconstruction*, Vistaar Publications, New Delhi.
30. Chambers, R. (1983): *Rural Development: Putting the Last First,* Longman, Harlow, London.
31. Nerfin, M. (ed.) (1977) : *Another Development: Approaches and Strategies,* Uppsala, Dag Hammarskjold Foundation.
32 Quoted in J. Putnam (2000) : *Bowling Alone: The Collapse and Revival of American Community*, New York: Simon and Schuster, p. 130.
33. Granovetter, Mark (1985): "Economic action and social structure: The problem of embeddedness", *American Journal of Sociology,* Vol. 9, p. 493.
34. Burt, R. (1992) : *Structural Holes*, Cambridge: Harvard University Press.
35. Loury, G. (1992): "The Economics of Discrimination: Getting to the Core of the Problem", *Harvard Journal for African American Public Policy.*
36 Ports, A. (1995): "Economic Sociology and the Sociology of Immigration: A Conceptual overview" in A. Ports (ed.), *The Economic of Sociology of Immigration: Essays on Networks, Ethnicity and Entrepreneurship,* Russell Sage Foundation.

37. Coleman, J. C. (1994) : *Foundations of Social Theory*, Cambridge, Mass: Harvard University Press.
38. Putnam, R.D. (2000) : *Bowling Alone: The Collapse and Revival of American Community*, New York: Simon and Schuster.
39. *Op. cit.*, Coleman (1994). p.302.
40. Fortes, A. (1998): "Social Capital: Its Origins and Applications in Modern Sociology", *Annual Review of Sociology*, Vol. 24, No. 1, pp. 1-24.
41. *Op.cit.*, Putnam (2000), pp. 287-293.
42. Woolcock, M. (2001): "The Place of Social Capital in Understanding Social and Economic Outcomes" Isuma: *Canadian Journal of Policy Research*, Vol. 2, No. 1, pp. 17.
43. *Ibid.*, pp. 22-23.
44. John Field (2003) : *Social Capital*, Routledge, London.
45 World Bank (1997): "*Social Capital*: The missing links?" in *Expanding the Measure of Wealth: Indicators of Environmentally Sustainable Development*, Washington, DC, p. 85.
46 Serageldin, I. (1996): "Sustainability as opportunity and the problem of social capital", *Brown Journal of World Affairs*, Vol. 3, No. 2, pp. 187-203.
47. Bastelaer, T. van (1998) : "Does Social Capital Facilitate the Poor's Access to Credit?", *Social Capital Initiative*, The World Bank, pp. 1-2.
48. Stiglitz , J. and Weiss, A. (1981) : "Credit Rationing in Markets with Imperfect Information", *American Economic Review*, Vol. 71, No. 3, pp. 393-410.
49. Montgomery, H and Weiss, J. (December, 2004): "Modalities for Microfinance Delivery in Asia and Latin America: Lessons for the People's Republic of China", Working Paper No. 29, Asian Development Bank Institute, p.2.
50. Tilly, R. (1989): "Banking Institutions in Historical and Comparative Perspective: Germany Great Britain, and United States in the Nineteenth and Early Twentieth Century", *Journal of Institutional and Theoretical Economics*, Vol.145, pp. 189-209.
51. *Op. cit.* Woolcock (1998), pp. 186-187.

3

Origin of SHGs, Microcredit Institutions and Poverty Alleviation in India : An Overview

> *"Money going through a woman in a household brought more benefits to the family as a whole than money entering the household through a man".*
>
> —*Muhammad Yunus (1998:88)*

According to Yunus[1], "Poverty has been created by the economic and social system itself that we have designed for the world. It is the institutions that we have built, and feel so proud of, which created poverty. It is the concepts we developed to understand the reality around us, which contributed to the creation of poverty, made us see things wrongly, and took us down a wrong path, causing misery for people. It is our policies borne out of our reasoning and theoretical framework, with which we explain interactions among institutions and people, which caused this problem for many human beings. It is the failure at the top, rather than lack of capability at the bottom which is the root cause of poverty".

The socio-economic deprivation includes economic, educational, health, social and other forms of deficiency experienced by the poor indicates the level of poverty. One of the causes of poverty is deprivation of income or purchasing power. Though goods and services are available in the market, the poorer sections in the society cannot afford them. The intensity of deprivation can be understood by the widening gap between the incomes of the affluent population and their counterparts. In this chapter, an attempt has been made to revisit some well-rehearsed but nevertheless relevant questions on poverty. What is the place of development and SHG growth in broad-based growth and poverty alleviation?

3.1. Definition of Poverty

The discourse on poverty is still a predominantly central phenomenon for economists, sociologists, political economists, and policy formulators, etc. However, the context of rural poverty is rapidly changing across the world, with high growth in some economies and stagnation in others. Persistence of poverty is to a large extent also related to a poor growth performance in national economies. Furthermore, in large parts of the world, poverty remains in absolute numbers, mainly in a rural and agriculture, in that most of the poor depend on the rural sector for their livelihood. Nevertheless, it is similarly striking that the declines are not totally dissimilar either some links between urban and rural poverty clearly exist. Poverty has various causes, including structural ones.

According to Singh (1989), poverty is a complex socio-economic state characterising particular families in a given society. Part of it is a social determinate because it depends substantially on the structure of class and family as well as social attitudes and values. Part of it is economic because it can be measured economically. It is regarded as both a condition of economic inefficiency and a condition of social and political exclusion. It surpasses the narrow limit of income and encompasses the wide complex of political and personal realities[2].

Poverty can be involved not only the lack of well-being but denial of opportunities for living a tolerable life[3]. According to World Development Report (2001), poverty implies lack of adequate food and shelter, deprivations that keep them away from a decent standard of living—better housing, sanitation, access to safe drinking water and so on. Poverty is a complex, multidimensional problem, with origins in both the national and international domains. Poverty is not purely an economic phenomenon. It has also a social dimension that can be referred to as human poverty. Human poverty includes dimensions such as poor health, limited educational opportunities, cultural backwardness, poor housing, lack of access to safe water, low life expectancy, limited access to public and private resources, and limited participation in community development. It adversely affects the ability of individuals and communities to gain access to and use of assets not just economic assets but also social and political[4].

3.2. Poverty Line and its Measurement

A poverty line represented by an income that commands a minimum calorie intake to individuals is first defined and then estimates are made of all those people whose income falls below this line. The method is known as Head Count Ratio (HCR) of poverty and is commonly used measure in Indian planning and development. The official estimates are, however, based on consumption expenditure generated by National Sample Survey Organisation (NSSO) instead of income to estimate the number of poor. The Planning Commission had accepted the poverty line that would be necessary to provide an individual a minimum per day intake of 2400 calories in rural and 2100 calories in urban areas. Converted in expenditure at the 1973-74 prices this was monthly expenditure of Rs. 49.1 in rural and Rs. 56.6 in urban India. In order to capture the inflationary implications over time, adjustments, using a price deflator, were made in the poverty line over time and space[5].

3.2.1. Absolute Poverty

Sachs in his book *The End of Poverty (2005)* defines absolute or extreme poverty means that households cannot meet basic needs for survival. They are chronically hungry, unable to access health care, lack of amenities of safe drinking water and sanitation, cannot afford education for some or all of the children, and perhaps lack rudimentary shelter—a roof to keep the rain out of the hut, a chimney to remove the smoke from the cook stove and basic articles of clothing. Unlike moderate and relative poverty, extreme poverty occurs only in developing countries[6]. In the study of poverty, defining poverty in terms of the nutrition-base poverty lines is not uncommon. The poverty line used in the United States is estimate with scale by three a minimum-budget estimate for food requirements (the scaling proxies for other requirements such as rent and clothing). In India poverty lines have traditionally been drawn by using estimates of expenditure necessary to guarantee a minimum consumption of calories that is below a limit of 2,100 calories per day in urban areas and 2,400 calories per day in rural areas. It is understood that, there is something absolute about the notion of poverty. Regardless of the society we live in, people need adequate levels of food, clothing, and shelter. Whereas it is certainly the case that there are variations in what might be considered adequate (shelter, in particular, might be subject to varying society-specific interpretations), nobody would deny the biological imperative of nutrition, for instance, or the near-universal norms of adequate clothing. At the same time it is unclear that the phrase "acceptable levels of participation in society" can be given absolute meaning, independent of the contours of the society under consideration.

3.2.2. Moderate Poverty

Generally, moderate poverty refers to conditions of life in which basic needs are met, but just barely. In some societies, the ownership of television may be deemed socially necessary for living a "full" life in other it is not. Likewise, minimal standards of leisure, access to scientific education, ownership of private means of transportation and so on, are all concerns that must be evaluated relative to the prevailing socio-economic standards. These considerations quite naturally give rise to the one for poverty lines that share certain common components, but vary from country to country. The World Bank has long used a complicated statistical standard, *i.e.*, income of $1 per day per person, measure at purchasing power parity (PPP is a theory which states that exchange rates between currencies are in equilibrium when their purchasing power is the same in each of the two countries. This means that the exchange rate between two countries should equal the ratio of the two countries' price level of a fixed basket of goods and services.) to determine the numbers of extreme poor around the world. Another World Bank category, *i.e.*, income between $1 per day and $2 per day per person, can be used to measure moderate poverty[7].

3.2.3. Relative Poverty

Relative poverty refers to the individual or group lack resources when compared with that of other members of the society. Since relative poverty is a matter of differences in levels of material resources that is inequalities in their distribution across a society. Relative poverty is normally constructed as a household income level below a given proportion of average national income. The relatively poor are found in high income countries but lack access to cultural goods, entertainment, recreation quality health care, education and other privileges for upward social mobility.

3.3. Indian Scenario of Poverty

In order to understand poverty in India, the official consensus since the late nineteen-seventies has been made to estimate the number of people who live in households with a consumption expenditure that is insufficient to command the minimum number of calories necessary for sustenance. This per capita daily calorific minimum has been defined as 2,400 calories in villages and 2,100 calories in cities. This is poverty line and all those who live below this line are the official poor. Every few years the National Sample Survey Organisation (NSSO) conducts surveys around the country to estimate the expenditure of different household classes. Another important problem in identifying the poor in India using the official poverty line is that the line is defined at an absolutely low level of income, corresponding to the expenditure required to purchase a minimum of calories. It is in no way an indicator of purchasing power to provide for a minimum decent standard of living. It is from these surveys that the Planning Commission periodically derives its numbers about the poor in rural and urban India. In the early 1950s, nearly half of India's population was living in poverty. Since then, poverty has been declining, though slowly, and today vast disparities between and within India's 28 States persist. More than 260 million people—about 26 per cent of the population—live below the official poverty line; seventy-five per cent of these live in the rural areas. Since first economic plan the nation has been experimenting with various alternatives to alleviate deep rooted poverty from the country. Such a high incidence of poverty is a matter of concern in view of the fact that poverty alleviation has been one of the major objectives of the development planning process[8].

It is estimated that women and children account for 73 per cent of those below the poverty line. At the same time, the ratio of females to males in India is 933 : 1,000. Increased female labour force participation, particularly among the lowest-income households, is the single most important coping strategy of poor households. Even while we say that 26 per cent of the people are below the poverty line, it must be remembered that identification of persons on the basis of a narrow definition of poverty based only on income, in a population that works predominantly outside the formal sector, is problematic. For instance, where income fluctuates from day to day, as it does for a vast majority of the Indian population, a single static poverty line is an inappropriate indicator of vulnerability[9]. Therefore, Alleviation of poverty in India is major challenge for the government as well as people concern about the extreme poverty. Poverty alleviation has been one of the guiding principles of the planning process in India. Before entering into the era of SHG in India, here are some observation of poverty reduction methods taken by Government of India followed by credit system in pre-colonial and post-colonial era.

3.4. Poverty Alleviation Programmes in India

Since First Five Year Plan (1951-56) alleviation of poverty has consistently been one of the foremost objectives adapted by the Government of India. It has also been realised since the beginning of the planning era that economic growth can reduce poverty by generating employment and income and labour intensive growth can reduce it even faster. Hence, country needs to have comprehensive National Poverty Reduction strategy. In India, many anti-poverty programmes have been implemented on *ad hoc* and isolated manner. A number of employment and income generation schemes were launched to provide employment in rural areas for sustaining livelihoods and eradicating poverty. The main programmes of the Five Year Plans had been reduction of relative disparities and in the First Plan, for instance, reduction in inequalities of income was accepted one of its objectives. In the Second Plan (1956-57 to 1960-61) also the reduction in inequalities of income and wealth distribution and a more even distribution of economic empowerment was accepted as one of the four major objectives. The other main objectives were: (i) an increase of 25 per cent in the national income; (ii) rapid industrialisation with particular emphasis on the development of basic and heavy industries; and (iii) large expansion of employment opportunities. The Third Plan (1961-62 to 1965-66) amid at securing a marked advance towards self-sustaining growth. Its major objectives were: (i) to secure an increase in the national income of over five per cent per annum; and (ii) to achieve self-sufficiency in foodgrains and increase agricultural production to meet the requirements of industry and exports. In fact, this plan has given more importance to heavy industries, such as steel, chemicals, fuel and power but not to rural development[10].

Initially, the earlier Five Year Plans had proceeded on the assumption that the normal programmes of development would improve the living standards of the poor through the trickle-down process. The trickle-down theory means that rapid growth of per capita income will trickle-down in improved living standards for the very poor. In the context of rural India, this theory has been anticipated to mean that the agricultural growth without major institutional reform will reduce poverty. Accordingly, Community Development Programme (1952), Intensive Agricultural District Programme (1960-61) were introduced. Intensive Agriculture Area Programme (1964) and High Yielding Varieties Programme (1966-67) were started to raise agricultural production[11].

The trickle-down theory was criticised because it failed to reduce any visible impact on the economic condition of the poor. It is argued that growth itself need not be poverty-reducing. In this context Bardhan argues that, in general, agricultural growth seems to be helpful to poverty eradication, but big farmer dominated growth dependent on private ownership, in the absence of land reforms, need not be so favourable to alleviation of poverty. It was becoming increasingly clear that the trickle-down process had failed in India.

In 1962, the perspective Planning Division of the Planning Commission released an important paper entitled "Perspective of Development 1961-1976, Implications of Planning for a Minimum Level of Living" with the approach of direct attack on poverty. This paper had paved the way for shaping the Fourth Plan (1969-74). The highlight of this paper was that, it mainly tried to draw attention towards the abject poverty in which the bulk of Indians lived, but more than that it made a forceful plea for removal of poverty. The approach of development can be regarded as a forerunner of the "direct attack on poverty" by means of poverty focused on pro-poor policies adopted since the Fourth Five Year Plan. This approach appears to be more promising and effective in reducing poverty both in the short and long runs. But poverty cannot be attacked directly without detailed knowledge of its location, extent and characteristics. The Fourth Plan highlighted the need for creation of employment opportunities and a more even distribution of income. It also showed a greater awareness of the need to alleviate poverty by direct means as would be obvious from the following observation of the Fourth Plan: "to some extent income disparities can be reduced through fiscal measures aiming at reduction of income at the top levels, but for us it is important to lay far greater stresses on positive steps for ameliorating the conditions of poorer people through planned economic development"[12].

In this Plan it was identified that the poor comprised landless agricultural labourers, small and marginal farmers and village artisans. Among them SCs and STs constitute the principal segment of the poor. This Plan could note that there are backward areas located mainly in areas with scanty rains, hill areas, some coastal regions, forest areas, etc.

Keeping these in mind, specific poverty eradication programmes for target groups and specific areas were started[13]. Such as Marginal Farmers and Agricultural Labour Agencies (MFALDA) and the Small Farmer Development Agency (SFDA) was set up in 1969 on the recommendations of Rural Credit Review Committee (RCRC). Main objective of the MFALDA programme is to support the marginal farmers in making the maximum productive use of their small holdings by undertaking horticulture, animal husbandry etc. Both these schemes were combined and renamed as District Rural Development Agency (DRDA) in 1979. In order to decrease the gap among the regions in the distribution of benefits from agricultural development in the country, Hill Area Development Programme (HADP) was started in 1970-71. Its focus was to control shifting cultivation, soil conservation, availing facilities of minor irrigation, land reclamation and development of tribal agriculture and animal husbandry. Employment Generation Scheme (EGS) 1972 embodied a commitment by the States to provide employment to person who comes forward to offer labour. Under this programme emphasis was given to both wage employment and enhancement of household income to set free from the clutches of cycle of poverty.

3.4.1. Minimum Needs Programmes (MNP, 1977)

The most important programme of the Fifth Five Year Plan (1974-79) was the Minimum Needs Programme (MNP) was introduced in 1977, a direct approach to attack on poverty which is known as *Garibi Hatao*. The fundamental objective was to provide basic minimum needs and growth with justice, where importance was given both to the growth of national income (GDP) as well as its redistribution. It envisaged the provision of free and subsidised services through public agencies to improve the consumption levels of those living below the poverty line and raise productive efficiency of both rural and urban workers. Its basic components are as of elementary health, water supply, roads, electrification, improvement of slums and nutrition, etc. Again importance was given to Village Development Programme (VDP) to increase productive capabilities in the rural areas and promoting the welfare and prosperity as well as equitable distribution of the benefit of development.

3.4.2. Integrated Rural Development Programme (IRDP, 1978)

This programme was started in 1978, and is the central pillar of poverty eradication since the Sixth Five Year Plan. It was the single largest anti-poverty programme aimed at the eradication of poverty among the target group of the poorest of the rural poor namely small and marginal farmers, agricultural and non-agricultural labourers rural artisans and craftsmen and SCs and STs who live below poverty line. The fundamental objectives of the IRDP are as follows: (i) to raise the production and productivity in agriculture and allied sectors; and (ii) to setting up agro-industrial complexes so that presently unemployed or underemployed person may get jobs in activities of agriculture. This programme was not integrated effectively and, therefore, the success is marginal and short-lived. Under IRDP scheme, subsidy loan were given to members of the SCs, STs and physically handicapped persons are entitled to subsidy upto 50 per cent of the cost of projects. As it was provided high subsidy to unplanned activities so it came to a disaster. Cattle loans were financed without adequate attention to other details of fodder availability and marketing of milk. The abiding legacy of the programme for India's poor has been that millions have become bank defaulters for no fault of their own. Today, they find it impossible to rejoin the formal credit sector. Under the IRDP, there is a separate component for micro-finance to women's groups under the programme of

Development of Women and Children in Rural Areas (DWCRA). Under DWCRA upto Rs. 25,000 were provided as revolving fund to a group of 10 to 15 women for investing in any group-based income generation activity[14]. The IRDP alone accounted for 40 per cent of the losses incurred by commercial banks in rural lending in 1988[15]. As a result the programme has paralysed and new programmes have come into being for rural credit and poverty alleviation.

3.4.3. Rural Landless Employment Guarantee Programme (RLEGP)

Eradication of rural poverty was the most important objective of the Sixth Plan (1980-85). The Rural Landless Employment Guarantee Programme (RLEGP) was launched on 15 August, 1983 to generate additional employment in rural areas particularly for the rural landless workers. Objectives behind the programmes are: to create productive and durable assets for strengthening rural infrastructure. To improve and expand employment opportunities for the rural landless, which will lead to rapid growth of rural economy and steady rise in the employment opportunities for the rural poor and to improve overall quality of the life in rural areas.

3.4.4 Employment Assurance Scheme (EAS)

In terms of social security Government of India in its Eighth Five Year Plan (1992-97) introduced various schemes. These are:

> Employment Assurance Scheme (EAS) in 1993 with the primary objective creation of additional wage employment opportunities during the period of acute shortage of wage employment, through manual work for the rural poor living below the poverty line.

The National Social Assistance Programme (NSAP) in 1995, with the objectives of providing social assistance benefits to poor households affected by old age, maternity care and death of primary bread winner. The programme supplements the efforts of the State government with the objective of ensuring minimum level of well-being.

The Training for Rural Youth for Self-Employment (TRYSEM) in1997, with the purpose to generating employment opportunities for the unemployed educated rural youth. The main thrust of this scheme is on equipping rural young in the age group of 18-35 years with necessary skills and technology to take up vocations of self-employed in the broad fields of agriculture and allied activities industry, services and business.

3.4.5. Swarnajayanti Gram Swarozgar Yojana (SGSY)

The Swarnajayanti Grameen Swarozgar Yojana (SGSY) which has been launched in 1999 is a holistic programme covering various aspects of self-employment, such as organisation of the poor into self-help groups, training, credit, technology, infrastructure and marketing. It is visualised that 50 per cent of the groups formed in each Block should be exclusively for women who will account for at least 40 per cent of Swarozgaris. Under the scheme, women are encouraged in the practice of thrift and credit which enables them to become self-reliant. Through assistance in the form of revolving fund, bank credit and subsidy, the *Yojana* seeks to integrate women in the economy by providing increasing opportunities of self-employment. Under the Sampoorna Grameen Rozgar Yojana an objective was set up that to provide additional wage employment in all rural areas and thereby provide food security and improve nutritional levels. Wage employment under this scheme is extended to below poverty line families. It is stipulated that 30 per cent of the employment opportunities should be reserved for women. The Indira Awas Yojana (IAY) aims at providing assistance for the construction of houses for people below the poverty line in rural areas. Under the scheme, priority is extended to widows and unmarried women. It is stipulated that IAY houses are to be allotted in the name of women members of the household.

In the Ninth Plan (1997-2002) emphases were given to capital formation and redistribution which would ensure food security and good life for all. The objectives of the Plan included, rural development with a view to generating adequate productive employment and eradication of poverty, accelerating growth process and ensuring food security to all. To fulfil these objectives Government of India introduced many schemes. These are as follows:

The Swarnajayanti Gram Swarozgar Yojana (SGSY) was introduced in April 1999. It has incorporated the IRDP, TRYSEM and DWCRA along with Millions Wells Schemes (MWS) into a single self-employment programme. It purposes at promoting micro enterprises and helping the rural poor into self help groups (SHG).

The objective of the Antyodaya Anna Yojana (AAY, 2001) scheme is economic upliftment of the poor families in last ladder among the poor. The poorest of the poor households from the BPL are provided foodgrains (wheat at Rs.2 per kg and rice at Rs. 3 per kg). Under this scheme initially target was given to the State and accordingly ration cards were issued to the beneficiaries, and being distributed to them from May 2001.

Pradhan Mantri Gramodaya Yojana (PMGY) introduced in the year 2001. It is focuses on village level areas, health, primary education, and drinking water, housing and rural roads with the objective of improving the quality of life of vulnerable section of the rural areas.

To reduce unemployment in rural areas Sampoorna Gramin Rojgar Yojana (SGRY), a centrally sponsored wage employment programme came into existence with effect from 25 September, 2001 by amalgamating two other wage employment programmes namely, Jawahar Gram Samridhi

Yojana (JGSY) and Employment Assistance Scheme (EAS). The fundamental objective of the scheme is to provide additional and supplementary wage employment and thereby providing food security and improving nutritional level in rural areas. Creation of durable community, social and economic assets and essential infrastructure in rural areas are the secondary objectives. The programme is being implemented in cost sharing basis between the Centre and State in the ratio 75 : 25 of the cash component. Fifty per cent of the total allocation is released in shape of foodgrains by Government of India on free of cost. Wages are paid through a mix of at least 5 kg of foodgrain and minimum 25 per cent in cash.

3.4.6. National Rural Employment Guarantee Act (NREGA)

It aims at social equity and justice ushering in fundamental changes in villages. The Act commenced from 2nd February, 2006 in 200 districts all over the country, including 19 districts of Odisha. The SGRY and the NFFWP have been subsumed under the NREGA in these districts. Under Sec. 4 of the Act, the State government shall formulate an Employment Guarantee Scheme for implementation of the Act following the guidelines prepared as NREGS (National Rural Guarantee Scheme) by the Central Government. The objective of the Act is to provide enhancement of livelihood security to the rural households by guarantying at least 100 days of wage employment in a year to every household whose adult member volunteer agree to do unskilled manual work. Besides, a durable asset is to be created implementation of the Act to strengthen the livelihood resource base of the rural poor. It is a centrally sponsored scheme with the funding shared between the Centre and State 75 : 25. In case of failure to provide employment within the stipulated period, i.e., within 15 days from the date of application, unemployment allowance has to be paid and the same is to be borne by the State government. The Gram Panchayat has a pivotal role in its implementation. It is responsible for planning, registration, issuing job cards, allocating employment, executing 50 per cent of the works and its monitoring, supervision and social audit. The scheme came into implementation in Odisha in March 2006 and the achievement under this scheme during 2006-07. In 2008, it has been proposed by the Central Government to implement all the districts of India.

3.5. Women Participation and Poverty Alleviation

Since the inception of First Five Year Plan (1951-56), various anti-poverty programmes have been implementing, as a result the degree of poverty has declined both at the national, urban and rural level. In deed, these policies and programmes recognised importance of women involvement for poverty reduction and made many provisions in implementation level. The post-liberalisation era in India witnessed the emergence of a new phenomenon, mainly in terms of social re-engineering and growing inclusion of the poor people at large and women folk in particular, who were keen on expanding their economic opportunities, i.e., the Self-Help Group (SHG).

Meanwhile, with success of NABARD's pilot project in 1992 on SHG has given a source to the rural women for self-employment and it has become one of the major mechanisms for poverty alleviation in India. SHG has become a substituted tool for poverty reduction and also become alternative collateral for the rural and urban poor to free from the clutches of moneylenders who charges high interest rate and monopoly of the local market.

3.6. Cooperative Credit Societies in India

Under Sir Purshottamdas Thakurdas in 1949, the Central

Banking Enquiry Committee found that the cooperative infrastructure was quite satisfactory and that commercial banks had not shown any appreciable interest in agricultural and rural credit and had not gone beyond *taluka* headquarters. In 1954, the All India Rural Credit Survey pointed out that the development of the cooperative credit movement had been inadequate in coverage and recommended its strengthening by developing a three-tier cooperative structure. Under Sir Mehta the Committee on Cooperative Credit was founded in 1960, it recommended the development of a strong and stable institutional framework for cooperative societies, suggesting they should follow sound business methods, distribute assets properly, maintain fluid resources, attract local deposits, developed proper lending norms, supervise the utilisation of credit, improve recovery, maintain a good audit report[16].

For the first time the Reserve Bank of India set up the All India Rural Credit Survey Committee (1951-52). While assessing the role of cooperatives, the committee found that agriculturalist money-lenders together supplied about 70 per cent of the total borrowing of agriculturalists. On the other hand, government agencies and cooperatives supplied only 6.4 per cent and commercial banks only 0.9 per cent. Therefore, the committee recommended an integrated recognisation of the cooperative credit system, which envisaged state partnership through contribution to the share capital of the cooperative credit institutions. Coordination between credit and other economic activities, especially marketing and processing; and administration through adequately trained and efficient personnel responsive to the needs of the rural people[17].

The cooperatives play a prominent role in the provision of credit to the agricultural sector. Though there are large numbers of banks are functioning and facilitating loans, still it is not enough for the million of cultivators and present SHGs. The credit cooperative operates in three tiers, i.e.,

State, district and village. At the State level, there is the apex cooperative Bank, which accesses funds from NABARD. It passes the funds on to the district cooperative banks, which in turn, provide funds to the Primary Agricultural Cooperative Societies (PACS) at the village level. PACS were permitted loans to the extent of only 10 times farmer's savings or margin money. There are 90,000 PACS in the country which are engaged in financing for productive purposes. In the rural areas, cooperative institutions enjoy some concessions which are not available to the normal commercial banks. Indira Misra argues that, although the "coverage of the PACS is quite large; their working is not uniformly good. Financial mismanagement, failure to mobilise local savings, inability to recover dues, and politicisation of their functioning are some of the known maladies the PACS suffer from"[18]. Now it is extending credit to SHGs.

In 1954, All India Rural Credit Survey (AIRCS) has carried out on formal credit institutions. Money lenders, traders and rich landlords accounted for more than 75 per cent of rural credit. Cooperative credit societies had already been in existence for 50 years but their share in rural credit was still less than 5 per cent. The 1945 cooperative planning committee had discerned early signs of sickness in India's cooperative movement, finding that a large number of cooperatives were saddled with the problem of frozen assets because of heavy overdues in repayment[19]. In the 1950s and 1960s, the way forward was seen to lie in cooperative credit societies. These cooperatives were to take the lead in the integrated scheme of Rural Credit suggested by the AIRCS. The share of cooperatives in rural credit did rise to cross 20 per cent in 1971. Presently, India's Cooperative Credit Structure (CCS), with over 13 crore members (including six crore borrowers), constitutes one of the largest rural financial systems in the world. The over one lakh Primary Agriculture Credit Societies (PACS) can, in many ways, be regarded as the veritable bedrock of India's rural economy[20]. The CCS services farm input distribution, crop production, processing and marketing as well as dairying weaving and textiles.

Shah *et al.* argued that however, the CCS has never realised the enormous potential opened up by its vast outreach. According to the task force on revival of rural cooperative credit institutions, this owes mainly to a "deep impairment of governance"[21]. While they were originally visualised a member-driven, democratic, self governing, self-reliant institutions, cooperatives have, over the years, constantly looked up to the State for several basic functions. The task force describes in detail how State governments have become the dominant shareholders, managers, regulators, supervisors and auditors of the CCS. The concept of mutuality (with savings a credit functions going together), that provided strength to cooperatives all over the world, has been missing in India. This "borrower-driven" system is best with conflict of interest and has led to regulatory arbitrage, recurrent losses, deposit erosion, poor portfolio quality and a loss of competitive edge for the cooperatives. Domination by richer elements in the rural elite that characterised cooperatives in the colonial period continues to be an abiding feature of these institutions even after independence.

In the 1950s the Government of India invested a great deal of faith in cooperative societies. But credit societies in particular did not succeed because of bureaucratic control, high incidence of default, especially by the rich. Because cooperative societies failed, the government could not disperse with private moneylenders. There is now talk of registering and regulating private moneylenders instead of abolishing them entirely.

3.7. Chit Fund System in India

In India, Chit Fund (CF) is a kind of savings and credit

practice among the main and petty businessmen. Normally, in chit fund scheme, a specific number of individuals come together to pool a specific amount of money at periodic intervals. This scheme is run by relatives, rural moneylenders and agriculture traders. As a group of individuals organised for mutual interest, it is called Rotating Savings and Credit Associations (ROSCAS) in South Asian countries[22]. Usually the number of individuals and the number of periods will be the same. At the end of each period, there will be an auction of the money. Members of the Chit fund will participate in this auction for the pooled money during that interval. The money will be given to the highest bidder. The bid amount will be divided by a number of members, thus determining per head contribution during that period. Usually the discount will continue to decrease over periods. The person getting money in the last period will receive the full scheme amount. Such chit fund schemes may be conducted by organised financial institutions or may be through unorganised schemes conducted among friends or relatives. There are also variations of chits where savings are done for a specific purpose.

3.7.1. Method of Functioning of Unorganised Chit Funds

Functioning of Chit funds are better explained using an example. Take a typical chit fund with 20 members contributing Rs.100 per week. This fund will run for 20 weeks. On the first week all members will contribute Rs.100. An auction meeting will be conducted, and the foreman of the chit fund will preside over it. The total amount that is pooled will be Rs.2,000. The auction will start with this amount. Bidders will start bidding by discounting this amount. Let us suppose that lowest any person bids Rs. 18,00 (a discount of Rs. 200). This amount (Rs. 18,00) is given to the winning bidder. Rest of the amount is divided by 20, bringing the discount per person to Rs. 14. This discount amount is returned to each member. Sometimes a part of this may be kept by the foreman as service charges, usually in organised chit funds.

3.7.2. Methods of Functioning of Organised Chit Funds

Chit funds in India are governed by various State or Central laws, like Travancore Chit Act of 1945, Chit Funds Act, 1982 and Madras Chit Fund Act, 1961. Organised chit fund schemes are required to register with the Registrar Firms, Societies and Chits. In north India the common type of chit fund is where small slips with each member's name are written and gathered in a box .When all members gather for a monthly or weekly meeting then person in-charge picks up one slip from the box in front of all the others and the person whose name comes up will be entitled to get the collection of that day. Afterwards that person's name slip is torn but after he has to come for subsequent meetings and give his share of the kitty.

Chit Funds are also misused by its promoters. There are many instances of the founders running away with the collected fund and absconding. Hence, chit funds have gained notoriety as "cheat" funds.

3.8. Paradigm Shift in the Rural Credit Systems

During 1966, numbers of bank were undertaken on commercial purposes and these were financed to large industries. The bulks of deposits collected were being deployed in organised sectors of industry and trade. But the farmers, small entrepreneurs and self-employed had to depend on informal moneylenders who used to exploit the clients by charging high rates of interest. In 1966, a scheme of social control was set up, whose main function was to periodically assess the demand for bank credit from various sectors of the economy to determine the priorities for grant of loans and advanced so as to ensure optimum and efficient utilisation of resources. However, the scheme did not provide any remedy.

On 19 July, 1969, the Government promulgated the Banking Companies (Acquisition and Transfer of Undertakings) Ordinance, 1969 to acquire 14 larger commercial banks with paid-up capital of Rs. 2,850 crore, deposits of Rs. 2,629 crore, loans of Rs.1,813 crore and with 4,134 branches accounting for 80 per cent of advances. Subsequently in 1980, six more banks were nationalised which brought 91 per cent of the deposits and 84 per cent of advances in public sector banking. At the time of nationalisation the socio-economic objectives were explicitly laid down and the banks were asked to contribute to the maximum possible extent towards to economic and social development of the country. The underlying philosophy of nationalisation was that "an institution, such as the banking system, which touches and should touch the lives of millions, has necessarily to be inspired by a larger social purpose and has to subserve national priorities and objectives"[23]. Therefore, the operations of banks should be in alignment with the national policy objectives of increasing production, diffusion of economic power, reduction of inequalities, and alleviation of poverty.

Subsidising credit rates has been one of the elements of the strategy for the economic development and rural upliftment. The principal justification for charging lower interest rates to certain categories of borrowers has been that farm-based investment activity in the short run does not always yield returns which enable regular servicing of loans while at the same time meeting minimum consumption requirements. In 1955, Subsidiary Banks Act passed, enabling the SBI to take over seven banks of the princely states as its associated banks. The formation of SBI and its seven associate banks was undertaken with the objective if accelerating the pace of the extension and attainment of the priority sector objectives. Prior to the nationalisation of banks, the commercial banks has a policy of benign neglected to agriculture credit[24].

Despite all its landing stage, there was not sufficient progress in regard to flow of consumption credit to the poor by the formal banking sector. Legislative reforms *vis-á-vis* universal membership in PACS was introduced; but the cooperative banks themselves became weaker and weaker in the subsequent years. The introduction of SHG in the 1970s and linking-SHGs with commercial banks introduced in the 1990s seems to have provided an alternative route to meet the credit needs of the poor.

3.9. Regional Rural Banks (RRBs)

To find a solution for the wide banking gap between commercial and non-commercial credit, particularly in meeting the credit requirements of the weaker sections of the society living in rural areas, such as small and marginal farmers, agricultural labourers, rural artisans and people involved in petty trades, etc., the Government of India established Regional Rural Banks (RRBs) through the Regional Rural Banks Act of 1976. The Government of India appointed a working group on rural credit under the Chairmanship of Narsimham. The Narsimham Committee observed that the cost of structure of commercial banks, the attitudes of their employees and the lack of a professional banking approach in the cooperative credit structure were the major problems in rural credit. It is also observed that the deposits collected by banks in rural areas were not totally deployed in the rural areas[25].

There are 196 RRBs, together covering 427 of the more than 516 districts and serve a client base close to 6.27 crore in the country (see Table 3.2). The RRBs prepare their area-specific programme of micro lendings and after assessing the present and potential credit requirements conduct techno-economic surveys. These banks are sponsored by various commercial banks in different districts. Despite the various measures taken by the Government and the RBI through social control and the nationalisation of major commercial banks, a large proportion of the rural poor remain outside the banking fold.

Looking into all aspects of consumption credit for the poor, the Export Committee on Consumption Credit (Under the Chairmanship of Shri B. Shivaraman, 1978) recommended for allowing a line of credit to poor households by the formal banking sector. The committee recommended a line of credit equal to Rs. 750 per household. The specific consumption demands identified by the Committee were: (a) medical expenses (33 per cent), (b) marriage (33 per cent), (c) education (13 per cent), (d) birth, death and religious purposes (10 per cent) and (e) general consumption (10 per cent)[26]. The committee recommended for a higher percentage (10 per cent) of risk cover by the government than usually done for other rural loans extended by the cooperative and commercial banks. On the estimated demand for consumption loan of Rs.170 crore in 1976. it provided for Rs.17 crore as Risk Fund. This fund, moreover, was required to be shared equally by the Central and the State governments.

3.10. Self-Employed Women's Association (SEWA) Cooperative Bank

The textile mills in Ahmedabad faced various problems, many of the casual women labourers become jobless and started searching for other market opportunities. In 1972, in the city, under the leadership of Ela Bhatt, 4,000 self-employed women started the Self-Employed Women's Association (SEWA), which was a trade union with the objective of fighting against market pressures. One of the primary demands of the union members was credit. In the beginning, the members tried to obtain credit from banks, but gradually they felt that they required a Bank or an organisation for their financial transactions, which is flexible enough for their needs, meeting their small credit needs repeatedly which can also safely keep their small savings; and where their poverty and illiteracy does not become a handicap for them. Therefore, in 1974, these women set up their own bank. SEWA bank is a creation of women, who have learnt to sign overnight[27]. Today, there are 33,000 women account holders. At the end of 2001, SEWA Bank had a working capital of Rs.10 crores in outstanding loans to about 2,00,000 women[28]. As a Bank, it provides credit to the members. It also helps in improvement of designs of the traditional craft items of the women, and in the sale of the products. It reflects the need for flexible credit by many women to sustain their micro-businesses and their household expenditure. Thus, this was the beginning of small credit era for the poorest of the poor for earning livelihoods. It also became a collateral free credit delivery systems and rates of interest also minimal.

The implementation of formal lending programmes towards the poor suffer from the difficulties such as of exact targeting, screening problems of distinguishing good and bad borrowers. Usually lending agencies would be able to ensure the productive usage of loans. Also, the high transaction costs incurred in lending to the poor made the formal lending agencies leave the poor unbanked. The India cooperative credit structure meant to empower the poor was not very successful as it was captured by a few powerful and because of excessive governmental interference and regulation. The search for an alternative to the formal banking sector and an effective financial system to cater to the needs of the poor for coping the poverty. The origin of microcredit or microfinance can be traced to the establishment of the SEWA cooperative bank in 1974, to provide banking services to the poor women employed in the unorganized sector in Ahmedabad in Gujarat[29]. This all happened because SEWA bank is a bank where the users are the owners and managers. Through identified leaders and organisers, continuous personal contact in the field is maintained with members. As owners, the members elect their own executive committee, make policies, decide interest rates and share profits. The bank is accountable to members as well as depositors and subject to audit by RBI and by the Cooperative Department of the State government of Gujarat[30]. SEWA Bank facilitates loans to three types of members:

- Hawkers and vendors (vegetable and fruit vendors, small shopkeepers, flowers and fish vendors)
- Home-based workers (weavers, carpenters, *bidi* rollers, women who process agricultural produce)
- Manual labourers and service providers (agricultural labourers, construction workers, paper-pickers and domestic workers).

The SEWA movement is committed to addressing a wide range of needs of its women members, known within SEWA as the "10 points" e.g., enhancing their income, employment and their ownership of assets, improving housing, health-care and the intake of nutritious food, providing child-care, organising women and building leadership and greater self-reliance[31].

3.11. Grameen Bank

Grameen Bank Project was born in the village of Jobra, Bangladesh, in 1976 by Professor Muhammad Yunus, the founder of Grameen Bank and its Managing Director. In 1983, it was transformed into a formal bank under a special law passed for its creation. It is owned by the poor borrowers of the bank who are mostly women. It works exclusively for them. Borrowers of Grameen Bank at present own 95 per cent of the total equity of the bank. Remaining 5 per cent is owned by the government.

Grameen bank clients follow the basis of group discipline. For example, Yunus started with "Ten Decisions" in 1982 and it has been increased to "Sixteen Decisions" in 1984. These "Sixteen Codes"[32] are the soul of Grameen. So meeting is most important to discuss group activities. If the group has some structure agenda to discuss and implement in future course of action, we can say that the SHGs is sustaining for its cause. The Sixteen Decisions are as follows:

1. We shall follow and advance the four principles of the Grameen Bank-discipline, unity towards constructing new houses at the earliest opportunity.
2. Prosperity we shall bring to our families.
3. We shall not live in a dilapidated house. We shall repair our houses and work towards constructing new houses at the earliest opportunity.
4. We shall grow vegetables all the year round. We shall eat plenty of them and sell the surplus.
5. During the plantation seasons, we shall plant as many seedlings as possible.
6. We shall plan to keep our families small. We shall minimize our expenditures. We shall look after our health.
7. We shall educate our children and ensure that we can earn to pay for their education.
8. We shall always keep our children and the environment clean.
9. We shall build and use pit-latrines.
10. We shall drink water from tubewells. If it is not available, we shall boil water or use alum to purify it.
11. We shall not take any dowry in our son's weddings,

neither shall we give any dowry in our daughter's wedding. We shall keep the centre free from the curse of dowry. We shall not practice child marriage.

12. We shall not commit any injustice, and we will oppose anyone who tries to do so.
13. We shall collectively undertake larger investments for higher incomes.
14. We shall always be ready to help each other. If anyone is in difficulty, we shall all help him or her.
15. If we come to know of any breach of discipline in any centre, we shall all go there and help restore discipline.
16. We shall introduce physical exercises in all our centres. We shall take part in all social activities collectively.

3.11.1. Loan Disbursing Methodology in Grameen Bank[33]

Grameen brought credit to the poor, women, the illiterate, and the people who pleaded that they did not know how to invest money and earn an income. Grameen created a methodology and an institution around the financial needs of the poor, and created access to credit on reasonable term enabling the poor to build on their existing skill to earn a better income in each cycle of loans.

Grameen Bank starts with the belief that credit should be accepted as a human right, and builds a system where one who does not possess anything gets the highest priority in getting a loan. Grameen methodology is not based on assessing the material possession of a person, it is based on the potential of a person. Grameen believes that all human beings, including the poorest, are endowed with endless potential. Grameen Bank does not require any collateral against its micro-loans. Since the bank does not wish to take any borrower to the court of law in case of non-repayment, it does not require the borrowers to sign any legal instrument. Its methodology of loan disbursements is "no collateral, no legal instrument, no group-guarantee or joint liability". Although each borrower must belong to a five-member group, the group is not required to give any guarantee for a loan to its member. Repayment responsibility solely rests on the individual borrower, while the group and the centre oversee that everyone behaves in a responsible way and none gets into repayment problem. There is no form of joint liability, i.e., group members are not responsible to pay on behalf of a defaulting member.

Grameen Bank (GB) has reversed conventional banking practice by removing the need for collateral and created a banking system based on mutual trust, accountability, participation and creativity. GB provides credit to the poorest of the poor in rural Bangladesh, without any collateral. At GB, credit is a cost effective weapon to fight poverty and it serves as a catalyst in the overall development of socio-economic conditions of the poor who have been kept outside the banking orbit on the ground that they are poor and hence not bankable.

3.12. Self-Help Groups : Formation and Function

Today, one can find variety of SHG in village *chopal* to Wall Street of USA, the concept of SHG has dominated in the worldwide. The model Self-Help Groups is one of the widespread tools for poverty alleviation in India. The SHGs are informal groups of persons who join hands together for sharing a common cause and concern. These groups are formed voluntarily and managed democratically. Their membership consists of homogeneous individuals. The objective of the SHG is the common good of members a possibly of others around them. Any group of individuals can decide and form an SHG and start functioning the same day. The SHGs are expected to evolve a strategy with a clear concept of mutual help between the members who are like-minded, belonging to similar socio-economic strata. SHGs are also expected to muster up resources for future use towards income generation activities. The general experience is that the SHGs have to pass through many phases in the course of becoming mature. In order to proceed methodically over a long period of time, the SHGs need to learn to maintain a record of their activities and financial transactions. In course of their dealings, they have to identify the serious from the non-serious members and ease out the latter. Before settling down to serious business they have to satisfactorily lay down common rules and codes of conduct.[34]

3.12.1. Phases of Self-Help Groups Formation

Indira Misra has illustrated four phases of SHG formation and its function. Theoretically there is every justification in anticipating that SHGs can be formed by any group of individuals, in practice the outside helping hand is a must. In any faulty move at the initial phase lie seeds of the SHGs destruction. The main cause and concern for any group formation is to wipe out the poverty so as to provide sustainable livelihoods for the poor.

In the formative stage, any person or NGO functionary can locate likeminded people who can form a group and ensure confidence in them to save some money by curtailing from the daily expenditures. Choosing likeminded people ensures that conflicts are reduced. Even the presence of a single who has discordant views may dissipate the energy of the members of the group in driving conflicts rather than in finding profitable economic opportunities. Second stage is the stage when members face opposition from the members of families, the local leaders and politicians. Third stage is normative. After settling the problems, the group members decide about the functioning of the groups. Decision about savings, opening of bank account, authorisation to maintain the account, frequency of meetings, convenient time for group meeting, participating in social agenda of the village have to be taken. The last stage is performative. Once the cycle of loan activity has been completed, the NGO and the SHG both gain stability. They can also expand their programmes and activities as per the requirement. The performative stage can go on indefinitely in a smooth manner on the basis of sound foundations laid in the earlier stages of SHG.

3.12.2. Functioning of SHG

SHGs are mostly informal groups where members pool savings and re-lend in the group on a rotational basis. The groups have a common perception of need and improvise collective action. Many such groups formed around specific production activities, promote savings among members and use the pooled resources to meet various credit needs of member. Where fund generation is low in initial stages due to low savings capacities, this is supplemented by external resources loaned by NGOs or donor agencies. Thus, SHGs have been able to provide primitive banking services to its members that are cost-effective, flexible and without defaults[35]. It is generally noticed that the main hesitation in starting a programme is the fear of accounts keeping. However, this aspect is not so difficult to handle only if the various requisite records are maintained methodically in writing. Some of the important functions of SHG manage are:

- Group members usually create a common fund by contributing their small savings on a regular basis.
- Groups evolve flexible systems of working and managing pooled money in a democratic way. If the group is formed by NGOs and its members are uneducated then an animator or an educated, knowledgeable person helps to manage their accounts.

- Loan requests are considered by groups in periodic meetings and competing claims on limited resources are settled by consensus.
- Loans are given mainly on trust with minimum documentation and without any collateral.
- The loan amounts are small, frequent, for short duration and are mainly for unconventional purposes.
- The rates of interest vary from group to group and the purpose of loan. It is higher than that of banks but lower than that of moneylenders.
- Besides collecting money, socio-economic issues are also discussed in the periodic meetings.
- It is essential that the records regarding the membership fee are maintained. First of all, the SHG has to determine in the first few meetings how much membership fee will be charged per month from every member.

The SHGs are not in a position to keep adequate staff for updating their bank transactions and individual accounts. For such exigencies, the SHGs can do well by engaging a local person, school teachers or students on a part-time basis for completing the passbook entries during the meeting itself, when the savings are brought by the group member. This is a vital exercise for NGOs channelising micro-credit. The person who deals all the SHGs formal work on behalf of NGOs is called as animator. Attending SHG meetings regularly should be compulsory. Leave of absence may be given only for strong reasons.

3.13. SHG Federation

A federation is a informal primary association in which members realise economies scale get strength as an interest group. A cluster level federation is a network of several SHGs and a structure evolved by SHGs themselves consisting of representatives from all member-SHGs, with the motive of supporting member-SHGs to attain the goals of economic and social empowerment of women members and their capacity-building. The group may have a cooperative credit society or a federation of cooperative societies. In case groups are a federation, the savings are collected by the group leader and brought to the federation office which maintains detailed accounts of group savings. Sharing a platform and gathering under a roof regularly engenders a spirit of friendship in members, which is so valuable to women who are otherwise so vulnerable and weak in the isolation of member's homes[36]. A majority of the well-functioning SHGs have bank linkage. SHG federation is not required to play the financial intermediary role as SHG-bank linkage is a sustainable relationship. Activities of SHG federation includes—it strengthen SHG member through training, information, on site support, book-keeping, accounting, marketing, financial management, advocacy and accessing government schemes. Federation also helps to resolve any conflicts that may arise within member-SHGs, assist in achieving sustainability of SHGs. It helps to promote new SHGs and facilitate women's empowerment by creating social, political awareness.

3.14. Models of Microcredit

For member's flexibility and smooth running of SHG, there are seven types of SHG models functioning in India and in South Asia. The models are as follows:

3.14.1. Model I : SHGs formed and financed by Banks

In this model, banks deal directly with the SHGs, provides financial assistance for on-lending to individual members. Here, rates of credit decided by members and by bank. Saving is the first priority. In this model, banks themselves take up the work of forming and nurturing the groups. Opening SHGs accounts and providing them bank loans. Upto March 2006, 20 per cent of the total number of SHGs financed was from this category. This showed an increase of 61.63 per cent in bank loan to SHGs over the position as on March 2005, reflecting an increased role of banks in promoting and nurturing of SHGs.

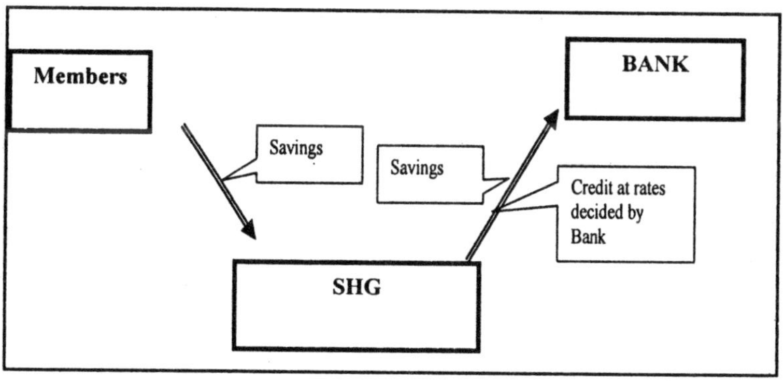

Figure 3.1: Model I- SHG

3.14.2. Model II : SHGs formed by Formal Agencies other than Banks, NGOs and others, but directly financed by Banks

In this model savings is the first priority. Member's pool money and deposit in the bank. The credit rates decided by the Banks not by the SHG. This model continues to have the major share, with 74 per cent of the total number of SHGs financed upto 31 March, 2006 falling under this category. Here, NGOs and formal agencies in the field of microfinance act only as facilitators. They facilitate organising, forming and nurturing of groups and training them in thrift and credit management. Banks give loans directly to these SHGs.

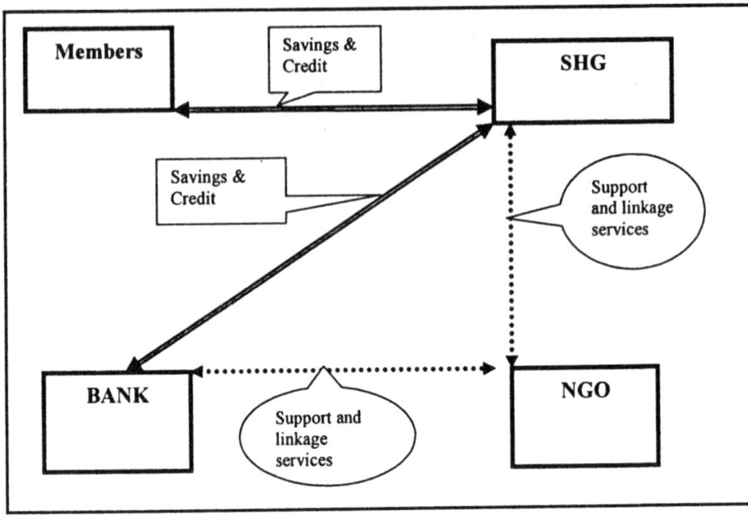

Figure: 3.2. Model II- SHG

3.14.3. Model III: SHGs financed Banks using NGOs and other agencies as financial intermediaries

In this model savings and credit decided by the SHG and also by the Bank. The NGO provides support and linkages services to the SHG to Bank and also provides training, etc. This is the model wherein the NGOs take on the additional role of financial intermediation. In areas where the formal banking system faces constraints, the NGOs are encouraged to approach a suitable bank for bulk loan assistance. This, in turn, is used by the NGO for lending to the SHGs. In areas where a very large number of SHGs have been financed by bank branches, intermediate agencies like Federations of SHGs are coming up as links between bank branch and member SHGs. These Federations are financed by banks, who, in turn, finance their member SHGs. The share of cumulative (increasing by one addition after another) number of SHGs linked under this model upto March 2006 continued to be relatively small at 6 per cent.

3.14.4. Modified NGO Model—BASIX (Andhra Pradesh) and SEWA (Gujarat)

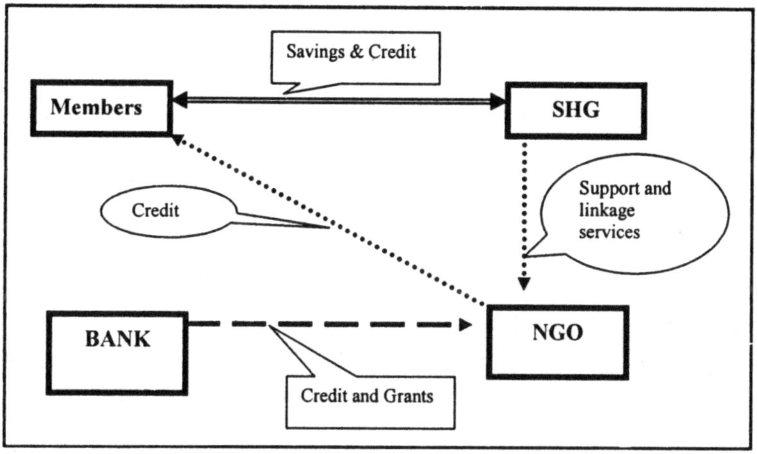

Figure: 3.3. Model III-SHG

Savings and credit decided by the group itself and savings goes to the NGO. The NGO can be a financial intermediary between the bank and a number of SHGs, with the NGO accepting the contractual responsibility for loan repayment to the bank and linkage between the bank and the SHG is indirect.

3.14.5. Indirect NGO Model -BOB-SEWA (Lucknow)

In this model savings are as usual with the bank and bank offer credit to the NGO. In return the NGO provides raw material and job work to the members.

3.14.6. IFAD Model (Tamil Nadu, Uttar Pradesh, Maharashtra)

Members save their money to the SHG and SHG deposit it in the bank. NGO provides training and linkages services to the SHG and Bank. There is a line department to support to the bank and members.

3.14.7. SGSY Model

In this model government involvement can find with the SHG. Savings and credit decided by the members, SHG and Bank. NGO get training from the Government and provides training and support services to the SHG and linked with the bank and line departments. The line departments have linkages with the Government and under SGSY scheme members get training.

3.15. SHG and Different Models of Bank Credit Linkage

Of the above seven model of SHGs credit linkage, model second is popular one. The Chart 3.1 shows that during 2005-06 model second has linked 74 per cent SHGs and disbursed loan. In this model SHGs member, first collect money and deposit in the bank and the rate of interest is decided by bank. The NGOs are the only training facilitators for income generating but bank transaction directly takes place between the SHGs and bank.

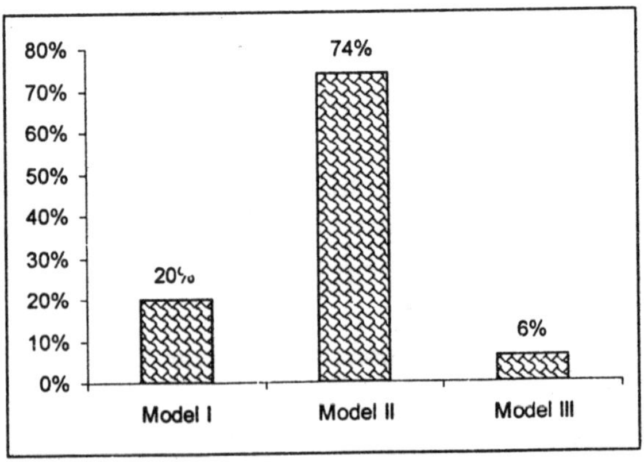

Bar Chart: 3.1 : SHG and Different Models of Bank Credit Linkage

Table: 3.1 : SHG-Bank Linkage-Model-wise Cumulative Position up to 31 March, 2006

Region	*Model I*		*Model II*		*Model III*		*Total (Rs. Million)*	
	SHGs formed and financed by Banks		*SHGs formed by formal agencies and NGOs but directly financed by Banks*		*SHGs financed by Banks through NGOs*			
	No. of SHGs	*Bank Loan*	*No. of SHGs*	*Bank Loan*	*No. of SHGs*	*Bank Loan*	*No. of SHGs*	*Bank Loan @*
Northern	11799	305.61	121109	3676.15	189	4.09	133097	3985.85
North-Eastern	47375	1377.56	10073	227.06	5069	52.39	62517	1657.01
Eastern	129521	3419.71	228769	5274.3	36061	660.18	394351	9354.19
Central	52763	1403.40	210031	6552.01	5121	94.66	267915	8050.07
Western	52705	1613.13	104298	3240.94	9251	397.32	166254	5251.39
Southern	155275	8247.74	971790	73030.19	87366	4398.99	1214431	85676.92
Total	**449438**	**16367.15**	**1646070**	**92000.65**	**143057**	**5607.63**	**2238565**	**113975.4**
Percentage	**20**	**14**	**74**	**81**	**6**	**5**	**100**	**100**

Source: Annual Report NABARD, 2005-06

3.16. National Bank for Agriculture and Rural Development (NABARD, 1982)

Since the widespread recognition of Grameen Bank in Bangladesh in 1970s and SEWA in India in 1980s brought new path of development and credit availability for the poor. This was the period when the old paradigm of directed agricultural credit with subsidized interest rates, rural and agricultural finance kept a low profile on the agenda of many governments and donors. In 1992, National Bank for Agriculture and Rural Development (NABARD) has renewed the credit delivery system, started a pilot project in the interest of the farmers. It picked up some five hundred SHGs. It has been described in Table 3.2.

National Agricultural Bank for Rural Development (NABARD) has been instrumental in the formation and nurturing of quality SHGs by means of promotional grant support to Non Government Organisations (NGOs), Regional Rural Banks (RRBs), District Central Co-operative Banks (DCCBs) Farmers' Clubs (FCs) and Individual Rural Volunteers (IRVs) and developing capacity building of various partners, which has brought about excellent results in the promotion and credit linkage of SHGs. Further, increasing number of partner institutions functioning as Self-Help Promoting Institutions (SHPIs) over the years resulted in the expansion of the programme throughout the country. The financial support provided by NABARD to its partner institutions and their progress in SHG promotion are revealed in above Table 3.2. During the year 2005-06, a total 219,060 SHGs were promoted by the five partner agencies of NABARD with the grant of Rs. 153.11 million in India. 1,28,762 SHGs were linked with the Bank credit.

3.16.1 Financial Grants to Regional Rural Banks (RRBs)

The local character and regional spread of RRBs given them

Table 3.2 : Grant Assistance extended to various Partners in SHG-Bank Linkage Programme by NABARD

Agency	*Sanctions during the Year 2005-06*			*Cumulative Sanctions*			*Cumulative Progress (Rs. Million)*		
	No.	*Amount*	*No. of SHGs*	*No.*	*Amount*	*No. of SHGs*	*Amount Released*	*SHG formed*	*SHGs linked*
Co-operatives	15	**8.61**	6,700	69	**31.64**	34,810	**7.63**	27,547	**11,258**
RRBs	8	**2.34**	2,255	109	**33.39**	41,190	**13.77**	48,281	**29,783**
NGOs	337	**62.70**	25,087	1,515	**256.50**	164,550	**124.96**	128,553	**80,511**
Farmers' Clubs	–	–	–	–	–	–	**5.48**	12,659	**6,509**
IRVs	415	**7.10**	4,275	757	**13.07**	8,800	**1.27**	2,020	**701**
Total	**775**	**81.25**	**38,317**	2,450	**334.60**	249,350	**153.11**	219,060	**1,28,762**

Source: Annual Report NABARD, 2005-06

an advantage in providing promotional and nurturing support to SHGs. Therefore, NABARD has been encouraging RRBs for this purpose from 1999 onwards. During the year, 8 RRBs in 6 States were sanctioned grant assistance of Rs.2.84 million for promotion and linkage of 2,255 SHGs, taking the cumulative total of grant sanctioned to Rs. 33.39 million for 109 RRBs in 21 States for promotion and linkage of 4,1,190 SHGs. Out of this, grant assistance aggregating Rs. 13.77 million was availed by banks, which resulted in promotion of 48,281 SHGs, of which 29,783 were provided with bank loans.

The Regional Rural Banks (RRBs) financed SHGs in a very significant way during 2005-06. All the 158 RRBs in the country participated in the SHG-Bank Linkage Programme. During the year 2006, maximum cumulative number of SHGs has been linked by RRBs Southern region (336678 SHGs), and cumulative Rs.23034.43 million has been disbursed as bank loan, followed by Eastern region 1,59,652 SHGs with cumulative Rs. 3,677.25 million, in Central region 1,28,390 SHGs with cumulative of Rs. 3,521.42 million, Northern region 45,772 SHGs with cumulative of Rs.1,256.41 million, North-Eastern region 35,108 SHGs with cumulative of Rs.570.88 million and Western region 34,424 SHGs with cumulative of Rs.1,161.08 million disbursed as on 31 March, 2006 (Table 3.3). During the year 2005-06, maximum number of SHGs have been linked by Pragjyotish Goanlia Bank in Assam (9190 SHGs) followed by Bolangir Anchlik Gramya Bank (7278 SHGs) in Orissa and Karnataka Vikas Gramin Bank (5819 SHGs) in Karnataka.

3.16.2. Financial Grants to Cooperative Banks

NABARD has been supporting capacity building, exposure and awareness creation initiatives among the cooperative to mainstream SHG-Bank Linkage in the Cooperative banking sector. During the year, 15 District Central

Table 3.3 : SHG-Bank Linkage-Physical and Financial Progress of Participating Regional Rural Banks up to 31 March, 2006

RRBs Region-wise	*Cumulative No. of SHGs provided with bank loan upto 31 March, 2005*	*No. of SHGs provided with bank loan during 2005-06*	*Cumulative No. of SHGs provided with bank loan upto 31 March 2006*	*Cumulative Bank loan disbursed upto 31 March 2005*	*Bank loan disbursed during 01 April 2005 to 31 March 2006*	*Cumulative Bank loan disbursed upto 31 March 2006 (Rs. Million)*
Northern	31701	14071	45772	841.95	414,46	1256.41
North-Eastern	18970	16138	35108	273.78	297.10	570.88
Eastern	111877	47775	159652	2081.64	1595.61	3677.25
Central	101060	27330	128390	2510.05	1011.37	3521.42
Western	23845	10579	34424	664..95	496.13	1161.08
Southern	276393	60285	336678	14623.10	8411.33	23034.43
Total	**563846**	**176178**	**740024**	**20995.47**	**12226.00**	**33221.47**

Source: Annual Report NABARD, 2005-06.

Cooperative Banks (DCCBs) in 5 Sates have been sanctioned grant assistance of Rs.8.61 million for promotion and linkage of 6,700 SHGs, taking the cumulative total grant assistance of Rs.31.64 million for 69 DCCBs for promotion and linkage of 34,910 SHGs. Out of this grant assistance, an amount of Rs.7.63 million has been released which resulted in the promotion of 27,547 SHGs and linkage of 11,258 SHGs.

In India, Cooperative Banks are other nodal agencies which are granting loans to the SHGs for poverty alleviation. In cumulative total number of SHGs linked with the CBs in India was 3,10,501 SHGs with cumulative of Rs.10,879.47 million as on 31 March, 2006. As per the Table 3.4 region-wise it revealed that Southern region was dominant that 1,41,774 SHGs has been linked with the cooperative banks and disbursed cumulative of Rs. 7,226.51 million. Followed by Eastern region (77,906 SHGs) with Rs.1,356.09 million, Western region (41,478 SHGs) with Rs.918.08 million, Northern region (25,794 SHGs) with Rs. 849.47 million and the North-eastern (3,543 SHGs) with the cumulative Rs. 64.63 million disbursed as loan as on 31 March, 2006. Cooperative Banks are comparatively late starters in the microfinance sector. The amendments made by many of the States in their respective Cooperative Societies Acts (CSA) enabled Cooperative banks to take up the activity of promotion and nurturing of SHGs. Influenced by the pioneering performance of District Central Cooperative Banks (DCCBs) in Hooghly (West Bengal) Chandrapur (Maharashtra) and South Canara (Karnataka) in the SHG-Bank Linkage (SBL) programme, many other DCCBs also evinced interest in SHG-Bank Linkage Programme (SBLP). The number of partners for the SHG-Bank Linkage in the Cooperative banking sector increased to 342 as on 31 March, 2006. During the year, maximum number of SHGs has been linked by Kolhapur DCCB (4,229) in Maharashtra followed by Hooghly DCCB (4,115) in West Bengal, Chandrapur DCCB (4,027) in Maharashtra and Mursheedabad DCCB (3,944) in

Table 3.4 : SHG-Bank Linkage-Physical & Financial Progress of Participating Co-operative Banks up to 31 March, 2006

Cooperative Banks Region-wise	*Cumulative No. of SHGs provided with bank loan upto 31 March, 2005*	*No. of SHGs provided with bank loan during 2005-06*	*Cumulative No. of SHGs provided with bank loan upto 31 March, 2006*	*Cumulative Bank loan disbursed upto 31 March, 2005*	*Bank loan disbursed during 01 April, 2005 to 31 March, 2006*	*Cumulative Bank loan disbursed upto 31 March, 2006 (Rs. Million)*
Northern	11773	8021	25794	545.62	303.85	849.47
North-Eastern	1419	2124	3543	34.40	30.23	64.63
Eastern	55153	22753	77906	750.50	605.59	1356.09
Central	14842	5164	20006	297.14	167.55	464.69
Western	18873	22605	41478	415.41	502.67	918.08
Southern	103077	38697	141774	4355.87	2870.64	7226.51
Total	**211137**	**99364**	**310501**	**6398.94**	**4480.53**	**10879.47**

Source: Annual Report NABARD, 2005-06.

West Bengal. The other DCCBs showing significant achievement cumulatively were Hassan DCCB and South Canara DCCB in Karnataka, etc.

3.16.3. Financial Grant to Non-Governmental Organisations (NGOs)

Recognising the core competence of the Non-Governmental Organisations (NGOs) in the formation and nurturing of good quality the SHGs, NABARD and external agencies continued to involve an increasing number of NGO partners to take up the function of Self-Help Promoting Institutions (SHPIs). The NGOs, which act as SHPIs as an add-on function, were provided with supplementary assistance in the form of promotional grant and infrastructural support.

Promotional grants were being provided to SHGs to upgrade themselves. During the year, grants aggregating Rs. 62.70 million were sanctioned to 337 NGOs for the promotion and credit linkage of 25,087 SHGs as against Rs. 42.66 million sanctioned to 317 NGOs for promotion and linkage of 24,234 SHGs during the previous year. The amount of cumulative grant support of Rs. 256.50 million has been sanctioned to 1,515 NGOs for promotion and linkage of 1,64,550 SHGs. As against this, a cumulative grant of Rs. 124.96 million was, so far drawn by the NGOs, which resulted in promotion of 1,28,553 SHGs and credit linkage of 80,511 SHGs.

3.16.4. Financial Grants to Individual Rural Volunteers (IRVs)

In India, on feedback received in respect of a pilot scheme for encouraging socially committed Individual Rural Volunteers (IRVs) in organising the rural poor into SHGs for alleviating poverty, it was decided to extend the scheme to 13 States which account for bulk of the rural poor. During the year, financial assistance of Rs. 7.10 million was sanctioned to 9 RRBs for promotion of 4275 SHGs through 415 volunteers. As on 31st March, 2006, the progress under the pilot scheme has been good. Total 124 IRVs have been actually associated who have promoted 2020 SHGs out of which 701 are credit linked. A grant assistance of Rs. 1.27 million has been released.

3.16.5. Financial Grants to Farmers' Clubs

The Farmers' Clubs, promoted by banks under the Farmers' Clubs Programme of NABARD enjoy local acceptability and goodwill by being informal ambassadors of the village to the banking system. Cumulatively, as on 31 March, 2006, the Farmers' Clubs promoted 12,659 SHGs, of which 6,509 have been credit linked, with the cumulative grant of Rs. 5.48 million.

3.17. The Rashtriya Mahila Kosh (RMK)

The RMK was created under the Societies Registration Act 1860 in the National Capital Territories (NCT) of Delhi on 30 March, 1993. On 31 March, 1993, a corpus fund of Rs. 31 crores was placed with the RMK. The Government resolution in this respect states that the focus of Government of India's endeavour to improve the status of women in India has been for their economic upliftment, particularly for the women working in the informal sector. Government of India's resolution dated 25.5.1993 states as follows: ". . . . it has been recognised that credit availability to such women has been critical constraint in their efforts for achieving economic self-reliance. With this end in view, the government has been considering the issue of facilitating the flow of credit to such women. This has also been one of the major recommendations of the National Commission on Self-employed Women and women in the informal sector"[37].

The main objectives of RMK are threefold

- To facilitate credit to women, treating credit as an instrument of socio-economic change;
- To sensitise existing credit delivery systems towards poor women's credit requirements, holding them out as vital and viable clientele, and
- To promote the networking of women's organisations for exchange of experience and development of skills and for social mobilisation.

The Women Development Corporation and women's cooperative societies could also perform these functions in case they were themselves managed on sound financial principles and met the infrastructural components.

3.18. Commercial Banks

The most recent entrants to the microfinance industry are the commercial banks. This modality includes many variants: transformed microfinance NGOs, government owned development banks, reformed State Banks and diversification into microfinance by existing commercial banks. In comparison, State Banks have generally underperformed. In the heyday of directed credit in the 1970s, subsidized loans often went to politically-favoured wealthy-landowners rather than poor farmers. Despite this repayment rates were low and many programmes operated at a loss. However, many State owned banks have extensive branch networks, enabling them to achieve significant outreach .[38] The ICICI Bank Ltd. in India, for example, has expanded its involvement in microfinance sector. In these cases and others where such requirements do not exist, the motive seems to be profits and diversification of business lines. During the year 2005-06, both public and private sector banks (47) combinely promoted and linked with banks loan was

3,44,567 SHGs and bank loan disbursed Rs. 28,284.30 million. Cumulative number of SHGs provided with bank loan was (1,18,840 SHGs) and cumulative amount was disbursed Rs. 69,874.49 million as on 31 March, 2006. Public sector banks are reaching to the people more than the private sector banks, if we compare, there are 27 public sector banks, and it has linked cumulative 11,41,570 SHGs and disbursed Rs. 64,396.78 million as on 31 March, 2006. It makes sense for commercial banks to lend to SHGs because of high repayment rate and record by the SHG members and because commercial banks set fairly high rates of interests. Also the banks are merge with deposits and the industrial do not absorb all the liquidity.

The SBI became a part of business for all the 27 Public Sector Banks (PSBs) and 20 private sector banks. SBI credit-linked the highest number of SHGs (1,42,034) during 2005-06, followed by Indian Bank (30,632) and Canara Bank (18,445). During the year, many more banks registered impressive growth in SHG-Bank Linkage. These are Indian Overseas Bank, PNB, AB, BoI and BB. The private sector banks which significantly supported SHG financing are ICICI Bank Ltd. (6,746 SHGs), Vysya Bank (1,531 SHGs) followed by Dhanalaxmi Bank (1,201 SHGs). The bank-wise position of SBL is demonstrated in the Table 3.5.

3.19. Banking Service for the Poor

In 1991, Reserve Bank of India (RBI) issued a circular requesting the bank branches to link 500 SHGs with banks under a pilot project. RBI again issued another circular in 1998, indicating that the SHGs linked with banks under the pilot project proved to be extremely successful; the loan given through the SHGs recorded a 100 per cent rate of recovery, and secondly, it was noticed that these loans were increasingly being used for income generating activities rather than consumption purposes. Henceforth, the banks

Table 3.5 : *Commercial Banks and SHG Linkages*

Commercial Banks	*No. of CBs*	*Cumulative No. of SHGs provided with bank loan upto 31 March, 2005*	*No. of SHGs provided with bank loan during 2005-06*	*Cumulative No. of SHGs provided with bank loan upto 31 March, 2006*	*Cumulative Bank loan disbursed upto 31 March, 2005*	*Bank loan disbursed during 01 April, 2005 to 31 March, 2006*	*Cumulative Bank loan disbursed upto 31 March, 2006 (Rs. Million)*
Public Sector Banks	27	810175	331395	1141570	38158.93	26237.85	64396.78
Private Sector Banks	20	33298	13172	46470	3431.26	2046.45	5477.71
Total	**47**	**843473**	**344567**	**1188040**	**41590.19**	**28284.30**	**69874.49**

Source: Annual Report NABARD, 2005-06.

were directed under "Service Area Approach" RRBs prepare detailed plans to meet the potential demand of the credit in their areas. They should try to encourage the SHG formation and linkage with banks as a normal activity to encourage the weaker sections of the society. As a result, all rural SHGs can open their bank accounts. Under the scheme, the SHGs are eligible to receive credit limits form the banks to the extent of four times of their savings. The interest rates relevant per annum indicated below are found at the time of field survey:

NABARD to Banks	@	6.5 per cent per annum
Bank to SHG	@	12.5 per cent per annum
Bank to NGO	@	10.5 per cent per annum
NGO to SHG	@	12 per cent per annum
SHG to Member	@	as decided by the SHG

In India, banking sector is regulated by the RBI under the provisions of Banking Regulating Act 1949. There are 27 nationalised banks, 35 private commercial banks and 29 foreign commercial banks, with around 35,000 branches in all. In addition, there are 196 Regional Rural Banks (RRBs) with about 15,000 branches, 28 State Cooperative Banks with nearly 650 branches and 361 District Cooperative Banks with about 11,000 branches. In addition, there are Urban Cooperative Banks working in urban areas.[39] The NABARD is the nodal bank, who supervises the functioning of RRBs and Rural Cooperative Banks, while commercial banks and Urban Cooperative banks continue to be supervised by the RBI. So far the most important steps taken by RBI and NABARD in respect of microcredit are: Their involvement with the IRDP, Support to tiny enterprises and agriculture under priority sector lending programme through Regional Rural Banks (RRBs), the adoption of self-help groups-bank linkage programme (SBLP) and collaboration and support to cooperative banks.

In 1992, to develop a supplementary credit delivery system to reach the poor in a cost-effective and sustainable manner, NABARD introduced a pilot project for linking up SHGs. As the rule of bank is "first suspect and than respect" to its customer. The broad principles were followed under the linkage scheme were:

- Savings first then credit. Without saving no credit.
- Savings as partial collateral.
- Bank loans to the SHG for on-lending to members.
- Credit decisions for on-lending to SHG members.
- Interest rates and other terms and conditions for loans to members to be decided by the group.
- Joint liability as a substitute for physical collateral.
- Ratio between savings and credit contingent upon credit worthiness and could increase over a period due to good repayment record, if needed.
- Small loans to begin with and different credit cycles clearly defined.

To review the linkage process, various studies were carried out by NABARD. The findings confirmed the following:

- Large number of participants were women clients (particularly resource poor regions).
- Membership in SHGs mostly came from the poorest sections of society.
- Demand for credit was frequent, for small amounts, at unpredictable times and not necessarily for purchasing income-generating assets.
- Even the very poor are able to save and savings increased with addition to their incomes.
- SHG intermediation led to reduction in the time spent

by the bank staff on identification of borrowers, documentation, follow-up and recoveries. This resulted in 40 per cent reduction in transaction cost which could increase further with increase in loan sizes.

- SHG intermediation significantly reduced transaction costs of the borrower due to elimination of cumbersome documentation procedures, time spent and costs incurred on repeated visits to banks.[40]

After observing the success rate of SHG and regular savings and repayment against credit, NABARD decided to amplify the scheme so as to improve the outreach of the formal banking system in cost effective manner. The aim being to enhance the quality of credit in rural areas and promote people's participation in self-help group and grassroots institutions. A number of studies document the positive economic impact of SHGs on indicators such as average value of assets per household, average net income per household, employment and borrowing for income generation activities (Puchazhendi and Satyasai 2000; Puchazhendi and Badatya 2002; Harper *et al.*, 1998). It has been shown that SHGs help inculcated the banking habit in rural women (Varman, 2005) the running of an SHG is also a great lesson in governance.

The SHG-bank Linkage model is the indigenous model of micro credit evolved in India and has been widely acclaimed as a successful model with a present coverage of over 1.4 million groups involving a cumulative credit flow of Rs. 6,300 crore as at the end of March, 2005 from the banking system. Being a savings first model, where credit discipline is inculcated in the group with their own funds, banks have found comfort in lending to such groups as they build up an adequate corpus of their own funds before they approach the bank for credit. In view of availability of social collateral and joint liability, banks have found the repayment experience encouraging enough to actually take charge of this programme. The SHGs has a set of bye laws devised and agreed by the members themselves. These include rules for monthly savings. Lending procedures periodicity and timing of meetings, penalties for defaulted. Meticulous accounts and records are maintained. The SHG itself functions like a small bank. The group lends money to its members. After a certain period (six months to a year) of disciplined functioning, it becomes entitled to a loan from the bank where it has an account.[41] It is also now widely organized that with increase in awareness and build-up of equity for savings and credit history, the poor would need credit in an increasing quantum depending on their stages of development. Keeping in view of long-term security of the households and as a means for inclusion in the mainstream of the financial sector, easier and wider availability of savings products has become imperative. With increasing rural-urban migration within and outside India, the need for remittance service to and from remote rural villages is also felt acutely. Protection against vulnerabilities of rural poor to disease, death, old age, also considered essential as social security measure. Thus there is need for comprehensive financial services encompassing savings, credit, remittance, insurance and pension products which the formal financial system has not been able to provide effectively in the rural areas.[42]

The Physical achievements of Self-help groups and bank linkage, financed by bank directly and indirectly to the groups during the year 2005-06, 7,81,958 new SHGs were formed and 6,20,109 were financed by the banks. 3,44,502 existing SHGs were refinanced by banks and 13.50 million poor families were accessed bank credit including repeat loan and 67.50 million estimated poor people covered during 2005-06. Cumulative number of SHGs financed by banks upto March 2006 was 2,238,565. 32.98 million poor families have accessed bank credit upto March 2006. Estimated 32.98

million poor people assisted upto March 2006 and about 90 per cent SHGs members are only women. Table 3.6 depicts number of SHGs formed during the last five years and slice chart illustrates their percentage of SHG formed during the year.

Table 3.6 : SHGs Financed by various Banks during the last five years (2001-06) in India

year	*No. of SHG*	*Percentage*
2001-02	197,653	10
2002-03	255,882	13
2003-04	361,731	18
2004-05	539,365	27
2005-06	620,109	32

Source: Annual Report NABARD, 2005-06

Table 3.6 shows that during 2005-06, these efforts have resulted in credit linkage of 620,109 (32 per cent) new SHGs with mainstream banks as against 5,39,365 (27 per cent) SHGs during 2004-05 thus registering 15 per cent growth over the previous year. The cumulative number of credit linked SHGs increased from 16,18,456 as on 31 March 2005 to 22,38,565 as on 31 March, 2006. The active clients who are regularizing their accounts are 90 per cent women and repayment rates also same per cent. The SHG-Bank linkage programme enabled an estimated 32.98 million poor households in the country gain access to microfinance for the formal banking system.

Total bank loans disbursed to SHGs during the year aggregated Rs. 44,990.83 million (including repeat loans of Rs. 21,686.32 million provided to existing SHGs already financed in the earlier years) as compared to Rs. 29,942.52 million disbursed during the previous year, registering a growth of 50.3 per cent over the previous year. The refinance drawn by banks from NABARD stood at Rs. 10,677 million during 2005-06. The cumulative progress in financing SHGs from 1992 onwards, in physical and financial terms is indicated in Table 3.7.

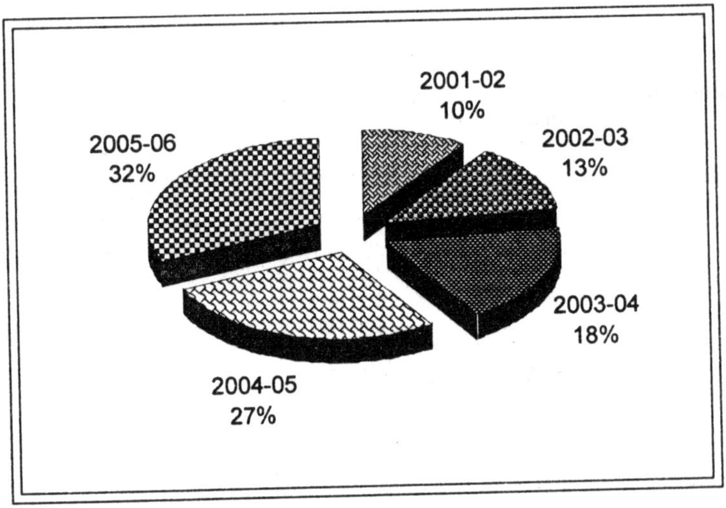

Chart 3.2 : SHGs Financed by Banks during the last Five Years, 2001-06

Table 3.7 : Self-Help Groups and Bank Linkage (2005-06) in India

Upto end of March	*SHGs financed*	*Bank Loan (Rs. Million)*
1992-99	32,995	571
1999-00	114,775	1,930
2000-01	263,825	4,809
2001-02	461,478	10,263
2002-03	717,360	20,487
2003-04	1,079,091	39,042
2004-05	1,618,456	68,985
2005-06	2,278,605	113,975

Source: Annual Report NABARD, 2005-06.

Above Table 3.7 illustrates the bank loans aggregating Rs.113, 975 million were disbursed to 22,38,565 SHGs with refinance support of Rs.41,597 million from NABARD, upto 31 March 2006. Around 90 per cent of the SHGs linked were exclusive women SHGs. Various studies have witnessed that the on-time repayment of SHG loans was over 90 per cent.

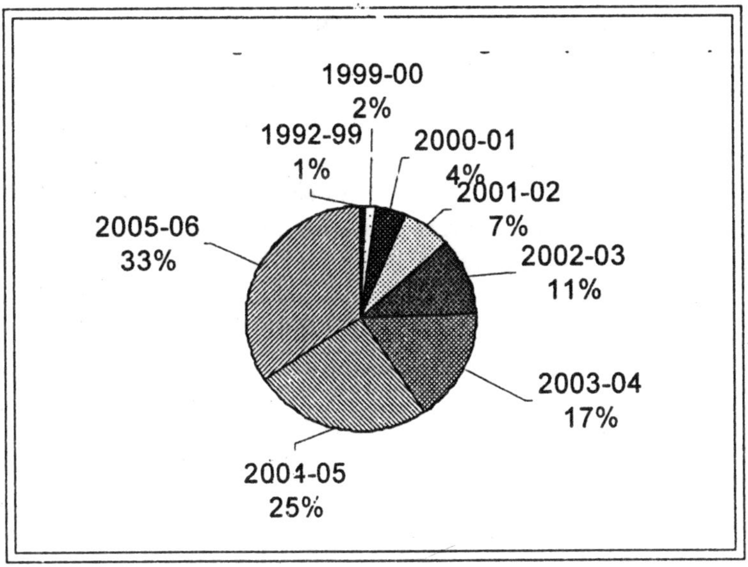

Chart 3.3 : SHG and Bank Linkage Cumulative Progress, 1992-06

3.20. SHG and Bank Linkage-Achievements in 2005-06

Forming and nurturing small, homogeneous and participatory SHGs of the poor has today emerged as a potent tool for human development. This process enables the poor, especially the women from the poor households, to collectively identify and analyse the problems they face in the perspective of their social and economic environment. It helps them to pool their meagre resources, human and financial, and prioritise their use for solving their own problems. The emphasis on regular thrift collection and its use to solve immediate problems of consumption and production not only helps to meet their most urgent needs, but also trains them to handle larger financial resources more skillfully, prudently and with a more lasting impact.[43]

3.21. Region-wise Spread of SHG-Bank Linkage up to 31st March, 2006 in India

The positive growth of SHG and Bank linkage was facilitated by the States or regions specific strategies developed by NABARD in consultation with its Regional Offices at the State level, Banks, NGOs and the State governments. Promotional efforts were launched in these States by NABARD through its Regional Offices, participating agencies. The year witnessed a perceptible increase of SHG-Bank Linkage across all the regions as revealed in Table 3.8.

Table 3.8 : Region-wise Spread of SHG-Bank Linkage

Region	*March 2001*	*March 2002*	*March 2003*	*March 2004*	*March 2005*	*March 2006*
Northern	9,012	19,321	34,923	52,396	86,018	133,097
North-Eastern	477	1,490	4,069	12,278	34,238	62,517
Eastern	22,252	45,892	90,893	156,237	265,628	394,351
Central	28,851	48,181	81,583	127,009	197,365	267,915
Western	15,543	29,318	42,180	54,815	96,266	166,254
Southern	187,690	317,276	463,712	674,356	938,941	1,214,431
Total	263,825	461,478	717,360	1,079,091	1,618,456	2,238,565

Source: Annual Report NABARD, 2005-06.

Table 3.8 shows that against 2,238,565 SHGs in India, South region has promoted and nurtured an overwhelmingly 1,214,431 SHGs as on March 2006, followed by Eastern region (394,351 SHGs), Central region (267,915 SHGs), Western region (166,254 SHGs), Northern region (133,097 SHGs) and in North-Eastern region (62,517 SHGs) as on 31 March, 2006.

3.22. Scheme for Financial Assistance to Banks for Rating of Micro Finance Institutions (MFIs)

In order to identify MFIs, classify and rate such institutions and empower them to intermediate between the lending banks and the clients, NABARD has decided to extend financial assistance to Commercial Banks and Regional Rural Banks by way of grant. The banks can avail the services of credit rating agencies, M-CRIL, ICRA, CARE and Planet Finance in addition to CRISIL for rating of MFIs. The financial assistance by way of grant for meeting the cost of rating of MFIs would be met by NABARD to the extent of 80 per cent of the total professional fees subject to a maximum of Rs. 80,000. The remaining cost would be borne by the concerned MFI. In addition to 20 per cent of the professional fee, the cost of local hospitality (including boarding and lodging) towards field visit of the team from the credit rating Agency, as a part of the rating exercise, would also be borne by the MFI. Those MFIs which have a minimum loan outstanding of more than Rs. 50.00 lakh (Rupees fifty lakh only) would be considered for rating and support under the scheme. Financial assistance by way of grant would be available only for the first rating of the MFI.

3.23. Refinance Support to Banks for Financing MFIs

The scheme is to provide 100 per cent refinance to banks for financing MFIs. Interest rate on refinance to Commercial Banks and Regional Rural Banks on their loans to MFIs for on lending to poor clients will be at lowest rate of interest. The stipulation that banks will charge not more than 9.0 per cent per annum rate of interest to the MFIs. As the banks are free to determine the rate of interest on their loans, the rate of interest on NABARD refinance will be 3 per cent less than that charged by the banks on their loans to MFIs. However, the minimum rate of interest on the refinance to banks for their loans to MFIs will be at interest rate on refinance applicable to the lowest slab stipulated by NABARD from time to time.

3.24. Scheme for Financing Matured SHGs for Farm Production and Investment Activities

The objective of the scheme is to facilitate the members of matured SHGs to meet their credit requirement for farm production and investment activities and to enable them to diversify their income generating activities. Term Loan and Cash Credit limit given by the banks for a period of five years to SHGs exclusively for farm production and investment activities covering agriculture sector and allied activities. Banks can also sanction composite loans by combining consumption credit to the extent of 30 per cent of the total limit. Matured SHGs which have successfully utilised bank loans and whose members have moved from consumption requirements to production requirements, may be considered for financing for farm production and investment activities. Due freedom may be given to SHGs to monitor and ensure end-use of credit as is usually practiced by banks under SHG Bank Linkage Programme. Refinance — 100 per cent of the bank loan under Automatic Refinance Facility (ARF). The refinance provided to the banks under the scheme will be payable in 5 years at half yearly intervals.

During 2005-06, these efforts have resulted in credit linkage of 620,109 new SHGs with mainstream banks as against 539,365 SHGs during 2004-05 thus registering 15 per cent growth over the previous year. The cumulative number of credit linked SHGs increased from 16,18,456 as on 31 March, 2005 to 22,38,565 as on 31 March, 2006. The active participation of women (90 per cent), and timely loan repayment (over 90 per cent) continue to be the prominent features of the programme. Proactive measures such as enlisting partnerships, capacity building of partner agencies, documentation and dissemination of best practices, etc., served to expand the programme. The year witnessed an all-round growth in the SHG-Bank Linkage programme in many non-southern States. The programme thus enabled an estimated 32.98 million poor households in the country gain access to microfinance from the formal banking system .[44]

On an experimental basis, Revolving Fund Assistance (RFA) to select NGOs and Micro Finance Institutions (MFIs) is provided by NABARD. So far, RFA of Rs. 273.20 million has been sanctioned to 32 agencies and Rs. 215.28 million has been released against which Rs. 92.49 million is outstanding as on 31 March, 2006. NABARD's emphasis on scaling-up the SHG-Bank Linkage programme in 13 priority States that account for 70 per cent of the country's rural poor has resulted in sevenfold increase in the number of SHGs credit linked during the period 2003-06. As a result, the share of States other than the southern States increased from 28 per cent as on 31 March, 2002, to 46 per cent as on 31 March, 2006.

In this chapter the potential and limitation of different poverty alleviation programmes have been analysed wherein it has also been examined the SHGs and microcredit institutions.

REFERENCES

1. Yunus, M (2003): "Halving Poverty by 2015— We can actually make it Happen", *The Round Table: The Commonwealth Journal of International Affairs*, Vol. 92, No. 370, pp. 363-75.
2. Singh, C. P. (1989): *Poverty Alleviation Programmes under the Plans*, Indus Publishing, p. 22.
3. UNDP (1997): "Human Development Report", p. 5.
4. Abdallah, S.M. and Kishk, F. M. (2005): "Impacts of Ecosystem Degradation on Livelihood: A Case Study of Northern Nile

Delta, Egypt" in Vineetha Menon, *et al.* (eds.): *Alleviating Poverty: Case Studies of Local Level Linkages and Processes in the Developing World*, Rainbow Publishers Ltd., India, p. 51.

5. Sah, D.C. and Bhatt, A. (2008): *Trapped in Poverty: Chronic Poor in Remote Tribal Areas*, Rawat Publications, New Delhi, India, pp. 1-21.
6. Sachs, J. (2005): *The End of Poverty: How we can make it happen in our Lifetime*, Penguin Books, London, p. 20.
7. Sachs, J. (2005): *The End of Poverty: How we can make it Happen in Our Lifetime*, Penguin Books, New Delhi.
8. Tenth Five Year Plan (2002-07, Government of India, p. 293.
9. Thukral, E. G. (2002): "Poverty and Gender in India: Issues for Concern", in Christopher Edumonds and Sara Medina (eds.) *Defining an Agenda for Poverty Reduction: Proceedings of the First Asia and Pacific Forum on Poverty*, Vol.1.
10. India 2008, Ministry of Information and Broadcasting, Government of India, p. 676-77.
11. Singh, C. P. (1989): *Poverty Alleviation Programmes under the Plans*, Indus Publishing, pp. 56-59. .
12. Quoted in Singh, C. P. (1989): *Poverty Alleviation Programmes under the Plans*, Indus Publishing, New Delhi, pp. 56-59.
13. Singh, C. P. (1989): *Poverty Alleviation Programmes under the Plans*, Indus Publishing, pp. 56-59.
14. *Op. cit.*, Misra (2003) pp. 21-22.
15. *Op. cit.*, Shah, *et al* (April 1997), p.1356.
16. *Op. cit.* Karmakar (1999), pp. 43-48.
17. *Ibid.*, p.48.
18. Misra, I. (2003): *Micro-Credit Macro Impact on Poverty*, National Publishing House, New Delhi, p.20.
19. Government of India (2005): "Report of the Task Force on Revival of Cooperative Credit institutions" Ministry of Finance, pp. 8-9.
20. *Ibid.*, pp.14-15.
21. *Op. cit.*, Shah, M., *et al.*, April 2007, p. 1353.
22. *Op. cit.*, Karmakar (1999), p. 347.
23. *Ibid.*, pp. 58-59.
24. *Ibid.*, pp. 64-65.
25. *Ibid.*, p.82.
26. Planning Commission, Government of India (2007): "Micro-Finance and Poverty Alleviation", Report of the Steering Committee (Eleventh Five Year Plan, 2007-12), pp. 8-9.

27. *Ibid.*, p. 107.
28. *Op. cit.*, Fisher, *et al.*, (2006), p. 61.
29. *Op. cit.*, Planning Commission, GOI (2007), p. 12.
30. Vyas, J. (2008): "Banking with Poor Self-employed Women", in K.G. Karmakar (ed.): *Microfinance in India*, Sage Publications, New Delhi, India, p. 262.
31. *Ibid.*, pp. 51-52.
32. Yunus, Muhammad with Alan Jolis (1998): *Banker to the Poor: The Autobiography of Muhammad Yunus*, Founder of the Grameen Bank, the University Press Ltd., Dhaka, Bangladesh, pp. 115-116
33. This portion extract from *http://www.grameen-info.org* (dated, 27.7.2008).
34. *Op. cit.*, Misra (2003), pp. 73-92.
35. *Op. cit.*, Karmakar (1999), pp. 230-31.
36. Reddy, C.S. (2008): "Emerging SHG Federations and Challenges" in K.G. Karmakar (ed.): *Microfinance in India*, Sage Publications, New Delhi, pp. 146-48.
37. *Op. cit.*, Misra, pp. 58-59.
38. Montgomery, H. and Weiss, J. (December, 2004). "Modalities for Microfinance Delivery in Asia and Latin America: Lessons for the People's Republic of China", working Paper No. 29, Asian Development Bank Institute, p. 2.
39. *Op. cit.*, Misra (2003), pp. 87-8.
40. *Op. cit.*, Karmakar (1999), p. 233.
41. *Op. cit.*, Shah, *et al.*, (April, 2007), p. 1358.
42. Reserve Bank of India (2004): Draft Report of the internal group to examine issues relating to "Rural credit and microfinance", p. 17.
43. NABARD, 2002.
44. Annual Report of NABARD, 2006, p. 18.

Annexure 3.1

SHG and Bank Linkage Programme (March 2001 to March 2006) in India

Sl.No.	Items	Mar-01	Mar-02	Mar-03	Mar-04	Mar-05	Mar-06
1	No. of new SHGs credit linked during the year	149,050	197,653	255,882	361,731	539,365	620,109
2	Cumulative No. of SHGs credit linked with banks	263,825	461,478	717,360	1,079,091	1,618,456	2,238,565
3	No. of SHGs provided with repeat bank loan	—	41,413	102,391	171,669	258,092	344,502
4	Percentage of women groups	90	90	90	90	90	90
5	No. of participating banks	314	444	505	560	573	547
	(1) Commercial Banks	43	44	48	48	47	47
	(2) Regional Rural Banks	177	191	192	196	196	*156
	(3) Co-operative Banks	94	209	265	316	330	342
6	No.of States/UTs	27	30	30	31	31	31
7	No. of Districts covered	412	488	502	563	572	583
8	No.of Partners	1,030	2,155	2,800	3,024	4,323	4,896
9	Bank Loan during the year	2,879	5,455	10,223	18,555	29,942	44,991
10	Of (9) above, repeat bank loan to the existing SHGs	—	924	3,318	6,978	12,676	21,686
11	Bank Loan (Cumulative)	4,809	10,263	20,487	39,042	68,985	113,975
12	Refinance (Cumulative)	4,007	7,965	14,188	21,242	30,920	41,597

Annexure 3.1 : (Contd.)

13	No. of families assisted (in million)	4.5	7.8	11.6	16.7	24.3	32.98
14	Average Bank Loan/SHG (Rs.)—New	18,227	22,918	26,985	32,004	32,012	37,582
	— Repeat	—	22,311	32,405	40,648	49,114	62,949
15	Average Bank Loan/Member**(Rs.)—New	1,072	1,432	1,687	2,286	2,287	2,684
	—Repeat	—	2,541	2,026	2,903	3,508	4,496
16	Model-wise linkage (Cumulative)						
	(1) SHGs formed and financed by banks	13%	16%	20%	20%	21%	20%
	(2) SHGs formed by NGOs and formal agencies but directly financed by banks	76%	75%	72%	72%	71%	74%
	(3) SHGs financed by banks through NGOs	11%	9%	8%	8%	7%	6%

Source: Annual Report NABARD 2005-06.

* Merger of some RRBs.

** The actual loan availed by SHG member is higher as this does not include own funds of SHG.

Annexure 3.2

SHG-Bank Linkage Programme—Regional Spread of Physical and Financial Progress as on 31st March, 2006 in India

(Rs. Million)

Region	*Cumulative No.of SHGs provided bank loan upto 31 March, 2005*	*No. of new SHGs provided with bank loan during 2005-06*	*No. of existing SHGs provided repeat bank loan during 2005-06*	*Cumulative No. of SHGs provided bank loan upto 31March, 2005*	*Cumulative bank loan upto 31March, 2005*	*Bank Loan during 2005-06@*	*Of. Col. B Repeat bank loan to existing SHGs*	*Cumulative bank loan upto 31 March, 2006*
Northern	86,018	47,079	4,308	133,097	2395.18	1,590.67	194.08	3,985.85
North-Eastern	34,238	28,279	267	62,517	1,019.61	637.40	20.49	1,657.01
Eastern	265,628	128,723	38,734	394,351	5,183.06	4,171.13	1,166.12	9,354.19
Central	197,365	70550	7,353	267,915	5,014.56	3,035.51	674.79	8,050.07
Western	96,266	69,988	12,434	166,254	2,950.77	2,300.62	508.53	5,251.39
Southern	938,941	275,490	281,406	1,214,431	52,421.42	33,255.50	19,122.30	85,676.92
All India	**1,618,456**	**620,109**	**344,502**	**2,238,565**	**68,984.60**	**44,990.83**	**21,686.31**	**113,975.43**

@ Includes Rs. 21,686.31 million provided to 344,502 existing SHGs in India.

Source: Annual Report NABARD 2005-06.

Annexure 3.3

SHG-Bank Linkage Programme—Agency-wise Cumulative Participation upto 31st March, 2006 in India

(Rs. Million)

Region	Commercial Banks		Regional Rural Banks		Cooperative Banks		Total	
	No. of SHGs	Bank Loan	No. of SHGs	Bank Loan	No. of SHGs	Bank Loan	No. of SHGs	Bank Loan @
Northern	61,531	1879.97	45,772	1256.41	25,794	849.47	133,097	3,985.85
North-Eastern	23,866	1,021.51	35,108	570.88	3,543	64.62	62,517	1657.01
Eastern	156,793	4,320.85	159,652	3,677.25	77,906	1356.09	394,351	9,354.19
Central	119,519	4,063.96	128,390	3,521.42	20,006	464.69	267,915	8,050.07
Western	90,352	3,172.23	34,424	1,161.08	41,478	918.08	166,254	5,251.39
Southern	735,979	55,415.97	336,678	23,034.43	141,774	7,226.52	1,214,431	85,676.92
India	1,188,040	69,874.49	740,024	33,221.47	310,501	10,879.47	2,238,565	113,975.43

@ Including Rs. 21,686.31 million provided to 344,502 existing SHGs in India.

Source: Annual Report NABARD, 2005-06.

Annexure 3.4

Self-Help Promoting Institutions in India

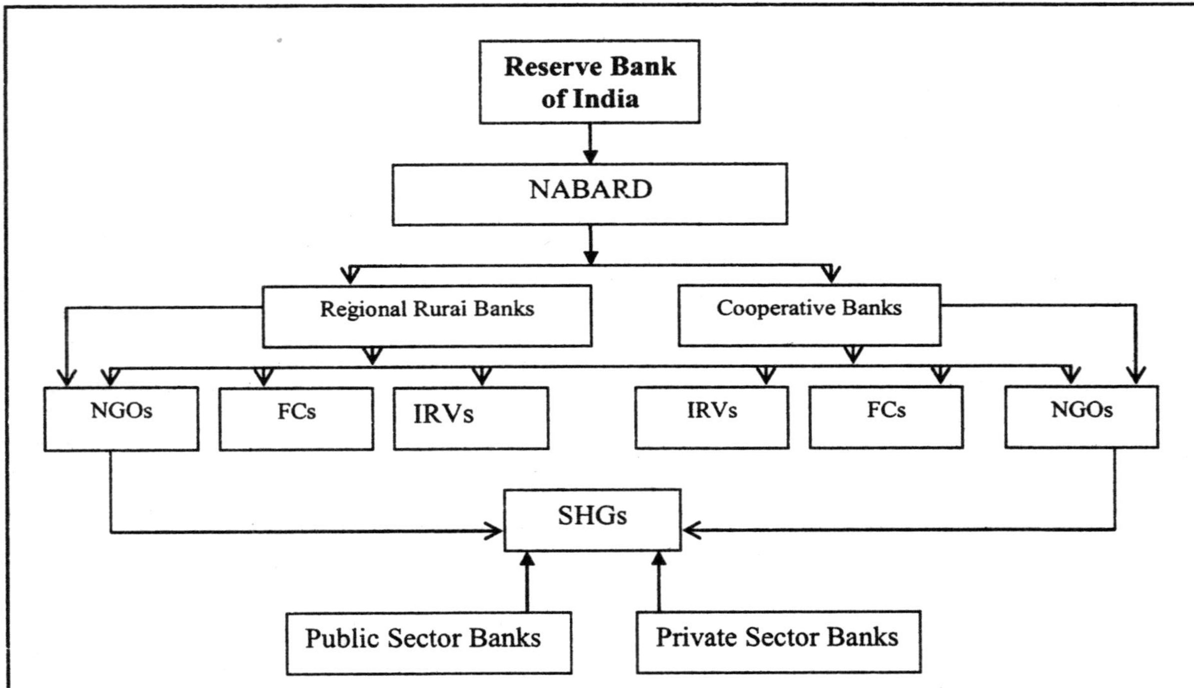

4

Socio-Economic Profile of Odisha

"It would be nice if the poor were to get even half of the money that is spent in studying them".

—Bill Vaughan, American columnist and author

As popular saying, "India lives in villages" so also "Odisha lives in villages"[1]. The statements seem to be more appropriate when considered from the analysis of available socio-economic data. As per 2001 Census, 85.01 per cent of the total population of the State lives in rural areas. The State of Odisha, created on the 1st April, 1936 in pursuance of Government of India (Constitution of Odisha) Order 1936. Presently, it has 30 districts.

4.1. Natural Resources of Odisha

The State of Odisha happens to be one of the most backward States in India. Though, along with the States of Bihar, Jharkhand, Chhattisgarh and Madhya Pradesh, Odisha is one of the most mineralised States in India. Its share in all-India estimated stock of some important minerals {Bauxite (59.50 per cent) , Chinaclay (31.50 per cent), Chromite (98.40 per cent), Coal (24.80 per cent), Dolomite (17.90 per cent),

Graphite (71.00 per cent), Iron Ore (32.90 per cent), Limestone (2.10 per cent), Manganese Ore (67.60 per cent)}[2]. In all cases, this share is much greater than the State's share in all-India area. The State occupies of 4.74 per cent of India's landmass, 36.71 million people as per 2001 Census, accounts for 3.57 per cent of the population of the country. The quality of soil, in general, is rather low, except in the coastal districts which contain highly fertile alluvial soil and the soils of the river valleys. This is a natural weakness of the State's economy as agriculture is its mainstay. It contributes 28 per cent of the net domestic product of the State. Furthermore, 65 per cent of the total population directly or indirectly engaged in agriculture for their livelihood and occupation[3].

As per socio-economic status of the State, it can be divided into two broad regions, i.e., the coastal region and inland districts. The former is fertile with high yielding capacity of agriculture comprising high proportion upper caste population. On the other hand, the inland districts are hilly and barren land with covering of forest; comprising ST and SC population with primitive stage of economic. It is needless to mention that socio-economic backwardness of a region is the root cause of mass poverty. As such the incidence of rural poverty in Odisha is found to be highest in India. In such scenario, it is, further, observed that the incidence of rural poverty in the KBK districts of Odisha is found to be more acute. This is clearly revealed from the poverty survey of the rural households conducted by the Panchayati Raj Department, Government of Odisha in 1992[4].

4.2. Features of Poverty in Odisha

Even within the economy, poverty varies in its degree or levels among the regions in accordance with the levels of progress and the degree of sustaining the progress achieved. Therefore, it is not uncommon to locate poor people in India, especially State like Odisha. The poverty is multidimensional and extends beyond money income to education, health care, skills enhancement, and political participation at all levels from the local to the global. It is also determined by access to natural resources, clean water and air and advancement of one's own culture and social organisation. However, alleviating poverty requires much more resources than now available to poor and developing countries. Poverty manifests itself in the form of "absolute poverty" that prevails in the State of Odisha (39.9 per cent BPL). Poverty is spatially concentrated in Odisha. Some regions such as southern Odisha are very poor, 89.14 per cent (NSS data 1990-2000). The nature and structure of the regions and human resources engagement in developmental programmes reflects State's progress and poverty level. The unequal distributional pattern of landholdings, ownership of assets and the agricultural productivity indicate the degree of progress and the level of poverty. Odisha is not only experiencing unequal distribution of land, assets and productivity but also vulnerable to repeated natural calamities like droughts, floods, and cyclones. The recurrent visitation of natural calamities further exacerbates distress of the people, particularly small and marginal farmers and landless labourers. A disproportionately large proportion of STs and SCs population in western and southern Odisha live rather precariously with very low economic base. The poverty reduction level is not satisfactory, even after accelerated measures taken to address their poverty, especially women and children are generally worst sufferer in these regions.

In Odisha, regions like the southern and northern are not well developed as compared to the coastal region. One of the important reasons for this is the higher concentration of unfertile land and STs population. In 1983, the percentage share of ST population in the coastal region of rural Odisha was 7.2 per cent, whereas, it was as high as 39.7 per cent in the southern region and 34.5 per cent in the northern region.

The poverty ratio in the coastal region was estimated at 64.0 per cent as against 85.5 and 79.1 per cent in the southern and northern regions respectively. The incidence of poverty among SC population was more or less same in all the three regions, i.e., 61-64 per cent. In case of general caste population, the incidence of poverty was comparatively much less in the coastal region than that in the southern and northern regions. Thus, in all the cases, the poverty ratio was found to be less in the coastal region.

A large number of rural communities, particularly in the hilly terrains of western and southern Odisha are physically excluded for want of connectivity and other infrastructural support (i.e., markets, urban areas, and road connectivity). As a result the poor in general and STs and SCs people in particular lack access to growth centres and service centres (i.e., schools, hospitals). Rural poverty is the highest in Odisha. Rural people depend mostly on agriculture and forest resources to eke out their subsistence. However, agricultural growth has been historically generally very low. Agricultural productivity is roughly half than that of the national average. Due to lack of purchasing powers of farmers, use of improved inputs (e.g., better seeds and fertilizers) is also far below the national average. Employment opportunities are rather very limited. Though extensive forest resources are important source of substance to majority of rural poor, they are highly degraded and lack desired financial and managerial inputs. Large forest areas are devoid of regeneration and, therefore, cannot provide livelihood support on sustained basis unless substantial investments are made in them. Want of adequate irrigation facilities (except in certain pockets) is another limiting factor that keeps agriculture under developed. Odisha lacks high quality infrastructure (e.g., railways, paved roads, ports). Optimal exploitation of its vast natural resources demands heavy investments in infrastructural development, and the State government's capacity to develop infrastructure is very limited.

4.3. Incidence of Poverty in Odisha

The incidence of poverty by social groups shows that there was higher concentration of poverty among the Scheduled Castes (SCs) and Scheduled Tribes (STs) population in both rural and urban areas, which can be seen from Table 4.1 percentage of poor was as high as 62 to 79 per cent among the SCs and STs in rural and urban areas as against 51 to 55 per cent for the entire population in 1983. The incidence of poverty among the ST population was near about two times more than that of the other caste population in the same year. The same situation was found even after a decade in 1993-94. The percentage of ST poor to total number of poor was 38.0 while the share of ST population to total population was 25 per cent in rural areas in 1993-94. In urban areas, the corresponding figures were 19.3 and 11.9. Though the per centage of population living below the poverty line declined in 1993-94 over the year 1983 among all social groups, but the incidence of poverty among SCs decreased considerably in 1993-94 over the year 1983. The poverty ratio of SCs reached near to that of all groups in 1993-94.

It is observed from Table 4.1 that though the incidence of poverty in Odisha is declining over time, it is still highest among all major States. As per the estimation made by Planning Commission, the percentage of population in Odisha below the poverty line in 2004-05 stood at 39.9 per cent as per mixed recall period method, followed by Bihar at 32.5 per cent and Madhya Pradesh at 32.4 per cent. The percentage of population below poverty line at all India level in 2004-05 has been estimated as 21.8 per cent as against 26.1 during 1999-2000. Further it is observed that the percentage of population below poverty line in some other States like Rajasthan, Haryana and Maharashtra have increased over 1999-2000. Further, the estimation also reflects that while percentage of population below poverty line in rural Odisha was lower than the urban Odisha; at all Odisha India level it was reversed.

Table 4.1 : Incidence of Poverty in Odisha vis-á-vis other major States (1977-78 to 2004-05)

(Based on MRP consumption)[5]

State	People Below Poverty Line (Percentage)					
	1977-78	*1983-84*	*1987-88*	*1993-94*	*1999-00*	*2004-05*
Andhra Pradesh	39.31	28.91	25.86	22.19	15.77	11.1
Bihar	61.55	62.22	52.13	54.96	42.6	32.5
Gujarat	41.23	32.79	31.54	24.21	14.07	12.5
Haryana	29.55	21.37	16.54	25.05	8.74	9.9
Karnataka	48.78	38.24	37.53	33.16	20.04	17.4
Kerala	52.22	40.42	31.79	25.43	12.72	11.4
Madhya Pradesh	61.78	49.78	43.07	42.52	37.43	32.4
Maharashtra	55.88	43.44	40.41	36.86	25.02	25.2
Odisha	**70.07**	**65.29**	**55.58**	**48.56**	**47.15**	**39.9**
Punjab	19.27	16.18	13.2	11.47	6.16	5.2
Rajasthan	37.42	34.46	35.15	27.41	15.28	17.5
Tamil Nadu	54.79	51.66	43.39	35.03	21.12	17.8
Uttar Pradesh	49.05	47.07	41.45	40.85	31.15	25.5
West Bengal	60.52	54.85	44.72	35.66	27.02	20.6
All India	**51.32**	**44.48**	**38.36**	**35.97**	**26.1**	**21.8**

Sources: Planning Commission, Government of India and Economic Survey (2007-08), Government. of Odisha.

4.4. People Living Below Poverty Line (BPL) in Odisha

Table 4.2 shows the percentage of people below poverty line as estimated by Planning Commission for Odisha from 1973-74 to 2004-05 with rural land urban break-up. It is observed that while the percentage of population BPL in rural Odisha is decreasing over the years, reduction in urban poverty is still slower. The slow rate of reduction of poverty in Odisha is attributed to several inherent problems which have been explored. Attempt has been made to accelerate poverty reduction by way of promoting broad-based industrial growth. The State government has targeted to reduce poverty by 15 per cent during the Eleventh Five Year Plan period.

Table 4.2 : Percentage of People Living in Below Poverty Line in Odisha

Year	*Odisha (Percentage)*			*India (Percentage)*		
	Rural	*Urban*	*Combined*	*Rural*	*Urban*	*Combined*
1973-74	67.28	55.62	66.18	56.44	49.01	54.88
1977-78	72.38	50.92	70.07	53.07	45.24	51.32
1983-84	67.53	49.15	65.29	45.65	40.79	44.48
1987-88	57.64	41.53	55.58	39.09	38.20	38.36
1993-94	49.72	41.64	48.56	37.27	32.36	35.97
1999-00	48.01	42.83	47.15	27.09	23.62	26.1
2004-05	39.80	40.30	39.90	21.80	21.70	21.80

Sources: Planning Commission, Government of India and Economic Survey (2007-08), Government of Odisha.

In the year 1992 for the purpose of survey of BPL (Below Poverty Line) households in rural areas the Government of Odisha had fixed up the maximum annual income of a family at Rs.11,000. On this basis, the BPL survey conducted in the State revealed that 79.10 per cent rural families in Odisha lived under poverty.

4.5. Structure of SHGs and Bank Linkage in Odisha

In order to provide credit opportunities to the poorest and marginal farmers, an initiative has been taken by cooperative credit institutions followed by the nationalization of major domestic banks and later the creation of the Regional Rural Banks (RRBs). Several measures, including establishment of the lead Bank Scheme, directed lending for the priority sectors, banking sector's linkage with the government sponsored programmes targeted at the poor. *Kisan* credit card and the Service Area Approach (SAA) were also introduced in the same time. Given the social responsibility to reach the rural areas and the poor, the banks and co-operative institutions with guidance from the Reserve Bank of India (RBI), the National Bank for Agriculture and Rural Development (NABARD) and other apex level institutions made serious efforts in meeting the needs and demands of the rural sector. As a result, the outreach of Indian banking system has seen rapid growth in rural areas[6]. The pigmy deposit scheme, which involved daily/weekly collection of tiny deposits at the depositors' doorstep by engaging local people as agents, was started in 1970s.

Poverty, which is the bane of Odisha, continues to prevail with the downtrodden and depressed sections of people. Despite the process of regulated planned development under active State intervention and predominance of public investment, socio-economic inequalities between place and people have sharpened over the years. In 1990s, SHGs became an alternative for sustaining livelihood. Various studies across the world have revealed to the potential and limitations of using micro-credit for achieving goals of poverty alleviation. According to Sen (1998) "microcredit has emerged as one solution to the problem paying attention to poverty alleviation even while retaining the anti-deficit radicalism"[7]. In this sense, a profile has been developed about the SHG and Bank linkage in Odisha. As on 31 March 2006, Odisha was promoted and nurtured 86,256 SHGs, of these cumulative bank loan disbursed Rs. 2,216.93 million. There are nine Regional Rural Banks (RRBs), 17 District Central Co-operative Banks and 35 Commercial Banks, which are taking part to promote and provide banking facilities to the SHGs. RRBs are the nodal agencies for promoting and nurturing SHGs through financing to the NGOs, IRVs, etc.

Table 4.3 illustrates the Regional Rural Banks (RRBs) financed SHGs in a very significant way during 2005-06. There are 158 RRBs in the country which have participated in the SHG-Bank Linkage programme. During the year 2005-06, maximum number of SHGs have been linked by Bolangir Anchalik Gramya Bank in undivided Bolangir district (7,278 SHGs) followed by Kalahandi Anchalik Gramya Bank in undivided Kalahandi district (4,135 SHGs). The other RRBs showing significant achievement are Utkal Gramya Bank

Table 4.3 : SHG- Bank Linkage—Physical & Financial Progress of Participating Regional Rural Banks in Odisha up to 31st March, 2006

Sl. No.	*Name of the Bank (RRB)*	*Cumulative no. of SHGs provided bank loan upto 31 March, 2005*	*No. of SHGs provided bank loan during 2005-06*	*Cumulative No. of SHGs provided bank loan upto 31 March, 2006*	*Cumulative Bank loan disbursed upto 31 March, 2005*	*Bank Loan disbursed during 2005-06 (Rs.Million)*	*Cumulative bank loan disbursed upto 31 March, 2006 (Rs. Million)*
1.	Baitarani Gramya Bank	5,586	1,674	7,260	94.60	75.24	169.84
2.	Balasore Gramya Bank	2,833	451	3,284	37.98	16.05	54.03
3.	Bolangir Anchalik Gramya Bank	10,901	7,278	18,179	210.20	207.88	418.08
4.	Cuttack Gramya Bank	4,829	1,974	6,803	83.70	86.31	170.01
5.	Dhenkanal Gramya Bank	3,385	973	4,358	94.70	61.82	156.52
6.	Kalahandi Anchalik Gramya Bank	12,189	4,135	16,324	208.46	149.55	358.01
7.	Koraput Panchabati Gramay Bank	13,911	3,395	17,306	342.08	196.40	538.48
8.	Puri Gramya Bank	4,102	1,264	5,366	64.89	68.04	132.93
9.	Rushikulya Gramya Bank	5,149	2,327	7,476	116.40	102.63	219.03
10.	**Odisha (Total)**	**62,785**	**23,41**	**86,256**	**1253.01**	**963.92**	**2216.93**

Source: Annual Report NABARD 2005-06.

(previously known as KPG Bank) in undivided Koraput district (3,395 SHGs), followed by Rushikulya Gramya Bank (2,327 SHGs), Cuttack Gramya Bank (1,974 SHGs), Baitarani Gramya Bank (1,674 SHGs), Puri Gramya Bank (1,264 SHGs), Dhenkanal Gramya Bank (973 SHGs), Balasore Gramya Bank (451 SHGs). During the year 2005-06 altogether 2,341 SHGs were linked with RRBs and provided Rs. 2,216.93 million as on March 2006 in Odisha. Maximum amount has been disbursed in undivided Koraput Panchabati Gramya Bank Rs. 538.48 million, followed by undivided Bolangir Anchlik Gramya Bank Rs.418.08 as on March 2006. Minimum amount disbursed in Balasore Gramya Bank (Rs. 54.03 million).

Table 4.4 shows that, in Odisha during the year 2005-06, 5,153 SHGs were provided bank loan, with amount of Rs. 397.67 million disbursed as on March 2006. The maximum number of SHGs were linked with the Koraput DCCB (4,261 SHGs) in undivided Koraput district and Rs.83.81 million has disbursed as on March 2006. Lowest numbers of SHGs were linked with Mayurbhanj DCCB (72 SHGs) and disbursed Rs. 0.81 million as on March 2006.

4.6. The Koraput Bolangir Kalahandi (KBK) Districts

A poor and backward State like Odisha having a substantial size of depressed population (39.9 per cent) and backward subsistence-oriented agricultural economy has failed to bridge the development disparities that have long existed between the people and space at the inter-district level. Till 1992, the State was divided into 30 districts. Among the 30 old and undivided districts only the four coastal districts namely Cuttack, Puri, Baleswar and Ganjam and two districts from the highland region namely Sundargarh and Sambalpur may be characterised as developed or advanced according to the existing development position of the State's economy. The undivided districts of Koraput, Bolangir and Kalahandi (popularly known as KBK districts) have since 1992-93 been

Table 4.4 : SHG- Bank Linkage—Physical & Financial Progress of Participating Co-operative Banks in Odisha up to 31st March, 2006

Sl. No.	*Name of the Bank (DCCB)*	*Cumulative no. of SHGs provided bank loan upto 31 March, 2005*	*No. of SHGs provided bank loan during 2005-06*	*Cumulative No. of SHGs provided bank loan upto 31 March, 2006*	*Cumulative Bank loan disbursed upto 31 March, 2005*	*Bank Loan disbursed during 2005-06*	*Cumulative bank loan disbursed upto 31 March, 2006 (Rs. Million)*
1.	Angul United DCCB	1599	719	2318	38.75	44.49	83.24
2.	Aska DCCB	190	4	194	1.95	0.70	2.65
3.	Balasore DCCB	1117	833	1,950	22.91	20.78	43.69
4.	Berhampur DCCB	564	320	884	32.20	18.19	50.39
5.	Bhawanipatna DCCB	73	58	131	1.36	1.60	2.96
6.	Bolangir DCCB	1165	174	1339	19.78	3.41	23.19
7.	Boudh DCCB	454	28	482	6.29	0.86	7.15
8.	Cuttack DCCB	373	225	598	9.32	4.56	13.88
9.	Keonjhar DCCB	236	173	409	5.08	3.47	8.55
10.	Khurda DCCB	145	247	392	5.94	8.27	14.21
11.	Koraput DCCB	3214	1047	4261	53.69	30.12	83.81
12.	Nayagarh DCCB	328	179	507	5.72	2.79	8.51
13.	Sambalpur DCCB	810	440	1250	13.78	10.51	24.29
14.	Sundergarh DCCB	1134	606	1740	15.54	10.34	25.88
15.	United Puri Nimapara DCCB	101	65	166	1.06	1.00	2.06
16.	Banki DCCB	63	25	88	1.95	0.47	2.42
17.	Mayurbhanj DCCB	62	10	72	0.62	0.19	0.81
	Total	**11628**	**5153**	**16781**	**235.92**	**161.75**	**397.67**

Source: Annual Report NABARD, 2005-06.

divided into eight districts. The old Koraput has been divided into four districts, i.e., Koraput, Malkangiri, Nabarangpur, and Rayagada; Bolangir district into two districts, i.e., Bolangir and Sonepur and Kalahandi have been divided into two districts, i.e., Kalahandi and Nuapada. These eight districts comprise of 14 Sub-divisions, 37 Tahsils, 80 Community Development Blocks, 1,437 Gram Panchayats and 12,293 villages. KBK geographical and administrative divisions have, summarised in Table: 4.5.

4.6.1. Socio-Economic Status of KBK

Among backward districts, the old and undivided district namely, Kalahandi, Bolangir, Koraput and Phulbani in the highland region are found to be chronically backward and highly underdeveloped (Meher, 1999:122). In recent years, the KBK in the southwestern part of Odisha have become vulnerable to recurring droughts and famine like situations, which lead to distress migration of the poor during non-agricultural seasons. Needless to explain, in a poor and backward State like Odisha, the KBK region is the most backward and poverty stricken belt. The economic development of the State cannot be brought to the take off stage, unless this region gets special attention by the planners and policy makers in terms of sector specific investments and family centred poverty intervention measures.

In Table.4.6 illustrates villages as per SC and ST population as on 2001 Census. The KBK districts account for 19.80 per cent population over 30.60 per cent geographical area of the State. 89.95 per cent people of this region still live in villages. Lower population density (153 persons per sq.km) in comparison to 236 for Odisha indicates difficult living conditions and an underdeveloped economy. Tribal communities dominate this region. As per 2001 Census, about 38.41 per cent people of these districts belong to Scheduled Tribes (STs) communities including four primitive

Table 4.5 : Geographical and Administrative Divisions of the KBK Districts

Sl. No.	*District*	*Area (Sq.Km.)*	*Number of*					
			Blocks	*TSP*	*Sub-div*	*Tahsils*	*GP*	*Villages (2001 Census)*
1.	Koraput	8,807	14	14	2	7	226	2028
2.	Malkangiri	5,791	7	7	1	3	108	1045
3.	**Nabarangpur**	**5,291**	**10**	**10**	**1**	**4**	**169**	**901**
4.	Rayagada	7,073	11	11	2	4	171	2,667
5.	Bolangir	6,575	14	**	3	6	285	1,794
6.	Sonepur	2,337	6	**	2	4	96	959
7.	Kalahandi	7,920	13	2	2	7	273	2,236
8.	Nuapada	3,852	5	**	1	2	109	663
Total	**8**	**47,646**	**80**	**44**	**14**	**37**	**1,437**	**12,293**

Source: District Statistical Handbook of KBK, 2005.
Note: ** Instead of Tribal Sub-plan, these districts use Modified Area Development Approach (MADA).

tribal groups, i.e., *Bondas* (Malkangiri district), *Dadai, Langia, Sauras* (Kalahandi and Bolangir districts) and *Dangraia Kandhas* (Koraput district). 44 Community development blocks are included in Tribal Sub-plan (TSP). In addition, 16.25 per cent persons belong to SCs as per 2001 Census.

Table 4.6 : Inhabited Villages as per SC & ST Population in KBK Districts

Sl. No.	*District*	*Inhabited Villages*	*No. Villages with SC and ST population*		
			More than per cent	*50% to 75%*	*Less than 50 per cent*
1	Koraput	1,922	1,163 (60.51)	382 (19.88)	377(19.61)
2	Malkangiri	979	796(81.31)	104(10.62)	79(8.07)
3	**Nabarangpur**	**876**	**475 (54.22)**	**254(29.00)**	**147(16.78)**
4	Rayagada	2,467	1,931(78.27)	246(9.97)	290(11.76)
5	Bolangir	1,764	280(15.87)	354(20.07)	1,130(64.06)
6	Sonepur	829	96(11.58)	97(11.70)	636(76.72)
7	Kalahandi	2,099	924(44.02)	395(18.82)	780(37.16)
8	Nuapada	648	194(29.94)	165(25.46)	289(44.60)
Total	**8**	**11,584**	**5,859(50.58)**	**1,997(17.24)**	**3,728(32.18)**

Source: District Statistical Handbook of KBK, 2005.
Note: Figures given in parentheses indicate percentage.

4.6.2 Families Below Poverty Line (BPL) in KBK

The region KBK is considered one of the poorest regions in the country. As per an estimate (based on 1990-2000 NSS data) 89.14 per cent people in Southern Odisha are below poverty line (BPL). As per the 1997 Census report about 72 per cent families live in less than one dollar a day. District-wise information about the number of BPL families as per 1992 and 1997 Census are demonstrated in the Table: 4.7.

There are several socio-economic indicators, which are manifested for the backwardness of the KBK: first, its geographical status as the districts comprises with full of hilly and barren meaning agriculture in this region is not productive and high squashy because of its undulating

Table 4.7 : Families Below Poverty Line (BPL) in KBK (Census 1992-97)

Sl. No.	*District*	*HCR (%)*	*1992 BPL Census*			*1997 BPL Census*		
			Total	*BPL*	*%*	*Total*	*BPL*	*%*
			Lakh Families			*Lakh Families*		
1	Koraput	92.24	1,88	1.63	86.59	2.65	2.22	83.81
2	Ma kangiri	–	0.80	0.68	84.81	1.09	0.89	81.88
3	Nabarangpur	–	1.52	1.38	90.56	2.15	1.59	73.66
4	Rayagada	–	1.42	1.22	86.04	1.88	1.36	72.03
5	Bolangir	48.89	2.39	1.81	75.82	3.30	2.01	61.06
6	Sonepur	–	0.92	0.57	62.29	1.10	0.80	73.02
7	Kalahandi	80.19	2.41	2.07	85.77	3.08	1.93	62.71
8	Nuapada	–	0.94	0.79	83.64	1.27	0.99	78.31
Total in Southern Odisha		87.14	12.28	10.14	82.60	16.52	11.79	71.40

Source: The KBK Districts Report, Planning Commission, Government. of India, 2005.
Note: HCR—Headcount Ratio as per 1999-2000 NSS data, Monaj Panda: 2002.

landscape, poor quality soil, dry nature of the land and scarce water resources; second, natural calamities, e.g., severe droughts and floods also often raise this region and some areas in quick succession; third, poor communication facilities; fourth, localized diseases, e.g., endemic malaria, highly under nutrition caused high morbidity and finally illiteracy, e.g., the literacy rate at 43.3 per cent is much lower than the State average of 63.1 per cent. The family literacy rate 29.1 per cent also compares unfavourably with the State average of 50.5 per cent. The KBK region as a whole had 24.31 per cent BPL families of the State, although the percentage of rural families in these districts constituted only 21.41 per cent of the total rural families in Odisha. Further, it is significant to observe in Table 10.5 that the percentage of depressed category BPL families (SCs & STs) in these districts is much higher than their actual share of such category of families in the KBK region[8].

As on March 2006, the cumulative number 64,550 SHGs were linked with bank credit and cumulative Bank loan disbursed Rs. 1,425.22 million in undivided Koraput-Bolangir-Kalahandi (KBK) districts. The highest cumulative number of (15,032) SHGs were linked with the bank loan and cumulative Rs. 329.25 million disbursed in Kalahandi district as on March 2006. In the sample study Nabarangpur district, the cumulative numbers of (7118) SHGs were linked with bank loan and cumulative Rs. 223.35 million disbursed as on March 2006. Sonepur is the poorest district in the KBK region as in the Table 4.8 it is revealed that as on March 2006, the district's cumulative 3,626 SHGs were linked with bank loan with cumulative Rs.101 million disbursed. In total 30 districts, (including Non-KBK districts) the cumulative 1,80,896 SHGs were linked with bank and Rs. 4,754.65 million disbursed as on March 2006 in Odisha.

In Odisha, 217 volunteers were associated for promoting 2,175 SHGs, for this purpose Rs. 3,330 million has benn sanctioned, 848 SHG were promoted with the help of Rs.0.76

Table 4.8 : SHG-Bank Linkage-District-wise Cumulative Physical & Financial Progress in Odisha up to 31st March, 2006

Sl. No.	Name of the District	Cumulative no. of SHGs provided bank loan up to 31 March, 2005	No. of SHGs provided bank loan during 2005-06	Cumulative No. of SHGs provided bank loan up to 31 March, 2006	Cumulative Bank loan disbursed up to 31 March, 2005	Bank Loan disbursed during 2005-06 @	Cumulative bank loan disbursed up to 31 March, 2006 (Rs. Million)
	KBK						
1.	Bolangir	6317	3063	9380	116.53	88.41	204.94
2.	Kalahandi	10352	4680	15032	175.05	154.2	329.25
3.	Koraput	6721	1810	8531	187.99	96.54	284.43
4.	Malkangiri	3207	1580	4787	63.7	42.15	105.85
5.	**Nabarangpur**	**5099**	**2019**	**7118**	**122.05**	**101.30**	**223.35**
6.	Nuapoda	5210	2773	7983	88.86	90.73	179.59
7.	Rayagada	6855	1238	8093	118.39	83.36	201.75
8.	Sonepur	2215	1411	3626	59.11	41.89	101
	Total	**45976**	**18574**	**64550**	**931.68**	**698.58**	**1425.22**
	Non-KBK						
9.	Angul	3851	1977	5828	87.78	131.19	218.97
10.	Balasore	5113	2008	7121	107.03	85.32	192.35
11.	Bargarh	4542	2111	6653	133.13	117.46	250.59
12.	Bhadrak	3034	1914	4948	67.41	55.38	122.79
13.	Boudh	2219	900	3119	39.13	29.32	68.45

Table 4.8 (Contd.)

14.	Cuttack	2821	1959	4780	55.27	95.02	150.29
15.	Deogarh	983	925	1908	20.46	25.45	46
16.	Dhenkanal	4830	2439	7269	127.09	119.45	246.54
17.	Gajapati	1684	770	2454	30.82	26.51	57.33
18.	Ganjam	7328	2982	10310	185.63	140.00	325.63
19.	Jagatsingpur	2406	1233	3639	45.17	40.27	85.44
20.	Jajpur	2154	1503	3639	37.30	37.56	74.86
21.	Jharsuguda	1179	978	2157	19.35	22.79	42.14
22.	Kandhmal	3256	1216	4472	47.77	34.28	82.05
23.	Kendrapara	3238	1808	5046	71.74	48.88	120.62
24.	Keonjhar	4861	2283	7144	89.35	97.75	187.10
25.	Khurda	3110	1585	4695	60.63	80.83	141.46
26.	Mayurbhanj	7037	2431	9468	115.29	233.16	248.45
27.	Nayagarh	2987	1107	4094	63.78	37.25	101.03
28	Puri	3936	1550	5486	77.23	58.55	135.79
29.	Sambalpur	2826	2343	5169	52.17	69.05	121.22
30.	Sundargarh	3885	3044	6929	52.74	52.57	105.31
	Total	**123256**	**57640**	**180896**	**2517.94**	**2236.71**	**4754.65**

Source: Annual Report NABARD, 2005-06.

@ Includes an amount of Rs. 21,686.31 million provided to 3,44,502 existing SHGs in India.

million as on 31 March, 2006. In real sense, 79 volunteers were associated for promoting SHGs and 187 SHGs were linked for credit. Table 4.9 illustrates that the total number of IRVs, SHGs are to be promoted and already promoted and amount sanctioned and released as on 31 March, 2006.

4.6.3 SHGs and Bank Facilities in KBK Region

The undivided Kalahandi-Bolangir-Koraput districts, popularly known as KBK for its socio-economic backwardness, as poorest of the poor are concentrated (detailed has explained in the KBK socio-economic profile). The KBK has continued to receive thrust in microfinance from the NABARD and other external agencies. During the year 2005-06, 18,574 SHGs were provided with bank loan, brought the cumulative number of groups credit linked to 64,550 SHGs, and 3 new NGOs were sanctioned promotional grant assistance of Rs.83 million for promotion and linkage of 350 SHGs in this region, taking the cumulative grant assistance sanctioned to Rs. 6.86 million to 40 NGOs for promotion and linkage of 2,282 SHGs. Besides, under the scheme of associating individual rural volunteers for SHG promotion and linkage, Kalahandi Anchalik Gramin Bank was sanctioned a grant assistance of Rs.0.39 million for promotion of 500 SHGs through 30 rural volunteers over a period of two years in Kalahandi, Nuapara, Kandhamal and Boudh districts of Odisha.

Like national scenario majority of people in Odisha live in villages. Despite having rich natural resources the State has remained as one of the most backward States in the country. Most of the manpower is engaged in agricultural and allied activities. Except river valleys and coastal alluvial soil rest of the land is rainfed, that is the agriculture sector contributes very low productivity.

The lack of adequate self-employment in Odisha has led to a large section of poor migrating to different parts of the

Table 4.9 : SHG-Bank Linkage-Grant Support to Individual Rural Volunteers (IRVs) in Odisha (special reference to KBK District) as on 31 March, 2006

Name of the Bank	*Year of sanction*	*No. of IRVs to be associated*	*No. of SHGs to be promoted and linked*	*Amount sanctioned*	*No. of SHGs promoted*	*No. of SHGs credit linked*	*Grant released*	*No. of Volunteers associated (Rs. million)*
KGB	2001	50	500	0.690	436	187	0.63	49
KAGB	2004	30	300	0.390	212	0	0.13	30
DGB	2005	25	250	0.325	0	0	0.00	0
SBI Odisha	2006	112	1125	2.025	0	0	0.00	0
Total in Odisha		**217**	**2175**	**3.330**	**848**	**187**	**0.76**	**79**
Grand Total in India		**737**	**9060**	**13.065**	**2020**	**701**	**1.27**	**124**

Source: Annual Report NABARD 2005-06.

country and also inadequate irrigation facility is another major cause which keeps agriculture at backward. Besides these factors, Odisha lacks high quality modern infrastructures. The significant success of SHGs, somehow reduce population migration in the State, but majority of people failed to adapt the SHG programme because their income level is very low.

REFERENCES

1. Misra, S.N. (2005) "Commercial Banks and Rural Development: Economic Reform Experiment in Odisha" in Mallik and Padhi (eds.) *Development, Deprivation and Welfare Policy: Essay in Honour of Prof.Baidynath Misra*, Rawat Publcations, New Delhi, p. 345.
2. *Odisha Development Report, 2002.* Parentheses are million tonnes.
3. *India Year Book (2007)*, p.1007. Alco see S.P. Panda (2005): "New Social Movements and Democracy: A study of Environmental Movements in Odisha" Dissertation submitted to JNU, New Delhi (unpublished).
4. *Socio-Economic Survey of Rural Households, 1992*, Panchayati Raj Department, Government of Odisha.
5. NSSO uses two different methodologies for measuring consumption rate. The first one from the consumption data collected using 30-day recall period (also known as reference period) for all the items. The other distribution is obtained from the consumer expenditure data collected using 365-day recall period for five infrequently purchased non-food items, namely, clothing, footwear, durable goods, education and institutional medical expenses and 30-day recall period for the remaining items. These two consumption distributions have been termed as Uniform Recall Period (URP) consumption distribution and Mixed Recall Period (MRP) consumption distribution respectively.
6 Draft Report of the Internal Group to examine issues relating to rural credit and microfinance, Reserve Bank of India, June 2005, p.1.
7. Rao, Smriti (2005): "Women SHGs and Credit for the Poor: A

Case Study from Andhra Pradesh", Ramchandran and Swaminathan (eds.) *Financial Liberalisation and Rural Credit in India,* Tulika Books, New Delhi, p.206.

8. *Socio-Economic Survey of Rural Households, 1992,* Panchayati Raj Department, Government of Odisha.

Annexure 4.1
The History of Nabarangpur

The history of Nabarangpur is inextricably interlinked with that of Koraput District. In a sense, its language, way of living, tradition, geographical location, flora and fauna and even climate is not distinct from the rest of the component of Koraput district. Koraput belonged to *Atavika* people who valiantly fought the Kalinga war in the third century BC. They remained independent and dreaded. *Kalinga* regained her former glory during Mahamegha Bahan dynasty in the first century BC. The third king of this dynasty Kharabela made the Kalinga empire and the Atavika land very strong. The successive dynasties – the Satavahans (second century AD) two Ikshvakus (third century AD) had their dominion dynasty belonged to the Nalas (third and fourth century AD), with a headquarters located at Pushkari, near the modern Umerkote town of Nabarangpur district. The Kesaribeda excavations bear testimony to the rule of King Bhabadatta Verman and King Arathapati. The inscriptions of Podagarh refer to King Skanda Verman .The Nala King are traced to the kings who ruled from Gwalior in Madhya Pradesh. Their fast growth landed them in Bastar-Koraput region. Around tenth century AD one Nala king Bhimesen was ruling over a region now located as the Koraput and Ganjam District.

The erstwhile Koraput was a small principality of Tri Kalinga under the Ganga era during the fifth century AD. The patches of Odra, Kalinga and Kosala were brought under the control of Ganga kings. This dynasty became prominent during the eleventh century AD with the rise of *Somanakshi*. Their suzerainty extended from the modern Sambalpur, Sonepur to Bastar-Koraput regions and they enjoyed control till the beginning of fourteenth century AD. Matsya Family ruling over *Vaddadi* region of modern Jeypore dominated the next generation. The famous king included Bhanudeva, Narasingha Dev and others which are evident from inscription of Simhachalam in Visakhapatnam district of Andhra Pradesh. The next dynasty belonged to the famous Silavansis, who ruled over *Vindhya* during fourteenth century AD. The earliest king Ganga Raju was ruling over Nandapur, a former capital of the Maharaja of Jeypore. Nandapur is famous for the throne of 32 steps erected in the line of king Vikramaditya of Ujjain, Jainism and Shaktism grew side by side in the kingdom of Nandapur. The last king of Silavansi was Pratap Ganga Raju who succeeded by Vinayak Dev of Surya Vansa which lasted till the end of the British Empire. Vinayak Dev was said to be married to the daughter of the last ruler of Silavansi Pratap Ganga Raju and ascended to the throne of Nandapur Vinayak Dev and his six succeeding generation of kings had only one son each and on advices from astrologers the headquarters of the kingdom was switched from Nandapur to Jeypore. During the Anglo-French conflict, Vikram Dev-I was successful in driving out the French from Malkangiri area and the Marathas from the Umerkote belt. King Vikram Dev I (1758 to 1781 AD) was succeeded by Ramachandra Dev-II (1781 to 1825) while his other two sons Jagannath and Narasingh Dev were placed in charge of Nabarangpur and Gudari regions. Jagannath Dev's son Arjun Dev and Narasingha Dev's son Chaitanya Dev were issueless. Hence, Nabarangpur and Gudari were remerged to Jeypore kingdom.

During the twentieth century Ramachandra Dev-IV (1920-31) was an honourable Lieutenant in World War-I. He was issueless and was succeeded by a benevolent, aged, scholar King Vikram Dev-IV, the son of Krishna Chandra Dev. During this period the Boundary Commission headed by Sir O'Donnel was entrusted with the task of writing the different Oriya speaking tracts. The Commission went round Jeypore, Paralakhumendi, Ganjam, and Visakhapatnam agency before finalizing. The State of Orissa was formed on 1st April, 1936 with Koraput as one of the six districts. In 1951, Vikram Dev-IV died at the ripe old age of 82 and the Estate Abolition Act was passed the next year. The Estate of Jeypore was taken over by Government of Odisha.

5

Umerkote Block : The Study Area

"Extreme poverty is the best breeding ground on earth for disease, political instability, and terrorism".

–Jeffrey Sachs

This chapter focuses to locate the socio-cultural and economic structure of the Nabarangpur district in general of study area "Umerkote Block" in particular. In presenting the socio-economic conditions of native STs and SCs and Bengali and the physical data of District, as well as contemporary processes that marginalised the natives of the region, followed by social order and livelihood struggles, I have attempted to connect the involvement of three communities (Bengali, STs and SCs) women in SHG system to livelihoods promotion.

5.1. Social Composition

The native inhabitants here are mostly tribals, encounter with the mainstream population (Oriya, Telugu, Marwari and Bengali) in the township has changed their lifestyle to some extent but a few of them like Paraja, Kondha, Gadava still live the primitive life style (food gathering and animal hunting). They mostly depend on cultivation and forest products. Some speak Oriya and Bengali in a corrupt form, difficult for the pure Oriya speaking people to understand. They are an admixture of several words and phrases from aboriginal dialects. Both Oriya and Bengali speaking people are trying to speak the tribal dialects, among them those who speak in corrupt form of the dialects are petty-businessmen and school teachers.

Nabarangpur district consists of Hindus, Christians and Muslims. The tribals worship the Hindu gods and goddesses. The Mohammedans, though small in population are believed to be the descendants of soldiers from Golkonda who invaded Jeypore. The Lutheran Mission Conversion actively converted several SCs to Christianity but not to the STs. Particularly, STs of Nabarangpur District are believers of tribal gods and goddesses, therefore, not a single tribal has been converted to Christianity. The American and German missionaries had a field day during the British Raj. They set up schools with boarding houses, dispensaries and built churches. In this District, Protestants, Catholics and other denominations of Christian are present. The Christian hospital popularly known as German Hospital of Nabarangpur town has been an attraction for patients from far-flung areas. Doctors of Germany, once served here, and the hospital's Golden Jubilee Celebration was held in 2003.

The social composition of the district consists STs are Bhumija, Kondha, Paraja, Gonda, Jani, Santhal and Bhatra; among SCs are Dombs, Manglis (cobbler), Ghasis (scavenger, bone collector), Chachri (salt seller), Blacksmith, and Bengali SCs (Namasudra); and among general categories are Oriya, Telugu, Bengali, Sundhi, Gauda, and Raj Gond. The Dombs (sub-caste of SCs) are widespread throughout the district and numerically they are next to Kondha. Dombs are weavers and drummers by profession and enjoy great influence over others by playing the different scales of music in *parab*, tribal temples, Mondei, *Jatra* and marriage ceremonies. The Dombs are mostly traders in cattle and chillis. The *Mirganis* appear to be sub-caste of Dombs. They differ from the Oriya Dombs in not killing cattle for food but they partake meat of naturally dead animals. They claim to be superior to Oriya Domb. They earn their livelihood by cultivation and weaving. Within the Oriya Domb, there is section of population who are known by *Khangar* Domb, they involve in theft and robbery. They claim themselves that they are the descent of Peta, Handi and Parshu (*Peta, Handi and Parshu were the three brothers who were famous for their act of daylight rubbery and theft in undivided Koraput district. Their native place is Kumli Kamta a village in Nabarangpur. Kamlu Gauda of Chikli village conspired all three brothers and killed them*). In the upper rank of the social strata there are *Sankhari*, who deal with *lac* and who make basket, chains and dolls out of it. They are good artists, artisans and traders. *Mali* are gardeners who grow and collect flowers for temple worship. They have now switched over to cultivation of sugarcane, tobacco, vegetables and the like on the banks of Indravati river. *Sundhi* are famous for distillation and selling of liquor. Tradition holds that they are the descendants of a Brahmin father and royal mother.

5.2. Dandakaranya Project and Bengali

Bengali were resettled in two phases by the Government of India after independence. The first phase was just after independence, when India faced the problem of emigration and resettlement of East Pakistani Hindu population in West Bengal. In second phase, the problem of emigration re-occurred when Bangladesh got her independence in 1971.The Dandakaranya Development Authority (DDA) was set up by a Resolution of the government dated 12 September, 1958 to look after the project. The Ministry of Rehabilitation carved out a contiguous area of about 80,000 square miles stretching over undivided Koraput district of Odisha and Bastar district of Chhattisgarh (previous Madhya Pradesh) for this project, which was given a mythical name "Dandakaranya" (Umerkote, Malkangiri, Raighar in Odisha) and Bastar (in Chhattisgarh). The Ministry in its note of 29 December, 1957, proposed to leave half of the area as forest and keep the other half for the settlement of 4 million persons, of which half may be the local *adivasis* and other half for displaced persons of East Pakistan (present Bangladesh). The proposal was approved by the National Development Council (NDC) in June 1957, it was later decided to prepare a master plan for integrated development of the rehabilitation area. With regard to its administration of the Rehabilitation Committee (RC)[1] directed that (a) an integrated scheme for the benefit of both displaced persons from East Pakistan (Bengali Hindu) and the native inhabitants; (b) the execution of the scheme be in the administrative charge of the Ministry of Rehabilitation; (c) the State Governments concerned would empower the Central Government and through the Chief Administrator to execute the schemes in their respective areas; and (d) a central authority consisting of the representatives of the Ministry of Rehabilitation and the State government concerned should be constituted. The authority would function under the direction of the Central Government.

Under the project some objectives have been taken by the Ministry of Rehabilitation (MR)[2] for integrated development of the areas. These are :

1. Improvement of communications between concerned State's capital and districts.
2. Balanced utilisation of land, including afforestation, soil conservation, reduction and development of colonies.
3. Sustainable agriculture and irrigation facilities.

4. Extensive pisciculture and domestication of livestock.
5. Provision of adequate market facilities.
6. Provision of schools and hospitals.
7. Development of electricity.

When the resettlement took place, the Bengali villages were settled in such a way that every village comprised of at least a Brahmin family, a Blacksmith, a Barber, and a Dhobi. The village consisted of about 60-70 households. The logic behind the settlement on caste lines was that, villagers required a Brahman for *puja* and prayers, Dhobi for washing and laundry, Barber for hair cutting and shaving, the Blacksmith for making sickles, iron ploughs and the like.

5.3. Failure of Integrated Development Schemes

In the time of settlement each Bengali family received 2-3 acres of irrigated and 4-5 acres of non-irrigated land. In 1966, large number of settlers left for West Bengal as they could not cope of with the environment and also it was dense forest with full of wild animals. Again the living style of local tribals was different from Bengali and culturally both of them are different. Another exodus took place between 1972 and 1978. By the time of resettlement it was estimated that there were altogether 36,513 families in the rehabilitation sites but this number was reduced to 25,153 after exodus in 1984.

According to Barik (2006) the settled groups acquired more benefits from the development programme compared to the local STs and SCs. Infrastructural facilities namely, roads, schools and hospitals, coupled with the technical know-how on modern agricultural technology related to maize production and pisciculture became the source of settlers' progress. The integrated development scheme itself showed partial treatment for the tribals. At the beginning of the project the tribal families were promised land but the idea was later scrapped. In the course of time, the DDA avoided implementation of tribal welfare to the present Chhattisgarh State. Odisha alone was given 29,120 acres of land for the settlement of 3,274 tribal families. It was revealed in the administrative report that the DDA did very little for the development of either the region or the tribes. Present study finds that after nearly five decades development plan and schemes the native tribals and SCs socio-economic condition has not been up to the mark than the Bengali. Presently, there was conflict between these two communities in Umerkote block, as the settlers occupied the cultural and economic spaces of the people who were already living there. The conflict primarily stemmed from attempts at over-accumulation of the available resources, especially agricultural land. Among the Bengali population, nearly 90 per cent availed SCs status by the government. The BSCs avail of all facilities offered by the government to Scheduled Castes and yet, they claim themselves to be superior to the local SCs and STs and maintain the basic notions of purity and pollution of caste.

5.4. Physical Features of the District

Nabarangpur was carved out from the mother district Koraput on 02.10.1992 for administrative reasons. The district was then a *taluka*[3] up to 1941 and later a sub-division of Koraput district from 1941 to 1991. Looking into the functional and administrative requirements, vastness of area and growing size of population, in pursuance of Revenue and excise department, Government of Odisha, the old Koraput district was divided into four new districts, i.e., Koraput, Nabarangpur, Rayagada and Malkangiri in 1992.

5.5. Location and Boundary

The District is located at 19° 14′ latitude and 82° 32′ longitudes and is situated at an elevation of 1876 ft. from the sea level. The District shares its boundaries with Kalahandi district in the East, Koraput district in the South. It is bounded by Bastar and Raipur district of Chhatisgarh in the west and north respectively. Its boundary stretches in the north to Kalahandi district and west to Jagadalpur district in Chhattisgarh east to Kalahandi and Rayagada and south to Koraput district with the river Indravati separating the two districts. Nabarangpur is located on the 2000 ft Plateau (about 2000 ft above mean sea level) like that of the historically, famous Jeypore town in the Koraput district. In the north, the Panabeda area, recently renamed, as Chandahandi is only 500 ft above the sea level shaves its climate and social life with the adjacent Kalahandi district. The remaining portion of Nabarangpur district is mainly flat with a few pockets of low hills. The highest peak Podagarh (a historic feature) is 30,50 ft high.

5.6. Forest Coverage in the District

Nabarangpur is generally bestowed with natural resources like forest, surface water but it lacks mines. About 46.5 per cent of the total geographical area of the District covered under forest. The forest provides timber and bamboos. Bamboo cultivation is encouraged under wasteland and watershed development programmes to boost the rural non-farm sector. Non-timber forest produce such as tamarind, *sal* leaves, *sal* seeds, *siali* leaves, *mohua*, *karanji* seeds and *kendu* leaves offer large scope rural employment when they are processed and utilised properly. There are four important forests from which the tribals and non-tribals get their daily fuel wood, e.g., Podagarh hill, Singsari reserved forest, Beheda reserved forest, Chandahandi forest, and Dabugaon reserved forest. There are patches of thick forests mostly containing *sal* seeds and those provide sustenance to dependent villages. Forest resources of the District are however, under constant pressure due to the practice of shifting cultivation amongst tribal and increased demand of timber and firewood by the people. Forestry and wasteland development is proposed to be given thrust in District Planning.

5.7. Geographical Area and Administrative Set-up

The district stretches over an area of 5294.5 sq. km (i.e., 3.4 per cent of the total geographical area of Odisha) and comes under the south Revenue Division (RD) of the State. At present, the District consists of one sub-division and 10 C.D blocks and four Tahsils. It has one Municipality and one Notified Area Council (NAC) at Nabarangpur and Umerkote respectively. Adding to this it consists of 897 villages out of which 880 are inhabited and the remaining 17 are uninhabited. The district is also declared as a scheduled area under the paragraph six of the Fifth Schedule of the Constitution of India. The grassroot democracy that is, Panchayat Raj Institutions (PRIs), got constitutional status by the 73rd Constitutional Amendment Act 1992. According to the provision of the Fifth Schedule of the Constitution which regulate Tribal and the Schedule areas it prohibits automatic extension of any provision made either by the Parliament or concerned States. For the purpose Parliament passed an Act in 1996 to extend Panchayat Raj provision to the schedule areas which are popularly known as Panchayat Extension to the Schedule Areas (PESA). Panchayats which cover under schedule areas have an elected constitutional body to represent in the Panchayat, like the non-schedule areas.

5.8. Demography of the District

As per the final population total figure for 2001 Census, the total population of Nabarangpur district was 10,25,766 of which 5,15,162 were males and 5,10, 604 were females (*Appendix 5.1*). The sex ratio of the District is 991, which is higher than the state average (i.e., 972), further a decennial growth of population by 21.15 per cent resulted in an increase of density of population from 160 per sq. Km. to 194 per sq km between 1091 and 2001. An overwhelmingly large section of the (94.22 per cent) population resides in the rural areas and only 5.78 per cent persons are living in urban areas. It also shows that the average size of household (average number of member in family) is more in urban areas, i.e., 4.7 than rural areas 4.5. The average size of household is more in Raighar (5.2) followed by Umerkote (5) and 4.6 in Jharigaon. Favourable sex ratio was found in five blocks of the District, namely, Tentulikhunti (1020), Chandahandi (1012), Papadahandi (1010), Nandahandi (1007) and Jharigaon (1006) respectively. In Umerkote block sex ratio is nearly 980 favourable because people are aware of family planning and parents give equal respect to both sex, i.e., male and female and it takes place more among the Bengalis.

5.9. Scheduled Castes and Scheduled Tribes Population in the District

The backwardness of the District is visualised from the concentration of SCs and STs population. The SC and ST population constitutes 69.13 per cent of total population of the District (*Appendix 5.2*). This is much higher than the State average of 38.7 per cent, as per the 2001 census. The proportion of STs to the total population is quite high (55.03 per cent) compared to the State average figure of 22.13 per cent. The SCs population (14.1 per cent) is a little less than the State level average i.e. 16.53 per cent. In the District, highest percentage of STs population comprises in six blocks, i.e., 65.02 per cent in Raighar, 62.63 per cent in Kosagumuda, 62.56 per cent in Umerkote, 62.24 per cent in Jharigaon, 59.28 per cent in Chandahandi, and 57.48 per cent in Papadahandi block respectively. Highest percentage of SCs population constitutes in three blocks, i.e., 17.94 per cent in Raighar,

15.96 per cent in Umerkote and 15.56 per cent in Nabarangpur Block respectively which is more than the district's percentage. Total of STs and SCs population, 71.42 per cent residing in rural areas and remaining 28.58 per cent live in Urban. The sanitary workers, cobblers, and cattle sellers among the SCs reside in the urban areas of Nabarangpur. It is further evident from the data that in almost all Blocks, the proportion of scheduled tribes is much higher than that of scheduled castes.

5.10. Literacy Rate

According to 2001 Census, the District literacy rate is one of the far lower (33.93 per cent) than the State level average 63.08 per cent. Its literacy rate in 1991 Census was 18.62 per cent, the rate has more than doubled in 2001 (Appendix 5.3). Literacy rate by sex is quite uneven in the District. The male literacy rate was 47.04 per cent whereas the female literacy rate was as low as 20.76 per cent as per the 2001 Census. In the District, 24 per cent STs and 45.36 per cent SCs population were found literate. There is no separate data available for Bengali scheduled castes and local scheduled castes. As mentioned 90 per cent Bengali are coming under the SC status. Therefore, the literacy rate is highest among the SCs than STs.

Overall literacy rate in the urban areas of Nabarangpur district is 73.71 per cent in 2001 Census. Block-wise literacy rate was found highest, i.e., Raighar (41.29 per cent) followed by Tentulikhunti (40.42 per cent), Chandahandi (39.08 per cent), Nandahandi (36.44 per cent), Nabarangpur (33.20 per cent), and 27.17 per cent in Umerkote block. Though Umerkote Block is dominated with Bengali population still its literacy rate is lower than other non-Bengali Block.

5.11. Landholdings Pattern

Agriculture is the main occupation for the people of

Nabarangpur district. Therefore, the distribution of operational holdings assumes much importance. It is mentioned in Table 5.1 that the class-wise number and area of operational holdings for the year 1995-96.The small and marginal farmers who constitute more than 80 per cent of the total number of farmers. They are operating in less than 50 per cent of the total operational area. The average size of operational holding ranges from 0.51 hectare in the case of marginal farmers to 16.85 hectares for large farmers. Hence, there is a clear indication of skewed distribution of operational holdings. The average size of operational holdings is found to be 1.25 hectares, which is close to the State level average (i.e., 1.30 hectares). Moreover, the average size of holdings is found to be 1.07 hectares and 1.29 hectares for the SCs and STs respectively. Those who hold 5.26 hectares and above are the medium landholders and they belong to OBC categories namely, *Sudhi, Mali, Teli, Gudia,* and *Telugu*. The larger (16.85 hectares and above) landholders are mainly belong to upper strata general categories, it includes, some Brahmin, few of Other Backward Classes (OBC), Khandayat, (Rajput) some Muslims, Marwari, migrant businessmen and who came to the district as a government service provider. Except OBCs like Sudhi and Mali, all large landholders came to the district either as a government employess or a petty businessmen. But in the course of time this section of people grasp not only large chunk of land from the native tribal and *Dalits* but also gradually dominated in local politics, and became decision maker by replacing the natives. The issues of exploitation of land, domination in politics and suppression of the cultural life to the natives has created conditions for ethnic conflict in the District. Of the 15,443 SC farmers, 1.53 per cent farmers the average size of operational holding are medium landholders (5.02 hectares) and 0.10 per cent farmers are large landholders (5.26 hectares) and 15.63 per cent farmers are semi-medium landholders (2.53 hectares). These groups of

Table 5.1 : Class-wise Number and Area of Operational Holdings in Nabarangpur District for the Year 1995-96

Sl. No.	*All Social Groups*			*Social Group S.C*			*Social Group S.T.*			*Avg. size of operational Holdings (in Ha)*
	Farmer	*No. of holders*	*Area operated (In Ha)*	*Avg. size of operational Holdings (in Ha)*	*No. of holders*	*Area operated (In Ha)*	*Avg. size of operational Holdings (in Ha)*	*No. of holders*	*Area operated (In Ha)*	
1.	Marginal	68602	35112	0.51	9280	4626	0.50	41726	21582	0.52
	Percentage to the total	53.28	21.80		60.09	27.87		50.14	20.05	
2.	Small (1.0-2.0)	35449	46562	1.31	3497	4485	1.28	24553	32326	1.32
	Percentage to the total	27.53	28.91		22.64	27.02		29.50	30.03	
3.	Semi-medium (2.0-4.0)	20018	50690	2.53	2413	6064	2.51	13748	35145	2.56
	Percentage to the total	15.55	31.47		15.63	36.54		16.52	32.65	
4.	Medium (4.0-10.0)	4337	22796	5.26	237	1190	5.02	2979	15700	5.27
	Percentage to the total	3.37	14.15		1.53	7.17		3.58	14.59	
5.	Large (10.0-20.0 & above hectare)	351	5914	16.85	16	231	14.44	213	2878	13.51
	Percentage to the total	0.27	4		0.10	1		0.26	3	
6.	All	128757	161074	1.25	15443	16596	1.07	83219	107631	1.29

Source: District Statistical Handbook, Nabarangpur District 2005, Directorate of Economics and Statistics, Odisha

SC farmers are mostly residing in Nandahandi, Kosagumuda, Nabarangapur, Tentulikhunti, and Papadahandi Blocks respectively. Of the 83,219 Scheduled Tribe farmers, 16.52 per cent farmers average size of operational holdings are semi-medium landholders (2.51 hectares), followed by 3.58 farmers are medium landholders (5.02 hectares) and 0.26 per cent farmers are large landholders (14.44 hectares) These farmers are located mostly in Raighar, Jharigaon, Kosagumuda, Nabarangapur, Umerkote and Papadahandi Blocks respectively.

5.12. Livelihood Promotion Strategy of Tribals

Expanding livelihood opportunities among the poor tribesmen and women is the surest way for economic progress. Agriculture and non-timber forest products (NTFP) collection are found to be the main sources of livelihood. Their staple foods are rice, ragi, corn, jackfruit, mango and varieties of *daal*. They drink intoxicants like, *mahuli* (brew made from mohua flowers), *tadi* (juice from date trees), *salap* (juice from Salop tree), *landa* (made of cereals), *handia* (rice beer). The *Kandha, Dangria Kondha* and *Paraja* consume meat of different animals and insects, such as, rabbit, squirrel, mouse, frog, shell, crab, non-poisonous snakes, insects, red ants egg, wild boar, different birds and monkeys. The method of hunting often leads to deforestation. When the tribals locate monkeys in a tree they deliberately cut the surrounded trees to isolate the monkeys and hunt them down. With the gradual ecological destruction and depletion of wild life the problem of acute food insecurity occurs, especially during droughts.

5.13. Person Living Below the Poverty Line

Being a backward and underdeveloped district of the State, the proportion of households living below the poverty line is quite large. This is seen from Table 5.2. According to the 1997 Below Poverty Level Census conducted by the Odisha government 73.7 per cent of the rural families are living below poverty level (BPL). Out of the BPL families in the District, 51.28 per cent are STs followed by 23.36 per cent SCs. Since the Below Poverty Level (BPL) Census is not updated and revised for all practical purpose the State government has accepted 1997 as the benchmark survey. This indicates that quite a sizeable proportion of rural families is poor and suffers from economic insecurity.

Table 5.2 also indicates share of Below Poverty Level (BPL) families to total families in respective Blocks of the district. Highest percentage of BPL families found in Jharigaon (89.3) followed by Papadahandi (82.8) and Nabarangapur (80.8). On the other hand, the lowest percentage shave of BPL families to total families in ascending order observed in Kosagumuda (59.5 per cent) followed by Umerkote (64.4 per cent) and Raighar (69.8 per cent) as per 1997 BPL census. It also observed that, highest percentage of Scheduled Tribe BPL families is concentrated in Raighar Block that is 65.41 per cent. This Block is completely dominated by Gond communities, who are also residing in the adjacent district of Bastar (Chhattisgarh), followed by 62.06 per cent in Jharigaon, 59.65 per cent in Umerkote and 59.47 per cent in Kosagumuda, highest number of Scheduled Castes BPL families is found in 29.31 per cent in Papadahandi block, followed by 27.19 per cent in Kosagumuda, 26.47 per cent in Tentulikhunti, and 22.24 per cent in Umerkote Block.

5.14. Occupational Distribution and Work Participation Rate

It is mentioned in Annexure 5.4 that the distribution of work in two types, main workers and marginal workers. "Work"[4] was defined as participation in any economically productive activity. Such participation was physical or mental in nature.

Table 5.2 : BPL Families in Nabarangapur District (with reference of Umerkote Block) (As per 1997 Census)

Sl. No.	*Name of the Block*	*GP*	*Total Rural Families*	*Total (BPL) Families*	*Percentage of BPL families by Social Group*		
					SC	*ST*	*Others*
1.	Chandahandi	14	16674	11890(71.3)	15.64	30.25	54.11
2.	Dabugaon	8	13494	10335(76.6)	18.37	56.04	25.59
3.	Jharigaon	21	22482	20072(89.3)	16.61	62.06	21.33
4.	Kosagumuda	24	31856	18945(59.5)	27.19	59.47	13.34
5.	Nandahandi	10	14029	10295(73.4)	25.90	44.23	29.87
6.	Nabarangapur	13	16622	13413(80.7)	26.10	53.18	20.72
7.	Papadahandi	22	29533	24439(82.8)	29.31	45.21	25.48
8.	Raighar	24	26015	18170(69.8)	21.48	65.41	13.11
9.	Tentulikhunti	15	21172	15948(75.3)	26.47	28.76	44.77
10.	**Umerkote**	**18**	**23552**	**15177(64.4)**	**22.24**	**59.65**	**18.11**
	Total of the District	169	215429	158684(73.7)	23.36	51.28	25.36

Source: District Statistical Hand Book, Nabarangapur, Odisha, 2001.
Note: Figures in parentheses indicates the percentage

Work involved not only actual work but also effective supervision and direction of work. According to this definition, the entire population has been classified into three main categories, i.e., Main Workers, Marginal Workers and Non-Workers. (i) Main workers were those who had worked for the major part of the year preceding the date of remuneration, i.e., those who were engaged in any economically productive activity for 183 days (or six months) or more during the year. (ii) Marginal workers were those who worked any time at all in the year preceding the enumeration but did not work for a major part of the year, i.e., those who worked for less than 183 days (or six months).

As per 2001 Census, out of 5, 07, 395 workforce, main and marginal workers constitute 52.19 per cent and 47.81 per cent respectively. The proportion of marginal workforce is quite high as compared to the State level figure-which is 32.83 per cent. High magnitude of marginal workers exhibits the fact that a large portion of the working population is underemployed. The District as a whole gives the clear picture that majority of workers are agricultural labourers (52.30 per cent) followed by cultivators (30.77 per cent). On the other hand, 2.22 per cent workers engaged in household industry. It is clear from the above figures the work participation rate is one of the highest (i.e., about 50 per cent). But relatively large share of marginal workers on the one hand, and high proportion of workers engaged as agricultural labourers on the other hand implicitly exhibits the fact that most of the workers are engaged in less productive activities.

5.15. Average Daily Wages of Rural Labourers in the District

Table 5.3 below provides the average daily wages of rural labourers in Nabarangapur district. The daily wage rate for men was Rs. 37.50 which has not been changed since 2001-03. In the year 2003-04, the wage rate has been increased just rupee one and it became Rs. 38.50. For women and children agricultural labourers, the wage rate has been fixed as Rs. 35-36 in the year 2001-04. Agricultural labourers prefer piece rate rather than the homely rate so that they can earn more in a day by producing more.

Under the National Rural Employment Guarantee Act (NREGA) 2005 of Government of India, the same wage rate has been for both men and women, i.e., Rs. 72.50 for 8 hours of work. The objective of the Act is to enhance the livelihood security in rural areas by providing at least 100 days of guaranteed wage employment in a financial year to every household whose adult member's volunteer to do unskilled manual work. The aim of the NERGA is to provide a strong social safety net for the vulnerable groups by providing a fall-back employment source, when other employment alternatives are inadequate. The need to integrate work priorities with a longer-term development strategy is reflected in Schedule I of the Act, which states that the "creation of durable assets and strengthening the livelihood resource base of the rural poor should be an important objective of the scheme".

Table 5.3 : Average Daily Wages of Rural Labourers in Nabarangapur District

Types of Rural Labourers	*Average Daily Wages per Manday (Rs.)*			
	Year 2001-02	*Year* 2002-03	*Year* 2003-04	*Under NREGA*
(A) Skilled				
Carpenter	65	66.25	70.50	00
Masson	72.50	72.50	76.50	00
Tractor Driver	67.50	68.54	71.25	00
(B) Agricultural Field labourers				
Men	37.50	37.50	38.50	72.50
Women	34.58	35.00	36.00	72.50
Children	35.00	35.00	36.00	00

Source: District Statistical Hand Book, Nabarangapur, Odisha, 2005.
Directorate of Economics and Statistics, Bhubaneswar, Odisha.

5.16. Agro-Climatic Region

Out of 10 C.D Blocks, 9 Blocks are covered under the Eastern *Ghat* highlands and one block comes under the Western undulating lands and thus the whole region comes under east coast plains and hills agro-climatic zone. Different kinds of soils like red, black and laterite are found in the districts. Whereas, fine and salty (a soil rich in salt) alluvial soil is found in Nabarangapur Tahsil, black soil is found in Umerkote Tahasil, On the whole the soil type is laterite and soil reaction is slightly acidic in nature. Soil erosion due to floods is one of the major concerns of the district. Rivers such as, Indravati, Turi, and Bhaskel, flow in this region. The District is mainly a flat plateau and the north-east monsoon scarcely affects the area. As a result, most part of the district, more particularly Nabarangapur and Umerkote Tahsils become extremely dry in the hot weather. The district on the average receives rainfall below the normal level. Table 5.4 shows average rainfall in millimetre. Average rainfall of the year is around 133.2 mm in 2005 followed by 186.96 mm in 2006 and 191.12 mm in 2007 respectively. Nabarangapur has very low irrigated area. About 15 per cent of the total cultivable land has got irrigation facilities. Indravati is a perennial river passing through the district. It provides irrigation drinking water and fish production and other modes of livelihood to villages situated on its bank. Bhaskel dam is the only medium irrigation project in the district, which is situated in Umerkote block with the irrigation potential of 3,500 hectares.

5.17. Agricultural Crops and Productivity

Agriculture is the major economic activity in the District. As per 2001 Census data, more than four-fifth of the total work force is engaged in this sector for their livelihood. Among the crops paddy is grown extensively, covering almost 55

Table 5.4 : Average Rainfall (mm) *in Nabarangapur District (2005-07)*

Months	*Years*		
	2005	*2006*	*2007*
January	64.22	0	0
February	16.16	0	0.80
March	0.45	27.7	13.02
April	29.72	43.4	54.21
May	52.39	87.35	65.62
June	212.38	163.2	590.30
July	416.4	742.8	370.10
August	256.3	578.90	721.20
September	442.2	438.70	394.40
October	90.07	102.50	83.60
November	18.26	59.05	0.30
December	0	0	0
Average	**133.20**	**186.96**	**191.12**

Source: Rainfall Report of Nabarangapur District, *www.Nabarangapur.nic.in* (accessed on 5/4/2008).

per cent of the total cropped area of the district. Season-wise paddy production of the year 2004-05 is shown in the Annexure 5.5. It shows that, of the total (1,61,789 hectares cultivated land), 29.38 per cent of the land was cultivated in autumn, and the yielding rate per hectare was 11.50 quintals. In the year 2004-05, total production of paddy was 35,29,991 quintals, of which 16.85 quintals of paddy was produced in autumn itself. In winter, 69.34 hectares of land was cultivated, of which 81.08 quintals of paddy was produced as per yield rate of 23.43 quintals per hectare. In summer, 12.64 hectares was cultivated and the yielding rate was 32.44 quintals per hectare. Total paddy was produced in winter 2.05 quintals. It was found that the yielding rate of paddy in summer was 32.44 per hectare was quite good in comparison to other two seasons, e.g., autumn (11.50 qt/hect.) and winter (23.43 qt/hect.). This variation seen because of low rainfall in the time of paddy sowing or heavy rainfall at the time of harvesting paddy. In Umerkote block, 16.67 per cent (of total cultivation land of the district) hectares of land were cultivated in the year 2004-05, and the yielding rate per hectare was 26.17 quintals. Total paddy produced was 7,68,643 (26.17) quintals. Next to paddy, maize is grown extensively in Raighar, Umerkote and Jharigaon Blocks. The district is known as the maize basket of the State (season-wise production of maize and other commercial crops is cited in Annexure 5.6 (*data was not available for the year 2004-07*). In the year 2003-04, total maize was cultivated in 19,807 hectares, yielding rate per hectare was 20.01 quintal, and total production was 3,96,388 quintals. This is the only district in Odisha where most of the Bengali farmers are engaged in maize cultivation. As staple food for the people is rice, so only on 75 hectares of land wheat was cultivated. Wheat cultivation takes place in Umerkote Block. Ragi cultivation takes place in the hilly areas and it is one of the added staple food for the tribals. Especially, people eat ragi in summer and also tribal prepare *landa* (ragi beer) and ragi cake for their festivals. In 2003-04, ragi was cultivated in 10,589 hectares of land and 54,142 quintals was produced. Other edible crops cultivated in this district are, greengram (1441 quintals), black-gram (40,658 quintals), horse-gram (23,223 quintals), *till* (black lentil), groundnut (5,400 quintals), sugarcane (4,21,984 quintals) and mustard.

There are three common varieties of crops in the district. They are paddy, maize, and several varieties of vegetables. These crops constitute the district's economy today. Rice is the staple food of Odisha and so is in the district of Nabarngpur. Among the commercial crops such as, molasses, varieties of vegetables and *daal,* maize is the most important commercial crops. Farmers cultivate finger millet, various types of beans and green gram for their daily consumption in their homeyard, ponds and on the river banks land. Small landholding farmers invest their own labour to prepare the paddy and maize fields for cultivation. They also have practices of sharing labour and seeds sharecropping and leasing out lands.

First, the farmer may work the land himself with the assistance of his family members, close relatives and friends. The relatives and friends who assist him will be reciprocated when they want assistance for preparation of their paddy and maize fields. This is a traditional method of labour exchange. The most usual form of labour exchange is called *Bethi*[5]. There are other forms of reciprocal labour where large number of people, usually women are collected for the paddy harvesting. In addition, most of farmers hire cows and buffaloes for ploughing and for reaping and threshing. But due to commercialisation of labour and consequences of starvation and hunger, the traditional way of labour exchange and rural life is gradually disappearing. Secondly, farmers can now employ labourers for the entire cultivation cycle. This method is open only to the richer farmers with cash in hand.

A farmer can cultivate his or her paddy lands on sharecropping basis. This method is a traditional form of cultivation called *Bhag Chash* (Sharecropping) among non-tribals and *Aadi* among tribals. The farmers who have more land or who are unable to cultivate lands for several reasons (occupation, unhealthy condition, especially duties like wedding in the family, etc.) give their lands to a kin, neighbours or friends for cultivating with an arrangement of sharing the harvest. Farmer can rent out the land and can get fixed amount of money in each season. The landowners, who do not have time to engage in sharecropping, rent out land. Those landholders, who are settled in the town, lease their agricultural land. A few farmers are cultivating paddy for commercial markets in the district.

Vegetables contribute to the rural economy of District significantly. There are two types of vegetable cultivation today such as, consumption-based or non-commercial vegetable and commercial vegetables. The non-commercial vegetable cultivation existed since the beginning of the village life in the district. The commercial vegetable cultivation started after resettlement. It is because of growth of population in the locality and development of infrastructure facilities, such as transport and communication to adjacent district and neighbouring cities (Raipur, Jagadalpur, and Berhampur). Commercialisation has accelerated with the availability of hybrid seeds and fertilizers. Commercial vegetables are beans and cabbage, tomato, carrot, beetroot, chillies, mushrooms, asparagus, ladyfinger, cauliflower, marrow, and brinjals.

5.18. Irrigation Facilities in Nabarangapur District

The district has enough potential of irrigation facilities from varieties of sources. Among the irrigation facilities, Bhaskel water reservoir a major irrigation facility located in Umerkote block of the district. The reservoir has connected with two canals on left bank and right bank. It releases water in the two sides in alternative years. Another small reservoir is called as Phuljhari, situated in Chandahandi Block. All the three rain-fed rivers namely, *Tel*, *Turi*, and *Nangi* flow in the block and they confluence near *Bidri*. River Bhaskel is a medium perennial river which gets water from the Bhaskel reservoir. There are lift irrigation (well and tubewells) facilities provided by the Government of Odisha and India to the farmers under different schemes throughout the District. These are the minor irrigation facilities, by which all the farmers of the District engage themselves with the occupation of agriculture round the year. Small number of farmers uses tube wells in the District. There are many methods of lift irrigation schemes depending upon the type of mechanism to lift the water. In old days water was lifted with the help of a person or a pair of bullocks. But now-a-days scheme for large areas irrigation some mechanical methods has been applied. Lift irrigation schemes done by

Pani Panchayat are with a principle that water is a natural common property. Every person in the village has a right to use it. In all schemes of Pani Panchayat water is shared equitably. Normally to lift water some energy required for pump operation. It may be electric power or diesel. Sometimes in some places water cannot be provided to the fields as the level of the field is higher than that the source of water. In this case water is required to be lifted at a convenient higher spot from which it can be supplied to the fields. Since 2002, Government of Odisha has started Biju Pani Panchayat Yojana (BPPY) to provide irrigation facilities to agricultural fields.

Table 5.5 : Irrigation Facilities in Nabarangpur District

District Year	*source-wise Irrigation Potential in Nabarangpur District (with reference to Umerkote Block), (Area in Hectares)*					
	**Major/Medium Irrigation projects*		***Minor Irrigation Projects (Rivers)*		****Lift Irrigation Projects*	
	Kharif	*Rabi*	*Kharif*	*Rabi*	*Kharif*	*Rabi*
2003-04	3500	1353	4709	480	2942	1260
2004-05	3500	1190	4975	475	2979	2046
Umerkote Block	**3500**	**1900**	**473**	**36**	**262**	**97**

Source: District Agriculture Office, Nabarangpur (District Statistical Hand Book, Nabarangapur, Odisha, 2005)
Note: * Bhaskel Dam, ** Rivers (Bhaskel, Tel, Turi, Nangi, Indravati, Bidri), *** Well, Tubewells

Table 5.5 shows that in the year 2004-05 for the Kharif season of crop cultivation total area land irrigated from the Bhaskel reservoir is 3500 hectares, followed by 1900 hectares for Rabi season in Umerkote Block. With the help of minor irrigation facilities, 473 hectares of land cultivated in Kharif season followed by 36 hectares in the Rabi season, and by lift irrigation, 262 hectares and 97 hectares areas of land cultivated in the season of Kharif and Rabi respectively. The district, Nabarangpur is situated on the bank of river Indravati, which originates in Thuamal Rampur plateau on Kalahandi district and flows in a south-west direction. The Upper Indravati Irrigation (Major) and Hydro Electricity Project is situated in the district of Nabarangapur but the Nabarangapur hardly benefits from the project both in terms of irrigation and hydro power. This dam project provides irrigation facilities to the adjacent district, especially Kalahandi. The farmers of Nabarangapur district irrigate their lands by drawing directly from the river. Major crops produce through irrigation are paddy, wheat, and maize. Apart from this, farmers cultivate commercial crops, like sugarcanes and varieties of vegetables on the banks of the river Indravati.

5.19. Markets or *Haat*

Haats (weekly markets) form the important rural marketing arrangement in India where farmers and artisans bring their products for sale and from where they buy items of daily use such as groceries, garments, vegetables, spices, cattle, birds and much more. It not only plays role of rural commercial exchange but it is a socio-cultural nerve-centres for villagers. It is a place from where villagers communicate with their relatives and also send information about the forthcoming local festivals (*Nuakhai, Chait Parav, Diali,* etc) and other social ritual such as attending relative funeral, marriage and *Ekusia* (baby birthday party celebrated after 21 days of baby birth. Some tribals also called it *Saatee*).

Self-help group members who start micro-enterprises face the challenge of accessing remote city markets. The *Haat* is easily accessible as it is held in the vicinity and it offers a ready market to women entrepreneurs. Sukhbir Singh[6] has cited 6 items that the *haat* offers: (1) easy access to markets;

(2) ready cash, thus ensuring a smooth cash flow and production cycle; (3) low marketing overheads; (4) high sales volume; (5) elimination of middlemen and hence better price realisation; and (6) better understanding of taste and choice of rural buyers.

Haat is right place for villagers to pass messages to their relatives who are residing in scattered villages around the region. In the *haat*, villagers occupied their particular place. As per their village names, they named that occupied place, for example, if the village name is *Kusumguda* then the occupied place will called as *Kusumgudia* (meaning villagers of the *Kusumguda* where they gather at weekly market day). So, it is easy to other villagers to find out who is sitting in what corner or side of the market and it also earn to pass messages about their relatives. There are daily markets which in local term are called as *Hatri* (It also pronounces as *Hatri*, it varies from place to place). It is only for the surrounding town dwellers and villagers which are residing within 3 km radius approximately. There are cattle markets, besides the commodity markets. In the cattle market, sellers sell their livestock and buyers buys cow, bullock, buffalo, goats and sheep. Specially, in this study area, pigs are not available in the markets. If anybody wants pig for festivals purpose he has to go to the particular village in which pigs are available.

Umerkote is the central business centre in the district, which is situated at 62 km away from district headquarters, i.e., Nabarangapur. Especially it is famous for maize production, paddy. Business of Umerkote, imports hybrid seeds, fertilizers, fodder, poultry, and garments from Raipur wholesale market (Capital of Chhattisgarh), Kolkata market and specie products from Berhampur market, and they sell to the middlemen, who operates in different markets, such as, Chandahandi, Dabugaon, Jharigaon, Kosagumuda, Nadahandi, Papdahandi, Raighar, Kundei, Kadinga, Anchalguma, Beheda, Maidalpur and Nabarangapur. All the population of the 18 Panchayats depend on the weekly

Monday market of Umerkote. Apart from this market, there are several weekly markets which are held on different days in a week, such as Pujariguda, Badakumari, Dhodra, Anchla, Kurshi, Tohara and Singsari. So far as the SHGs are concerned, members can sell their products such as vegetables, chillies, turmeric, salt, bamboo baskets, minor forest products and so on in the market. From this income, they contribute to their collective fund.

5.20. Banking Facilities

Banks are the catalytic agents of economic development. Banks mobilise deposits on the one hand, and channelise the same in the form of development of the region is marked by the member of bank branches operated in that area. Table 5.6 exhibits Block-wise branch network of co-operative banks, Regional rural banks and Commercial banks in Nabarangapur district. Table 5.6 reveals that in total 27 branches of these banks are operating in one lakh population. The distribution of bank branches is highly uneven one as is revealed from Table 5.6 in terms of operational area of each branch which ranges from 4449.4 sq km in case of Jharigaon block to 95.0 sq km. in case of Tentulikhunti block. On an average each bank branch is serving 173.9 sq km of geographical area of blocks. On the other hand, the 135.1 sq. km of geographical area is served by one branch for the district as a whole, which means banking facilities are not adequately available which could be attributable to the backwardness of this region.

5.21. People's Involvement with the SHG System

In 1990s, when SHG system was booming in the country, at the same period, NABARD extended its offer to the district. From 1999 onwards, the IRDP has been replaced by the Swarnajayanti Grameen Swarozgar Yojana (SGSY) and SHG

Table 5.6 : Block-wise Number. of Banking Service in Nabarangpur District

Sl. No.	Name of the Block	Number of Branches			Total	Bank Branches per lakh population
		Cooperative Bank	RRB	Commercial Bank		
1.	Chandahandi		2		2	3.3
2.	Dabugaon		2		2	3.6
3.	Jharigaon		1		1	0.8
4.	Kosagumunda		3		3	2.2
5.	Nabarangapur		2		2	3.0
6.	Nandahandi		2		2	3.8
7.	Papadahandi	1	3	2	6	5.4
8.	Raighar		3		3	1.9
9.	Tentulikhunti		1	3	4	5.9
10.	Umerkote		2		2	1.5
	Block Total	1	21	5	27	2.8
	Urban	3	2	3	8	13.5
	District	**4**	**23**	**8**	**35**	**3.4**

Source: Potential Credit link plan (2005-06), Nabarangpur District, NABARD Regional Office, Odisha.

took over as an alternative mechanism for poverty alleviation. By the credit people engaged themselves in different occupations and sustained their livelihood. About 1,50,00 SHGs are functioning in this district, with the help of various Self-Help Promoting Institutions (SHPIs). According to Karmakar, the phenomenal growth rate of the SHGs, which shows that, "the rural people are keenly involved in their growth and are able to sharpen their micro-entrepreneurial skills with the help of their micro-savings. Thus, the SHG movement has come to stay and is especially needed for women's empowerment"[7].

Table 5.7 depicts the grants and support provided by NABARD to NGOs for promotion and linkage of SHGs in Nabarangapur District. All together, five NGOs are working in Nabarangapur District, and Rs. 0.911 million has been

Table 5.7 : Grant Support to NGOs for Promotion and Linkage of SHGs in Nabarangpur District as on 31st March, 2006

Sl. No.	*Agency (NGO)*	*Year of sanction*	*No.of SHGs to be promoted and linked*	*Amount sanctioned (Rs. M)*	*Progress Mode as on 31 March, 2006*			
					Grant Released (Rs. M.)	*No.of SHGs. Promoted*	*No. of SHGs with SBI A/Cs*	*No. of SHGs credit linked*
1	SEDP/PG (BHU)	2002	80	0.12	0.1	80	75	48
2	DA	2003	100	0.183	0.037	0	0	0
3	GIDE	2003	200	0.36	0.281	106	200	61
4	SARD	2004	100	0.18	0.117	90	73	15
5	IWDS	2005	50	0.088	0.046	20	20	2
	Total		**530**	**0.911**	**0.571**	**296**	**370**	**126**
	On going projects	35	3129	5.07	2.578	2215	2114	805
	Completed	14	1345	1.786	1.64	1496	1065	1477
	Total in KBK	**49**	**4474**	**6.856**	**4.218**	**3711**	**3179**	**2282**

Source: Annual Report NABARD 2005-06.

sanctioned to promote and nurture 530 SHGs in Nabarangpur district. So far 296 SHGs have been promoted with the help of Rs.0.571 million and 126 SHGs were linked with Bank in the District. The NGO, Socio-Economic Development Programme (SEDP) is working in the study area at Umerkote Block. So far SEDP has promoted 80 SHGs. Of them 48 were linked with banks for credit. The amount sanctioned for promoting 80 SHGs was Rs. 0.120 million and as on 31 March, 2006, Rs.0.100 million has been released. The Non-Governmental Organisation Global Unit for Integrated Development Education (GIDE) has promoted 106 SHGs and 61 were linked with the bank against 200 SHGs to be promoted and linked as on 31 March, 2006. Rs. 0.360 million was sanctioned in 2004 but Rs. 0.281 million was released as on March, 2006. Social Action for Rural Development (SARD) has given target to promote 100 SHGs in 2004 and amount was sanctioned Rs. 0.180 million, it promoted 90 SHGs and of which 73 SHGs were linked with SBI but only 15 SHGs were fulfilled criteria for bank credit facility. Democratic Association (DA) an NGO which has shown zero result that it has targeted to promote 100 SHGs in 2003 and Rs. 0.183 million was sanctioned. Indian Women Development Society (IWDS) other NGO was targeted to promote 50 SHGs but it only promoted 20 SHGs with the sanctioned amount of Rs. 0.088 million. KBK as whole, Rs. 6,856 million has sanctioned for promoting 4,474 SHGs. As on March 2006, 3,711 SHGs were promoted with the help of Rs. 4,218 million and 2,282 SHGs were linked with banks for credit. Microcredit is the key to development initiatives for the poor and unemployed particularly in the developing countries. It has significant role in providing livelihoods for the poorest of the poor.

5.22. Festivals

Festivals are occasions for the expression of community

identity. In the area several festivals and fairs are observed. Nabarangapur is a plural society and it has been celebrating many festivals.

5.22.1. Mela or Jatra

Melas and *jatras* are anointed with different gods and deities. In *melas* and *jatras* there are markets attracting salesmen from all over the area. For adolescent tribal boys and girls, *jatras* provide the space for the exchange of gifts such as, rings, towels and sweets, symbolising greeting. When they establish the bond they refer each other not by their personal names but with symbolic names such as *mitri* (friend) *baliphul* (exchange of sand flower), *kadamali* (exchange of a garland made with grass seed), *mendhaphul* (exchange of sheep flower), *gajamunga*. They meet several times in different festivals and if they like each other they seek the approval of their parents for marriage. There are also instances of elopement (locally known as *udlia*[8]).

Dussera (Dasahara)[9] is an important ten-day long Hindu festival, a time honoured ritual in which Goddess *Durga*, epitome of power and energy, Motherhood of the whole universe, is worshipped with due fervour and solemnity. The Maharaja of Jeypore (Sub-Division of Koraput district) used this occasion for the concourse of his subjects. Deities from various areas, towns and villages, are symbolically brought through decorated large bamboo poles to the accompaniment of drums and often musical instruments. On the day of *Vijaya Dasami*, special elaborate offerings are made to the deity which includes the age-old practice of animal sacrifice to the Goddess. People are always in their colourful costumes and rejoice on the grand occasion. In Umerkote Block, tribals called it *Lakhbinda* (shooting an aim, symbolised that killing the devil god Ravan). *Lakhbinda* is held on the day of *Dasahara* near the cattle market in Umerkote. On that day, tribal Pujari fastoms a Brinjal on the top of a long bamboo pole and tribals and non-tribals use bows and arrows, homemade gun, sticks and stones to hit the brinjal targets. The person who aims is honoured in the temple and is given gifts of clothes and money. For Bengali community too Durga Puja is an important festival. Maa *Bhandargharani*[10] of Nabarangpur is the presiding deity of the locality. The name signifies the preserver of wealth and protector of lives. She is also worshipped in nearby villages. Tuesday and Saturday are marked for special worship. Devotees throng temple precincts on every conceivable occasion to seek her blessings. Major festival of the District is Rath Jatra (car festival) of Umerkote which attracts all corners of the people from undivided Koraput district.

Maa *Pendrani*[11] of Umerkote is born out of a myth. A small village *Pendrahandi* near Umerkote worships a pure soul Pendrani, an engaged girl of Pendra, who was a victim of secret human sacrifice by her own brothers. As the story goes, Pendra was from Kalahandi who was engaged with Pandri (a beautiful girl) of a farmer family of Pendrahandi village and he was staying with his parents-in-laws as *Gharjooanai* or *Gharjaamai* (before getting married to a girl, the tribal young man works in the girls house for 3-4 years). It was in the cultivation time heavy rain repeatedly damage the hedge. Despite their efforts Pandri's brother are unable to prevent the paddy crop from getting washed away. To please mother earth the brothers conspire to sacrifice Pendra. Pandri comes to know of the heinous act of her brothers and woebegone she commits suicide in the place where Pendra was buried.

Her spirit is believed to be roaming about the villages helping those who trust her. People adore her sacrifice and have built a temple for her in Umerkote. *Puja* and prayer takes place in every Sunday and devotees from almost all corner of undivided Koraput distirct come to this temple for seeking her blessing. Annual *Jatra* (festival) of Pendrani takes place in the month of August, where tribals and non-tribals gather and worship the goddess.

Mahashivaratri attracts devotees from all walks of life – urban rich to rural poor. *Papadahandi* temple is a pilgrim centre to celebrate such occasion in the District and in Umerkote it is in *Deulkona* (*Deul* means temple and *Kona* means corner). This is another great festival for the tribals to participate and enjoy. The mythologies of Shiva, Parvati and Ganesh are brought alive in folk drama. Festivals of other communities too evoke reverence. The Moharam of the Muslims is a day of prayer and remembrance. Huge processions are taken round the township and mass prayers are held at mosques. Inter-community greetings are exchanged in a spirit of brotherhood. Christmas marks the beginning of a long festival running upto the New Year's Day.

5.22.2. Mondei: Tribal Festival

Mondei[12] is the widely celebrated festival of Nabarangapur district. This festival usually celebrated after harvesting the crops. This festival is observed at different popular locations throughout the district gathering men and women of the area and far off. Tribals of all villages come with decorated *Biman* (a chair for the deity) and long bamboo pole.

Presently District Council of Culture is observing its Annual District Cultural Festival in the same name during 1st, 2nd and 3rd of November every year. Gram Panchayat level and Block level celebrations precede the main District level festival for more than a fortnight It has already become a State level Tribal Festival gaining National and International recognition having enough potential to attract tourists both from inside and abroad. Various activities are included in this festival to accommodate multi-veracity programmes to suit tastes of all classes of people. Rural Sporting, Mountain Trekking, Kavi- Sammelan, Crafts Mela, Artist Camps, Pallishree Mela, Development Exhibition, Open Quiz, Folk dances all over Odisha, colourful and locally typical as well as popular processions, etc., give full exuberance and keep people spellbound during these days.

5.22.3. Padagada Mondei

Padagada is a Gram Panchayat in Umerkote Block, where an annual festival held in the month of March. Like other tribal festivals it is also an important festival in this region. Tribal devotees come with their *Biman* and *Laathi* (Bamboo Pole) to this festival. The tribals make a bonfire and dance around it. Same type of festival takes place in Haat Bharandi in Raighar Block where the participants are both tribals and Bengalis, as less number of Oriya speaking people found here.

5.22.4. Dhodra Mondei

This is another important *Mondei* for the tribals and non-tribals which takes place in the month of March. Most of the non-tribals (Bengali, Oriya, Marwari, and Muslim) set up varieties of shops. All the tribals of the Umerkote region gather in Dhodra festivals in their traditional clothes. They bring with them the decorated *Biman* and bamboo pole as it symbolizes their home deity without this the Mondei does not make any sense. For three days and nights, the managing committee of Dhodra mondei arranges tribal folk dance, drama and songs competition. The importance of Dhodra mondei is that tribals buy gifts for their relatives and get together.

5.22.5. Maati (Earth) Maa and Bihan Jatra (Seed Festival)

This is a festival which takes place in the second week of May. The importance attached with the festival is that, before cultivation, the farmers offers prayer in front the *Maati Maa*

(Earth deity) to satisfy her so that she can provide good crops in the forthcoming harvesting season. This festival is celebrated by all the villagers. The festival takes place outside the village and only the male members of the village participate in the festival. They make animal sacrifice and offered wine to the deity. The men drink and indulge in bawdy language and gestures. Women are forbidden from the celebration as they fear that it may lead to draughts, epidemics and famines. The *Pujari* (the priest) plays a crucial role in the festival. In the end of the festival the *Pujari* symbolically distributes seeds to all the villagers. Before sowing seeds the farmer sows the symbolic seeds.

5.22.6. Gram Debta *(Village Deity)*[13]

In the tribal society, the Gram Debta is an important deity of the village. She is the village goddess and the villagers address it in different names known as Gram Debta, Mata or Thakurani. The Goddess is usually installed at the centre of the village. In some villages, she is also found at the entrance under banyan tree, mango tree or thatched hut which is called as village temple. She is represented by a sacred stone which smeared with vermillion. In all rituals or offerings, the tribals worship and make the first offerings to the Goddess. Also, the first yield of their crops, vegetables and fruits are offered to *Gram Debta*. It is a belief that the Gram Debta guards the village from evil spirits. It is also believed that, if any thing goes against the established custom and taboo, the consequences may be epidemics, mass fever, small pox and diarrhoea.

5.22.7. Chait Parab

The Chait Parab is one of the popular festivals in the tribal society. The festival has been traditionally named after the month of *Chaitra*, which falls in the month of mid-March to

Mid-April. In this festival the Jani and Disari plays important role to worship and organize the festival. The festival continues for about one week and the villagers cherish and enjoy throughout the period without doing any job. As per their tradition and rituals, they offer the newly ripe mangoes to the deities before they eat. One of the significance of the festivals is communal hunting. In the communal hunting, the Disari or Pujari of the village decides the day for hunting. On the fixed day, the villagers go for hunting and while returning from forest, all the members perform a ritual in the forest to please forest deities. The festival ends with a ritual performed by the women for the well-being of their husbands and children.

5.22.8. Phus Parab

The Phus *parab* is another important festival in the tribal society. This festival also named after the month *Pausha* which falls in the month of mid-December to mid-January. The significance of this festival is that, the Jani or Disari offers prayer to the village deities to keep the cattle healthier and protect from wild animals.

5.23. Research Area

Umerkote Block with the geographical area of 512.87 square km located in the hilly terrain of south-west of Odisha. Majority of the inhabitants (62.56 per cent) in the Block are tribal people. Of the total 1,36,739 population (Census 2001), 64 per cent are living below poverty line. It has 106 inhabited villages, of which about 27-28 are Bengali settled. The Block is situated at a distance of 62 km from the district headquarters Nabarangapur, and about 570 km from State capital, i.e., Bhubaneswar. It is socially and culturally closer to the neighbouring State, Chhattisgarh than with coastal Odisha. The Block is more heterogeneous then coastal Odisha because apart from the local tribes, Bengalis, Telugus from Andhra Pradesh and Marwaris reside here. Many of the tribes like Gonds and Bhatras follow Chhattisgarhi culture. The region's agriculture is linked with major markets in Raipur and Jagdalpur (in Chhattisgarh). The distance from the State capital and bad hilly roads make it difficult for people in the region to be connected to the coastal districts of Odisha. The Block has now become commercially significant for the State because of the high production of maize and paddy in the area. Umerkote has attracted Marwari, Telugu and Oriya businessmen and is developing into a major business centre. Umerkote now has a Notified Area Council (NAC).

Nabarangpur district though one of the most backward districts in the State, yet has potentialities of development. The potentialities of growth exist both in farm (primary sector), non-farm sector (Secondary sector and Tertiary sector) and allied sector. Bulks of the farmers are as successful paddy and maize growers. While paddy is cultivated traditionally, in recent years quite a large number of farmers are found to be in maize production. Some people are engaged with horticulture and collecting forest product. That apart, people are engaged with allied activities (dairy farming, poultry farming, animal husbandry and pisciculture).

Table 5.8 : Research Area (Umerkote Block) at a Glance

A.	GENERAL INFORMATION		
	(i)	Geographical area (sq.km.)	512.87
	(ii)	Number of Gram Panchayats	18
	(iii)	Number of inhabited villages	106
	(iv)	Number of households (2001)	27436
	(v)	Number and per cent of BPL families (1997)	15177 (64%)
	(vi)	Distance on road from district Hq. (km.)	62
	(vii)	Composite development index (CDI)rank	5
B.	DEMOGRAPHIC INFORMATION (2001)		
	(I)	Distribution of Population by Gender	
		Total population	136739
		Total males	69057

(Contd...)

Table 5.8 : (Contd...)

		Total females	67682
		Sex Ratio (female per 1000 males)	980
	(II)	Distribution of Population by Social Groups	
		Scheduled Castes (Including BSC)	21817(15.96%)
		Scheduled Tribes	85542(62.56%)
		Others	29380(21.49%)
	(III)	Literacy Rate	
		Overall Literacy Rate	27.17
		Male Literacy Rate	38.13
		Female Literacy Rate	15.96
	(IV)	Distribution of Workers and Work Participation Rate	
		Total Workers	69984
		Total Main Workers	34100(48.73%)
		Total Marginal Workers	35884(51.27%)
		Total Non-workers	66755
		Work Participation Rate	51.18
C.	Cultivable Area (hect.)		185824
	Total areas under paddy cultivation (hect.)		16.67
	Total areas under maize cultivation (hect.)		10.65
D.	One Industry— Mangalam Timbre		

Source: District Statistical Hand Book, 2005.

REFERENCES

1. Barik, R. K. (2006) : 'Faulty Planning in a Tribal Region: The Dandakaranya Development Authority', in G.C. Rath (Ed.) : *Tribal Development in India: The Contemporary Debate,* Sage Publications, New Delhi, p.96.
2. *Ibid,* p.97.
3. A small sub-division, where an assigned hereditary King used to rule.
4. Census 2001, Government of India.
5. Reciprocal arrangements whereby obligations are carefully reckoned in precise terms, the term vary from region to region.
6. Singh, Sukhbir (2008): "SHG-Bank Linkage Programme: Progress and Prospects" in Karmakar (ed.) *Microfinance in India,* Sage Publications, New Delhi, 2008.
7. *Op cit.,* Karmakar (2008) p.40.
8. In other words it is known as love marriage.
9. Dasahara has its symbolic meaning that *Das* mean ten headed Ravan and *Hara* mean killing the devil.

10. *Bhandar* means a room in the house where tribals keep their agricultural products, and *Gharni* means wife, who is the home maker. It symbolises to the goddess of wealth and protector of lives.
11. The name of the tribal goddess Pendrani has named after her own name Pandri and her fiancī's name Pendra. Sometimes the suffix "ni" for particular married woman name as per her husband's name. For example, Pandri is her own name but after her engagement with Pendra, villagers started calling her Pendrani. Generally this suffix is used among STs and SCs.
12. The word is derived from the Hindi word *'mandi'* which means a small market, now understood to mean large congregation of people followed with worshipping a common deity amid pre-historic rituals, a fair and entertainment activities with compulsory folk dances and tribal opera for the whole night. Mandi is pronounced in different name in divided Koraput. For example, in Koraput it is called "Parab", Malkangiri.
13. Naik, R. (2004) : *Planning Processes and People's Participation: Study of Tribal Sub-plan*, Gagandeep Publications, New Delhi, also see, Raj K. Khosla (2006) : "Forest Resource Management in the Koraput District of Odisha: An Analysis of Panchayati Raj Institutions in Scheduled Areas", Thesis submitted in JNU, New Delhi (unpublished).

Annexure 5.1

Demographic Profile of Nabarangpur District: 2001 Census

Sl. No	Name of the Block	No. of house-holds	All Social Group			Sex Ratio	Average size of house-hold	Density of population (Per Sq. Km.)	Population in the age Group (0-6) years			Children (0 to 6 years) Dependency rate
			Male	Female	Persons				Male	Female	Total	
1.	Chandahandi	16,043	30,350	30,726	61,076(6.32)	1,012	3.8	237	5,086	5,015	10,101 (5.65)	16.54
2.	Dabugam	12,894	27,791	27,848	55,693 (5.76)	1,002	4.3	256	5,188	5,254	10,442 (5.84)	18.77
3.	Jhorigam	27,174	61,756	62,104	123,860(12.82)	1,006	4.6	276	12,190	12,549	24,739 (13.83)	19.97
4.	Kosagumda	30,068	67,821	66,848	134,669 (13.93)	986	4.5	245	11,715	11,853	23,568(13.17)	17.50
5.	Nabarangpur	15,487	33,110	32,588	65,698 (6.80)	984	4.2	237	5,675	5,698	11,373 (6.36)	17.31
6.	Nandahandi	12,400	26,045	26,232	52,277 (5.41)	1,007	4.2	245	4,090	4,202	8,292 (4.64)	15.86
7.	Papadahandi	26,111	55,301	55,878	111,179 (11.50)	1,010	4.3	249	10,211	10,388	20,599 (11.51)	18.53
8.	Raighar	30,370	79,519	77,827	157,346 (16.28)	979	5.2	113	15,605	15,132	30,737 (17.18)	19.53
9.	Tentulikhunti	16,552	33,663	34,350	68,013 (7.04)	1,020	4.1	179	5,880	5,746	11,626 (6.50)	17.09
10.	Umerkote	27,436	69,057	67,682	136,739 (14.15)	980	5.0	267	13,809	13,612	27,421 (15.33)	20.05
	Total (Rural)	214,538	484,413	482,083	966,496 [94.22]	995	4.5	206	89,449	89.449	178,898 [95.64]	18.51
	Urban	12,448	30,749	28,521	59,270 [15.78]	928	4.7	–	4,139	4,011	8,150 [4.36]	13.75
	District	227,026	515,162	510,604	1,025,766	991	4.5	194	93,588	93,460	187,048	18.23

Source: Census of India 2001: Census Directorate, Odisha.

Note: (1) Figures in round brackets show block-wise share of the total; and (2) Figures in brackets show the share of urban and rural areas in the district total.

Annexure: 5.2

Block-wise and Gender-wise SC & ST Population in Nabarangpur District : 2001

Sl. No	Name of the Block	Scheduled Caste			Scheduled Tribes			% to Total population		
		Male	Female	Total	Male	Female	Total	SC	ST	Total
1.	Chandahandi	3,189	3,290	6,479 (4.92)	10,174	10,102	20,276 (3.63)	10.61	33.20	43.81 (3.88)
2.	Dabugaon	2,944	2,942	5,886 (4.47)	16,385	16,600	32,985 (5.91)	10.58	59.28	69.86 (5.63)
3.	Jharigaon	6,909	7,038	13,947 (10.58)	38,392	38,696	77,088 (13.80)	11.26	62.24	73.50 (13.19)
4.	Kosagumuda	7,752	7,691	15,443 (11.72)	42,463	41,875	84,338 (15.10)	11.47	62.63	74.09 (14.45)
5.	Nabarangpur	5,254	4,969	10,223 (7.76)	18,991	18,811	37,802 (6.77)	15.56	57.54	73.10 (6.96)
6.	Nandahandi	3,673	3,607	7,280 (5.52)	10,945	11,077	22,031 (3.94)	13.93	42.14	56.07 (4.25)
7.	Papadahandi	5,594	5,780	11,374 (8.63)	31,642	32,265	63,907 (11.44)	10.23	57.48	67.71 (10.91)
8.	Raighar	14,449	13,775	28,224 (21.42)	51,507	50,793	102,300 (18.32)	17.94	65.02	82.95 (18.91)
9.	Tentulikhunti	5,568	5,535	11,103 (8.43)	15,813	16,445	32,258 (5.78)	16.32	47.43	63.75 (6.28)
10.	Umerkote	11,116	10,701	21,817 (16.56)	43,147	42,395	85,542 (15.32)	15.96	62.56	75.51 (15.55)
	Total (Rural)	66,448	65,328	131,776 (91.10)	279,468	279,059	558,527 (98.95)	13.63	57.79	71.42 (97.34)
	Urban	6,534	6,344	12,872 (8.90)	3,004	2,949	5,953 (1.05)	18.54	10.04	28.58 (2.66)
	District	72,982	71,672	**144,654**	282,008	564,480	**846,488**	14.10	55.03	**991142** (69.13)

Source: Census of India 2001, Census Directorate of Odisha

Note: (1) Figures in round brackets show block-wise of the total and (2) figures in square brackets show the share of urban and rural areas in the district total.

Annexure 5.3

Literacy Rate and Gender Gap in Literacy in Nabarangpur District: 2001 Census

Sl. No	Name of the Block	Literates			Percentage of Literacy			Gender Group
		Male	Female	Overall	Male	Female	Overall	
1	Chandahandi	14595	5328	19923	57.77	20.72	39.08	37.05
2	Dabugaon	8269	5921	11190	36.58	12.93	24.14	21.32
3	Jhorigam	16257	5686	21943	32.80	11.47	22.14	21.32
4	Kosagumda	20689	6645	27334	36.87	12.08	24.60	24.79
5	Nabarangpur	13149	4886	18053	47.93	18.17	33.20	29.76
6	Nandahandi	11435	4595	16030	52.08	20.86	36.44	31.23
7	Papadahandi	19566	8068	27634	43.39	17.74	30.51	25.66
8	Raighar	35591	16688	52279	55.69	26.62	41.29	29.07
9	Tentulikhunti	15558	7236	22794	56.00	25.30	40.42	30.73
10	Umerkote	21065	8632	29697	38.13	15.96	27.17	22.16
	Urban	22120	15559	37679	83.13	63.48	73.71	19.65
	District	198294	86244	284538	47.04	20.67	33.93	26.36

Source: Census of India 2001 and Census Directorate, Odisha.

Annexure 5.4

Distribution of Workforce and Work Participation Rate in Nabarangpur District (with reference to Umerkote Block)

Sl. No.	Name of the Block	Main Workers (percentage)			Marginal Workers (percentage)			Total Workers (percentage)			Work Participation rate (percentage)		
		Male	Female	Total	Male	Female	Total	Male	Female	Total	Male	Female	Total
1	Chandahandi	81.79	18.21	100	32.85	67.15	100	58.54	41.46	100	58.49	40.92	49.92
2	Dabugaon	86.50	13.50	100	32.72	67.28	100	57.33	42.67	100	58.18	43.22	50.69
3	Jharigaon	81.79	18.21	100	27.77	72.23	100	55.90	44.10	100	56.90	44.65	50.76
4	Kosagumuda	85.87	14.13	100	28.05	71.95	100	56.32	43.68	100	60.48	47.59	54.08
5	Nabarangpur	80.46	19.54	100	33.85	66.15	100	56.66	43.34	100	56.51	43.92	50.26
6	Nandahandi	83.96	16.04	100	36.60	63.40	100	59.12	40.88	100	55.27	37.95	46.58
7	Papadahandi	82.36	17.64	100	33.89	66.11	100	56.67	43.33	100	57.31	43.37	50.31
8	Raighar	75.96	24.04	100	27.39	72.61	100	56.18	43.82	100	55.13	43.93	49.59
9	Tentulikhunti	77.74	22.26	100	33.86	66.14	100	56.39	43.61	100	54.43	41.26	47.78
10	**Umerkote**	**81.64**	**18.36**	**100**	**30.11**	**69.89**	**100**	**55.22**	**44.78**	**100**	**55.96**	**46.30**	**51.18**
	Total	81.32	18.68	100	30.79	69.21	100	56.49	43.51	100	**56.91**	**44.05**	**50.50**
	Urban	84.40	15.60	100	36.56	60.31	100	77.69	22.31	100	48.92	15.14	32.67
	District	**81.51**	**18.49**	**100**	**30.87**	**69.13**	**100**	**57.30**	**42.70**	**100**	**56.43**	**42.43**	**49.46**

Source: Census of India 2001 and Census Directorate, Odisha.

Note: Data was not available for non-workers.

Annexure 5.5

Season-wise Estimated Area in Hectares, Yield-Rate and Production in Quintals of Paddy in the District (with reference to Umerkote Block)

Paddy Production in Quintals in the District

Season		*Year 2003-04*	*Year 2004-05*
Autumn	Area in Hectares	52952 (32.72)	51768 (29.38)
	Yield Rate in Qt/Hect.	8.03	11.50
	Production in Quintals	954837 (23.48)	595134 (16.85)
Winter	Area in Hectares	107147 (66.22)	122165 (69.34)
	Yield Rate in Qt/Hect.	28.59	23.43
	Production in Quintals	3063710 (75.35)	2862350 (81.08)
Summer	Area in Hectares	1690 (1.04)	2235 (12.64)
	Yield Rate in Qt/Hect.	24.79	32.44
	Production in Quintals	46965 (1.15)	72507 (2.05)
Total in the District	Area in Hectares	161789	176168
	Yield Rate in Qt/Hect.	25.13	20.04
	Production in Quintals	4065512	3529991
Umerkote Block Total	Area in Hectares	NA	29372 (16.67)
	Yield Rate in Qt/Hect.	NA	26.17
	Production in Quintals	NA	768643 (2.17)

Source: District Statistical Hand Book, Nabarangpur, Odisha, 2005.

Annexure 5.6

Season-wise Estimated Area, Yield Rate and Production of Different Crops (A–Area in Hectares, Y–Yield rate in Quintals per Hectares. & P–Production in Quintals)

Year (2003-04)

Sl. No.	*Crop*		*Total*	*Autumn*	*Winter*	*Summer*
1	Wheat	A	75	–	–	75
		Y	17.32	–	–	17.32
		P	1299	–	–	1299
2	Maize	A	19807	17125	520	2162
		Y	20.01	19.87	21.79	20.75
		P	396388	340195	11331	44862
3	Ragi	A	10589	7210	3365	14
		Y	5.11	5.38	4.53	7.81
		P	54142	38790	15243	109
4	Greengram	A	513	–	25	488
		Y	2.81	–	2	2.85
		P	1441	–	50	1391
5	Blackgram	A	8669	–	8669	–
		Y	4.69	–	4.69	–
		P	40658	–	40658	–
6	Horsegram	A	5734	–	5734	–
		Y	4.05	–	4.05	–
		P	23223	–	23223	–
7	Till (black lentil)	A	5	–	5	–
		Y	2.06	–	2.06	–
		P	10	–	10	–
8	Groundnut	A	679	551	–	128
		Y	7.95	7.92	–	8.09
		P	5400	4364	–	1036
9	Musturd	A	5	–	5	–
		Y	0.73	–	0.73	–
		P	4	–	4	
10	Potato	A	118	–	118	–
		Y	95.55	–	95.55	–
		P	11275	–	11275	–
11	Jute	A	–	–	–	–
		Y	–	–	–	–
		P	–	–	–	–
12	Sugarcane	A	859	–	859	–
		Y	491.25	–	491.25	–
		P	421984	–	421984	–

Source: District Statistical Hand Book, Nabarangpur, Odisha, 2005.

6

Socio-Economic Features of Respondents and Households Sample under Study

"One day our grandchildren will go to museums to see what poverty was like".

—Muhammad Yunus, Grameen Bank Founder, Bangladesh

In the previous chapter an attempt has been made to describe the socio-economic structure of the district particularly focused on the sample under study[1]. This chapter illustrates the salient features such as, social and economic background of the households in general and of the selected women respondents in particular. The respondents for this study are women. The terms "respondent" and "household" are used interchangeably in the following analysis. This section deals with the social status of the sample under study, e.g., respondents own profile and her household structures and assets. For the convenience of the study, people's engagement with the SHG and enhancing income, which leads to poverty alleviation, three communities have been selected from the Umerkote Block, viz., Scheduled Tribe[2], Scheduled Caste[3] and Bengali[4].

6. 1. Social Features of the Sample under Study

As already mentioned Umerkote Block is predominantly a

tribal dominant area, it was expected obvious of their highest involvement with the SHGs. Out of 209 women respondents, the highest concentration of 60.3 per cent (126) were Scheduled Tribe women followed by local Scheduled Caste women who constitute 18.2 per cent (38), while the Bengali Scheduled Caste women form 17.7 per cent (37) and only 3.8 per cent (8) of the respondents from the general category.

Table: 6.1 : Social Groups

Social[5] Groups	*Statistics*		
	Frequency	*Percentage*	*Cumulative Percentage*
ST	126	60.3	60.3
SC	38	18.2	78.5
BSC	37	17.7	96.2
General	8	3.8	100.0
Total	209	100.0	–

6.1.1. Age Group of the Respondents

Due to the absence of recording birth dates the age of the respondents are based on their own guess. In the process of this study, I cross-checked their responses against various prominent events that have occurred in their lives. In Table 6.2 shows that for ST women the highest percentage of the respondents, i.e., is 46 per cent (58) found for the age group between 30-35, followed by 27 per cent (34) for those in the 26-29 age group and, 16.7 per cent (21) are in the age group of 40-45, and 7.9 per cent (10) respondents are age group of 36-39. It shows that among the ST women, 30-35 age groups are more active to participate in the SHG activities compared to the younger group of 26-29 and the middle aged women of 40-45. Of the 38 SCs women, 52.6 (20) are under the age group of 30-35, followed by 23.7 per cent (9) 40-45 age group, 10.5 per cent (4) each respondents are in the age group of 22-25 and 26-29 respectively. Likewise, among the 37 Bengali

Table 6.2 : Age of the Respondents and Social Groups

Age of the respondents	*Statistics*	*Social Groups*				
		ST	*SC*	*BSC*	*General*	*Total*
22 25	Count	3	4	2		9
	% within the Community	2.4%	10.5%	5.4%	—	4.3%
	% of Total	1.4%	1.9%	1.0%		4.3%
26 29	Count	34	4	17	3	58
	% within the Community	27.0%	10.5%	45.9%	37.5%	27.8%
	% of Total	16.3%	1.9%	8.1 %	1.4%	27.8%
30 35	Count	58	20	15	3	96
	% within the Community	46.0%	52.6%	40.5%	37.5%	45.9%
	% of Total	27.8%	9.6%	7.2%	1.4%	45.9%
36 39	Count	10	1	2	2	15
	% within the Community	7.9%	2.6%	5.4%	25.0%	7.2%
	% of Total	4.8%	0.5%	1.0%	1.0%	7.2%
40 45	Count	21	9	1		31
	% within the Community	16.7%	23.7%	2.7%	—	14.8%
	% of Total	10.0%	4.3%	0.5%		14.8%
Total	Count	126	38	37	8	209
	% within the Community	100.0%	100.0%	100.0%	100.0%	100.0%
	% of Total	60.3%	18.2%	17.7%	3.8%	100.0%

SC respondents, 45.9 per cent (17) are in the age group of 26-29, followed by 40.5 per cent (15) respondents are 30-35 age groups. In the same community, 5.4 per cent (2) each is under the age group of 22-25 and 36-39 respectively. It shows that those women who are under the age group of 30-35, are taking more interest to join into the SHG. In the sample of 209, general caste respondents are only 3.8 per cent (8). Among general caste women, 37.5 per cent (3) each are under the age group of 26-29 and 30-35 respectively, and 25 per cent are under the age group of 36-39.

Table 6.2 also shows that, 45.9 per cent (96) of total (209) respondents are under the age group of 30-35, emphasizing that they are keen to join the SHGs to enhance their income. Likewise, 27.8 per cent (58) of total respondents are under the age group of 26-29, and 14.8 per cent (31) are in the middle aged group are between 40-45 years old. Moreover, age is important from the banks point of view to lend loans for income generation activities to the SHG and also for the individual concerned.

6.1.2. Marital Status of Respondents

As per the sample size of the study, all the respondents (100 per cent) are married women irrespective of social groups. This is perhaps because the married women provides better stability in the membership in the SHG than an unmarried girl could, as she is also the member of the household where she has less responsibilities, especially in household management matter. Unlike the unmarried, the married women can guarantee permanent membership for the SHG. Another point of preference for married women may be that she is more responsible and sincere to the household's progress.

6.1.3. Religious Background of the Respondents

Mostly, Self-Help Groups are informal and homogeneous,

Table 6.3 : Religion of Respondents

Religion of the Respondents	*Statistics*	*Social Groups*				*Total*
		ST	*SC*	*BSC*	*General*	
Hindu	Count	126	32	37	8	203
	% of Total	60.3%	15.3%	17.7%	3.8%	97.1 %
Christian	Count	—	6	—	—	6
	% of Total		2.9%			2.9%
Total	Count	126	38	37	8	209
	% of Total	60.3%	18.2%	17.7%	3.8%	100.0%

where members are invited from the same community and religion. This is because homogeneity of membership may ensure group solidarity, mutual trust and security and, therefore, can function smoothly. Having belonged to the same religion also increases belongingness and leads to social harmony and economic progress.

Table 6.3 shows that an overwhelmingly 97.1 per cent (203) respondents belong to Hindu religion, and only 2.9 per cent (6) of respondents are Christians. The tiny percentage of Christians in the sample is due to the recent conversions in the area and mostly from the SCs. This classification of religion is based on the way in which the respondents replied regarding their present religious status. As it is mentioned in the district profile that the tribals of this region celebrates varieties of festivals in the forest as well as in the village temple before sowing seeds in the agriculture field and after harvesting the crops and also their believe in epics the *Ramayana*, indicates that they claim themselves as Hindu.

6.1.4. Caste and Sub-Caste of Respondents

Before proceeding to the sub-caste of the respondents, it is worthwhile to discuss about the caste systems in this region. The caste system is hierarchical determining the social status in the group. Broadly, these castes can be classified into four groups—the highest castes, the upper castes, the lower castes and the lowest castes. The highest castes are the Brahmins and the upper castes are Kshatriya. As this study areas is concerned, Brahmins can be seen in two categories that, Oriya Brahmins, those who are dominant in the temple worship and the Bengali Brahmins who perform rituals in the Bengali villages only. They are not the part of the priest in the local tribal temples. Among the upper castes, e.g., Kshatriya, two categories are found such as among Oriya speaking people, they called it Khondyat or Rajput, and among Bengali, it is known as Kayast. Among the lower castes are Vaisya and lowest castes are Sudra. Among the Vaisya groups—traders like, Marwari, Teli (among Oriya) and Dakua (among Bengali) are prominent. Each of these lower castes and lowest castes has its own innumerable sub-castes. Among the native lowest castes Sudra, there are a number of sub-castes, namely, Oriya Domb, Khangar Domb, Mirgani Domb, Mangli or Chamar, Chachri, etc. Among Bengali the lowest caste—Namasudra is the only sub-caste seen in this area. Among the tribals who come under the Hindu fold, their sub-castes namely, Bhumia, Kondha, Paraja, Gonda, Bhatra, Jani Sundhi, Gauda, and Blacksmith. Raj Gond, are numerically very less but they claim themselves upper castes that is Rajput. Thus, each caste has a social unit. It is autonomous in nature and has its own Panchayat which enforces conduct appropriate to that caste. If there is an infringement of the caste rules the individuals or even the group is punished by fine or in extreme cases by ex-communication (*bahishkara*). Of course, rituals are also provided and for the re-entry of those punished individuals back into the groups. For SC categories, if an individual has banished from the caste he can re-entry to the caste by paying fine what imposed by the Panchayat. The re-entry ritual ceremony is done by the tribal priest. By social status the Jani or Pujari of the village enjoys highest status as he is the only person to perform all the prayers and *puja* offerings in the village. The term sub-caste or *jati* is used here for this study. The term sub-caste or *jati* denotes to a sub-communities, who live in the same village. They are likely to have more frequent communication with each other than with *jati* fellows in other villages. According to Mandelbaum (1972), "a sub-caste or *jati* is an endogamous, hereditary social group that has a name and a combination of attributes. All members of a *jati* are expected to act according to their *jati* attributes, and each member shares his *jati's* status in the social hierarchy of a village locality"[6]. The members of each

Table 6.4 : Sub-Caste and Sub-Tribe of Respondents

Sub Caste & Sub-Tribes of Respondents and Social Groups

Sub-Caste & Sub-Tribes	*Statistics*	*Social Groups*				
		ST	*SC*	*BSC*	*General*	*Total*
Bhatra*	Count	42	—	—	—	42
	% within the community	33.3%				20.1%
	% of Total	20.1 %				20.1%
Weaver	Count		2	—	—	2
	% within the community		5.3%			1.0%
	% of Total		1.0%			1.0%
Namasudra	Count	—	—	37	—	37
	% within the community			100.0%		17.7%
	% of Total		17.7%			17.7%
General	Count	—	—	—	8	8
	% within the community				100.0%	3.8%
	% of Total				3.8%	3.8%
Kandha **	Count	34	—	—	—	34
	% within the community	27.0%				16.3%
	% of Total	16.3%				16.3%
Dom	Count	—	36	—	—	36
	% within the community		94.7%			17.2%
	% of Total		17.2%			17.2%

(Contd...)

Table 6.4 : *(Contd...)*

	Paraja **	Count	2	—	—	—	2
		% within the Community	1.6%				1.0%
		% of Total	1.0%				1.0%
	Bhumija*	Count	26	—	—	—	26
		% within the Community	20.6%				12.4%
		% of Total	12.4%				12.4%
	Gond*	Count	18	—	—	—	18
		% within the Community	14.3%				8.6%
		% of Total	8.6%				8.6%
	Saora **	Count	4				4
		% within the Community	3.2%				1.9%
		% of Total	1.9%				1.9%
Total		Count	126	38	37	8	209
		% within the Community	100.0%	100.0%	100.0%	100.0%	100%
		% of Total	60.3%	18.2%	17.7%	3.8%	100%

Note : Within the tribes, there are sub-tribes who hold lower social status and are untouchable within the ST community. For example, * (Bhatra, Bhumija, and Gond) hold higher social status than **(Paraja, Saora and Kandha).

endogamous group follow certain characteristic patterns of behaviour and have certain assigned attributes. The group members, among them have a specialised occupation, according to which the group is ranked in the local hierarchy. Therefore, every person is a member of his village and also of his *jati*.

Table 6.4 shows the sub-caste of the respondents in each social group. Out of 126 ST respondents, *Bhatra* are 33.3 per cent (42) followed by *Kondha* 27 per cent (34), *Bhumija* 20.6 per cent (26), *Gond* 14. 3 per cent (18), Saora 3.2 per cent (4) and 1.6 per cent (2) are *Paraja*. Likewise, for total 38 SC respondents, 94.7 per cent (36) belong to Domb and only 5.3 per cent (2) are weavers. All the 37 Bengali SCs are *Namasudra*. Under the General category are the *Raj Gond*[7] and the *Kayastha*[8].

6.1.5. Education Level of Respondents

Table 6.5 shows the education level of the respondents. Under the sample study, 61.7 per cent (129) respondents are illiterate. While others 17.2 per cent (36) are literate but never attended a school; they have received informal education under the Total Literacy Mission Programme (TLMP) of the Central Government. Another 10 per cent (21) have attended up to primary school, and 11 per cent (23) have completed upper primary level education. The educated respondents, are Bengalis, either Namasudra or upper caste Bengalis.

Bengali community benefited education from the Dandakaranya Project (DP) launched in Umerkote in 1950s and 1960s. Under this project a primary school was established in every village so the resettlement can avail education. Again the programme of study used in these schools was Bengali script. So it was not quite possible to the native tribal and SC to learn Bengali script. After 1970s not a single school was constructed in tribal villages and that explains why majority of the STs and SCs undersampled

Table 6.5 : Education Level of Respondents

Education level of Respondent	*Statistics*	*Social Groups*				
		ST	*SC*	*BSC*	*General*	*Total*
literate	Count	27	9	—	—	36
	% within the community	21.4%	23.7%			17.2%
	% of Total	12.9%	4.3%			17.2%
illiterate	Count	99	28	—	2	129
	% within the community	78.6%	73.7%		25.0%	61.7%
	% of Total	47.4%	13.4%		1.0%	61.7%
Primary (I-V)	Count	—	1	19	1	21
	% within the community		2.6%	51.4%	12.5%	10.0%
	% of Total	0.5%	9.1 %	.5%	10.0%	
Upper Primary	Count	—	—	18	5	23
	% within the community			48.6%	62.5%	11.0%
	% of Total		8.6%	2.4%	11.0%	
Total	Count	126	38	37	8	209
	% within the Community	100.0%	100.0%	100.0%	100.0%	100.0%
	% of Total	60.3%	18.2%	17.7%	3.8%	100.0%

were deprived from education facility. This is also the reason that under the sample study an overwhelmingly 61.7 per cent (129) of respondents found illiterate. Presently, there are numerous schools and also colleges established in the district as well as in the Blocks.

Analysing Table 6.5 in terms of social groups, of 60.3 per cent (126) ST respondents, 21.4 per cent (27) respondents are literate and rest 78.6 per cent (99) are illiterate. Likewise, out of 38 SC respondents, 23.7 per cent (9) respondents are literate and majorities 73.7 per cent (28) are illiterate, and only 2.6 per cent (1) has completed primary level education. Among BSC respondents, out of 37 respondents, 51.4 per cent (19) completed primary level education followed by 48.6 per cent (18) got upper primary education. Among the general category sample of 8 respondents, 62.5 per cent (5) have completed upper primary education and 12.5 per cent (1) has received primary education. Only 25 per cent (2) respondents, who are in general category, are illiterate, and, belong to *Rajgond* community.

6.2. Occupation of the Respondents

Occupation describes the principal activities in which a person is engaged to eke out her livelihood. The respondents were engaged as daily-wage labourers, labouring on their own agricultural fields, food gathering, cattle rearing and dairy farming, fishery, sellers of vegetables and dry fishes in the daily village market and such other activities. Table 6.6 shows that out of 209 respondents, 23.4 per cent (49) primarily earn their livelihoods from dailywage labour. Those respondents earn their livelihood from dairy farming are 11 per cent (23), followed by 13.4 per cent (28) women help their husband in the agriculture field. There is a very small percentage of 2.4 per cent (5) earns livelihoods from food gathering activities. Currently, 49.8 per cent (104) of the respondents are engaged in working on own agricultural field and simultaneously generating their incomes through SHG activities.

In terms of occupation distribution in each caste or community it was found that out of 126 ST Respondents, 65.1 per cent (82) engaged in their own agricultural field and allied activities for income generation. While 20.6 per cent (26) help their husband in agricultural field, 8.7 per cent (11) are seasonal daily-wage labourers, 1.2 per cent (2) respondents are engaged with dairy farming and 4 per cent (5) gather forest products to sell in the Bengali villages and towns. These respondents gather forest products like bamboo sprout for eating, *Chanr Kali* (a sweet and sour fruit), *Kendu fruit, Kailari Saag* (sweet leaves), *red ant eggs, edible roots and fruits, mushrooms, Thirli aamb* (Forest sour mango) *Ghooli* (small snail), and the like. Out of 38 SC respondents, 86.8 per cent (33) work as seasonal daily-wage workers. These respondents work under Bengali and Oriya land owners and also work as labourers in the construction of roads and public buildings. 13.2 per cent (5) of the SC respondents are working in their own agricultural fields and in allied activities such as selling vegetables, dry fish, chilli powder, turmeric powder, and ladies cosmetics products, and the like. Whereas, out of 37 Bengali SC respondents, 51.4 per cent (19) are dependent on dairy farming, followed by 40.5 per cent (15) who are working in their own agricultural fields, and allied activities (wood collection, hand sewing carpets) and the remaining 8.1 per cent (3) are seasonal dailywage labourers. Among 8 general caste respondents, 25 per cent (2) each are engaged with seasonal dailywage labour, dairy farming, helping husband in the agricultural field and allied activities respectively.

6.2.1. Annual Income of the Respondents (Approximate)

An attempt has been made to assess the annual income of

Table 6.6 : Occupation of Respondents

Respondents Occupation	*Statistics*	*Social Groups*				
		ST	*SC*	*BSC*	*General*	*Total*
Seasonal dailywage labourer	Count	11	33	3	2	49
	% within the community	8.7%	88.8%	8.1%	25.0%	23.4%
	% of Total	5.3%	15.8%	1.4%	1.0%	23.4%
Dairy farming	Count	2	—	19	2	23
	% within the community	1.6%		51.4%	25.0%	11.0%
	% of Total	1.0%		9.1%	1.0%	11.0%
Helping husband in the agriculture field	Count	26	—	—	2	28
	% within the communiy	20.6%			25.0%	13.4%
	% of Total	12.4%			1.0%	13.4%
Food gathering	Count	5	—	—	—	5
	% within the community	4.0%				2.4%
	% of Total	2.4%				2.4%
Working own agri field and seasonal dailywage	Count	82	5	15	2	104
	% within the community	65.1%	13.2%	40.5%	25.0%	49.8%
	% of Total	39.2%	2.4%	7.2%	1.0%	49.8%
Total	Count	126	38	37	8	209
	% within the community	100.0%	100.0%	100.0 h	100.0%	100.0%
	% of Total	60.3%	18.2%	17.7%	3.8%	100.0%

the respondents. The annual incomes of the respondents are generated from their engagement with varieties of occupations. Table 6.7 deals with the annual income of the respondents. It shows that 18.2 per cent (38) are unpaid home workers, 71.8 per cent (150) earn in between Rs. 5,000 to 7,000 annually and remaining 10 per cent (21) earn approximately Rs. 8,000-12,000 per annum. In terms of distribution within castes and communities, it was found that, of the 126 ST respondents, 26.2 per cent (33) consist of unpaid workers, who work in their own fields or homes. An overwhelming 69 per cent (87) of ST respondents earn somewhere between Rs. 5,000-7,000 per annum working as dailywage labourers, agricultural labourers and as petty traders. The remaining 4.8 per cent (6) earn approximately between Rs. 8,000-12,000 per annum. These respondents earn their annual income from dairy farming. Likewise, among 38 SC respondents, 92.1 per cent (35) earn an annual income in between Rs. 5000-7000. These respondents earn through dailywage labour and allied activities. Only 7.9 per cent (3) of SC respondents earn between Rs. 8,000-12,000 per annum. This particular percentile of SC respondents are engaged in business activities like, selling vegetables, dry fish, etc., in the local daily and weekly markets and also vending in nearby villages.

Out of 37 Bengali SC respondents, 8.1 per cent (3) are unpaid home workers. These respondents are either helping their husbands in their agriculture fields or looking after home. Among the BSCs, 67.6 per cent (25) respondents earn Rs. 5,000-7,000 per annum, and 24.3 per cent (9) earn Rs. 8,000-12,000 per annum approximately. These groups are very much active in dairy farming and livestock (poultry including duck rearing) activities. Among General Category, out of 8 respondents, 25 per cent are unpaid home workers extending a helping hand to their husbands in their own agriculture fields and looking after homes. Each of the

Table 6.7 : Annual Income of Respondents (Approximately)

Annual Income of Respondents		*Social Groups*				
		ST	*SC*	*BSC*	*General*	*Total*
Unpaid homework	Count	33	—	3	2	38
	% within the community	26.2%		8.1%	25.0%	18.2%
	% of Total	15.8%		1.4%	1.0%	18.2%
Rs. 5,000-7,000	Count	87	35	25	3	150
	% within the community	69.0%	92.1%	67.6%	37.5%	71.8%
	% of Total	41.6%	16.7%	12.0%	1.4%	71.8%
Rs.8,000-12,000	Count	6	3	9	3	21
	% within the community	4.8%	7.9%	24.3%	37.5%	10.0%
	% of Total	2.9%	1.4%	4.3%	1.4%	10.0%
Total	Count	126	38	37	8	209
	% within the community	100.0%	100.0%	100.0%	100.0%	100.0%
	% of Total	60.3%	18.2%	17.7%	3.8%	100.0%

remaining two in this category earn Rs. 5,000-7,000 and Rs. 8,000-12,000 per annum respectively from dailywage and dairy farming and livestock (poultry, goats and sheep) activities.

6.3. Housing Structure of Respondents

As described in the district profile, Umerkote Block is basically a plain land. Except in the town almost all villages consist of either huts[9] or semi-pucca[10] houses. One can, however, find one or two pucca[11] houses in every Bengali villages and old tribal villages except in the hill areas. Basically, STs like *Kondha* and *Paraja* reside near to the forest in a hut and some landless people also reside in huts even in towns. In Odisha, the hut is locally called as *Kudia*. This is built with wood, bamboos, strong forest grass and *Siali* and *Badla* leaves are used in covering the roof tops. These leaves are very broad and strong and protect the dweller from hot summers and heavy rains. Walls are prepared with crisscrossing bamboo frames that are filled out with mud. Semi-pucca houses are called *Kati Ghar.* Their walls are made with processes mud and their roofs are covered with *Jhikar or Khapar* (home made tile). *Pucca* house walls are built with raw or brunt bricks, floorings are done with concrete cement, and roofs are either covered with tin chequered tiles. The semi-pucca houses which are owned by the Bengalis were being provided to them in the time of resettlement. By dint of hard labour and agriculture and business activities, some of them are able to construct their own pucca house replacing the old one.

Table 6.8 shows that 33 per cent (69) are residing in huts, 64.1 per cent (134) in semi-pucca houses and 2.9 per cent (6) in pucca houses. Some ST lives in separate community clusters in the forest, such as, Kondha and Paraja. Their villages are named after the communities who settled first in the area such as *Santa Guda* (*Santa* represents the community and *Guda* means bird's nest) and animals like

Table 6.8 : Housing Structure of Respondents

Housing Structure	*Statistics*	*Social Groups* *ST*	*SC*	*BSC*	*General*	*Total*
Hut Count	48	21			69	
	% within the Community	38.1 %	55.3%	—	—	33.0%
	% of Total	23.0%	10.0%			33.0%
Semi Pucca	Count	78	17	33	6	134
	% within the Community	61.9%	44.7%	89.2%	75.0%	64.1%
	% of Total	37.3%	8.1 %	15.8%	2.9%	64.1
Pucca Count	—	—	4	2	6	
	% within the Community			10.8%	25.0%	2.9%
	% of Total			1.9%	1.0%	2.9%
Total	Count	126	38	37	8	209
	% within the Community	100.0%	100.0%	100.0%	100.0%	100%
	% of Total	60.3%	18.2%	17.7%	3.8%	100%

Bhalu Guda (*Bhalu* means bear). Villages are also named after persons, communities, tribal deity and trees. For example, few villages are called *Pujari Guda* (*Pujari* are tribal priests, dominated by the particular *Pujari* community), *Majhi Guda*, (dominated by Majhi community) *Kailari Guda* (*Kailari* is a tree with edible leaves). Of the 126 Scheduled Tribe respondents, 38.1 per cent (48) reside in huts, 61.9 per cent (78) have now become upwardly mobile to live in semi-pucca dwellings.

Among 38 SC respondents, 55.3 per cent (21) are residing in huts, and remaining 44.7 per cent (17) are residing in semi-pucca houses. These houses are either built by themselves or provided by the government under the Indira Awas Yojana (IAY) scheme. Typically, they are found at the tail-end of the villages, perhaps due to pollution barriers in villages. These villages are named after their caste, such as *Domb Sahi* (*Domb* is the sub-caste of SC and *Sahi* means a street), *Chamar Para* (*Chamar* is the sub-caste of SC and *Para* means ward), Lahara *Para* (Blacksmith ward), and the like.

Out of 37 Bengali Scheduled Caste respondents, 89.2 per cent (33) respondents are residing in a semi-pucca house. These houses were built when the Dandkaranya Project was started in 1950s and 1960s, but even after 50-60 years majority of Bengali are residing in the same houses. They have only changed the roof tops that were made of tin. Remaining 10.8 per cent (4) respondents are residing in pucca houses. Among 8 general category respondents, 75 per cent (6) are residing in a semi-pucca houses and the remaining 25 per cent (2) are residing in pucca houses.

6.3.1. Availability of Electricity Facility

Questions were also asked of the respondents regarding availability of basic facilities like safe drinking water, toilets, electricity and the like. Table 6.9 depicts about access to electricity facilities. In the sample of 209 households, only

Table 6.9 : Availability of Electricity to the Households

Availability of Electricity	*Statistics*	*Social Groups*				
		ST	*SC*	*BSC*	*General*	*Total*
Yes	Count	3	—	34	7	44
	% within the community	2.4%		91.9%	87.5%	21.1%
	% of Total	1.4%		16.3%	3.3%	21.1 %
No	Count	123	38	3	1	165
	% within the community	97.6%	100%	8.1%	12.5%	78.9%
	% of Total	58.9%	18.2%	1.4%	0.5%	78.9%
Total	Count	126	38	37	8	209
	%within the community	100.0%	100%	100.0%	100.0%	100.0%
	% of Total	60.3%	18.2%	17.7%	3.8%	100.0%

21.1 per cent (44) have electricity connections to their homes and overwhelmingly 78.9 per cent (165) are not having electricity. Among the ST households, only 2.4 per cent (3) are connected with electricity. Among SC households, however, 100 per cent houses are without electricity. Whereas, among Bengali SC houses, 91.9 per cent (34) are connected electricity, whereas 8.1 per cent (3) households are found without electricity. Likewise, in the general category household 87.5 per cent (7) are connected with electricity and remaining 12.5 per cent (1) house has not been connected with electricity. However, the kerosene *dibris* (the glassless lamp made up of tin) is the only alternative for the households which do not have electricity connection. Besides kerosene, some household use oils extracted from forest fruit-seeds which are not edible. For example, *Jada Tel* (a type of oil) is used for two purposes, to light in the evening and groom their hair. Another type of oil used for lighting homes is *Dooma Jada Tel* (*Dooma* means Ghost, *Jada* means a forest fruit Jatropha).The Gram Vikas, a State level NGO has provided *Gobar* (cow and buffalo dung) Gas plants, to generate electricity, but due to lack of technical knowledge and interest among the tribals it has not been used.

6.3.2. Availability of Drinking Water

An attempt has also been made to know from the respondents that from where they fetch water for potable use. Table 6.10 indicates that, 60.8 per cent (127) respondents fetch water from ponds (*Bandh* and *Nahar*)[12] and handpump (*Nal-Chuan*). As the river is situated very far from the villages, only 27.3 per cent (57) of the respondents fetch potable water from the river (locally, the river is called *Nandi*) and handpump. In the summer the handpump gets dry and ST people residing in the forest areas do not have other option than depending on the nearby river which is about 8 km

Table 6.10 : Availability of Drinking Water

Availability of drinking water	*Statistics*	*Social Groups*				
		ST	*SC*	*BSC*	*General*	*Total*
Tubewell & Pond	Count	60	38	26	3	127
	% within the community	47.6%	100.0%	70.3%	37.5%	60.8%
	% of Total	28.7%	18.2%	12.4%	1.4%	60.8%
River & handpump	Count	55			2	57
	% within the community	43.7%	—	—	25.0%	27.3%
	% of Total	26.3%			1.0%	27.3%
River,well & handpump	Count	10	—	6	1	17
	% within the community	7.9%		16.2%	12.5%	8.1
	% of Total	4.8%		2.9%	0.5%	8.1
River, well, pond, & handpump	Count	1	—	5	2	8
	% within the community	0.8%		13.5%	25.0%	3.8%
	% of Total	0.5%		2.4%	1.0%	3.8%
Total	Count	126	38	37	8	209
	% within the community	100.0%	100.0%	100.0°%	100.0%	100%
	% of Total	60.3%	18.2%	17.7%	3.8%	100%

away. These respondents do not fetch water from ponds even though they are nearer, because it is unclean as people wash clothes and cattle in them. 8.1 per cent (17) collect water from river, wells and handpump and rest 3.8 per cent (8) fetch water from all means (river, pond, well, handpump). In the summer some of the ponds get dry and some are not in use for drinking purposes and again in rainy season these rivers and ponds become impure because of overflowing of hill water with mud. Under sample study some Bengali villages and tribal villages are settled near to the river bank, therefore, they avail water from all the above-mentioned sources for their daily use.

If we analyse the data as per social groups we will find that out of 126 ST respondents, 47.6 per cent (60) respondents fetch water from ponds and handpump; and 43.7 per cent (55) from river and handpump, and 7.9 per cent (10) fetch water from river, well and handpump. These people reside closer to the rivers like *Bhaskal Nandi* (over which a water reservoir has been built and is being used for irrigation purposes) *Nangi Nandi, Tel Nandi* and the confluence of these three rivers is called as *Bidri Ghat* (Bidri river bank). All Scheduled Caste respondents, fetch water from ponds or handpump. Handpumps are provided to the villages under different schemes of the Government of India. In the corner of every street, there is handpump for villagers. Those people who are residing in that street only fetch water from the handpump. For example, the tube-well is in *Domb* street, or *Chamar* street only the Dombs or the Chamar can draw water from it; the ST people do not touch the handpump. Both the communities (STs and SCs) fetch water from ponds but use different banks of the same pond. Out of 37 Bengali respondents, 70.3 per cent (26) respondents replied that they fetch water from ponds and handpump, followed by 16.2 per cent (6) fetch water from river, handpump and ponds, and remaining 13.5 per cent (5) fetch water from all means for their daily use. Among general category, out of 8 respondents, 37.5 per cent (3) replied that they fetch water from handpump and ponds, followed by 25 per cent (2) each fetch water from river, handpump, wells and ponds and remaining 12.5 per cent (1) fetch water from wells, handpump and ponds.

6.3.3. Availability of Cooking Devices for Households

Table 6.11 shows the use of cooking devices, social groups, percentage and figures of the sample households. Among the total social groups, out of 209 sample size, 96.7 per cent (202) households are using fuel wood, cow and buffalo dung and maize stick as cooking devices. Gas is not supplied to these villages and in any case few can afford it.

Surprisingly, 3.3 per cent (7) of Bengali households use gas cylinders. Almost all members of every household gather forage and fuel wood from the forest, when they have the time. Old men and women, who do not go out for work, young people and even school going children go out to collect fuel wood from the forest and store them for use during the rainy season and the winter to overcome the bitter cold. As forest are far away from the villages and in rainy season it is not possible to cross the rivers and also difficult to enter into it. Gradually as the forest is decreasing and the local people especially Bengalis, SC and some ST of the region are increasingly depending on alternative means like dry fodder and cow dung for cooking. The other reason for forest degradation is shifting cultivation by the tribals. Bio-gas plants were provided by the Gram Vikas to some of the tribal households but after using a couple of month, these people did not take interest on it and thus, it become useless. Because, tribal people lack maintenance of machinery parts.

6.3.4. Availability of Toilet Facility

Table.6.12 provides data of access to toilet facilities. Only

Table 6.11 : Availability of Cooking Devices for Households

Cooking Devices	Statistics	Social Groups				
		ST	*SC*	*BSC*	*General*	*Total*
Wood/ dung/miaze stick	Count	126	38	33	5	202
	% within the community	100.0%	100.0%	89.2%	62.5%	96.7%
	% of Total	60.3%	18.2%	15.8%	2.4%	96.7%
All (Including Gas)	Count	—	—	4	3	7
	% within the community			10.8%	37.5%	3.3%
	% of Total			1.9%	1.4%	3.3%
Total	Count	126	38	37	8	209
	% within the community	100.0%	100.0%	100.0%	100.0%	100.0%
	% of Total	60.3%	18.2%	17.7%	3.8%	100.0%

Note: All (including gas/wood/dry sticks/maize sticks/dung).

27.8 per cent (58) of the respondents have safety toilet. Among the Bengali community, including BSC households owned concrete latrines. When they resettled in this District, they were using dry toilet and as gradually their economic conditions well up and at least in terms of sanitary of own house and compound, Bengali community are more conscious than other communities in this area.

Except 1.9 per cent (4) ST households, an overwhelmingly 58.4 per cent (122) does not have any toilet facility. Lack of awareness in the sanitary levels and also affordability for toilet is very difficult to the tribal people. In my field study, I found that in one of the nearby villages, Gram Vikas an NGO had provided community safety toilets. The villagers' initial enthusiasm in using these toilets gradually waned. The villagers could not keep these toilets clean as they turned people away from using them. Again hiring a scavenger for cleaning the toilet is not possible for them. Other problem is that all scavenger are residing in the town and it is not quite possible to them to travel about 15-20 km daily for cleaning the toilet. Among SC, of the 38 households, 5.3 per cent (11) owned dry latrines. After using some time they fill up the toilet with mud and built a new one. It is seen among the Raj Gond households, who are in the social group of general caste, are not using toilet.

6.4. Household[13] Composition of Respondents

Traditionally, families live in a large single home is called "joint family" but in modern times accommodations are often in individual, homes within a shared compound is called "nuclear family". The joint family includes father and mother, sons, grandsons and great-grandsons with their spouses, as well as the daughters, granddaughters and great-granddaughters until they are married. Thus, often it comprising of several married couples and their children. In the Hindu social units, several generations of kindred

Table 6.12 : Availability of Toilet Facility

Toilet		*Social Groups*				
Facility	*Statistics*	*ST*	*SC*	*BSC*	*General*	*Total*
Yes	Count	4	11	37	6	58
	% of Total	1.9%	5.3%	17.7%	2.9%	27.8%
No	Count	122	27	—	2	151
	% of Total	58.4%	12.9%		1.0%	72.2%
Total	Count	126	38		8	209
	% of Total	60.3%	18.2%	17.7%	3.8%	100.0%

living together under the same roof or in a joining compound. The head of the joint family, called *Kutumba*, or *Mukhya* or *Karta*, is the father, supported by the mother, and in his absence, the elder son, guided by his mother and supported by his spouse. From an early age of the eldest son, he is given special training by his father to assume this future responsibility as head of the family. In the case of death of a father, the sacred law allows for the division of family wealth between sons.

Sometimes division of family wealth also takes place when sons are involved in different professions and live in different towns, and get all along under one roof, or when the family becomes unmanageably large. The main characteristics of the joint family are that its members (1) share a common residence, (2) share the food cooked in the same kitchen, (3) hold their property in common and, (4) ideally, profess the same religion, sect and *sampradaya*.

All the second generation families consisting of husband, wife and their children live under the guidance of the head of the joint family. All work together unselfishly to further the common good. Each joint family extends out from its home to include a second level of connections as an "extended family".

The study area is predominantly occupied by the tribal Hindus[14], whose family composition is either joint or nuclear. Most of the families live in the same compound; gradually joint families are becoming nuclear families because of different sort of socio-economic problems. Below Table 6.13 indicates the household composition of the respondents. Out of total 209 respondents, 70.8 per cent (148) respondents are residing in nuclear families and remaining 29.2 per cent (61) respondents are residing in joint families. If we see the data as per social category then we will find that out of 126 ST respondents, 76.2 per cent (96) respondents are staying with nuclear families, and remaining 23.8 per cent (30) are residing in joint families. Traditional tribal joint families are

Table 6.13 : Household Composition of Respondents

Household Composition	*Statistics*	*Social Groups*				*Total*
		ST	*SC*	*BSC*	*General*	
Nuclear	Count	96	27	21	4	148
	% within the community	76.2%	71.1%	56.8%	50.0%	70.8%
	% of Total	45.9%	12.9%	10.0%	1.9%	70.8%
Joint Count	30	11	16	4	61	
	% within the community	23.8%	28.9%	43.2%	50.0%	29.2%
	% of Total	14.4%	5.3%	7.7%	1.9%	29.2%
Total	Count	126	38	37	8	209
	% within the community	100.0%	100.0%	100.0%	100.0%	100.0%
	% of Total	60.3%	18.2%	17.7%	3.8%	100.0%

fragmenting because of family disputes, for example, sons tend to apply pressure on their parents to partition after they get married. Family disputes especially disputes over land contribute to the break up. Among SCs, 71.1 per cent (27) are residing in nuclear families. These respondents are residing separately, as most of them are dailywage labourers and they do not share their incomes with their other brothers. Remaining 28.9 per cent (11) are residing together in the joint family. The household compositions of the Bengali SC are mixed, meaning they stay in the same compound or built house in the same plot of the compound. The compounds are just a fenced plot. It is seen with the help of the data that 56.8 per cent (21) Bengali SC respondents are residing in nuclear families, other 43.2 per cent (16) respondents are residing in joint families. They start earning at their very early age and do not mind to stay separately. Some educated BSC maintain family discipline and stay together in joint families. Among general caste, familial bond is more important to maintain the socio-economic status of the family. Those who are not economically sound enough, they stay separately. In this study out of 8 general respondents, 50 per cent (4) respondents each are residing in a joint family and nuclear family respectively. Raj Gond a sub-caste of general caste hardly break away from their joint families.

6.4.1. Households size of the Respondents

An attempt has been made to analyse the household size of the respondents, which indirectly indicates the household size of the Umerkote Block. Table 6.14 shows that of 209 households, 36.8 per cent (77) households' size is five members consisting of husband, wife, and unmarried children and in some cases include parents of the male spouse. Other 23.4 per cent (49) having a household size of four members, 12.4 per cent (26) are with eight members, 8.1 per cent (17) are with six members household size and

Table 6.14 : Households Size of the Respondents

Household Size	*Statistics*	*Social Groups*				
		ST	*SC*	*BSC*	*General*	*Total*
3	Count	2	3	1	1	7
	% within the community	1.6%	7.9%	2.7%	12.5%	3.3%
	% of Total	1.0%	1.4%	0.5%	0.5%	3.3%
4	Count	30	11	8	2	49
	% within the community	23.8%	28.9%	16.2%	25.0%	23.4%
	% of Total	14.4%	5.3%	2.9%	1.0%	23.4%
5	Count	56	10	10	1	77
	% within the community	44.4%	26.3%	27.0%	12.5%	36.8%
	% of Total	26.8%	4.8%	4.8%	0.5%	36.8%
6	Count	10	2	5	—	17
	% within the community	7.9%	5.3%	13.5%		8.1%
	% of Total	4.8%	1.0%	2.4%		8.1%
7	Count	6	4	1	—	11
	% within the community	4.8%	10.5%	2.7%		5.3%
	% of Total	2.9%	1.9%	0.5%		5.3%
8	Count	14	6	4	2	28
	% within the community	11.1 %	15.8%	10.8%	25.0%	12.4%
	% of Total	6.7%	2.9%	1.9%	1.0%	12.4%

(Contd...)

Table 6.14 : *(Contd...)*

9	Count	6	1	4	1	12
	% within the community	4.8%	2.6%	10.8%	12.5%	5.7%
	% of Tctal	2.9%	0.5%	1.9%	0.5%	5.7%
10	Count	2	1	4	—	7
	% within the community	1.6%	2.6%x	10.8%		3.3%
	% of Total	1.0%	0.5%	1.9%		3.3%
11	Count	—	—	—	1	1
	% within the community				12.5%	0.5%
	% of Total				0.5%	0.5%
12	Count	—	—	2		2
	% within the community			5.4%		1.0%
	% of Total			1.0%		1.0%
Total	Count	126	38	37	8	209
	% within the community	100%	100%	100%	100.0%	100.0%
	% of Total	60.3%	18.2%	17.7%	3.8%	100.0%

5.7 per cent (11) are nine members household. One per cent (1) of the respondent household is having 12 members, and finally, a 0.5 per cent (one household) with 11 members. Table 6.14, signifies that among ST households, 44.4 per cent (56) households' size is 5 members. These are the respondents whose age is around 22-29 years old and having 2-3 children. Followed by 23.8 per cent (30) ST households' size are four members. Households consist with eight members are 11.1 per cent (14) and 4.8 per cent (6) household size consist with nine members. These are the households which are larger households than the SC. Among SCs, out of 38 household, 28.9 per cent (11) households size are four members, followed by 26.3 per cent (10) are five members household. These households are smallest because, unlike ST, they easily take to family planning and sterilisation.

In Table 6.14 it is seen that the household size of the BSC respondents are 27 per cent (10) household size are five numbers, followed by 16.2 per cent (6) with four members, 13.5 per cent (5) with six member and, 10.8 per cent (4) each household size consist eight and nine members respectively. These households comprised with unmarried younger brothers and sisters, and in-laws. Among general caste, the household size shows that, 25 per cent (2) each household consist with four members and eight members households, followed by 12.5 (1) household consist with three members and five members, nine members and eleven members respectively. Those households with the largest members are from the Raj Gond community. Some SCs are more individualistic because they usually go for nuclear household and they are being influenced by their employer.

6.4.2. Head of the Household of Respondents

Below Table 6.15 reveals data about the head of the household of the respondents. Out of 209 respondents, majority of 85.2 per cent (178) households headed by male spouse, 8.6 per cent (18) households are headed by husband's father. (in local term father-in-law is called as *Satra* by SC and ST). Only 4.8 per cent (10) households are headed by the female respondents themselves, and the remaining 1.4 per cent (3) households are headed by husband's brother (the local term for brother-in-law is *Soosra by* SC & ST and *Bhasoor* by Bengali communities). It is clear that these households are typically patriarchal in nature. A unique custom among the Bengalis is to partially cover their faces with their saree in the presence of their *Sasur* or *Bhasoor.* SC women don't cover their face but they have an avoidance relation with their husband's father or husband's brother.

As per social group it consists among 126 ST households, 89.7 per cent (113) households are headed by respondents' husband, followed by 4.8 per cent (6) households headed by the father-in-law, 4 per cent (5) households headed by respondent herself and remaining 1.6 per cent (2) households headed by brother-in-law. Those households of ST which are headed by respondents are tribal households and they belong to Kondha and Paraja sub-communities. Households headed by husbands of the respondent belong to Bhatra, Majhi and Gond communities. Among SC, of the 38 households, 78.9 per cent (30) households are being headed by husband, followed by 13.2 per cent (5) households headed by father-in-law and remaining 7.9 per cent (3) households headed by respondent herself. An overwhelmingly 81.1 per cent (30) BSC households are headed by husband, followed by 16.2 per cent (6) households headed by father-in-law and remaining 2.7 per cent (1) household headed by respondents herself. Among general caste, of the 8 household, 62.5 per cent (5) are headed by husband and remaining 12.5 per cent (1) each household headed by father-in-law, respondents herself and brother-in-law respectively.

Table 6.15 : Head of the Household of Respondents

Head of Household	*Statistics*	*Social Groups*				
		ST	*SC*	*BSC*	*General*	*Total*
Husband	Count	113	30	30	5	178
	% within the community	89.7%	78.9%	81.1 %	62.5%	85.2%
	% of Total	54.1%	14.4%	14.4%	2.4%	85.2%
Father-in-law	Count	6	5	6	1	18
	% within the community	4.8%	13.2%	16.2%	12.5%	8.6%
	% of Total	2.9%	2.4%	2.9%	0.5%	8.6%
Self	Count	5	3	1	1	10
	% within the community	4.0%	7.9%	2.7%	12.5%	4.8%
	of Total	2.4%	1.4%	0.5%	0.5%	4.8%
Brother-in-law	Count	2	—	—	1	3
	% within the community	1.6%			12.5%	1.4%
	% of Total	1.0%			0.5%	1.4%
Total	Count	126	38	37	8	209
	% within the community	100.0%	100.0%	100%	100.0%	100.0%
	% of Total	60.3%	18.2%	17.7%	3.8%	100.0%

6.4.3. Number of Children in each Household of Sample under Study

Table 6.16 indicates the number of children in each household. Out of 209 households, 41.6 per cent households having 3 children followed by 40.7 per cent households with 2 children, and 15.8 per cent (33) having 4 children. In the same table, it can be observed that out of 126 ST households, little less than half, 48.4 per cent (61) of the households are having 3 children and more than one-third, i.e., 34.9 per cent (44) households are having 2 children, 15.1 per cent (19) with 4 children and the remaining 1.6 per cent (2) households are having 1 child. Those respondents having 1 or 2 children are under the age group of 22-25. Among SC respondents, one household was found with as many as five children— four daughters and a son. The respondent claims that she had to give birth to four daughters expecting for a male child. Remaining households are having 2 to 3 children. The SC respondents feel that it is difficult for them to look after more children, as most of them are dailywage labourers. Of the 38 SC households, 36.8 per cent (14) households are two children, followed by 34.2 per cent (13) households are 3 children and 26.3 per cent (10) households are having 4 children. Among Bengali respondents Table 6.16 shows that out of 37 Bengali SC respondents, 59.5 per cent (22) are having 2 children and remaining 29.7 per cent (11) households having 3 children. There are 8.1 per cent (3) households with 4 children and 2.7 per cent (1) household is without kid. As it was found during the field study that the respondent was newly married. Of the 8 general caste households, 62.5 per cent (5) are having 2 children, followed by 25 per cent (2) are 3 children and remaining 12.5 per cent (1) household is having 4 children.

6.4.4. Children's Educational Status

Table 6.17 illustrates the educational status of the

Table 6.16 : Number of Children in each Household of Sample under Study

Number of Children	*Statistics*	*Social Groups*				
		ST	*SC*	*BSC*	*General*	*Total*
0	Count	—	—	1		—1
	% within the community			2.7%		0.5%
	% of Total			0.5%		0.5%
1	Count	2	—	—	—	2
	% within the community	1.6%				1.0%
	% of Total	1.0%				1.0%
2	Count	44	14	22	5	85
	% within the community	34.9%	36.8%	59.5%	62.5%	40.7%
	% of Total	21.1 %	6.7%	10.5%	2.4%	40.7%
3	Count	61	13	11	2	87
	% within the community	48.4%	34.2%	29.7%	25.0%	41.6%
	% of Total	29.2%	6.2%	5.3%	1.0%	41.6%
4	Count	19	10	3	1	33
	% within the community	15.1%	26.3%	8.1%	12.5%	15.8%
	% of Total	9.1 %	4.8%	1.4%	0.5%	15.8%
5	Count	—	1	—	—	1
	% within the community		2.6%			0.5%
	% of Total		0.5%			0.5%
Total	Count	126	38	37	8	209
	% within the community	100%	100%	100.0%	100.0%	100%
	% of Total	60.3%	18.2%	17.7%	3.8%	100%

respondent's children. Among 126 ST respondents, 17.5 per cent (22) are sending their children either to Tribal Welfare (TrW) school or village school. An overwhelmingly 82.5 per cent (104) respondents replied that their children have either dropped out at the primary level or have never attended the school. The children who dropped out are mainly from the TrW and *Jongli* (forest) schools. It was proposed to set up *Jongli* schools for tribals residing in the forest area, but not a single school could have been established in the forested villages. Instead they were established nearby the Bengali villages or in the revenue villages. Hence, the tribals instead of sending their children to the far away schools preferred to engage them in the domestic work like looking after domestic animals, or sent or collect fire wood and other products. The Kondha, Paraja, Gond, Bhatra tribals practice child marriage. The prospective groom has to go for work for a couple of years or more in his bride's father's house to gain the approval of his in-laws.

Girl children, especially, are hardly sent to the school. Those who attend school belong either to the Majhi or Gond community or are residing in the "revenue village" (A revenue village usually consists of a number of hamlets, agglomeration of habitation, occupied a definite boundary, and recognised by the district and State administration. It also represents a sociological unit) where a school is located nearby. Among SC respondents, Table 6.17 shows that 50 per cent (19) respondents send their children to school and rest 50 per cent (19) do not. Some are sending their children to the village schools being influenced by the Bengalis and some other who cannot afford expenses are sending them to TrW school to minimise their family expenditure. In TrW schools and *Jangli* Schools, scheduled tribes and scheduled castes children get free education with food and clothing. Among Bengali SC Table 6.17 shows that, out of 37 respondents, 86.5 per cent (32) respondents are sending their children to school. Unlike the tribals, the Bengali parents

Table 6.17 : Children's Educational Status

Children studying	*Statistics*	*Social Groups*				
		ST	*SC*	*BSC**	*General*	*Total*
Yes	Count	22	19	32	6	79
	% within the community	17.5%	50.0%	86.5%	75.0%	37.8%
	% of Total	10.5%	9.1 %	15.3%	2.9%	37.8%
No	Count	104	19	5	2	130
	% within the community	82.5%	50.0%	13.5%	25.0%	62.2%
	% of Total	49.8%	9.1 %	2.4%	1.0%	62.2%
Total	Count	126	38	37	8	209
	% within the community	100.0%	100.0%	100%	100.0%	100.0%
	% of Total	60.3%	18.2%	17.7%	3.8%	100.0%

* BSC = Bengali S.C.

are better educated, and economically better off and schools are available in their own villages. Only children of the economically disadvantaged Bengalis are dropout of schools. Among general category, out of 8 respondents, 75 per cent (6) are sending their children to school and the remaining 25 per cent (2) are those with girl child are not sending their daughters to the school. Altogether, the data shows that a majority, i.e., 62.2 (130) per cent of the respondents are not able to send their children to schools on account of the stated reasons.

6.4.5. Children Employed in Homework

Table 6.18 shows the children's work profile of the respondent household. As we have earlier seen that majority of respondents are not sending their children to school. The reasons specified are that either they have engaged their children in domestic work or that the children are too young to go to school. An attempt has been made to explore the status of the children not going to school. 76.1 per cent (159) respondents' children not employed in homework because they are too young and remaining 23.9 per cent (50) are employed in the domestic work. Among 126 ST respondents, 26.2 per cent (33) replied that their children aged between 8-17 years are helping them in domestic work.

Among the 38 SC respondents, 36.8 per cent (14) replied that the same aged children are helping in different ways. Among ST households, children are engaged in collecting fire wood, edible roots and fruits, catching fish, crabs, looking after own livestock, supplying cooked food to parents working in their own agriculture field. Among SC households, children are engaged with collecting fuel woods, eatable roots and fruits. As majority of SC respondents are landless daily-wage labourer (discussed in the subsequent table). Their children work in Bengali-owned agriculture fields and collect fodder to sell it in the Bengali villages.

Table 6.18 : Children Employed in Homework

Children Employed in Homework	*Statistics*	*Social Groups*				
		ST	*SC*	*BSC*	*General*	*Total*
Yes	Count	33	14	2	1	50
	% within the community	26.2%	36.8%	5.4%	12.5%	23.9%
	% of Total	15.8%	6.7%	1.0%	0.5%	23.9%
No	Count	93	24	35	7	159
	% within the community	73.8%	63.2%	94.6%	87.5%	76.1%
	% of Total	44.5%	11.5%	16.7%	3.3%	76.1%
Total	Count	126	38	37	8	209
	% within the community	100.0%	100%	100.0%	100.0%	100.0%
	% of Total	60.3%	18.2%	17.7%	3.8%	100.0%

However, only 5.4 per cent (2) respondents replied that their children have to look after their cows and bullocks.

6.5. Husband Profiles

SHGs are aimed at enhancing savings and credit-worthiness of the poor women so that they can save their surplus income and take loans subsequently to enhance their income generation capacity. All women are not active in income generating activities, but only take loans from SHG funds, and it is widely suspected that they are supporting their husbands' business ventures. Hence, the husbands' socio-economic profile becomes significant.

6.5.1. Education Level of Husbands

Table 6.19 depicts the educational level of the respondents' husbands. Out of 126 ST respondents, 87.3 per cent (110) report that their husbands have not been to school. In general they are engaged in tilling land, crop harvesting, cleaning land, adopting shifting cultivation, collecting forest produce, hunting animals (rabbits, squealer, bats, wild boars, deer, *langoors* and the like), and catching different type of birds, mice, lizards and snakes for food. The remaining 12.7 per cent (16) consist of those who studied in schools in the Bengali villages. Among SCs, it is found that of 38 respondents, 81.6 per cent (31) replied that their husbands' are illiterate, followed by 18.6 per cent (7) are found completed primary level education. Basically, SCs are landless labourers and they usually work on the land owned by the Bengalis. Agriculture is the main source of income and livelihood for majority of the Bengali of this district.

Among the Bengali SC, out of 37 respondents, 64.9 per cent (24) completed upto upper-primary level, followed by 32.4 per cent (12) who have studied upto primary level, and the remaining 2.7 per cent (1) have attended high school

Table 6.19 : Education Level of Husbands to Respondents

Education Level of Husbands	*Statistics*	*Social Groups*				
		ST	*SC*	*BSC*	*General*	*Total*
Illiterate	Count	110	31	—	2	143
	% within the community	87.3%	81.6%		25.0%	68.4%
	% of Total	52.6%	14.8%		1.0%	68.4%
Primary	Count	16	7	12	–	35
	% within the community	12.7%	18.4%	32.4%		16.7%
	% of Total	7.7%	3.3%	5.7%	–	16.7%
Upper Primary	Count	—	—	24	5	29
	% within the community			64.9%	62.5%	13.9%
	% of Total	11.5%	2.4%	11.5%	2.4%	13.9%
10th Fail	Count	—	—	1	1	2
	% within the community			2.7%	12.5%	1.0%
	% of Total			0.5%	0.5%	1.0%
Total	Count	126	38	37	8	209
	% within the community	100.0%	100.0%	100.0%	100.0%	100%
	% of Total	60.3%	18.2%	17.7%	3.8%	100%

though they could not pass. Because of the Dandakaranya Project of the Government of India, all the Bengali SC husbands are educated. Among general caste, it is seen in the above data that out of 8 respondents, 62.5 per cent (5) replied that their husbands have completed upper-primary, and 12.5 per cent (1) replied that her husband had studied up to the tenth class. These people could not continue their studies beyond because, they had to support their families, and they had to go to town for attending higher secondary schools by crossing dense forests facing dangers of attacks from bears and leopards. Of the total 209 respondents, it is found that 68.4 per cent (143) respondents' husbands are illiterate. However, 16.7 per cent (35) respondents' husbands have completed primary school and remaining 13.9 per cent (29) replied that their husbands' completed upper-primary school education.

6.5.2. Occupations of Respondents' Husbands

An attempt has been made to study the occupational background of the respondents' husbands. Table 6.20 reveals that out of 209 respondents, half (52.2 per cent) of the respondents replied that their husbands are engaged in agricultural work throughout the year. Besides growing a crop on their own land they grow vegetables on the river bank. Followed by 27.8 per cent (58) replied that they do work in their lands, the rest of the time they go for seasonal dailywage work.

In Table 6.20 data has been described according to the social groups. Among STs, out of 126 respondents, 59.5 per cent (75) replied that their husbands' occupations are farming. These STs reside in the revenue villages and they are full time farmers. Remaining 40.5 per cent (51) respondents replied that their husbands' are engaged in earning livelihood by doing whatever job they get. These ST people reside in the forest villages and soon after they

Table 6.20 : Occupations of Respondents, Husbands

Occupation of husband	*Statistics*	*Social Groups*				
		ST	*SC*	*BSC*	*General*	*Total*
Daily wage labour	Count	—	13	—	—	13
	% within the community		34.2%			6.2%
	% of Total		6.2%			6.2%
Skilled labour (Mason & Carpenter)	Count	—	17	—	—	17
	% within the community		44.7%			8.1 %
	% of Total		8.1 %			8.1%
Small Grossary shop owner	Count	—	2	—	—	2
	% within the community		5.3%			1.0%
	% of Total		1,0%			1.0%
Farmer	Count	75	4	25	5	109
	% within the community	59.5%	10.5%	67.6%	62.5%	52.2%
	% of Total	35.9%	1.9%	12.0%	2.4%	52.2%
Fishing	Count	—	—	5	—	5
	% within the community			13.5%		2.4%
	% of Total			2.4%		2.4%
Dairy farming	Count		1	3	—	4
	% within the community		2.6%	8.1%		1.9%
	% of Total		0.5%	1.4%		1.9%

(Contd...)

Table 6.20 : *(Contd...)*

Occupation of husband	*Statistics*	*Social Groups*				
		ST	*SC*	*BSC*	*General*	*Total*
Farmer and seaonal dailywage labour and fuelwood seller	Count	51	1	3	3	58
	% within the community	40.5%	2.6%	8.1 %	37.5%	27.8%
	% of Total	24.4%	0.5%	1.4%	1.4%	27.8%
Truck Driver	Count			1		1
	% within the community	—	—	2.7%	—	0.5%
	% of Total			0.5%		0.5%
Total	Count	126	38	37	8	209
	% within the community	100.0%	100%	100%	100.0%	100.0%
	% of Total	60.3%	18.2%	17.7%	3.8%	100.0%

complete sowing their own agriculture fields, they go to the Bengali villages to work as dailywage labourers. Some of them also sell fuel wood in the Bengali villages and in the nearby town. Table 6.20 shows that the SC people take up any kind of work that they can get. Out of 38 SC respondents, 34.2 per cent (13) replied that, they are landless so their husbands' are full time dailywage labourers. In the monsoon season they work for Bengali land owners and in summer they work in irrigated lands owned by upper-caste people who settled in the nearby towns but come to villages at times to supervise their own agricultural operations. They are Brahmins, Marwaris, Khandyats or Khestriyas, Kayasths , Raj-Gonds, and Telugu traders and lawyers. These dailywage labourers also work in brick kilns and some are engaged making home tiles. Among the SC community it was found that 44.7 per cent (17) of the husbands are skilled labourers (mason and carpenter). The people learnt masonry and carpentry while they worked as helpers of skilled masons and carpenters. Under the sample study of SC, 5.3 per cent (2) have owned small grocery shops. They reported that they got funds under the TRYSEM scheme in 2003 and presently they are getting their finance through the SHGs. Remaining 10.5 per cent (4) replied that their husbands are working in their own lands, and 2.6 per cent (1) each engaged with dairy farming and sells fire wood. Among Bengali SC, 67.6 per cent (25) are engaged with cultivation, 13.5 per cent (5) engaged themselves in fishing and farming, followed by 8.1 per cent (3) respondents' husband have owned dairy farm and simultaneously doing farming and in the spare time working in other agriculture fields. These people earn their livelihood from fishing in different ponds and different places. Occasionally, they go out to fish to other places. These people lease ponds from Panchayats. They may also hire fishing net for the purpose. Occasionally they buy sea-fish from suppliers in Andhra Pradesh and sell them in the nearby villages. In the monsoon season, they cultivate their land and whenever they go out for fishing, the agricultural land is taken care of by the women and children at home. Of the 8 general castes, 62.5 per cent (5) respondents' husband engaged themselves in agriculture and remaining 37.5 per cent (3) works in their own agricultural field and also they go for the dailywage work.

6.5.3. Annual Income of Husbands' of Respondents (Approximately)

Table 6.21 reveals annual income of the husbands' of respondents. Out of 209 respondents, 12.9 per cent (27) respondents replied that their husbands income is in between Rs.16,000-20,000 per annum, 37.3 per cent (78) replied that their husbands earn Rs. 21,000-25,000 per annum, 30.6 per cent (64) earn annual income of Rs. 26,000-30,000, followed by 19.1 per cent (40) respondents replied that their husbands earn Rs. 31,000-36,000 per annum approximately. Table 6.21 shows that the tribals who are earning in the range of Rs.16,000-20,000 per annum stand 4.8 per cent (6) out of the total ST respondents. They earn this amount from various sources and fall under the occupation category of farming and simultaneously selling fuel wood and daily-wage workers. Among ST respondents, 49.2 per cent (62) of ST respondent's husbands' are earning Rs. 21,000-25,000 per annum. They are small landholding farmers. Followed by 32.5 per cent (41) earn income between Rs. 26,000-30,000 per annum. They are engaged in dairy farming and cattle trading. These farmers also hold medium level lands, and remaining 13.5 per cent (17) earn Rs. 31,000-36,000 per annum by selling own products, vegetables in the summers and winters.

As most of the SC respondents' husbands are dailywage labourers, it is seen under the study that out of 38 SC respondents, 55.3 per cent (21) replied that their husbands' annual income is Rs.16,000-20,000 approximately, followed by 34.2 per cent (13) husbands annual income is Rs. 21,000-25,000. They earn from working in construction sites and

Table 6.21 : Annual Income of Husbands' of Respondents (Approximately)

Annual Income of Husbands Rs.	*Statistics*	*Social Groups*				
		ST	*SC*	*BSC*	*General*	*Total*
16,000-20,000	Count	6	21	—	—	27
	% within the community	4.8%	55.3%			12.9%
	% of Total	2.9%	10.0%			12.9%
21,000-25,000	Count	62	13	3	—	78
	% within the community	49.2%	34.2%	8.1 %		37.3%
	% of Total	29.7%	6.2%	1.4%		37.3%
26,000 30,000	Count	41	4	15	4	64
	% within the community	32.5%	10.5%	40.5%	50.0%	30.6%
	% of Total	19.6%	1.9%	7.2%	1.9%	30.6%
31,000 36,000	Count	17	—	19	4	40
	% within the community	13.5%		51.4%	50.0%	19.1%
	% of Total	8.1 %		9.1 %	1.9%	19.1%
Total	Count	126	38	37	8	209
	% within the community	100.0%	100.0%	100.0%	100.0%	100.0%
	% of Total	60.3%	18.2%	17.7%	3.8%	100.0%

carpentry, and the like. The remaining 10.5 per cent (4) respondents replied that their husbands' income is Rs. 26,000-30,000 per annum approximately. These are the people who are engaged in dairy farming, running small grocery shops and allied activities. Among BSCs, it is seen that most of the respondents' husbands are engaged with farming, fishing and dairy farming, etc. Out of 37 BSC respondents, 51.4 per cent (19) replied that their husbands' annual income is Rs. 31,000-36,000 approximately. They earn from selling vegetables, fish, dairy farming, etc. Another 40.5 per cent (15) replied that their husbands' income per annum is Rs. 26,000-30,000 approximately, and remaining 8.1 per cent (3) respondents replied that their husbands' annual income is Rs. 21,000-25,000 approximately. Among general caste, out of 8 respondents, 50 per cent (4) each replied that their husbands' annual income is Rs. 26,000-30,000 and Rs. 31,000-36,000 respectively. Table 6.21 further depicts that Bengali community are more prosperous than the other communities.

6.6. Household Assets

An attempt has been made in the study to explore the total household assets. Normally, household assets constitute landholding pattern and animal husbandry. As most of the tribal villages are very old one and their landholding size is quite-well. Among Bengali, it was in the time of resettlement each family availed 5 acres of land and with the increase of household size they have divided the land between the family members. Other assets of Bengali community are their animal husbandry. (For this study number of hens and ducks has been excluded).

6.6.1. Landholding Size

In respect to landholding and asset ownership of the respondents, Table 6.22 reveals that out of 209 households,

43.1 per cent (90) households have owned 2-3 acres of land, followed by 34.9 per cent (73) occupied more than 3 acres of land, 13.4 per cent (28) have owned less than one acre, and 8.6 per cent (18) owned 1-2 acres of land. Ownership of landholding has been categorically shown in Table 6.22. Among ST households it is seen that, of the 126 households, 55.6 per cent (70) of them owned about 2-3 acres of land, followed by 37.3 per cent (47) households owned more than 3 acres of land, and remaining 7.1 per cent (9) households have owned about 1-2 acres of land. As it is mentioned that majority of Scheduled Castes either daily-wage labourers or semi-skilled labourers, and that reveals from Table 6.22 households landholding pattern. Out of 38 SC households, 65.8 per cent (25) owned less than one acre of land, 15.8 per cent (6) owned 1-2 acres of land, 7.9 per cent (3) have owned 2-3 acres of land and remaining 10.5 per cent (4) owned more than 3 acres of land. Among Bengali SC, out of 37 households, 45.9 per cent (17) households have owned more than 3 acres of land, followed by 40.5 per cent (15) owned 2-3 acres of land, 8.1 per cent (3) owned less than one acre of land and remaining 5.4 per cent (2) households have owned 1-2 acres of land.

Fluctuation of households' landholding has seen under the sample study because, when in 1950s-60s Dandakaranya settlement project was started, at that time it was proposed 5 acres of land for each Bengali family, but gradually when households size has increased and division of family members started the landholding size also decreased. Those households holding more than 3 acres of land are small family. To get more cultivated land, these people depending on local tribals. As most of the tribals specially, forest dwellers have owned forest land on the process of shifting cultivation. After cultivating 2-3 years they give this land on contract to the Bengali farmers. Sometimes they also lease the land for money to spend in their sons' or daughters marriage, purchasing new clothes for verieties of festivals,

Table 6. 22 : Landholding Size of Households

Landholding size	*Statistics*	*Social Groups*				
		ST	*SC*	*BSC*	*General*	*Total*
<1 acre	Count		25	3		28
	% within the community	–	65.8%	8.1%	–	13.4%
	% of Total		12.0%	1.4%		13.4%
1 2 acres	Count	9	6	2	1	18
	% w thin the community	7.1 %	15.8%	5.4%	12.5%	8.6%
	% of Total	4.3%	2.9%	1.0%	0.5%	8.6%
2 3 acres	Count	70	3	15	2	90
	% within the community	55.6%	7.9%	40.5%	25.0%	43.1%
	% of Total	33.5%	1.4%	7.2%	1.0%	43.1%
3 > acres	Count	47	4	17	5	73
	% within the community	37.3%	10.5%	45.9%	62.5%	34.9%
	% of Total	22.5%	1.9%	8.1 %	2.4%	34.9%
Total	Count	126	38	37	8	209
	% within the community	100.0%	100.0%	100.0%	100.0%	100.0%
	% of Total	60.3%	18.2%	17.7%	3.8%	100.0%

to buy cows, buffaloes, bullocks, cycle or radio, and also goats or sheep to offer the village deity, which they have promised earlier for the recovery of good health of their relatives. Most of the Bengali farmers get land from these tribals and produce lots of maize (production of maize has been discussed in district profile). Those households engaged with agriculture occupation are having more than 3 acres of land also get land on contract farming from people who are having more land. Method of agriculture land contracts are two types. One method is that person who owned land gets one-third of the produce and two-third goes to the cultivator. All operating costs are born by the cultivator. In second method, owner of the land gives land and bears seeds and labour expenses, and the produce is distributed equally. Among general castes, landholding pattern shows that, out of 8 households 62.5 per cent (5) owned more than 3 acres of land, followed by 25 per cent (2) holding 2-3 acres, and remaining 12.5 per cent (1) household have owned 1-2 acres of land.

6.6.2. Livestocks

6.6.2.1. Pair of Cow and Bullock owned by Households

An attempt has been made in the study to know about households livestocks. Below Table 6.23 reveals livestocks of the households. It shows that, out of total (209) respondents, 40.7 per cent (85) households have owned pair of bullocks, followed by 39.7 per cent (83) households owned two pairs of bullocks, 19.1 per cent (40) households owned three pairs of bullocks and remaining 0.5 per cent (1) households has owned four pairs of bullocks. Social group-wise data shows that, out of 126 ST households, two pairs of cows or bullocks are owned by 49.2 per cent (62) households, followed by one pair of bullock owned by 37.3 per cent (47) and remaining 13.5 per cent (17) households have owned three pairs of bullocks and cows. Households, those who have owned two and three pairs bullocks and cows are those traditional farmers who solely depend on tilling land with the help of bullocks and cows. Those households who owned pair of bullocks do not have much agricultural land so, soon after completing tilling own land and sowing seeds, they work in other farmers' agricultural land. It was observed among scheduled castes that out of 38 households, 89.5 per cent (34) have owned pair of bullock, and remaining 10.5 per cent (4) have owned two pairs of bullocks. They borrow this pair of bullock from the village *Sahukar* or *Mahajan* on contract basis. In local dialogue it is called *Bankia*. The cost of bullock cover either by freely tilling the agriculture land of *Sahukar* or paying half of the daily earnings. For example, if a person earns Rs.40 per day by using the bullock, than he has to pay half (Rs.20) to the *Sahukar*. This is a system completely based on faith of both the party. If the person who has taken bullock on contract basis and failed to pay half of earnings then there is a chance to lose the bullock, so people always try to keep good relationship with the *Sahukars*.

Among Bengali SC, out of 37 households, 59.5 per cent (22) households have owned three pairs of bullocks and cows. The cows which are infertile also used for tilling purposes by the SCs but tribals like, Gond, Bhatra and Majhi believe it as a taboo. However, 29.7 per cent (11) households have owned two pairs of cows or bullocks. These households keep cows for milking purpose and the remaining 10.8 per cent (4) household owned one pair of bullock. Among general categories, households, 12.5 per cent (1) each keeps three and four pairs of cows or bullocks respectively. They keep cows for dairy farming and bullocks for tilling lands and remaining 75 per cent (6) households have owned two pairs of cows. These households cultivate their land by the help of tractor which they hire from the moneylenders of the town or they use buffaloes for that purpose.

Table 6.23 : Pair of Cow and Bullock owned by Households

Pair of Cow and Bullock	*Statistics*	*Social Groups*				
		ST	*SC*	*BSC*	*General*	*Total*
1	Count	47	34	4	—	85
	% within the community	37.3%	89.5%	10.8%		40.7%
	% of Total	22.5%	16.3%	1.9%		40.7%
2	Count	62	4	11	6	83
	% within the community	49.2%	10.5%	29.7%	75.0%	39.7%
	% of Total	29.7%	1.9%	5.3%	2.9%	39.7%
3	Count	17	—	22	1	40
	% within the community	13.5%		59.5%	12.5%	19.1 %
	% of Total	8.1 %		10.5%	0.5%	19.1%
4	Count	—	—	—	1	1
	% within the community				12.5%	0.5%
	% of Total				0.5%	0.5%
Total	Count	126	38	37	8	209
	% within the community	100%	100.0%	100.0%	100.0%	100.0%
	% of Total	60.3%	18.2%	17.7%	3.8%	100.0%

6.6.2.2 Pair of Buffaloes owned by Households

Table 6.24 shows buffalo owned by households. Of the 209 households of total social groups, 57.4 per cent (120) do not have any buffalo. Remaining 28.2 per cent (59) households have owned pair of buffaloes followed by 14.4 per cent (30) owned two pairs of buffaloes. These households keep buffalo for multiple purposes like tilling land, pulling cart and wood log. They do not keep buffalo for milking purpose as they feel uneasy with the smell of buffalo milk. If we see the data table social group-wise then we will find that out of 126 scheduled tribe households, 38.9 per cent (49) have owned one pair of buffalo, followed by 21.4 per cent (27) have owned two pairs of buffaloes. Whereas, 39.7 per cent (50) ST households do not owned buffalo and they are mostly belong to the hilly tribes. Among SCs, of the 38 households, 13.2 per cent (5) have owned pair of buffalo. Of the 37 Bengali SCs, 10.8 per cent (4) have owned pair of buffalo, followed by 5.4 per cent (2) owned two pairs of buffaloes but an overwhelmingly 83.8 per cent (31) households do not have buffalo. Those general caste, who do not have own buffalo are 75 per cent. They do not keep buffalo because somebody is needed to take care of buffaloes. Whereas, 12.5 per cent (1) each household has owned two pairs buffaloes. Mostly these households are Raj Gond. For them buffaloes are supporting assets for tilling land and also for pulling cart.

6.6.2.3. Goats and Sheep owned by Households

Table 6.25 reveals the households which own goats and sheep. People domesticate animals to increase their income sources and also a component of food. As observed people of this study area domesticate verieties of animals like cow, bullock, buffalo, goat, sheep, and pig and birds (hen, pigeon and duck) for multiple purposes. Of the 209 households, 29.2 per cent (61) have owned two pairs of goats and sheep,

Table 6.24 : Pair of Buffaloes owned by Households

Pair of Buffalo	*Statistics*	*Social Groups*				
		ST	*SC*	*BSC*	*General*	*Total*
0	Count	50	33	31	6	120
	% within the community	39.7%	86.8%	83.8%	75.0%	57.4%
	% of Total	23.9%	15.8%	14.8%	2.9%	57.4%
1	Count	49	5	4	1	59
	% within the community	38.9%	13.2%	10.8%	12.5%	28.2%
	% of Total	23.4%	2.4%	1.9%	0.5%	28.2%
2	Count	27	–	2	1	30
	% within the community	21.4%	–	5.4%	12.5%	14.4%
	% of Total	12.9%	–	1.0%	0.5%	14.4%
Total	Count	126	38	37	8	209
	% within the community	100.0%	100.0%	100.0%	100.0%	100.0%
	of Total	60.3%	18.2%	17.7%	3.8%	100.0%

followed by 21.1 per cent (44) owned three pairs, 12.9 per cent (27) households have owned four pairs, and remaining 8.6 per cent (18) households have owned one pair of sheep or goat. Among ST households, of the 126 households, 34.1 per cent (43) households owned two pairs of goats and sheep, followed by 23.8 per cent (30) owned three pairs, 11.9 per cent (15) households owned four pairs, remaining 11.1 per cent (14) households owned a pair of sheep or goat. This community domesticates animals for multipurpose utilization. First, tribals like, Gond, Bhatra, and Majhi do not eat meat of cow, bullock and buffalo, so goats, sheep and pigs are substitute for them. Secondly, tribal people celebrate verieties of festivals round the year and they offer animals to their worshipped deities in the festivals. However, 19 per cent (24) ST households do not own any animal.

Finally, animals are domesticated to increase the asset holdings so that at the time of need they sale them to meet their demands. For example, they are used for buying seeds and fertilizers in the time of cultivation, repayment of loans, etc. Tribals like Kondha residing in the forest villages domesticate animals for both the purposes, eating as well as commercial purposes. These tribals sale more goats and sheep for buying household gadgets like radio and bi-cycle and also for repayment of loans, which are taken from SHG funds or from moneylenders. Their meat substitutes are forest animals like, rabbit, mouse, and monkey, etc. Among 38 SC households, 10.5 per cent (4) households own two pairs of goats and sheep, followed by 7.9 per cent (3) households each has owned one and three pairs of goats and sheep respectively, and the remaining 2.6 per cent (1) household owned four pairs of goats. Generally, Scheduled Caste households are economically very poor and they don't hold much of agricultural land so for their household requirements they sell domesticated animals. It is observed that, initially they take goat or sheep from the moneylenders and *Shaukars* on sharing basis (locally, the practice is called *Aadi*, half of share). Moneylenders and *Shaukars*, invest on

Table 6.25 : Goats and Sheep owned by Households

Goats & Sheep in number	*Statistics*	*Social Groups*				
		ST	*SC*	*BSC*	*General*	*Total*
0	Count	24	27	6	2	59
	% within the community	19.0%	71.1%	16.2%	25.0%	28.2%
	% of Total	11.5%	12.9%	2.9%	1.0%	28.2%
1	Count	14	3	1	—	18
	% within the community	11.1 %	7.9%	2.7%		8.6%
	% of Total	6.7%	1.4%	0.5%		8.6%
2	Count	43	4	13	1	61
	% within the community	34.1 %	10.5%	35.1 %	12.5%	29.2%
	% of Total	20.6%	1.9%	6.2%	0.5%	29.2%
3	Count	30	3	8	3	44
	% within the community	23.8%	7.9%	21.6%	37.5%	21.1%
	% of Total	14.4%	1.4%	3.8%	1.4%	21.1%
4	Count	15	1	9	2	27
	% within the community	11.9%	2.6%	24.3%	25.0%	12.9%
	% of Total	7.2%	0.5%	4.3%	1.0%	12.9%
Total	Count	126	i 38	37	8	209
	% within the community	100.0%	100.0%	100.0%	100.0%	100.0%
	% of Total	60.3%	18.2%	17.7%	3.8%	100.0%

goats and lends to the villagers for domestication on sharing basis, so that they can use these goats for meat in their sons' or daughters' marriage. Among Bengali households, sheep are not domesticated and not used for eating purposes, as they do not like the smell of sheep. However, 71.1 per cent (27) SC do not own any goats or sheep. Of the 37 Bengali SC households, 35.1 per cent (13) owned two pairs of goat, followed by 24.3 per cent (9) households owned four pairs of goat, 21.6 per cent (8) owned three pairs and remaining 2.7 per cent (1) household has owned one pair of goat. However, 16.2 per cent (6) BSC households do not own any goats or sheep. Among 8 general caste households, 25 per cent (2) do not domesticate goats or sheep. First these households lack manpower; and secondly they are upper-caste Hindus (Bengali Kayastha), as they feel domesticating sheep or goats, or pigs may pollute their homes. But they eat goat, hen, and duck meat. Remaining 37.5 per cent (3) general households have owned 3 pairs of goat or sheep, followed by 25 per cent (2) households owned four pairs and 12.5 per cent (1) has owned a pair of goat. The tabulated data shows that, most of the social groups domesticate animals for multipurpose but majority respondents agreed that domestic animals enhance their incomes.

6.26. Annual Households' Income of Respondents (Approximately)

Here, the approximation of annual incomes of the households is estimated by including all their income sources. The following Table 6.26 reveals the annual income of the households. Of the 209 households, 38.8 per cent (81) households earn approximately Rs. 25,000-29,000 per annum, followed by 31.6 per cent (66) households earn Rs. 30,000-35,000, 17.7 per cent (37) household earn Rs. 36,000-40,000 per annum approximately, and remaining 12 per cent (25) households' income per annum is Rs.18,000-24,000 approximately.

If we see the above Table. 6.26 community-wise, we will

Table 6.26 : Annual Households' Income of Respondents (Approximately)

Annual Income of Households (Rs.)	*Statistics*	*Social Groups*				
		ST	*SC*	*BSC*	*General*	*Total*
18,000-24,000	Count	6	19	—	—	25
	% within the community	4.8%	50.0%			12.0%
	% of Total	2.9%	9.1 %	–	–	12.0%
25,000-29,000	Count	63	15	3	—	81
	% within the community	50.0%	39.5%	8.1%		38.8%
	% of Total	30.1 %	7.2%	1.4%		38.8%
30,000-35,000	Count	40	4	17	5	66
	% within the community	31.7%	10.5%	45.9%	62.5%	31.6%
	% of Total	19.1 %	1.9%	8.1 %	2.4%	31.6%
36,000-40,000	Count	17	0	17	3	37
	% within the community	13.5%	0.0%	45.9%	37.5%	17.7%
	of Total	8.1 %	0.0%	8.1 %	1.4%	17.7%
Total	Count	126	38	37	8	209
	% within the community	100.0%	100.0%	100.0%	100.0%	100.0%
	% of Total	60.3%	18.2%	17.7%	3.8%	100.0%

find that of 126 STs households, 50 per cent (63) households earn Rs. 25,000-29,000 per annum approximately, followed by 31.7 per cent (40) households earn Rs. 30,000-35,000, 13.5 per cent (17) households earn Rs. 36,000-40,000 and remaining 4.8 per cent (6) households earn Rs. 18,000-24,000. Among SCs, out of 38 households, 50 per cent (19) of the households per annum income are Rs. 18,000-24,000, followed by 39.5 per cent (15) households earn Rs. 25,000-29,000 and remaining 10.5 per cent (4) households per annum income are Rs. 30,000-35,000 approximately. Among Bengali SCs, of the 37 households, 45.9 per cent (17) households each earn the income brackets Rs. 30,000-35,000 and Rs. 36,000-40,000 per annum approximately. Remaining 8.1 per cent (3) households earn Rs. 25,000-29,000 per annum. Of the 8 general castes, 62.5 per cent (5) households per annum income are Rs. 30,000-35,000 and remaining 37.5 per cent (3) households earn Rs. 36,000-40,000 approximately.

In this chapter socio-economic conditions of the respondent have been analysed. The findings of this chapter indicate that Bengali households are prosperous than the STs and SCs. Educational level shows that most of the ST and SC women and men are illiterate than the Bengali SC. It also shows that most of the ST and SC women are agricultural labourer than Bengali women and annual income of the Bengali community are far better than the STs and SCs.

REFERENCES

1. Detail on district profile and study area (Umerkote Block) with data has analysed in Chapter Five.
2. ST and SC are the native people of the district Nabarangpur and can understand each other's language which are local dialect but ST claims they are superior by caste than the SC and matrimonial relationship cannot take place between them.
3. Rather saying Oriya SC, just the term SC has been used for the study, because, if we say Oriya SC then it will indicate to

the Oriya speaking or the mainstream Oriya. So far as Oriya SC is concerned, except some government and non-government servants and petty-businessmen who reside in the towns of this district, all are local SC. So finding out local SC's participation in SHG and economic activities and comparing their performance with the Bengali community and also with the ST, the term SC has used. In general, there is no caste discrimination among the Bengali community and Oriya of this district and claims themselves superior by caste than the ST and particularly BSC claims superior caste than the local SC. There is no caste discrimination among the BSC and Oriya speaking SC or the mainstream SC (SC, those who use surname, e.g., Sethi, Behera, Malik, etc., though they belong to Dhobi or Dabha, Muchi (cobbler), Dhibar (fishermen) community) of Odisha, can participate in each other's ritual ceremonies.

4. The code Bengali Scheduled Caste (BSC) has been used for this study, to find out the community-wise participation in the SHG and economic activities.
5. Throughout the study 'social group' and "social community" have been used interchangeably. It is also given importance to "Social Group" because Social Capital leads to Self-Help Groups.
6. Mandelbaum, D.G. (1972): *Society in India*, Vol.I. *Continuity and Change*, Vol. II. Popular Prakashan, Mumbai, Bombay, pp.14-15
7. This is the community who used to work for the King in Nabarangpur, though they are tribal but they claim themselves upper caste and also maintain highest caste status in this region.
8. Kayastha are Bengali community. Their surnames are Das, Mandal, Ray and Ghosh.
9. Huts in both the wall and roof are made of materials which have to be replaced frequently. Wall may be made of grass, thatch, leaves, reeds, bamboo, mud, polythene, unburnt bricks or wood. Roof may be made from grass or leaves.
10. Semi-pucca houses in which wall made of permanent materials such as, unburnt bricks and mud. Roof may be made of tiles and asbestos.

11. Pucca houses in which both wall and roof are made of permanent materials, like, material for wall can be burnt bricks, stone with lime or cement or cement concrete. Roof may be made of tiles, slate, shingle, corrugated or galvanised iron or zinc etc.
12. Basically, in this district, ST and SC use the term Bandh for Pond and Nahar for big pond and Naala for the canal.
13. A household is usually a group of persons who normally dwell together under the same roof and take their meals from a common kitchen unless the exigencies of work prevent any of them from doing so. There may be one member household, two-member households or multi-member households. For the study purposes each one of these types is regarded as "household" and it may become difficult to apply the definition of household strictly. Again the informer or the respondents are women. Therefore, the household or woman represents a socio-economic unit for the present study.
14. The way tribal people worshipping gods and goddesses, village deities that surely comes under the Hindu fold of worshipping gods and goddesses, only difference is of chanting *mantra* in the temple and under the tree. Tribals are known for about the mythology of gods and goddeses, for example, Ram, Siva, Ganesha, Hanuman, etc., but they only worship tribal gods and goddeses in different forms such as, stone, trees, and animals, and also spirits. Brahmins can join to the tribal's worshipping place but they cannot chant *mantra*, it is the tribal *Pujari* who performs all the rituals. For example, it is mentioned in the chapter four that there is spirit deity called Pendrani in Umerkote block and is well known among the Hindus in KBK region and it is owned by the tribal. A prime element in this discrepancy is the concept of *Varna*. It is the popular theory which is based on Hindu scripture, that society is composed of people in four ranked categories called *Varnas*, that is, Brahmins, Kshatriya, Vaisya and Sudra. In reality, all Hindus are not subsumed in these categories, and frequently there are differences of opinion in a village about who belong to which category. Though, it is insufficient as a sociological theory, this definition "tribal Hindus" is an appropriate one for the tribes as they are not coming within the four-fold theory of Hindu *Varna* script.

7

Women in Self-Help Groups and Impact on Development

"We not only want a piece of the pie, we also want to choose the flavour, and to know how to make it ourselves."

–Ela Bhatt, SEWA (1992)

This chapter highlights on formation of self-help groups, women's participation in the SHGs and performance of SHGs and in relation to development. I focused here on why the women decided to join into SHGs and who pervaded them to join SHGs in the operations of SHGs strategies they adopt, the degree of autonomy they enjoy and I also saw the kinds of problems and constraints they face in conducting their affairs. Women as a group are socially and economically disadvantaged. Most of the women in the sample, not only lacked formal education, but they also work in a sector of the economy where their demand is very less and their earnings are minimal. Most of them are engaged in various types to eke out their livelihoods. As the base of the study is about women participation in SHGs. The main question raised is that as an institution it is superior to indigenous moneylenders and whether their reliance on the indigenous moneylenders has declined because of the women SHGs.

SHGs are informal groups of people, who pool their savings and re-lend the money within the group on a rotational basis, depending upon the consumption, production or investment need of the members. SHGs have a common perception of need and improvise collective decisions and actions. Many such groups are formed around specific production activities to promote savings among members and use the pooled common resources to meet emergent credit needs of members.

7.1. Self-Help Group Formation

An attempt has been made to explore who motivated to women for SHGs. There are a number of government as well as and private agencies Non-Governmental Organisations (NGOs) that help poor women and men in forming and promoting the SHGs. In this study, women are the key interviewers.

Below Table 7.1 shows that, of the 209 respondents, 20.6 per cent (43) respondents replied that, the husband that pampered her to join a SHG, 19.1 per cent (40) replied that it was an Integrated Child Development Scheme (ICDS) official who rendered advise to them to form a SHG, followed by 17.7 per cent (37) respondents who were pervaded by a fellow member to join her SHG. However, 15.8 per cent (33) respondents told that it was Socio-Economic Development Programme (SEDP), a National level NGO working in West Bengal and Odisha, functionaries suggested them to form group, 13.4 per cent (28) respondents replied that, it was the Village Level Worker (VLW) in Block Office, a government employee who look after the village matters, 7 7 per cent (16) replied that, it was Society for Agriculture, Health and Education, Animal Husbandry and Rural Development (SAHARA), a State level NGO working in Odisha advised to join into a group, and remaining 5.7 per cent (12) replied that it was Integrated Tribal Development Agency (ITDA),

Table 7.1 : Agency or Person Motivating Respondents to Join Self-Help Group

Agency or person suggested to join in group	*Statistics*	*Social Groups*				*Total*
		ST	*SC*	*BSC*	*General*	
Block Office	Count	11	—	13	4	28
	% of Total	5.3%		6.2%	1.9%	13.4%
ICDS	Count	9	24	7	—	40
	% of Total	4.3%	11.5%	3.3%		19.1 %
SEDP	Count	32		1	—	33
	% of Total	15.3%	—	0.5%	—	15.8%
SAHARA	Count	16	—	—	—	16
	% of Total	7.7%				7.7%
ITDA	Count	12	—	—	—	12
	% of Total	5.7%				5.7%
Fellow member	Count	20	9	6	2	37
	% of Total	9.6%	4.3%	2.9%	1.0%	17.7%
Husband	Count	26	5	10	2	43
	% of Total	12.4%	2.4%	4.8%	1.0%	20.6%
Total	Count	126	38	37	8	209
	% of Total	60.3%	18.2%	17.7%	3.8%	100.0%

a government department promote tribals socially and economically official suggested them to join into the Self-Help Group.

After finding the success report from Self-Employed Women's Association (SEWA), Planning Commission, Government of India proposed that SHG could be mechanisms for poverty alleviation. It is envisaged that 50 per cent of the Groups formed in each Block should be exclusively for women who will account for at least 40 per cent of Swarozgaris. Therefore, it was found that, government organisations motivated nearly 40 per cent of the respondents. Again under Swarnajayanti Gram Swarozgar Yojana (SGSY) scheme, it was proposed that if the groups performance is good in terms of savings and credit than the group will get grant of Rs. 10,000.

7.2. Group Formation Year

After getting information and suggestions from different sources about self-help groups, like minded members from same community and having roughly the same level of income from a SHG. The SHG is formally registered, after several meetings, and members consent, they get the group register. Table 7.2 below tabulates SHGs registration year and communities, that which year the group has been formed.

Table 7.2 shows that, of the total 20 groups under sampled, 15 per cent (3) ST group were formed and registered in 1999, followed by 15 per cent (3) STs and 5 per cent (1) Bengali SC group was registered in 2000. Groups formed and register in 2001 are 25 per cent (5) STs, 5 per cent (1) SC and 5 per cent (1) general caste respectively. In year 2002, two scheduled tribes groups and two scheduled caste groups, followed by one Bengali scheduled caste group were formed and registered and one Bengali scheduled caste group was registered in 2003. It was observed from the above

Table 7.2 : Year of SHGs Formation and Community Background of Members

Group Formation Year	*Statistics*	*Social Groups*				*Total*
		ST	*SC*	*BSC*	*General*	
1999	Count	3	—	—	—	3
	% of Total	15.0%				15.0%
2000	Count	3	—	1	—	4
	% of Total	15.0%		5.0%		20.0%
2001	Count	5	1	—	1	7
	% of Total	25.0%	5.0%		5.0%	35.0%
2002	Count	2	2	1	—	5
	% of Total	10.0%	10.0%	5.0%		25.0%
2003	Count			1	—	1
	% of Total			5.0%		5.0%
Total	Count	13	3	3	1	20
	% of Total	65.0%	15.0%	15.0%	5.0%	100.0%

Source: SHGs record book of Block office and cross checked with the group register.
Note: For this study 20 SHGs consisting of 209 members have been selected from 643 groups registered till 2006 in the Block Office of Umerkote, Nabarangpur, Odisha.

table that 35 per cent (7) groups were formed and registered in 2001. That was the period when maximum number of groups were formed and registered by different government agencies and NGOs. It also shows that awareness about SHGs had by that time spread to the remote corners of rural society.

7.3. Monthly Savings of the Respondent in the Groups Fund

The savings pattern of the SHG varies widely ranging from weekly to monthly deposits. In terms of amount, generally it ranges from as low as Rs.10 a month to Rs.100 a month per member. The amount savings and frequency of savings (which coincide with the frequency of meetings) are also influenced by the ideas shared by the promoters of SHGs, level of poverty prevailing among the members, nature of surplus resources being generated from the economic activities undertaken by members. In order to authenticate the monthly savings of the member, data has been analysed in Table 7.3 from the sample under study.

Table 7.3 shows that out of 209 respondents, 38.8 per cent (81) respondents replied that they save Rs. 30 per month, followed by 30.1 per cent (63) respondents save Rs. 40 per month, 26.3 per cent (55) respondents save Rs. 20 per month and remaining 4.8 per cent (10) respondents save Rs.50 per month. Percentage within social groups can be observed from Table 7.3 that, of the 126 STs, 57.1 per cent (72) of the respondents save Rs. 30 per month followed by 27 per cent (34) respondents save Rs. 20 and remaining 15.9 per cent (20) respondents replied that they save Rs. 40 per month. Among the SC, of the 38 respondents, 55.3 per cent (21) replied that they save Rs. 20 per month, followed by 26.3 per cent (10) respondents save Rs. 40 per month and remaining 18.4 per cent (7) respondents save Rs. 30 per month. However, among Bengali Scheduled Caste, of the 37 members, 78.4 per cent (29) respondents save Rs. 40 per

Table 7.3 : Monthly Savings of the Respondents in the Groups Fund

Monthly Savings Rs.	*Statistics*	*Social Groups*				
		ST	*SC*	*BSC*	*General*	*Total*
20	Count	34	21	—	—	55
	% within the community	27.0%	55.3%			26.3%
	% of Total	16.3%	10.0%			26.3%
30	Count	72	7	—	2	81
	% within the community	57.1%	18.4%		25.0%	38.8%
	% of Total	34.4%	3.3%		1.0%	38.8%
40	Count	20	10	29	4	63
	% within the community	15.9%	26.3%	78.4%	50.0%	30.1%
	% of Total	9.6%	4.8%	13.9%	1.9%	30.1%
50	Count	—	—	8	2	10
	% within the community			21.6%	25.0%	4.8%
	% of Total			3.8%	1.0%	4.8%
Total	Count	126	38	37	8	209
	% within the community	100%	100.0%	100.0%	100.0%	100.0%
	% of Total	60.3%	18.2%	17.7%	3.8%	100.0%

month and remaining 21.6 per cent (8) respondents save Rs. 50 per month. Among the general caste, from Table 7.3 it is illustrated that, of the 8 respondents, 50 per cent (4) of them save Rs. 40 per month and remaining, 25 per cent (2) each respondent saves Rs.30 per month and Rs. 50 per month respectively. Table 7.3 shows that, monthly saving rate is highest among the member who pay monthly fees Rs. 30 and but it is less for member who saves Rs. 50. For example, members who save Rs. 30 per month are 81, the amount collected at the end of the month will be Rs. 2,430 but if we see among the member who save Rs.50 per month are 10 and their total saving is Rs. 500. It shows that less income group saves more and high income group saves less. Subsequent Table 7.4 shows that, the source from where the members get the above-mentioned amount.

7.4. Sources of Savings

A pre-condition for joining SHGs is to save small amounts on a regular basis. This regular savings habit is existential for selecting members of SHGs. Savings mobilised by the SHG from among the members is either lent among themselves or kept in the savings deposit account with the SHGs. Having recognised that the poor can save and save cumulatively; the time has possibly come to offer diverse savings products to the SHGs, and in turn to the members. At this stage it would be worth sharing a field level interaction with the SHG members that wherefrom the member gets money to save in the group fund. Table 7.4 shows the sources of savings of the sample under study.

From Table 7.4 it can be observed that, member those who join into the group saves amount from different sources, for example, some SHGs member saves money after reducing from household's expenses and also *curtailing* from the everyday household expenditures. Meaning of *curtailing* in local term STs like, Gond, Bhatra and Majhi, and including

Table 7.4 : Sources of Savings by the Respondents

Sources of Savings	*Statistics*	*Social Groups*				*Total*
		ST	*SC*	*BSC*	*General*	
Reducing from expenses	Count	53	23	1	2	79
	% within the Community	42.1 %	60.5%	2.7%	25.0%	37.8%
	% of Total	25.4%	11.0%	5%	1.0%	37.8%
From own income	Count	54	15	12	3	84
	% within the Community	42.9%	39.5%	32.4%	37.5%	40.2%
	% of Total	25.8%	7.2%	5.7%	1.4%	40.2%
From husband's income	Count	19	–	24	3	46
	% within the Community	15.1 %		64.9%	37.5%	22.0%
	% of Total	9.1 %		11.5%	1.4%	22.0%
Total	Count	126	38	37	8	209
	% within the Community	100.0%	100.0%	100.0%	100.0%	100.0%
	% of Total	60.3%	18.2%	17 7%	3.8%	100.0%

SCs called as *Khomla* and other STs like, Kondha called it *Kundi itamai Dabu (Kundi* means a oval shape basin and *Dabu* means rupee); woman curtails the amount from daily expenditures and it remains unknown to husband and she would not disclose how much amount she saved in secret place, at the time of emergency only she gets that amount. Woman do not disclose about the amount because she scared her husband may take away the amount and spend in unproductive ways, like buying home made distillery or gambling, etc., in Bengali language it is called (*Lakshmi Ghat*, it is place inside the house where she offers prayer, she keeps a Pot in which she puts the amount what she has curtailed from her daily household expenditures. Even if husband is drunkard one, he dose not touch the pot). Of the 209 sampled study, 40.2 per cent (84) respondents replied that, they save monthly fees for group fund from own income, followed by 37.8 per cent (79) respondents contribute monthly fees to the group fund from curtailing from household daily expenditures and remaining 22 per cent (46) members save from husbands' income. Table 7.4 also shows percentage within social groups and sources of savings. Of the 126 ST respondents, 42.9 per cent (54) replied that they save from their own income, followed by 42.1 per cent (53) save from curtailing from their daily expenditures and remaining 15.1 per cent (19) replied that they save from their husbands' income. Among the Scheduled Caste, of the 38 respondents, 60.5 per cent (23) replied that they pay their monthly fees to the group fund from curtailing the household daily expenditures and remaining 39.5 per cent (15) replied that, they managed their monthly fees from own income. It is interesting among Bengali Scheduled Castes that, of the 37 respondents, 64.9 per cent (24) pay monthly fees to the group fund from their husbands' income, followed by 32.4 per cent (12) save from own income and remaining 2.7 per cent (1) curtails from daily household expenditures. Among the general caste, of the 8 respondents, 37.5 per cent (3) respondents each save from their own income and from husbands' income respectively, and remaining 25 per cent (2) respondents save monthly fees for group fund after curtailing from household daily expenditures.

7.5. Purposes of Savings

Income is a key determinant of persons' and propensity to save. Poor people accept varieties of jobs which are often available intermittently. Either rich household or poverty ridden households save for many reasons. Savings are mainly used to meet contingencies requiring large scale expenditure that may crop up all of a sudden or for meeting targeted amount of investment. Poor women keep apart a fist full of rice (before putting rice in cooking pot, woman keeps apart a fist full of rice in separate pot for using in near future when there is nothing to feed children in the home) and a rupee out of rupees hundred curtailing from household expenditures for short-term use. Through all these means of savings not only give women a sense of self-esteem, giving them greater voice within their families and greater recognition and status both within and beyond their households. Purposes of savings have been described in Table 7.5.

Table 7.5 shows that those respondents who are in Scheduled Tribe categories, of the total 126 respondents, 67.5 per cent (85) respondents save to meet family necessary requirements and remaining 32.5 per cent (41) save for enhancing family income. Among Scheduled Caste, of the 38 respondents, 44.7 per cent (17) respondents save for meeting household necessary requirements, and remaining 55.3 per cent (21) respondents replied that they save for enhancing household income. However, among Bengali Scheduled Caste, of the 37 respondents, 51.4 per cent (19) respondents replied that they save for meeting household's necessary requirements, and 48.6 per cent (18) respondents

Table 7.5 : Purpose of Savings

Purpose of savings	*Statistics*	*Social Groups*				
		ST	*SC*	*BSC*	*General*	*Total*
For meeting necessary family requirements	Count	85	17	19	6	127
	% within the community	67.5%	44.7%	51.4%	75.0%	60.8%
	% of Total	40.7%	8.1%	9.1%	2.9%	60.8%
For Investing in Petty business	Court	41	21	18	2	82
	% within the community	32.5%	55.3%	48.6%	25.0%	39.2%
	% of Total	19.6%	10.0%	8.6%	1.0%	39.2%
Total	Court 126	38	37	8	209	
	% within the community	100.0%	100.0%	100.0%	100.0%	100.0%
	% of Total	60.3%	18.2%	17.7%	3.8%	100.0%

replied that, they save money for generating family income. Among the general caste, of the 8 respondents, 75 per cent (6) replied that, they save for meeting the basic requirements in near future and remaining 25 per cent (2) replied that, they save to enhance their household income.

7.6. Group's Meeting Management and Member Present in the Meetings

A norm of the SHGs is that all members should attend the meeting which is organised weekly or monthly. As per the members convenience meetings are held once in a month. It is not quite possible to attend weekly and so it was found in this study area that almost SHGs member meet once in a month. It is the responsibility of the President and the Secretary of the SHG to call monthly meeting. As many of the members are barely literate, they require an animator (a boy or girl who is literate and trained about SHG functioning and book keeping) who are appointed by NGOs to mobilise the SHG members and conduct monthly meetings. The SHG pays the animator on a monthly basis. An animator receives roughly Rs. 20 from each SHG every month. Generally, SHGs transaction books maintenance is so complicated that irrespective of literate or illiterate, all SHG seeks help from an animator. Following Table 7.6 shows that the number of members present in the monthly group meeting. The data has been tabulated after cross-checking records of 20 SHGs under sample (209 members) study.

Table 7.6 shows that, of the 209 respondents or members, 80.4 per cent (168) respondents were attended all monthly meetings, and remaining 19.6 per cent (41) respondents missed some meetings. From Table 7.6, it can be observed that, members attend monthly meeting are interchangeably as all members cannot attend the group meeting because members are busy with earning livelihoods. For example, coming late from agriculture fields, forest, absence from the

Table 7.6 : Attendance of SHG Monthly Meetings

No. of member attend monthly group meeting	*Statistics*	*Social Groups*				
		ST	*SC*	*BSC*	*General*	*Total*
Present in all meetings	Count	97	29	36	6	168
	% within the community	77.0%	76.3%	97.3%	75.0%	80.4%
	% of Total	46.4%	13.9%	17.2%	2.9%	80.4%
Missed some meetings	Count	29	9	1	2	41
	% within the community	23.0%	23.7%	2.7%	25.0%	19.6%
	% of Total	13.9%	4.3%	0.5%	1.0%	19.6%
Total	Count	126	38	37	8	209
	% within the community	100%	100.0%	100.0%	100.0%	100.0%
	% of Total	60.3%	18.2%	17.7%	3.8%	100.0%

village on a particular day for the purpose to meet and see relatives in other village or attending patient. It shows that majority of the members are interested in attending the group meeting but because of some emergencies work they do not attend the meeting. Normally, Bengali community is more aware about the happening of the society and also particularly SHG is concerned. Commercial Banks are not disbursing loan on the name of the husband or father-in-law of the BSC respondents because they are defaulter of past bank loans. As SHG is the only method through which Bengali are getting loan from the banks. So it made conscious them to attend regularly to the SHG meetings, by which they will come to know the day-to-day happening. Especially, in busy season like monsoon, when almost agricultural labourers are busy in agriculture fields, they return from agriculture fields in the evening and keep themselves engage with cooking and serving family members, therefore, the meetings of SHGs take place any Monday. Usually, on fourth Monday of the month they don't go for work as it is weekly marketing day.

7.7. Person decides Agendas for Meeting

President and Secretary are the main office bearers of the SHGs. They liaison with the bank in which the SHGs open an account. In true sense they are the real informer to the group member about lending money to own SHG member or outside the SHG. Their duty is to go to the bank, in which they have group account. Without these office bearers consent, bank transactions are not possible. Member or even non-member of the SHGs, contact either to the President or the Secretary to seek loans. It is their responsibility to organise meetings and set up the agenda. All the SHG members are not only aware about their rights that they have to take loan from the SHG fund but also they know their responsibility that they have to contribute monthly fees. Generally, office bearers are chosen from the SHG members itself. The SHG member asked any literate, or bit talkative whom the member of the concerned group's think confidence enough to talk to the bank official and also to the government official, or who is influential in terms of households' assets in comparison to rest of the SHG member to preside and hold the post of the office. Regular training on book-keeping is organised for SHG and NGO animator by Micro Finance Institutions (MFIs) by the help of NABARD, which is the nodal agency for SHG formation and loan disbursement.

7.8. Decision Taking Procedure in the SHG Meetings

The office bearers be it the President or the Secretary may initiate a programme but the approval of all the members for the programmes becomes necessary if it has to succeed. If they wish to provide loan to a non-member, then in the meeting they decide collectively on the interest to be charged like, the amount of loan to be sanctioned and the collateral, if it is to the SHG member itself then the member should see her track record, repayment record, before making a decision.

7.9. Year of Banking Linkage and Loan Facilitation

The SHGs links with commercial banks work well when mutual expectations are fulfilled. Before giving loans to SHGs, banks examine the accounts of SHGs maintain with them and when they are satisfied with the credit worthiness of the SHGs, they grant them loans. Even the amount of loan offered to an SHG is calibrated with the latter's performance in terms of the balance in its account. Table 7.7 provides an idea of the time the bank takes to provide cash credit linkages to SHGs.

The fundamental principles under the SHG and Bank linkage schemes are: savings first and then credit. SHGs savings is the main collateral for getting loan from the bank. Small amount of bank loans begins against the deposit of

Table 7.7 : Account Opening Year and the Year of Cash Credit Linkage with Commercial Banks

A/C opening year	*Years of Waiting for Bank Loan*			
	<1 year	*1 year*	*2 years*	*Total*
2000	1	–	–	1
2001	4	4	–	8
2002	1	8		9
2003			2	2
Total	**6**	**12**	**2**	**20**

SHGs after verifying SHGs own lending and repayment reports. Bank loan disbursements completely based satisfactory result of repayment rate of the SHGs. Table 7.7 shows that 8 SHGs have had to wait for one year to get bank loans because, their saving amount is not at satisfactory level of the commercial banks. For example, if it is compared with Table 6.3 of monthly savings amount of the respondents then it can be seen that 5 SHGs monthly savings is Rs. 20 and 8 SHGs monthly savings is Rs.30. Therefore, with this minimum deposits of SHGs take time to get loan from the bank. As banks disburse loan to SHGs against their deposit which dependence on the satisfactory level performance of SHGs. Interestingly, BSCs SHG members are doing better as loan allocation by banks to their husband or father-in-law has been stopped by the bank because of their past default.

7.10. Promotion of Self-Help Groups from Grade-I to Grade-II in Umerkote Block (2001-2003)

After formation of SHG, it opens an account in the bank for depositing their monthly collection, an incentive schemes has been decided on the basis of performance of the SHGs. The scheme includes promoting SHGs to higher grades so that they become eligible for larger amount of loans, if they register good performance in terms of loan recovery. The government under several of its development schemes such as the Swarnajayanti Gram Swarozgar Yojana (SGSY), Integrated Child Development Scheme (ICDS), Integrated Tribal Development Programme (ITDP) and Integrated Rural Development Programme (IRDP) support SHGs with grants if it qualifies to what is called Grade I in its performance and further if it is promoted Grade II, a subsidy is provided to the SHG in the form of a plow, spray machines, power tiller, cow and such other assets so that the members individually and the SHG collectively benefit. There are some criteria to SHGs to qualifying for Grade I to Grade II. These are as follows:

(i) regular savings of the SHG in the Bank ;
(ii) internal and bank loan repayment rate;
(iii) regularity in meetings and attendance; and
(iv) proper SHGs book-keeping (SHG Flap-book: a complete group transaction record kept in one ledger; member Passbooks: for savings, deposits and loans; financial statements: indicating the financial position of the SHG, and loan receipts voucher).

As mentioned in (Appendix 7.1.) promotional years (2001-2003) are shown in the rows and group formation years (1997-2003) and number of SHGs being formed and graded is provided in columns. In 1997, out of 12 SHGs registered, 8 SHGs were passed to Grade-I in 2002, of these 8 SHGs, 5 SHGs were promoted to Grade-II in the same year. Remaining 4 SHGs from 12 SHGs, fulfilled eligibility criteria for Grade-I in the year 2003, and out of these 4 SHGs, 3 SHGs selected for Grade-II in the same year.

In 1998, the number of SHGs that got registered was 11, of these 11 SHGs, 10 fulfilled the criteria for Grade-I, and out these 10 SHGs, 8 passed to Grade-II in 2002, and the remaining only SHG passed Grade-I and promoted to Grade-II in 2003.

In 1999, 14 SHGs were registered, of these, 6 SHGs reached to Grade-I in 2002 and of the 6 SHGs, 5 SHGs passed to Grade-II in 2002, and remaining 8 SHGs passed Grade-I in 2003. 6 SHGs became eligible for Grade-II in 2003 year.

In 2000, 77 SHGs got registered with bank. Of these SHGs, 39 fulfilled criteria to pass to Grade-I in 2001, and of these 39 SHGs, 25 were promoted to Grade-II in 2001. In 2002, 22 SHGs were selected for Grade-I, and of these SHGs, 19 SHGs were promoted to Grade-II in 2002 and remaining 16 were passed to Grade-I in 2003, of these, 14 SHGs were promoted to Grade-II in 2003.

In 2001, 114 SHGs were registered with the bank, of these SHGs, 22 passed to Grade-I in 2001, and out of 22 SHGs, 14 were promoted to Grade-II in 2001, followed by 41 SHGs from 114 SHGs passed Grade-I, and of these 41 SHGs, 25 SHGs were promoted to Grade-II in 2002. Out of 114 SHGs registered in 2001, 51 SHGs passed Grade-I in 2003 and of these 51 SHGs, 46 SHGs were promoted to Grade-II in 2003.

In 2002, 124 SHGs were registered and of these SHGs, 26 SHGs passed Grade-I in 2002, of these SHGs, 18 SHGs were promoted to Grade-II in 2002, followed by 98 SHGs which were passed to Grade-I in 2003, of these SHGs, 84 SHGs were promoted to Grade-II in 2003. The Appendix 6.1 shows that, during 2001-02 a large number of SHGs got registered and several were even promoted. Of these 401 registered SHGs, 238 were formed in 2001-02. There is a greater awareness among the people and also willingness to take risk to repay loans. In 2003, 49 SHGs were registered and of these, 31 SHGs were passed to Grade-I. Out of these 31 SHGs, 26 SHGs were promoted to Grade-II in 2003.

7.11. Promotion of Self-Help Groups from Grade-I to Grade-II (2001-2004) under Sample Study

Table 7.8 shows the promotional years of SHGs which are taken for research purpose. Of the total 20 groups which are registered since 1999-2003, 9 SHGs fulfilled criteria for

Grade-II in 2003 and remaining 11 SHGs fulfilled criteria for Grade-II in 2004. It can also be observed that in 2001, 7 SHGs were registered and out of these 7 SHGs, 3 SHGs passed to Grade-II in 2003, and remaining 4 SHGs passed to Grade-II in 2004.

It shows in both (Appendix 7.1. and Table.7.8) tables that, majority of self-help groups were registered in the year 2001-02. Gradation of SHGs begins in the last quarters of financial year as it is a government scheme through which SHG receives grants and subsidy loan as per their bank transaction.

Table 7.8 : Promotion of Self-Help Groups from Grade-I to Grade-II Sample under study (2001-04)

Registration of SHG		*Year of Grade-I Pass*	*Year of Grade-II Pass*		*Total*
Year	*No. SHG*		*2003*	*2004*	
1999		2002	1	–	1
	3	2003	–	2	2
2000	4	2002	4	–	4
2001		2001	1	–	1
	7	2002	1	–	1
		2003	1	4	5
2002	5	2003	1	4	5
2003	1	2003		1	1
Total	20		9	11	20

Source: List of SHGs in Umerkote Block (Block Office)

7.12. Total Savings of SHGs registered in the Period 1999-2004

Following Table 7.9 shows total savings of SHGs sample under study. Total savings includes own fund, bank loan and grants from governments. Grants are provided from different funds like, SGSY, ITDA, ICDS, and IRDP, etc. also provided subsidies loan under different schemes for varieties of economic activities. Table 7.9 shows that the overall performance of some SHGs the grant amount is half the savings of SHGs. This is an attraction for the SHGs formation and putting the unbankable to the bank transaction (savings and credit) and also a poverty eradication programme under the SGSY scheme of Government of India.

Table 7.9 : Total Savings of SHGs Registered in the Period 1999-07

Sl. No.	*Name of Bank*	*A/C No.*	*Own Fund (Rs.)*	*BANK Loan (Rs.)*	*ITDA Grant (Rs.)*	*SGSY Grant (Rs.)*	*Total * (Rs.)*
1	KCCB, UKT	2012	40000	25000	5000	5000	**75000**
2	KCCB, UKT	2306	57500	25000	5000	5000	**92500**
3	KCCB, UKT	1961	35000	25000	5000	5000	**70000**
4	KCCB, UKT	2590	26000	10000	5000	5000	**46000**
5	KCCB, UKT	1993	15000	25000	5000	5000	**50000**
6	KCCB, UKT	2114	30000	25000	5000	5000	**65000**
7	KCCB, UKT	2124	21000	19000	5000	5000	**50000**
8	KCCB, UKT	1676	26000	30000	5000	5000	**66000**
9	KCCB, UKT	2170	20000	25000	5000	5000	**55000**
10	SBI, UKT	37/11000	16000	48000	5000	5000	**74000**
11	KPGB, Beheda	2074	20000	45000	5000	5000	**75000**
12	KPGB, Dhodra	149	10000	25000	5000	5000	**45000**
13	KPGB, Dhodra	201	7000	15000	5000	5000	**32000**
14	KPGB, Dhodra	98	10000	25000	5000	5000	**45000**
15	KPGB, Dhodra	183	20000	10000	5000	5000	**40000**
16	KPGB, Dhodra	97	15000	10000	5000	5000	**35000**
17	KPGB, Dhodra	113	10000	15000	5000	5000	**35000**
18	KPGB, UKT	119	5000	15000	5000	5000	**30000**
19	KPGB, UKT	172	20000	25000	5000	5000	**55000**
20	KPGB, UKT	1/27	6000	10000	5000	5000	**26000**
	Total (Rs.)	–	409500	452000	100000	100000	1061500

Note: * Total includes (own fund, bank loan and grants).

Sources: State Bank of India, Umerkote, Nabarangpur.

Koraput Central-Cooperative Bank, Umerkote, Nabarangpur.

Utkal Gramya Bank (previously Koraput Panchabati Grameen Bank), Umerkote, Nabarangpur.

Utkal Gramya Bank (previously Koraput Panchabati Grameen Bank) Dhodra, Nabarangpur.

Utkal Gramya Bank (previously Koraput Panchabati Grameen Bank) Beheda, Nabarangpur.

SHGs record, Umerkote Block Office.

Above Table 7.9 also shows that there are some SHGs

have accumulated over Rs. 40,000. These are SHGs whose per month savings are Rs. 40 and Rs. 50. The SHGs which are over 5-7 years old and with the experience gained by SHG member in handling individual savings, group funds, dealing with bankers and bank officials, keeping track of loans shows that these SHGs are more successful than other. Basically, SHGs which are formed and run by BSCs are more successful than STs or SCs. There are also some SHGs whose own savings is less than Rs.10,000, as their monthly saving rate is very less i.e., Rs. 20, also their credit investments sectors are petty-business, from which they only generates hand to mouth income.

7.13. Purposes of Loaning: Required and Received from SHG Fund

The basic norm of SHG is that directly providing credit to the members from the small savings for meeting the current household's requirements, viz., school fees of children, medicinal expenses, etc. It also minimises the current credit dependency on moneylenders who charges high rate of interest. Lending from SHGs fund ensures to sustain the group and also gain access to more funds from the government and the banks. Across SHGs, it is noticed that SHG members have simultaneously taken more than one loan depending on the priority of requirements. In the following Tables (7.10 to 7.13), an attempt has been made to examine the reasons for which loans have been taken. For example, those who are having land-use the loan for cultivation purposes, those who do not have land-use the loan to improve their economic conditions. Here, total savings of group includes, own fund, bank loan and government grants because whatever loan goes to the individual member it is from group's fund only. As SHGs is concerned, bank issues loan in the name of the SHG but not to any individual member. It is the sense of duty of SHG member that whom to give loan. Loan from SHG fund are availed by the members as per their requirements and capability to repay in time. Here is the analysis of loans taken by the group member as per their requirements.

Table 7.10 illustrates the requirements of amount for agriculture purpose. Out of 209 respondents, including all social groups, 26.31 per cent (55) respondents did not require loans for agriculture purposes, as they have landholdings of less than one acre. Followed by 18 members from STs and one from SCs required Rs.1000 and they receive the same amount. Those Respondents who have required Rs.2,000 were 48 members, out of these 48 members, 12.5 per cent (6) STs and 2.1 per cent (1) member from SC received Rs.1,000 and 6.3 per cent (3) STs received Rs.1,500, 75 per cent (36) STs and 2.1 per cent (1) each from SC and Bengali Scheduled Castes received Rs. 2,000 for cultivation. Total 43 respondents required Rs. 3,000, of these 43 members, 62.8 per cent (27) ST respondents and one general member received Rs. 2,000 and 30.2 per cent (13) STs received Rs. 3,000 for cultivation. Those members who have required Rs. 4,000 were 9.56 per cent (20), of these members, 60 per cent (12) STs and 5 per cent (1) SC received Rs. 2,000 and 10 per cent (2) STs and 15 per cent (3) SCs received Rs. 3,000 and remaining 10 per cent (2) STs received Rs. 4,000.

Including all social groups, 8 members required Rs. 5,000 for agriculture purpose, only 25 per cent (2) Bengali SCs member received the same amount. Remaining 12.5 per cent (1) SC and ST each received Rs. 4,000 and 25 per cent (2) STs and 12.5 per cent (1) SC received Rs. 3,000 and 12.5 per cent (1) member received Rs. 2,000. It shows that those households are having 2-3 acres of land, required money from group fund for agriculture purposes, as this is an alternative source on less rate of interest for them not to borrow credit on high rate of interest from moneylenders. It is also seen that some members have taken large amount and some have taken very less. The reason is that members get loans on priority of

Table: 7.10 : Loan Required for Agriculture and Loan Amount Received

Loan required	Loan Received	Loan amount	Number and per cent	Social Groups				Total
				ST	SC	BSC	General	
0	Received	0	Count	2	32	16	5	55
			% of Total	3.6%	58.2%	29.1%	9.1%	100.0%
	Total		Count	2	32	16	5	55
			% of Total	3.60%	58.2%	29.1%	9.1%	100.0%
1000	Received	1000	Count	18	1	–	–	19
			% of Total	94.7%	5.3%	–	–	100.0%
	Total		Count	18	1	–	--	19
			% of Total	94.7%	5.3%	–	–	100.0%
2000	Received	1000	Count	6	1	–	–	7
			% of Total	12.5%	2.1%	–	–	14.6%
		1500	Count	3	–	–	–	3
			% of Total	6.3%	–	–	–	6.3%
		2000	Count	36	1	–	1	38
			% of Total	75%	2.1%	–	2.1%	79.2%
	Total		Count	45	2	–	1	48
			% of Total	93.8%	4.2%	–	2.1%	100.0%
3000	Received	1000	Count	1	–	–	–	1
			% of Total	2.3%	–	–	–	2.3%
		1500	Count	1	–	–	–	1
			% of Total	2.3%	–	–	–	2.3%
		2000	Count	27	–	–	1	28
			% of Total	62.8%	–	–	2.3%	65.1%
		3000	Count	13	–	–	–	13
			% of Total	30.2%	–	–	–	30.2%

(Contd...)

Table: 7.10 (*Contd.*)

Loan required	*Loan Received*	*Loan amount*	*Number and per cent*	*Social Groups*				*Total*
				ST	*SC*	*BSC*	*General*	
	Total		Count	42	–	–	1	43
			% of Total	97.7%	–	–	2.3%	100.0%
4000	Received	2000	Count	12	1	–	–	13
			% of Total	60.0%	5.0%	–	–	65.0%
		3000	Count	2	–	3	–	5
			% of Total	10%	–	15%	–	25%
		4000	Count	2	–	–	–	2
			% of Total	10.0%	–	–	–	10.0%
	Total		Count	16	1	3	–	20
			% of Total	80%	5%	15%	–	100%
5000	Received	2000	Count	–	–	1	–	1
			% of Total	–	–	12.5%	–	12.5%
		3000	Count	2	1	–	–	3
			% of Total	25.0%	12.5%	–	–	37.5%
		4000	Count	1	1	–	–	2
			% of Total	12.5%	12.5%	–	–	25.0%
		5000	Count	–	–	2	–	2
			% of Total	–	–	25.0%	–	25.0%
	Total		Count	3	2	3	–	8
			% of Total	37.5%	25.0%	37.5%	–	100.0%
6000	Received	4000	Count	–	–	2	–	2
			% of Total	–	–	50.0%	–	50.0%
		5000	Count	–	–	1	–	1
			% of Total	–	–	25%	–	25%

(*Contd...*)

Table: 7.10 (*Contd.*)

Loan required	Loan Received	Loan amount	Number and per cent	Social Groups				Total
				ST	SC	BSC	General	
		6000	Count	–	–	1	–	1
			% of Total	–	–	25%	–	25%
	Total		Count	–	–	4	–	4
			% of Total	–	–	100%	–	100%
7000	Received	3000	Count	–	–	1	–	1
			% of Total	–	–	25%	–	25%
		4000	Count	–	–	1	–	1
			% of Total	–	–	25%	–	25%
		5000	Count	–	–	2	–	2
			% of Total	–	–	50%	–	50%
	Total		Count	–	–	4	–	4
			% of Total	–	–	100%	–	100%
8000	Received	4000	Count	–	–	1	–	1
			% of Total	–	–	33.3%	–	33.3%
		5000	Count	–	–	1	–	1
			% of Total	–	–	33.3%	–	33.3%
		6000	Count	–	–	1	–	1
			% of Total	–	–	33.3%	–	33.3%
	Total		Count	–	–	3	–	3
			% of Total	–	–	100%	–	100%
9000	Received	6000	Count	–	–	1	–	1
			% of Total	–	–	50%	–	50%
		7500	Count	–	–	1	–	1
			% of Total	–	–	50%	–	50%
	Total		Count	–	–	2	–	2
			% of Total	–	–	100%	–	100%

(Contd...)

Table: 7.10 (*Contd.*)

Loan required	*Loan Received*	*Loan amount*	*Number and per cent*	*Social Groups*				*Total*
				ST	*SC*	*BSC*	*General*	
10000	Received	7000	Count	–	–	1	–	1
			% of Total	–	–	100%	–	100%
	Total		Count	–	–	1	–	1
			% of Total	–	–	100%	–	100%
12000	Received	8000	Count	–	–	–	1	1
			% of Total	–	–	–	50%	50%
		7500	Count	–	–	1	–	1
			% of Total	–	–	50%	–	50%
	Total		Count	–	–	1	1	2
			% of Total	–	–	50%	50%	100%

requirements and also willingness to take risk, i.e., to repay the loans in time.

Table 7.11 shows members loan requirements for animal husbandry. It was mentioned in chapter five that people keep livestock for different purposes. For example, it is an allied source of income for households. People used to borrow money from moneylenders at high rates of interest for buying animals for different purposes. For example, bullock and buffalo for tilling land, cow for dairy farming, and for offering animals (goats, sheep, buffalo, pig, hen, duck) to the village or forest deity before the sowing season or at the time of harvesting. In order to keep good relationships with the village *Mahajan* people pay annual visit with goats or sheep, as he is the person who is helpful when anyone needs money. For example, those who does not have bullock to plough land, they borrow pair of bullock from village *Mahajan,* and after completion of crop harvesting pay visit to the *Mahajan* with goats and bag of harvested crops during the festival called *Diali Parav* (It is a festival of STs and SCs that, celebrate harvesting, specially to offer first harvested crops to cow, bullock and buffalo). Nevertheless, self-help group is an alternative source that, from which members are availing loans at a lower rate of interest for buying animals which is not only a source of income, but also a way of maintaining traditions. The data has been described according to social groups and loan requirements and received for animal husbandry.

It was mentioned about livestock of households in chapter five, that some of the households, specially, STs and SCs keep animals on share basis. Normally Bengali community does not keep goats or sheep, as they do not allow the smell of these animals to their houses. It is seen in Table 7.11 that out of 209 members, 59.33 per cent (124) members do not require any loan for animal husbandry. Above analysis shows that, generally Bengali community asked highest amount of loan and their number is also

Table 7.11 : Loan Required and Received for Animal Husbandry

Loan required	*Loan received*	*Loan amount*	*Number & per cent*	*Social Groups*				*Total*
				ST	*SC*	*BSC*	*General*	
0	Received	0	Count	70	26	23	5	124
			% of Total	56.5%	21.0%	18.5%	4.0%	100.0%
	Total		Count	70	26	23	5	124
			% of Total	56.5%	21.0%	18.5%	4.0%	100.0%
1000	Received	1000	Count	31	3	–	1	35
			% of Total	88.6%	8.6%	–	2.9%	100.0%
	Total		Count	31	3	–	1	35
			% of Total	88.6%	8.6%	–	2.9%	100.0%
2000	Received	1000	Count	4	–	–	1	5
			% of Total	19.0%	–	–	4.8%	23.8%
		2000	Count	11	4	1	–	16
			% of Total	52.4%	19.0%	4.8%	–	76.2%
	Total		Count	15	4	1	1	21
			% of Total	71.4%	19.0%	4.8%	4.8%	100.0%
3000	Received	1000	Count	4	–	–	–	4
			% of Total	40%	–	–	–	40%
		2000	Count	3	2	–	–	5
			% of Total	30%	20%	–	–	50%
		3000	Count	–	1	–	–	1
			% of Total	–	10%	–	–	10%
	Total		Count	7	3	–	–	10
			% of Total	70%	30%	–	–	100%
4000	Received	2000	Count	3	1	1	–	5
			% of Total	50%	16.7%	16.7%	–	83.3%

(Contd...)

Table 7.11 : *(Contd..)*

Loan required	Loan received	Loan amount	Number & per cent	Social Groups				Total
				ST	SC	BSC	General	
		2500	Count	–	–	1	–	1
			% of Total	–	–	16.7%	–	16.7%
	Total		Count	3	1	2	–	6
			% of Total	50.0%	16.7%	33.3%	–	100.0%
5000	Received	2000	Count	–	–	1	–	1
			% of Total	–	–	25%	–	25%
		3000	Count	–	–	2	–	2
			% of Total	–	–	50%	–	50%
		4000	Count	–	–	1	–	1
			% of Total	–	–	25%	–	25%
	Total		Count	–	–	4	–	4
			% of Total	–	–	100%	–	100%
6000	Received	4000	Count	–	1	–	–	1
			% of Total	–	100%	–	–	100%
	Total		Count	–	1	–	–	1
			% of Total	–	100%	–	–	100%
7000	Received	4000	Count	–	–	2	–	2
			% of Total	–	–	50%	–	50%
		5000	Count	–	–	2	–	2
			% of Total	–	–	50%	–	50%
	Total		Count	–	–	4	–	4
			% of Total	–	–	100%	–	100%

(Contd...)

Table 7.11 : *(Contd..)*

Loan required	*Loan received*	*Loan amount*	*Number & per cent*	*Social Groups*				*Total*
				ST	*SC*	*BSC*	*General*	
8000	Received	8000	Count	–	–	1	–	1
			% of Total	–	–	100%	–	100%
	Total		Count	–	–	1	–	1
			% of Total	–	–	100%	–	100%
10000	Received	4000	Count	–	–	1	–	1
			% of Total	–	–	100%	–	100%
	Total		Count	–	–	1	–	1
			% of Total	–	–	100%	–	100%
12000	Received	5000	Count	–	–	1	–	1
			% of Total	–	–	50%	–	50%
		7000	Count	–	–	–	1	1
			% of Total	–	–	–	50%	50%
	Total		Count	–	–	1	1	2
			% of Total	–	–	50%	50%	100%

considerably high, whereas it is lowest among the rest of the categories of members. The reason is that, Bengali communities are more aware about taking care of milking cow than STs and SCs. The reason is that many of the Bengali men are well trained in veterinary sciences.

Table 7.11 can summarise that, low amount of loans are asked by maximum number of STs and SCs because they used the loan amount in small income generating activities such as , vegetable growing and selling, seasonal fruits, dry fish vending in the village and town in daily and weekly markets, and also for vending in the village. Basically, Bengali SCs required medium to high loan for income generating activities, such as buying equipments (fishing net, bucket, and basket) for fisheries and other allied activities. Generally, general categories people required higher amount of loan for the purpose of buying fertilizers and seeds and other needs.

Table 7.12 depicts about the respondents those who have taken loan in time of emergencies (meeting medical expenses, buying a bullock as one of the pair may lost, attending relatives' funeral, etc.). Out of 209 respondents, 53 respondents have not taken loan for emergency purposes, and remaining 156 respondents required loan range from Rs. 500 to Rs. 5,000 for emergencies. It has been seen that only 2 ST members have required Rs. 500 each and both of them received the same amount to mitigate their emergencies situations. However, there are larger number (88 respondents) of members those who required Rs. 1,000, are 78.4 per cent (69) STs, 20.5 per cent (18) SCs and one BSCs, irrespective of their categories all member received Rs. 1,000. Forty-one member each required Rs. 2,000 for emergencies, but 9.8 per cent (4) STs member received Rs. 1,000 each and 17 (41.5 per cent) STs, 34.1 per cent (14) SCs and 14.6 per cent (6) BSCs received Rs. 2,000 each to lessen their emergencies. Seventeen members required Rs. 3,000 each for emergencies purposes, out of these members, there was only

Table 7.12 : Loan Required and Received for Emergencies

Loan required	*Loan received*	*Loan amount*	*Number and per cent*	*Social Groups*				*Total*
				ST	*SC*	*BSC*	*General*	
0	Received	0	Count	25	2	20	6	53
			% of Total	47%	4%	38%	11%	100%
	Total		Count	25	2	20	6	53
			% of Total	47.2%	3.8%	37.7%	11.3%	100.0%
500	Received	500	Count	2	–	–	–	2
			% of Total	100%	–	–	–	100%
	Total		Count	2	–	–	–	2
			% of Total	100%	–	–	–	100%
1000	Received	1000	Count	69	18	1	–	88
			% of Total	78%	21%	1%	–	100%
	Total		Count	69	18	1	–	88
			% of Total	78%	21%	1%	–	100%
2000	Received	1000	Count	4	–	–	–	4
			% of Total	9.8%	–	–	–	9.8%
		2000	Count	17	14	6	–	37
			% of Total	41.5%	34.1%	14.6%	–	90.2%
	Total		Count	21	14	6	–	41
			% of Total	51.2%	34.1%	14.6%	–	100.0%
3000	Received	2000	Count	–	–	–	1	1
			% of Total	–	–	–	5.9%	5.9%
		3000	Count	9	2	4	1	16
			% of Total	52.9%	11.8%	23.5%	5.9%	94.1%
	Total		Count	9	2	4	2	17
			% of Total	52.9%	11.8%	23.5%	11.8%	100.0%

(Contd...)

Table 7.12 : *(Contd..)*

Loan required	*Loan received*	*Loan amount*	*Number and per cent*	*Social Groups*				*Total*
				ST	*SC*	*BSC*	*General*	
4000	Received	2000	Count	–	–	–	–	1
			% of Total	–	14.3%	–	–	14.3%
		2500	Count	–	–	1	–	1
			% of Total	–	–	14.3%	–	14.3%
		3000	Count	–	1	1	–	2
			% of Total	–	14.3%	14.3%	–	28.6%
		3500	Count	–	–	3	–	3
			% of Total	–	–	42.9%	–	42.9%
	Total		Count	–	2	5	–	7
			% of Total	–	28.6%	71.4%	–	100.0%
5000	Received	4000	Count	–	–	1	–	1
			% of Total	–	–	100%	–	100%
	Total		Count	–	–	1	–	1
			% of Total	–	–	100%	–	100%

5.9 per cent (1) general caste respondent received Rs. 2,000 and remaining, 52.9 per cent (9) STs,11.8 per cent (2) SCs, 23.5 per cent (4) BSCs, and 5.9 per cent (1) general caste received Rs. 3,000 to meet their emergencies. Rs. 4,000 required by 7 members from different communities. Out of 7 members, 14.3 per cent (1) SCs received Rs. 2,000 and 14.3 per cent (1) BSCs member received Rs. 2,500, and 14.3 per cent (1) member each from SCs and BSCs received Rs. 3,000 but in the highest cap 42.9 per cent (3) BSCs member received Rs. 3,500. Only one BSCs member required Rs. 5,000 and received Rs. 4,000 to meet households' emergency situations. Most of the Bengali in this region is better off than the STs and SCs.

Above data analysis reveals that, scheduled tribes and scheduled castes people required fewer amounts to meet their emergencies as compared to rest of the communities. It does not mean that these people don't require large amount for their emergencies, but the reason is that they get loan from their own fund which is very little. Moreover, their emergency requirements "amount" is also very low, such as attending funeral, medical expenses, and land disputes, etc.

7.14. Methods of Repayment of Loan

The loans were sanctioned for periods ranging between three months to eight months. Normally, repayments were fixed on monthly intervals. Those members who repay monthly intervals are specially petty-salespersons, as they use for business. Those people who take loan for cultivation purposes repay loans after harvesting.

Table 7.13 shows the methods of repayment of loans in SHG programme. Of the 209 respondents, 16.7 per cent (35) respondents, repay their loans from their own income. It is mentioned about the occupation of the respondents in chapter five. It shows that respondents earn their livelihoods from different sources, dailywage labour, petty-business

Table 7.13 : Methods of Repayment of Loan

Methods of Repayment of loan	*Statistics*	*Social Groups*				
		ST	*SC*	*BSC*	*General*	*Total*
From own income	Count	26	2	4	3	35
	% of Total	12.4%	1.0%	1.9%	1.4%	16.7%
From husbands' income	Count	100	36	33	5	174
	% of Total	47.8%	17.2%	15.8%	2.4%	83.3%
Total	Count	126	38	37	8	209
	%of Total	60.3%	18.2%	17.7%	3.8%	100%

such as vegetable vending, dry fish vending, etc. These members also take loans as per their capacity to repay the amount. An overwhelmingly 83.3 per cent (174) members repay their loans from husbands' income as these women take loan for cultivation purpose and also for allied activities. These members have taken loans for multiple uses, such as cultivation and dairy farming, and petty-business.

7.15. Penalty for Default Members

Specially, those Bengali people who used to get loan from banks discontinued because of their increase rate of past default. Disbursing personal loan has been stopped by the banks to these Bengali because most of them are still to repay their past loans. In this critical juncture, SHG become an alternative source for getting loan. Even though, SHG is an informal institution to get loan on low interest rate but there are SHGs who have made certain rules to get back the loan from their defaulters. Normally, vendors and dailywage labourers do not defaulter as their credit requirement is small against their savings and also because they do not take big risk. Strict rules are followed by Bengali SHGs, that if a member does not clear the loan with interest on stipulated time then they charge Rs.5 per cent extra on the existing loan. So, in order to avoid this risk all members repay their loan in time.

7.16. Repayment and Default

Table 7.14 depicts that of the total (209) members of the 20 SHGs under study, an overwhelmingly 94.3 per cent (197) members from all social groups repaid the amount whatever they have taken from the groups' fund and 5.7 per cent (12) members have not paid. This was the data taken from the last loan they cleared before taking the fresh loan. It is seen that most of the members are conscious about their loan and

Table 7.14 : Repayment and Default

Repayment and Default	*Statistics*	*Social Groups*				
		ST	*SC*	*BSC*	*General*	*Total*
Paid	Count	121	35	33	8	197
	% within the community	96.0%	92.1%	89.2%	100.0%	94.3%
	% of Total	57.9%	16.7%	15.8%	3.8%	94.3%
Not Yet Paid	Count	5	3	4	–	12
	% within the community	4.0%	7.9%	10.8%		5.7%
	% of Total	2.4%	1.4%	1.9%		5.7%
Total	Count	126	38	37	8	209
	% within the community	100.0%	100.0%	100.0%	100.0%	100.0%
	% of Total	60.3%	18.2%	17.7%	3.8%	100.0%

group sustainability. If we see the data social group-wise, among STs respondent, of the 126 members, repayment rate is considerably high that is 96 per cent, followed by SCs, 92.1 per cent of the total number of 38 members.

Normally, these groups' savings are very less and also their loan amount in comparison to other social group is very little. Among BSCs, of the 37 members, repayment rate is 89.2 per cent. The conservative thinking that loans taking from individual, groups, banks or moneylenders is considered to be a grave risk. If a person dies without repaying her or his debts, her sons and heirs feel it their duty to do so, otherwise soul of the dead will not rest in peace. Also, the fear of non-repayment of loan from the SHG fund may lead to alienation from the SHG. Defaulters may also be denied to financial help from fellow villagers.

7.17. Presently Households depending on Moneylenders

The traders and commission agents including village *Mahajan* are the major moneylenders in the rural economy. Traders give loan in terms of seeds, fertilizers and pesticides and commission agents (CA) provide advance money towards purchase of output from farmers and include elements of forward trading. However, village moneylenders or the *Mahajan* give loans to his clients on the basis of personal relations. These credit arrangements are all on voluntary basis as the formal banking system does not readily finance to rural people. Other needs of the rural people is for consumption purposes as well as for meeting urgent religious, social, educational and medical needs and again banks do not normally disburse loans for such purposes.

Table 7.15 shows that, even after joining into the SHG and generating some income from the tiny savings, still some people depend on the village moneylenders. People depending on moneylenders because, they are instant

Table 7.15 : Present Dependency on Moneylenders

Present dependency on Moneylenders	*Statistics*	*Social Groups*				
		ST	*SC*	*BSC*	*General*	*Total*
Sometimes	Count	49	11	24	3	87
	% within the community	38.9%	28.9%	64.9%	37.5%	41.6%
	% of Total	23.4%	5.3%	11.5%	1.4%	41.6%
No more	Count	58	17	11	5	91
	% within the community	46.0%	44.7%	29.7%	62.5%	43.5%
	% of Total	27.8%	8.1 %	5.3%	2.4%	43.5%
Never Count		19	10	2		31
	% within the community	15.1%	26.3%	5.4%	—	14.8%
	% of Total	9.1%	4.8%	1.0%		14.8%
Total	Count	126	38	37	8	209
	% within the community	100.0%	100.0%	100.0%	100.0%	100.0%
	% of Total	60.3%	18.2%	17.7%	3.8%	100.0%

sources of money in time of most emergency. Of the 209 respondents or households, there are 41.6 per cent (87) households who are still depending on moneylenders as per their requirements. Among the total respondents, 38.9 per cent (49) STs, 28.9 per cent (11) SCs, 64.9 per cent (24) Bengali SCs, and 37.5 per cent (3) general category were relying on moneylenders. It shows that, whatever, money the households are getting from the SHG fund is not sufficient to meet their needs.

There are members of SHGs who used to borrow money from the moneylenders. They have discontinued that after availing loans from SHGs fund. Data shows that, 43.5 per cent (91) of the total respondents of 209, discontinued borrowing money from moneylenders. It shows that, whatever amount they are getting from the group funds is meeting their requirements. There are 14.8 per cent (31) respondents, who never availed credit from moneylenders, because they don't have anything to mortgage for their requirements are minimal which they manage from their own income. As per the data, there are 15.1 per cent (19) STs have not borrowed money from the moneylenders as they are residing in the forest villages and their requirements is very less and also the moneylenders do not give money without guarantee. Among the SC, 26.3 per cent (10) respondents never got chance to get money as the rate of interest is high and willingness to take risk is not possible to them, as except their labour they don't have anything to mortgage. Among Bengali SCs, 5.4 per cent (2) respondents felt that their culture of self-sufficiency never allowed them to get money from *Golakatu* (throat cutter moneylenders) on high rate of interest.

7.18. Rate of Interest Charged by Moneylenders per Month

During the field study for this research it was discovered that villagers used to borrow credit from the village moneylenders at high rate of interest against mortgaging their belongings, such as utensils, land, jewellery, radio, cycle and the like. With the severe competition between moneylenders and SHGs, the dominance of the moneylenders has gradually declined and also the rate of interest in the village has declined. It was revealed that moneylenders used to charge interest depending on the degree of closeness to the clients, such as, Rs. 7-10 per cent for Rs.100 per month. But the nature of rate of interest has come down to Rs. 7 to 4 per cent for Rs. 100 per month. Table 7.16 shows the opinion of the respondents, that what rate of interest the moneylenders are charging currently.

Table 7.16 shows members' statement that, if they have to borrow credit from the village moneylenders, then what rate of interest they have to pay. It is mentioned above that client and moneylender relationship is purely personal level relations and as per that relation only rate of interest fix. Generally, in this area moneylenders are from Bengali community amongst whom anyone of household member is in government service, Generally, in this area moneylenders belongs from Bengali, Telugu, Oriya, communities, and amongst whom, anyone of household member is a government employee Marwari are the only community who engage with business and also lends money to all social groups. Normally, Marwari do not give loans to small farmers, therefore, those who have small landholding, they depend on the commission agents. Basically, CAs found from Oriya, Telugu and Bengali people who are small traders and well known to both the party, i.e., the Marwari and the clients. Of the 209 respondents, 51.7 per cent (108) replied that if they have to borrow credit then they need to pay Rs. 5 per cent for Rs.100 per month, and 27.8 per cent (58) replied that, they pay Rs. 6 per cent for Rs.100 per month. Followed by 17.2 per cent (36) replied as their relationships with the moneylenders are quite close, so they get credit on Rs. 4 per cent for Rs.100 per month and remaining 3.3 per cent (7) respondents replied that if they have to borrow credit then they need a guarantee and they pay rate of interest at Rs.7 per cent for Rs.100 per month. It is observed from the above

Table 7.16 : Rate of Interest Charged by Moneylenders Per Month

Rate of Interest Per Month	*Statistics*	*Social Groups*				
		ST	*SC*	*BSC*	*General*	*Total*
4%	Count	23	2	11	–	36
	% within the community	18.3%	5.3%	29.7%	–	17.2%
	% of Total	11.0%	1.0%	5.3%	–	17.2%
5%	Count	63	18	19	8	108
	% within the community	50.0%	47.4%	51.4%a	100.0%	51.7%
	% of Total	30.1 %	8.6%	9.1 %	3.8%	51.7%
6%	Count	37	16	5	–	58
	% within the community	29.4%	42.1%	13.5%	–	27.8%
	% of Total	17.7%	7.7%	2.4%	–	27.8%
7%	Count	3	2	2	–	7
	% within the community	2.4%	5.3%	5.4%	–	3.3%
	% of Total	1.4%	1.0%	1.0%	–	3.3%
Total	Count	126	38	37	8	209
	% within the community	100.0%	100.0%	100.0%	100.0%	100.0%
	% of Total	60.3%	18.2%	17.7%	3.8%	100.0%

analysis that still there are people who are depending on moneylenders to solve their current financial problems.

7.19. Impact of SHG at Individual Level

The SHG programme has been successful as important agents of poverty alleviation by a member of different measures. The most common measure of a SHG's performance is member's loan repayment rate, since this has a large bearing on whether mechanisms like small savings sustainable. One basic fact of the SHGs formation is to secure livelihoods and also help each other SHG members in the time of need. There is a clear community bias in forming SHGs. The most outstanding factor of SHGs is that it is a way through where women can save which can be used in time of emergencies. Data analysis clearly indicates that, fairly higher percentages (94.3 per cent) of SHG members were repaid their loans. A remarkable feature of the SHGs is that, the total savings and their sincere repayment methods which help members to get loans on rotation basis. Equilibrium savings and interest rate with rotational credits among members convey stability of SHG and sense of common purposes and consensus proved SHG is one of the alternative mechanisms for poverty alleviation.

7.20. SHGs under Study and Women Empowerment

Following section deals with the field data with analysis of sustainability of SHG and Empowerment. The analyses are based on the opinion of the respondents and also their performance in individual level. Lack of substantial methods to measure empowerment of women, here, data has analysed on the basis of their responses on the questions asked in the process of field survey. Self-Help Group movement has been encouraged by the Odisha government and has emerged as a powerful tool for socio-economic empowerment of people living below poverty line and for removal of poverty.

7.20.1. Awareness about the Government Schemes Proposed for Poverty Alleviation

The participants for this study were women. So an attempt has been made whether she is aware about the government schemes which are proposed for poverty alleviation being a member of the self-help group. SHG is places where member not only saves money and takes credit but also discuss different day-to-day activities.

Table 7.17 shows that, of the 209 respondents, 81.3 per cent (170) member replied that, they were aware about the poverty alleviation schemes, and remaining 18.7 per cent (39) replied that they did not know about the proposals. It shows that, even if these people are attached with the group, they were not aware about the programme and project plan by government to remove rural poverty.

7.20.2. Availed Benefits from the Proposed Schemes

Table 7.18 indicates that, of the 209 respondents, 61.7 per cent (129) respondents were agreed that, they knew about the schemes and they availed it. There were some respondents who availed house facility under rural housing programme of Indira Awaas Yojana. Almost all households have ration card under below poverty line schemes but 38.3 per cent (80) replied that they were not getting their share every month.

The discontinuity of ration distribution was major problem for those families which were residing in the forest areas. Lack of communication facilities and information problem, these people were not getting their shares. Of the total 209 respondents, 23.4 per cent (49) ST respondents replied that they know about the scheme, but they did not get right information so they missed their shares, followed by 7.7 per cent (16) SCs, 5.3 per cent (11) Bengali SCs, and 1.9 per cent (4) general castes are not availing the proposed schemes.

Table 7.17 : Awareness about the Government Schemes Proposed for Poverty Alleviation

	Statistics	Social Groups				
		ST	*SC*	*BSC*	*General*	*Total*
Awareness by Govt. schemes proposed for PA — Yes	Count	98	32	33	7	170
	% of Total	46.9%	15.3%	15.8%	3.3%	81.3%
No	Count	28	6	4	1	39
	% of Total	13.4%	2.9%	1.9%	0.5%	18.7%
Total	Count	126	38	37	8	209
	% of Total	60.3%	18.2%	17.7%	3.8%	100.0%

Table 7.18 : Availed Benefits from the Proposed Schemes

		Statistics	*Social Groups*				*Total*
			ST	*SC*	*BSC*	*General*	
Availed benefits from the schemes	Yes	Count	77	22	26	4	129
		% of Total	36.8%	10.5%	12.4%	1.9%	61.7%
	No	Count	49	16	11	4	80
		% of Total	23.4%	7.7%	5.3%	1.9%	38.3%
Total		Count	126	38	37	8	209
		% of Total	60.3%	18.2%	17.7%	3.8%	100.0%

The SHG federation is a democratic body formed with a certain number of SHGs functioning in a specific geographical area with the objective of uniting such SHGs for common cause and for achieving these causes which an individual SHG would not be able to do. A federation is an association of primary organisations. Primary organisations may join together to realise economies of scale or to gain strength as an interest group. A cluster level federation is a network of several SHGs and a structure or body evolved by SHGs themselves consisting of representatives from all members of SHGs, with the motive of supporting member of SHGs to attain the goals of economic and social empowerment of women members and their capacity-building. In other words, it is another forum for SHGs to step up development of women members taking advantage of collective effort of member SHGs enabling holistic and need-based economic and social development. Non government organisations took the leadership role in promoting them on a pilot basis. Considerable donor funds were invested in evolving the SHG federation model by leading NGOs. The concept of federation emerged from the felt need of the SHGs that have been functioning well and were keen to come together for sharing and learning.

7.20.3. Creation of Self-Help Group Federation

Considering the above federation formation method, an attempt has been made to know from the respondents that which institutions can help the member to form federation.

Table 7.19 shows that, of the 209 respondents, 55 per cent (115) of the members replied that, by only government intervention federation can be created. When cross question was put, why not other institutions, the answer was that, they don't rely on the NGO functionaries, and also the bank official as they charge cost for promotion of federation. Bank official also look down upon to *Adivasi* (tribal) as they feel

Table 7.19 : Creation of Self-Help Group Federation

	Statistics		*Social Groups*				
		ST	*SC*	*BSC*	*General*	*Total*	
Creation of SHG forum (federation)	By group interction	Count % of Total	10 4.8%	5 2.4%	4 1.9%	—	19 9.1%
	By Govt. intervention	Count % of Total	68 32.5%	25 12.0%	20 9.6%	2 1.0%	115 55.0%
	By bank staff inter vention	Count % of Total	1 0.5%	—	—	—	1 0.5%
	By NGO functionary intervention	Count % of Total	29 13.9%	—	—	1 0.5%	30 14.4%
	by group and NGO meetings	Count % of Total	1 0.5%	—	—	—	1 0.5%
	by all	Count % of Total	17 8.1%	8 3.8%	13 6.2%	5 2.4%	43 20.6%
	Total	Count % of Total	126 60.3%	38 18.2%	37 17.7%	8 3.8%	209 100.0%

that tribals are not creditworthy. Mostly 32.5 per cent (68) tribal women agreed that the federation can be created by government functionaries.

As SHG is part of self-management and sustainability of groups, clusters and federations promoted by the community banking programme share the costs of management out of their own savings and credit operations. By providing regular access to savings, credit and insurance services, the programme is able to rescue many poor people from the clutches of moneylenders and arrest the income drain. In addition, the programme helps members to enhance their income and create assets. Many older groups and federations go beyond providing savings, credit and insurance services and meet the other social and developmental needs of members.

7.20.4. Interaction with other SHGs

The whole approach of the SHG formation is to help each other at the time of requirements and promote socio-economic development in individual level and also in group level. Social interaction takes place in the group level (Table 7.20). An attempt has been made in this study that whether women member interact with other groups regarding SHGs activities.

As there are some nodal SHG who takes all work initiative to help the fellow member to generate income. For example, government has handed over distribution of monthly ration to SHG but all groups were not so active that they can avail the right. Main concerns here is that, do the women groups get help from the other groups? Table 7.20 shows that, of the 209 respondents, 69.9 per cent (146) members replied that, they sometimes interact with other group members, followed by 30.1 per cent (63) replied that they interact during their meeting at Bank, Block office and training centres.

Table 7.20 : Interaction with other Groups

Statistics			*Social Groups*				
			ST	*SC*	*BSC*	*General*	*Total*
Interaction with other groups	Yes	Count	36	11	11	5	63
		% of Total	17.2%	5.3%	5.3%	2.4%	30.1%
	Sometimes	Count	90	27	26	3	146
		% of Total	43.1 %	12.9%	12.4%	1.4%	69.9%
Total		Count	126	38	37	8	209
		% of Total	60.3%	18.2%	17.7%	3.8%	100.0%

7.20.5. Effectiveness of Self-Help Groups on Village and Community Affairs

Self-help group is not only mechanism to fulfil individual interest but also a group solidarity tool, which engage in village and community affairs. As village consists with different communities and present day women groups are taking initiative to village matters. For example, group member look after the Anganwadi centres, contributing financial help to the old people, and providing ration facilities to helpless old women. Under the sample study, it was found that one Bengali group which is distributing Public Distribution Systems (PDS) in the village is helping four old people who don't have anybody to look after them.

It was tried to find out whether the groups were contributing their time and money to village affairs, like, development work (cleaning village well, repairing village temple, road, forest, and generating community fund). Table 7.21 indicates that, of the 209 respondents, 32.1 per cent (65) respondents replied that their groups engaged with village affairs but 68.9 per cent (144) respondents replied that their groups did not contribute money from group fund in any affairs.

As SHG is strategy, a process by which rural poor, vulnerable and disadvantage people not only get economic benefits but also fulfil their psychological factors. SHG is a movement through which disadvantaged women get place to uplift themselves from the clutches of poverty and also from the exploitation of moneylenders. During the field study an attempt has been made that whether those women who are engaged with SHG got freedom to choose the job they want to do. Does these women availed economic freedom within the households?

Table 7.21 : Effectiveness of Self-Help Groups on Village and Community Affairs

Statistics			*Social Groups*				
			ST	*SC*	*BSC*	*General*	*Total*
Effect of SHG on village and community affairs	Yes it is	Count	51	1	10	3	65
		% of Total	24.4%	0.5%	4.8%	1.4%	31.1%
	Not so far	Count	5	37	27	5	144
		% of Total	35.9%	17.7%	12.9%	2.4%	68.9%
Total		Count	126	38	37	8	209
		% of Total	60.3%	18.2%	17.7%	3.8%	100.0%

7.20.6. Freedom on Economic and Choice of Job

Table 7.22 reveals that 93.8 per cent (196) respondents replied that they had got freedom to pursue any job that they want to. They don't face any hindrance from their family member. There are 5.7 per cent (12) member replied that they have not got that freedom. They have their own work at home and again their husbands did not want to engage their wives to work outside. An important facet of the SHG movement is to empower women in all aspects of life.

There are still traditional families who don't allow their women go to the bank or Block office. Women suffer from low status in majority of society but among STs its minimal. ST women of the this area, their hard working level only measure their status and as far as ST women is concerned they don't have any obstacle, even if she belongs to large landholding family, she goes to the forest to collect fruits and root on her leisure time.

7.21. Impact of SHGs in Livelihood Promotion Activities

SHG programme is an additional initiative for livelihoods promotion and supportive opportunities for the poor people and also an alternative mechanism to help each other. Under the study an attempt has been made to explore that whether this SHG method is helping the household to increase their livelihood. Table.7.23 shows that, of the 209 respondents, 78.5 per cent (164) replied that somehow it is helping them to get some extra income, followed by 16.7 per cent (35) respondents agreed that it had helped them enough, that they are able to buy cow and bullock and at least they are not going to moneylenders for loan.

Those respondents who gave negative response were 4.8 per cent (10) and most of them are from the scheduled tribes who are residing in the forest villages. Those STs who agreed that SHG has helped in livelihood promotion activities

Table 7.22 : Freedom on Economic and Choice of Job

Statistics			Social Groups				
			ST	*SC*	*BSC*	*General*	*Total*
Economic independence and choice of job	Yes	Count	122	36	31	7	196
		% of Total	58.4%	17.2%	14.8%	3.3%	93.8%
	No	Count	4	1	6	1	12
		% of Total	1.9%	0.5%	2.9%	0.5%	5.7%
	Don't know	Count	—	1	—	—	1
		% of Total		0.5%			0.5%
Total		Count	126	38	37	8	209
		% of Total	60.3%	18.2%	17.7%	3.8%	100.0%

Table 7.23 : Impact of SHGs in Livelihood Promotion Activities

		Statistics	*Social Groups*				
			ST	*SC*	*BSC*	*General*	*Total*
Impact of SHGs in livelihood promotion activities	Somewhat	Count	98	32	28	6	164
		% of Total	46.9%	15.3%	13.4%	2.9%	78.5%
	Very much	Count	19	6	9	1	35
		% of Total	9.1 %	2.9%	4.3%	0.5%	16.7%
	Not at all	Count	9	—	—	1	10
		% of Total	4.3%			0.5%	4.8%
Total		Count	126	38	37	8	209%
		% of Total	60.3%	18.2%	17.7%	3.8%	100.0%

owned two village pond and they earned extra income from the fishery. Among SCs, 2.9 per cent (6) replied that they joined in the SHG programme help them to earn their livelihoods and also they are sending their children to school.

7.22. Decision on Family Expenditures

After exploring households' assets, respondents' income, respondent's husbands' income and total households annual income, here an attempt has been made to find out who has larger say in major expenditures decision making. Of the 209 households, Table 7.24 shows that an overwhelmingly 76.6 per cent (160) respondents replied that, before going to spend households income for any major thing both husband and wife together take decision. For example, buying animals, seeds, fertilizer, clothes to celebrate festivals, lending money to any relatives or fellow villagers, or saving in SHG fund, buying books for school going children, radio and bicycle or ornaments and the like. Followed by 19.1 per cent (40) respondents replied that they consult all adult members including male, female. Remaining 3.3 per cent (7) respondents replied that, it is their husbands who decide major expenditure of the households.

Table 7.24 shows the data for social groups also, of 126 STs, majority 88.1 per cent (111) of households' expenditure is decided by both wife and husband. However, 9.5 per cent (12) respondents replied that they consult all adult members while spending their household income. Other 2.4 per cent (3) respondents replied that it is the husband who decides about the expenditure. Among 38 Scheduled SCs respondents, 68.4 per cent (26) replied that it is the couple that takes the decision, followed by 21.1 per cent (8) decides jointly by all family members and 5.3 per cent (2) respondents replied that their husbands have full sway over household incomes. It was found among the SCs under study that 5.3 per cent (2) replied that the respondent herself decides major

Table 7.24 : Decision on Family Expenditures

Decision on Household Expenditures	*Statistics*	*Social Groups*				
		ST	*SC*	*BSC*	*General*	*Total*
Husband	Count	3	2	1	1	7
	% within the community	2.4%	5.3%	2.7%	12.5%	3.3%
	% of Total	1.4%	1.0%	0.5%	0.5%	3.3%
Self	Count	—	2	—	—	2
	% within the community		5.3%			1.0%
	% of Total		1.0%			1.0%
Jointly family member	Count	12	8	18	2	40
	% within the community	9.5%	21.1%	48.6%	25.0%	19.1%
	% of Total	5.7%	3.8%	8.6%	1.0%	19.1%
Husband and respondent	Count	111	26	18	5	160
	% within the community	88.1 %	68.4%	48.6%	62.5%	76.6%
	% of Total	53.1 %	12.4%	8.6%	2.4%	76.6%
Total	Count	126	38	37	8	209
	% within the community	100%	100.0%	100.0%	100.0%	100.0%
	% of Total	60.3%	18.2%	17.7%	3.8%	100.0%

expenditure of the households, as her husband is very old and also she earns more than her husband. Among Bengali SCs, all adult members' consents must be required for major household expenditure. Of the 37 Bengali SCs, 48.6 per cent (18) respondents replied they decide family expenditure jointly and couple together respectively and remaining 2.7 per cent (1) replied that it is her husband who decides major family expenditure. Among general caste, except one respondent, all agreed that whatever has to be spent for family causes, they need all the members' concurrence so that conflicts could be avoided.

This chapter examines respondents interest in SHG programme, formation year and maintenance of SHG functions, methods of savings and lending, main aim of savings, total savings of the SHGs, household dependency on moneylenders, the tool-SHG impact on households and individual level, women as an agent of poverty reduction and her freedom in the household and society, her awareness about the government schemes, her choice of job, etc. It is found that low amount of loans are asked by maximum number of STs and SCs because they used the loan amount in income small generating activities such as, vegetable growing and selling, seasonal fruits, dry fish vending in the village and town in daily and weekly markets, and also for vending in the village. Basically, Bengali SCs required medium to high loan for income generating activities, such as buying equipments (fishing net, bucket, and basket) for fisheries and other allied activities. Generally, general categories people required higher amount of loan for the purpose of buying fertilisers and seeds and other needs. It shows that, STs and SCs people required minimum amount to meet their emergencies as compared to rest of the communities. Moreover, their emergency requirements "amount" is also very low, such as attending funeral, medical expenses. While empowerment may be the answer to some problems, it can solve all problems and will itself create new ones.

In the case of SHG and its functioning, only two women hold the total power of the group. For example, one is the group head or leader (president) and other one is secretary. On be half of group, the bank account will be opened jointly on the name of the president and secretary. These two are the office bearer and rest of the group members are just members. These two are responsible for the whole transaction of the bank. So, rest of the members are far away from the empowerment process. In this case, the members are only passive elements. Women may be energized by their group activities. However, activities must be scheduled at the convenience of the women, and additional burdens should be minimised as much as possible. If conscientization and empowerment are not part of the group process, there may in fact be little or no long-term gain to compensate for the time loss from women's participation in community activities.

Annexure 7.1

Upgradation of Self-Help Groups in Umerkote Block (2001-2003)

SHG Registration (Grading Year)		2001				2002				2003			
		Grade-I		Grade-II		Grade-I		Grade-II		Grade-I		Grade-II	
Year	No	No.	% Upgradation	No	%. Upgradation	No.	% Upgradation	No.	% Upgradation	No.	% Upgradation	No.	% Upgradation
1997	12	–	–	–	–	8	67	5	63	4	33	3	75
1998	11	–	–	–	–	10	91	8	80	1	100	1	100
1999	14	–	–	–	–	6	43	5	83	8	57	6	75
2000	77	39	50.6	25	64.1	22	29	19	86	16	21	14	88
2001	114	22	19.3	14	63.6	41	36	25	61	51	45	46	90
2002	124	–	–	–	–	26	21	18	69	98	79	84	86
2003	49	–	–	–	–	–	–	–	–	31	63	26	84
Total	**401**	**61**	**15.2**	**39**	**63.9**	**113**	**28.2**	**80**	**70.8**	**209**	**52.1**	**180**	**86.1**

Source: SHGs Record Register, Block Office Umerkote, Nabarangpur District, Odisha.

8

Conclusion

"Massive poverty and obscene inequality are such terrible scourges of our time — times in which the world boasts breathtaking advances in science, technology, industry, and wealth accumulation — that they have to rank alongside slavery and apartheid as social evils."

—Nelson Mandela, Former President (Republic of South Africa)

The concept of micro credit and its organised delivery on a large scale to economically backward clients through groups on collateral free small amount of loan was popularised by the Grameen Bank that was launched by Muhammad Yunus during the mid 1970s when he launched the Grameen Bank programme in his native Bangladesh. The SHG phenomenon is the outcome of pragmatic search for solutions to poverty within the framework of capitalism. It shows that the poor can tap their 'social capital' to overcome oppression and poverty and that the poor are not just helpless victims of the system. In a way the thesis defends and even strengthens capitalism but it can also be seen as a way by which the poor can collectively bring about a revolution and put an end to their own exploitation.

India is still predominantly a rural society and as per

the 2001 Census, 72.22 per cent of its population live in rural areas. This work is mainly concerned about the people who have been excluded from formal financial benefits, social, economic and political life and whose experiences, contributions, concerns and dreams are rarely considered in planning for the future. Poverty is especially severe in rural areas, where social services and infrastructure are limited or non-existent. A great majority of those live in rural areas are poor and depend on agriculture for their livelihood. They are either peasants cultivating tiny plots of land or landless labourers. The incidence of poverty in Odisha is outrageous, i.e., 43 per cent of the total population. The outrage is not just that deprivation, suffering and death is unavoidable; it is also that a situation coexists with affluence.

The horror of poverty is so deep rooted in India that, even after the Tenth Five Year Plan, 26 per cent of the people are still living below the poverty line. The fundamental and long-recognized development challenge for India is to achieve sustained economic growth with equity. The poor must participate in development and benefit from the growth process if poverty is to be eliminated.

The SHG movement and continuity of savings and credit in Umerkote Block of Nabarangpur is examined in detail with the theoretical tool of "Social Capital Theory". Apart from this theory, other theories are also discussed in this research to look into the rural development and women's empowerment. These are as follows:

Development is a process by which the members of a society increase their personal and institutional capacities to mobilise and manage resources to produce sustainable and justly distributed improvements in their quality of life consistent with their own aspirations.

Marxists argue that economic development was stimulated as major feudal landholders transformed themselves into capitalist entrepreneurs. Simultaneously the feudal oppression was lifted from the shoulders of the peasants, who would in due course form a working class, which could be recruited for a socialist revolution. The best known new-Marxist development theories are the dependency theories and the world systems theories.

Modernisation was the dominant sociological theory of development from much of the 1950s to 1960s. Its principal claim was that development was a process in which "societies" defined as nation-states. The claims of modernisation theory can be traced back to both eighteenth century Enlightenment and the classical sociology of the nineteenth and early twentieth centuries. The developing countries of the world are termed "traditional" and their counterpart at higher stage of economic and technical developed countries known as "modern". The phenomenal growth of knowledge, sciences and technology created modern state. Rostow (1960) put forward a five-stage theory of development, in which nation-states rigidly pass through a similar development sequence. The five stages he proposed are; traditional society preconditions for take-off; the take-off, the drive to maturity and the age of high mass consumption. The preconditions for take-off and the take-off stages were considered to be the two most important, with the former removing obstacles to growth through the development of entrepreneurial ambition and reinvestment, and the latter consolidating these key features of development process.

The *Development of Underdevelopment* (1967) thesis went further and argued that the reason why some countries developed was precisely because they had exploited the underdeveloped countries. Frank's theory has been criticised. In fact the critics have shown that some third world countries 'developed' when they opened their economies to capital development.

Dependency theory resemblances Franks but it stresses on the fact that the third world lacks capital for which it is dependent on the 'core'. Hence, to break this 'dependence' the third world has to promote autonomous development by investing within.

Gandhian idea of development is based on the foundational ethics of *ahimsa* (non-violence). In Gandhian era, the concept of development was not so highlighted, there for he used the term progress rather than development, more with respect of ethics and cosmic integrity. According to Gandhi, "by economic progress we mean material advancement without limit, and by real progress we mean moral progress, which again is the same thing as progress of the permanent elements in us". As such he never made an academic contribution to "development". However, he pleaded for an organised effort to change the ruling paradigm and move towards a superhuman stage. According to him, "the cosmic-moral organisation, faith is the path of spirituality and spirituality in its true sense is the motive force behind development" (*The Collected Works of M.K. Gandhi*, Vol. 87:2470). Gandhian development of society is with the human only that every human being has a right to live and, therefore, to find the wherewithal to feed himself and where necessary to clothe and house himself.

Essentially, *structural adjustment* is the process by which the International Monetary Fund (IMF) and the World Bank base their lending to underdeveloped economies on certain conditions, pre-determined by these institutions. The pre-conditions concern the drafting and implementation of economic policies that are acceptable to the institutions themselves. The prevalence of Structural Adjustment Policies (SAPs) as a curative measure for the macro-economic imbalances with third world economies mark the triumph of mono-economies over structuralism.

Marxists criticises that Structural Adjustment Policies are the major cause of poverty for developing countries. Many third world nations are in debt and poverty partly due to the policies of International Institutions such as the International Monetary Fund (IMF) and World Bank. By the influence of this programme, the developing countries, increased their dependency on the developed countries. SAPs have been imposed to ensure debt repayment and economic restructuring. But the way it happened has made poor countries to reduce spending on things like health, education and development while debt repayment and other economic policies have been made the priority. In effect, the IMF and WB have demanded that poor nations, lower the standard of living of their people.

The *welfare approach* is the oldest and still the most popular social development policy for the developing world in general and poor and vulnerable in particular. It was introduced in the 1950s and 1960s. Its aim was to bring women into development as better mothers. According to Hardiman and Midgley (1982), MacPherson and Midgley (1987) and Moser (1993) that women are seen as passive beneficiaries of development. The reproductive role women is recognised and policies seek to meet practical gender needs through that role by top-down handouts of food aid, measures against malnutrition and family planning. The welfare approach is based on three assumptions. First, women are passive recipients of development, rather than participants in the development processes. Secondly, that motherhood is the most important role for women in society; and thirdly, that child-rearing is the most effective role for women in all aspects of economic development.

The *equity approach* recognises that in general, "poor are active participants in the development process and women in particular are more active partners". "Equity" is the original Women in Development approach introduced in the 1976-85 UN Women's Decade. The purpose of the equity approach is to gain equity for women in the development processes. This approach focuses on women's poverty and the failure of modernisation to redistribute income. It is also known as the "basic needs" approach, and views underdevelopment as the central problem. Efforts are concentrated on enabling women to become income generators, generally through small-scale enterprises. However, (Boserup, *et al.*, 1970; Tinker 1976; Moser 1993) these efforts do not take account of women's special needs, and still see women's participation as less important than men's.

In the arena of Women in Development, *efficiency approach* is third predominant approach. Its main purpose is to ensure that development is more efficient and effective through women's economic contribution. By post-1980s onward, this approach has become popular. Although the so-called development industry realised that women were essential to the success of the total development effort it did not necessarily follow that development improved conditions for women.

In many respects *empowerment approach* has arisen from dissatisfaction with the original Women in Development as equity approach, because of its perceived co-option into the anti-poverty and efficiency approaches. However, the empowerment approach differs from the equity approach. This relates not only its origins but also in the causes, dynamics and structures of women's oppression which it identifies and in terms of the strategies it proposes to change the position of third world women. Origins of the empowerment approach are derived less from the research of First World women and more from the emergent feminist writings and grassroots organisational experience of Third World women. The empowerment approach acknowledges inequalities between men and women and the origins of women's subordination in the family. It also emphasises the fact that women experience oppression differently according to their race, class, colonial history and current position in the international economic order. This approach recognises the triple role of women and seeks through bottom-up women's organisations to raise women's consciousness to challenge their subordination.

The Women in Development (WID) is originated with the

publication of Esther Boserup's *Women's Role in Economic Development* (1970). This is an early analysis by a western feminist of the sexual division of labour in the Third World and it is relating to the negative impact of development strategies on women. She argued that women in agriculture societies earned status as food producers. The modernization process, supervised by colonial authorities filled with Western nations of the sexual division of labour, placed new technologies under the control of men, thereby marginalizing women, reducing their status and undercutting their power and income. Modernisation was not automatically progressive.

Alternative development has been concerned with introducing alternative practices and redefining the goals of development. This has been successful in the sense that key elements of both have been adopted in mainstream development. Even if not consistently practised it is now generally accepted that development efforts are more successful if the community participates. NGOs now play key roles on the ground and in development cooperation. This success reflects not simply the strength of NGOs and grassroots politics but also the 1980s rollback of the state, the advance of market forces and the breakdown of regulation. All the same, the goals of development have been generally redefined. It is now widely accepted that development is not simply a matter of GDP growth and human development is a more appropriate measure of development. This also means that alternative development has become less distinct from conventional development discourse and practice since alternatives have been absorbed in mainstream development. However, alternative development has failed to develop a clear perspective on micro-macro relations, an alternative macro approach, and a coherent theoretical position, although, it is often claimed that there is an alternative development paradigm.

The idea of *social capital* is both appealing and promising.

Precisely, because it offers a potential strategy for obviating these concerns while bridging theoretical and disciplinary parts. Therefore, an attempt has been made to put a logical structure for integrating social capital into development theory and policy by observing and explaining the empirical studies conducted at the micro and macro level. Under the empirical study facts and figures has been collected and explored the conditions on which social capital is a method for poverty alleviation through self-help group model.

In general, social capital theory can be a model for social situations and a model for self-help groups and microfinance. Social situations cover a range of group interactions in different settings. We assume that people have certain goals and that they attempt to realise those goals through their actions. The focus of the study is on how individual's attempts to achieve their goals by one another's actions and that by the help of microfinance institutions. Therefore, in this study special attention has been given to the social capital theory. Society is not only a system of moral norms and defined statuses which embody those norms; it is also a system in action. As individuals and groups meet, as they strive, as they attempt to solve problems, their statuses and even their moral norms are to some extent changed. The social capital of a society includes the institutions, the relationships, the attitudes and values that govern interactions among people and contribute to economic and social development.

Microcredit literature review on social capital examines the empirical evidence on the relationship between social capital and the performance of credit delivery programmes in the developing world. Moreover, microcredit through SHG is a strategic alternative tool for poverty alleviation. The concept of SHG is catching up as the most viable means in recent years to empower economically backwards, poorest of the poor, especially women at the periphery. Women have shown extraordinary dynamism in organizing themselves in group activities for income generation, better bargaining power and improvement in the quality of life. Membership in a group provides women a legitimate forum beyond the private domestic sphere and inputs to which they previously lacked access. It permits a gradual building of women's capacity to interact effectively and redistribute economic opportunity. It is against this backdrop that the SHGs have merged as an alternate structure to cater to the needs of the women.

Economists, anthropologists and sociologists in particular are using the concepts of development as well as social capital to explain the comprehensive improvement of empowerment of vulnerable section of society, especially women. However, taking into consideration the unequal development of the modern world, they have employed several other concepts directly related to development.

As mentioned there were several policies implemented since First Five Year Plan (1951-56) to reduce poverty from the country. These policies got momentum in the Five Year Plans with varieties of schemes and programmes to reduce poverty. The origin of SHGs has existed in rural society of India much prior to the period when rural planners formulated this concept. In India, the concept of SHGs can be traced back to the Gandhian Gram Swaraj movement. It is mainly concerned with the poor and it is of the people and for the people. The genesis of these could be traced to nutritional aid in Indian village community. In traditional rural societies, self-help takes various forms. So, self-help in essence is a form of cooperation. Mahatma Gandhi, highlighted the same concept and stressed the self-help aspect in this Sevagram project during 1921.

The formal sector is widely diverse. At one end of the spectrum is the highly personalised system of financial flows among relatives and friends, situated within a scheme of reciprocity in which loan transactions do not carry interest charges. These loans largely address day-to-day cash flow problems to meet the consumption and production needs of the household. Then there are cooperatives, credit unions rotating savings and credit associations, and other self-help organization that are owned and operated by their members. These alliances typically make use of pooled funds to make loan and sometimes provide other financial services to member provided by input suppliers and output buyers to their client-producers.

Self-help group is a small economically homogeneous affinity group of rural poor, which voluntarily agrees to contribute to a common fund to be lent to its members as per group decision, which common fund to be lent to its members as per group decision, which works for group solidarity, self and group awareness, social and economic empowerment in the way of democratic functioning. Since 1970s, SHGs in India reach almost nook and corner and connected million of households. It is true that some SHGs and the SHG programmes do not perform well as well as some microfinance institutions. If the purpose is to determine whether the Indian SHG model is a sustainable one, it is more relevant to look at the programmes that are performing well than those that are not. One can expect that over time, the weak SHG programmes will stagnate or close and most outreach will be dominated by well-managed programmes. This is what has happened among conventional microfinance institutions over the past three decades. Self help groups are quoted as an alternative to institutional credit to the poor, the main objectives of self help group is to promote savings among poor and provide small and short term loans to its members at low rates of interest to meet their urgent and small business needs.

It was found that the money contributed by the members of self help groups were pooled together and used as a revolving fund, and regular loans were given to its members on a priority basis decided by the members themselves. Now the SHGs members get loans at low rates of interest and they are free from the clutches of the money lenders. At least four general elements (i) the group product, including the efficiency of the group's productivity; (2) the group, including collective interaction and cohesiveness; and (3) the contributions of individual participants.

It is clear that SHGs can be financially sustainable, and most were profitable. Although costs of promotion and support have been subsidised, SHGs compare favourably with many other microfinance approaches[1] in terms of the subsidy required per client and financial sustainability. The study analysis indicates that most of the SHGs would be financially sustainable even if they had to pay the cost of external promotion and support. Primary purpose for formation of self help groups was to undertake social and other developmental activities. Thrift, credit and income generating activities were taken up later. Access to timely and adequate credit, transparency with simple procedures, elimination of middlemen and group empowerment has been the other motivating factors for group formation.

Generally, regularity of savings is witnessed among the good groups, with the exception of areas where lack of livelihood opportunities force the poor to migrate to other areas. SHG is a method of ensuring financial discipline, which results in improved repayment rates. It expands resources available to the poorest, so that they have more options for their work and life. Tiny savings in the SHG fund is an asset that raises capacity to borrow as well as achieve the status as a breadwinner within the community. Savings are an autonomous means of economic growth for the women. It enables a woman to control the growth of her business and supplement it with loans. Savings are a fallback, a form of social security in times of crises. Whenever cash is urgently needed in time of sickness or death she had her savings to fall back on.

With increasing number of SHGs and their membership,

NGOs termed as an associative economy. It differs from cooperatives in the sense that the latter operate, *de facto* as public sector enterprises with little autonomy and member participation, while the former emerge out of people's own initiatives and are run wholly by them. A self-help lead to self-reliance of SHGs. Self-reliance is a state whereby a group having achieved such a state no longer depends on the benevolence or assistance of third parties to secure its interests. Thus a self-reliant group is one that has developed sufficient productive and organizational capacity to design and implement a strategy, which effectively contributes to the betterment of its independent status. However, it does not mean autarky. In the present society, interaction with other groups and institutions is unavoidable. It implies a style of interaction based on equality. Thus self help held promotion is a deliberate effort to facilitate the emergence and foster the functioning of SHGs so as they become self-reliant institutions of poor people.

For economically backward people, SHG is the collateral substitution for replacing the conventional collateral and security forms that are traditional and tangible with non-conventional formats. In order to formulate policies, take decision or make laws, a small group of beneficiaries become more appropriate. As an effective mechanism for mobilization of rural women and also for building up organizations, the most accepted concept is the self help group concept. Through the process of unionisation and provision of credit, saving and employment services could strengthen women and prepare them to fight together the bureaucratic constraint. Political pressures enforce management action and empower themselves through awareness, leading to a better quality of life of the people.

The SHGs jointly addressed a number of community welfare issues like approaching the concerned authorities for schools and electrification of the village and solving their drinking water problem and conducting camps for animal health activities. SHG being comprised of group of persons, gets empowered to solve most of their problems of non financial nature like raw material, input supply, marketing, better adoption of technology, education and training for realizing the human potential for development.

Empowerment also enables women's groups to shape themselves as social activities by trying to check malpractice and discrimination in the implementation of different scheme in the system. Training of rural women is important so as to increase their involvement in development process chance their skill and make them equal partners in national development. The major objectives of training of rural women should be to equip them with better skills and enhance their knowledge so as to prepare them to face new challenges due to technological developments. The discourse of SHGs is catching up as the most viable means in recent years to empower women, especially at the grass root level. Women have shown extraordinary dynamism in organising themselves in group activities for income generation, better bargaining power and improvement in the quality of life. Membership in a group provides women a legitimate forum beyond the private domestic sphere and inputs to which they previously lacked access. It permits a gradual building of women's capacity to interact effectively and redistribute economic opportunity. The SHGs have now merged as an alternate structure to cater to the needs of the women. The equality of women with men remains myth till women becomes economically self-reliance. Women need to be viewed as productive members of the society, sharing equal authorities and responsibilities.

SHG bank linkage programme, connected on common fund through regular savings, supplemented by outside borrowings, loans for traditional and non-traditional production and consumption activities, terms of credit decided by consensus in group meetings. Collateral consists of mutual confidence and trust, simple documentation, peer pressure and group dynamic to ensure repayments. Rural poor women have succeeded in evolving an innovative alternative banking practice, i.e., first saving then credit by the assistance of microfinance institutions. The age old phenomena that poor are not creditworthiness has been challenged in 1970s when informal financial institutions like Grameen Bank in Bangladesh and SEWA in India took part to accommodate poor rural women in income generating activities. Resources mobilisation by SHG through shares, savings and deposits of various forms has attracted commercial banks to provide loan to the poor people. HSBC (Stan Chart), ICICI Bank, HDFC Bank, IDBI Bank, any many more commercial banks, currently it is operating with the poor in the remote corners of India[2].

The strategy of SHGs was introduced in 1974 by SEWA a pilot study at a formal level initiated in 1992 by NABARD got recognition in 1999 with launching of SGSY by Government of India in all developmental programmes. The SGSY was intended to be an improvement on earlier efforts of poverty alleviation to escape the pitfalls encountered under the IRDP. Thus the SGSY was conceived as a holistic programme of microenterprise development, covering all aspects of self-employment, by means of organising the poor into SHGs, providing for their capacity building, planning of cluster activities, infrastructure build up, technology, credit and marketing. The Planning Commission of India, realising the usefulness of SHGs for poverty alleviation and potentiality of poor people's creditworthiness and its popularity, introduced in every development programmes. It is observed incidence of poverty in Odisha 70.07 per cent (1977-78), 65.29 per cent (1983-84), 55.58 per cent (1987-88), 48.56 per cent (1993-94), 47.15 per cent (1999-2000) and 39.9 per cent in 2004-05 that the percentage of population of BPL in rural Odisha is decreasing over the years, reduction in urban poverty is still slower. The slow rate of reduction of poverty in Odisha is attributed to several inherent problems which have been explored.

8.1. Major Findings

The results of present study partly match with the previous findings of Samanta *et al.* (2007), Das (2005), NABARD (2006), Singh (2008), Mahajan (2008), Kashyap (2008), Karmakar and Mohapatra (2008), Kabir (1999), Hulme and Mosley (1996), Khandaker (1998), Park and Ren (2001), Nelson and Wright (1995), Moser (1993), Friedmann (1992) Mayoux (2001) that participation of women in SHGs has made a significant impact on their empowerment both in social and economic aspect. The women members were able to increase their income levels and contribute to the development of the family. Particularly in this study it was found that in the process, many women members expressed that they were participating in the financial decision of the family, which they were not allowed during the pre-bank linkage period. It was observed that regularity in attending meetings and the savings habit was a disciplinary measure in SHGs. Though SHGs is one of the mechanisms for poverty alleviation but caste, class, and economic status is the measuring stick for the inclusion of members in the SHGs. This study differs from the above studies as not a single study has given comparative social economic status of the members. This study has taken place in a multi social community level where the poverty level has seen located with the individual respondents and a comparison has been brought up.

Nabarangpur district is best to a wide range of castes, sub-castes especially the SCs often remain marginalised and subordinate to the upper castes and also to STs and BSCs as well as different socio-religious denominations. In respect of type of participants in the SHGs women members were taken for study from three communities, such as STs (60.3 per cent), SCs (18.2 per cent), Bengali SCs (17.7 per cent) and general category includes both Raj Gond and Bengali (3.8 per cent). Data shows that the highest share among households in the Block consists of STs. It was observed that majority of the SHG members were STs (60.3 per cent) and most of them belongsed to Bhatra sub-tribes (20.1 per cent). It can be said sub-caste or sub-tribes as Majhi are sub-caste within the STs and they wear thread but not the Bhatra. Again within STs there is caste status, Kandha are the lowest sub-tribes, they are not being allowed to Bhatra, Majhi and Gond kitchen nor they are allowed to touch dead body. Therefore, as purity and pollution is concerned there is stratum within the STs. Among SCs, Bengali SCs of Namasudra sub-caste were the second highest (17.7 per cent) and Domb were the third (17.2 per cent). It was found that majority (64.1 per cent) of them were residing in a nuclear households in semi-pucca houses of which most of them were owned by Bengali SCs, lower rate of sanitary facilities, with lower level of electricity connectivity, medium level of household dependency ratio. It was also found that most of the households were headed by husband. It was observed that most of respondents were middle aged group with medium (34 per cent) level of literacy. Broadly, social status of a household remains associated with the resources at its disposal and the caste that it belongs to. Distribution of government schemes and other resources generally remains in favour of the upper and middle castes, especially to Oriya and Bengalis, while the overall situation of the ST and SC groups remains poor. Many among the BSCs however enjoy better economic status compared to the STs and SCs. Such social environment helps sustain relations of production that get articulated through patronage and exploitation. It was found that one-third of SHG were formed by Block Office with the help of its officials and one-fifth was formed by two NGOs, viz., SEDP and SAHARA and also motivated by husband. More than one-third of SHGs were formed in 2001 and one-fourth in 2002.

The amount of savings is also influenced by the ideas shared by the promoters of SHGs, level of poverty prevailing among the members, nature of surplus resources being generated from the economic activities undertaken by members. It was found that as lower daily incomes do not help to save more so the saving rate was lower among the STs and SCs. It was observed that, members attend monthly meeting interchangeably as all members cannot attend the group meeting because members are busy with earning a livelihood. For example, coming late from agriculture field, from forest, absence from the village on that particular day due to visiting relatives in other village or attending patient. It shows that majority of the member are interested in attending the group meeting but because of some emergencies work they do not attend the meeting. Normally, Bengali community is more aware about the activities of the society and also particularly SHG is concerned. Commercial Banks are not disbursing loans in the names of the husband or father-in-law of the BSC respondents because they are defaulters. SHG is the only source from which the Bengalis are getting loans from the banks. Most of the SHGs were linked with commercial banks in 2002 and they disbursed loans after properly monitoring members at group level memberships. Gradation of SHGs takes place for significant performance of SHGs and grants provided to them. It was found that grant amount is half the savings of SHGs. Under SGSY scheme grants were provided to the SHGs for using the amount in income generating activities which is the part of poverty alleviation programme.

The basic norm of SHG is that directly providing credit to the members from the small savings for meeting the current household's requirements, viz., school fees of children, medicinal expenses, etc. It also minimises the current credit dependency on moneylenders who charge high rates of interest. Lending from SHGs fund ensures to sustains the group and also gains for them access to more funds from the government and the banks. It is noticed that SHG members have simultaneously taken more than one loan depending on the priority of requirements. SHGs provide loans mainly for agricultural purposes such as, buying fertilizers, insecticides, bullocks and buffaloes, hybrid seeds, for petty-business and animal husbandry for supporting income generation. SHG members also borrow loans for specific social occasions which are obligatory in nature. For example, births and deaths, pregnancies, and marriages. However, in actual practice raising of such loans are not unilinear, often they are raised from multiple sources such as moneylenders, relatives and friends. Loans raise from moneylenders and pawn brokers who charge differential rates of interest depending on the nature, type and time of loans asked for. SHGs provide collateral free loans whereas, moneylenders ask for guarantee. Mortgaging land and at times even mortgaging the standing crop for raising loans during emergencies such as, deaths and births, and marriages is not uncommon. Such practices are more common among the BSCs than among the STs and non-BSCs. Borrowing from moneylenders was viewed to be somewhat convenient despite their charging high rates of interest, for even while many are unable to repay on time, moneylenders wait especially when the borrower belongs to the village itself. During festive occasions also people especially tribal groups raise loans from moneylenders.

Many factors are associated with the higher repayment rates under micro-finance programmes. Group-based lending introduces peer pressure and monitoring and creates social pressure to enforce loan contracts. Moreover, micro-finance is not merely an intervention of lending and borrowings. It emphasizes for building capabilities of programme participants through savings, credit and other financial services. Thus, it leads towards a path of social development. It was observed that an overwhelmingly (94.3 per cent) members from all social groups repaid the amount whatever they had taken from the groups' fund. The conservative thinking that loans taking from individual, groups, banks or moneylenders is considered to be a grave risk. If a person dies without repaying her or his debts, her sons and heirs feel it their duty to do so, otherwise soul of the dead will not rest in peace. Also, the fear of non-repayment of loan from the SHG fund may lead to alienation from the SHG. Defaulters may also be denied financial help from fellow villagers.

It was observed that repayments were fixed on monthly intervals. Those members who repay monthly intervals are specially those who operate petty-business. Those people who take loan for cultivation purposes repay loans after harvesting. An overwhelmingly (83.3 per cent) member repays their loans from husbands' income as these women take loans for cultivation and also for allied activities. These members have taken loans for multiple uses, such as cultivation and dairy farming, and petty-business.

Even though, SHG is an informal institution to get loan at low rates of interest but there were SHGs who have made certain rules to get back the loan from their defaulters. Normally, vendors and dailywage labourers do not default as their credit requirement is small against their savings. They also do not take big risks. Strict rules are followed by Bengali SHGs, that if a member does not clear the loan with interest on stipulated time then they are charged Rs. 5 per cent extra on the existing loans. So, in order to avoid this risk all members repay their loan in time.

Regarding overall women's empowerment, the impact of microcredit programme seems to be encouraging in both private and government institutions. Self-help promoting institutions (SHPIs) promote sustainability of services which are outreach to the poors and women as well. Such as, a sense of control, competence, coherence, confidence, self-esteem, entitlement, responsibility, participation, solidarity and community. Situational components can include control over resources; interpersonal, work and organisational skills; decision-making powers; self-sufficiency, mobility and ability to get around in society, increased status, financial and social support, information, income; improvements in living conditions such as child care, school attendance of children and housing improvements. It was found that most Bengali women are far ahead in terms of outside connection and the performance was significantly associated with family encouragement and achievement motivation.

Sustainability of SHG can be viewed at several levels—institutional, group and individual and can relate to organisational, managerial and financial aspect. A sustainable livelihood for each and every SHG member is mission of the SHG. These SHG members are looking for ways to stabilise their lives and livelihoods in a way that it enhances their dignity and contributes to the broader well being of the family members. Sustainability of SHGs has been viewed with regard to its performance. The decade of SHG progress is not a chance of choice but roughly the time required for capacity building, empowerment and livelihood processes to be personally experienced by each member through challenges faced in their lives. If each member of the concerned group credited for 3 to 5 times cycles of loan and repayment rate is satisfactory, then only we can say that the group is sustaining. It was observed that almost all SHGs have crossed five years of terms and all members taken loan for more than three cycles in this period. Some members in the SHGs who are slightly more enterprising also make good use of the bank loans available, to exnand their livelihood portfolio.

Joining the SHGs means that, expecting for some major gain in terms of extra benefit at the individual level as well as at the group level. SHGs are an additional initiative for livelihoods promotion and supportive opportunities for the poor people and also an alternative mechanism to help each other.

The SHG federation is a democratic body formed with a certain number of SHGs functioning in a specific geographical area with the objective of uniting such SHGs for common cause and for achieving these causes which an individual SHG would not be able to do. A federation is an association of primary organisations. Primary organisations may join together to realise economies of scale or to gain strength as an interest group. A cluster level federation is a network of several SHGs and a structure or body evolved by SHGs themselves consisting of representatives from all members of SHGs, with the motive of supporting members of SHGs to attain the goals of economic and social empowerment of women members and their capacity-building. In other words, it is another forum for SHGs to step up development of women members taking advantage of collective effort of member SHGs enabling holistic and need-based social, political and economic development. Empowerment can also be analysed at the group level, although little attention has been paid to its components. Groups' sustainability and empowerment includes the ability to name problems, to identify actions leading to solutions to understand and get what is needed from others, and to establish links with other groups, i.e., meaning group interaction for federation creation. Thus a successful sustainability of SHG programmes can increase membership and strengthen relationships with local banks, NGOs, political leaders, and government functionaries. It can help the group and individual member not to borrow money from moneylenders on high interest rate. It will build up capacity of practical knowledge, solid information, real competencies, concrete skills, material resources, genuine opportunities and tangible results.

It was found that family encouragement towards SHG

was more among the Bengali SCs than STs and SCs. It was not because of husband domination but because of lack of awareness and uneasy to take risk. It was observed that among the individual level constraints encountered by SHG members were lack of education especially STs and SCs in comparison to BSCs much higher. Improper price for the produced goods unscrupulous by middlemen were the constraints faced by the SHGs members. There is a clear community bias in forming SHGs. It was found in the study that of the 20 groups, none of the Bengali SHG members had taken membership to STs or SC and *vice-versa*. SHG members like to join into their own community, where they can feel confident while taking part in any discussion regarding the SHG.

The SHG movement has provided a voice to tribal women and brought out their entrepreneurial skills, demonstrated by microenterprises and their income generating activities, such as dairy farming, pisciculture, vegetable cultivation and the like. Initiation of informal credit delivery system has increased access of tribals to credit for income generation. It has inculcated savings and repayment habits. SHGs have been successful as agents of poverty alleviation by a number of different measures. The most common measure of a SHG's performance is member's loan repayment rate, since this has a large bearing on whether mechanisms like small savings are sustainable. One basic fact of the SHGs formation is to secure livelihoods and also help each other SHG members in the time of need. The most outstanding factor of SHGs is that it is a way through which women can save which can be used in time of emergencies. Data analysis clearly indicates that a fairly higher percentage (94.3 per cent) of SHG members have repaid their loans. A remarkable feature of the SHGs is that, the total savings and their sincere repayment methods which help members to get loans on a rotation basis. Equilibrium savings and interest rate with rotational credits among members convey stability of SHG and a sense of common purposes have proved that the SHG is one of the most effective alternative mechanisms for poverty alleviation.

As SHG is part of self-management programmes, clusters and federations promoted by the community banking programme share the costs of management out of their own savings and credit operations. By providing regular access to savings, credit and insurance services, the programme is able to rescue many poor people from the clutches of moneylenders and arrest the income drain. In addition, the programme helps members to enhance their income and create assets. Many older groups and federations go beyond providing savings, credit and insurance services and meet the other social and developmental needs of members. In the case of SHG and its functioning, only two women hold the total power of the group. For example, one is the group head or leader (president) and the other one is secretary. On be half of group, the bank account can be opened jointly in the names of the president and secretary. These two are the office bearers and rest of the group members are just members. These two are responsible for the whole transaction of the bank. So, rest of the members are far away from the empowerment process. In this case, the members are only passive elements. Women may be energised by their group activities. However, activities must be scheduled at the convenience of the women, and additional burdens should be minimised as much as possible. If conscientisation and empowerment are not part of the group process, there may in fact be little or no long-term gain to compensate for the time loss from women's participation in community activities.

Micro-finance programmes are trying to become self-sustained gradually. High rate of recovery under micro-finance programmes proves a hypothesis that the economically backward people are creditworthy and thus bankable. Micro-finance can be the best intervention for the poverty alleviation and employment generation all over the world like Bangladesh and India. At the same time government sponsored schemes of poverty alleviation are there in which subsidy is one of the components. From time to time Government announce these populist schemes to strengthen their vote banks. There is a fear that such subsidised schemes can hamper the growth of microfinance in India.

Poverty alleviation is a gigantic task at personal level and as well as government programmes. Now NGOs and MFIs are playing important role in reducing poverty and generating employment in developing countries through micro-finance. Governments of both the Centre and States have also created conducive environment and regulatory framework for the spread of micro-finance. In India government has taken initiative for micro-finance development. Besides ICICI Bank and other private financial institutions have come forward for the growth of micro-finance sector. Targeted micro-finance programmes also help to increase assets, savings and net worth of households. Most importantly, by promoting a shift from land-based activities to non-traditional economic activities, promotes productivity and create employment opportunities in the rural economy. The study documents that due to Grameen Bank of Bangladesh and SEWA in India's initiative, overall levels of employment have increased, labour force participation among women has increased and self employment has increased.

REFERENCES

1. Detail on microcredit or microfinance institutions have been included in the introduction chapter and third chapter.
2. *Sa-Dhan* (December 2006-February 2007), Quarterly compendium of News Clippings on Microfinance and related Environment, Vol.3, No. 1.

Bibliography

Books

Adams, Dale; Douglas Graham, and J.D. von Pischke. (1984), *Undermining Rural Development with Cheap Credit.* Boulder, CO: Westview Press.

Agafonoff, Alexander (1994), *Banco Solidario S.A. : Micro-Enterprise Financing on a Commercial Scale in Bolivia,* Research School of Pacific and Asian Studies, Australian National University.

Asian Development Bank (2000), *Role of Central Banks in Microfinance in Asia and the Pacific Asian Development Bank.*

Austin, James E. (2000), *The Collaboration Challenge,* Jossey-Bass.

Asian Development Bank (2000), *The Role of Central Banks in Microfinance in Asia and the Pacific,* Asian Development Bank, Manila.

Backer, G. S. (1981), *Treatise on the Family,* Cambridge, MA: Harvard University Press.

Balkenhol, Bernd (Ed.) (1999), *Credit Unions and the Poverty Challenge: Extending Outreach, Enhancing Sustainability,* International Labour Office.

Barrow, Christopher J. (2001), *Social Impact Assessment: An Introduction,* Edward Arnold.

Baviskar, B. and Attwood, D. (1995), *Finding the Middle Path: The Political Economy of Cooperation in Rural India.* Boulder, GO: Westview Press.

Becker, Gary (1981), *Treatise on the Family.* Cambridge: Harvard University Press.

Bedi, R. (1992), *Theory, History, and Practice of Cooperation.* Meerut (U.P., India), R. Lall Book Depot.

Besley, Timothy, (1995), "Saving Credit and Insurance", In *Handbook of Development Economics,* Vol. 3A (ed.) Jere Behrman and T.N. Srinivasan, pp. 2125-207, Amsterdam: Elsevier.

Bhatt, Nitin (2002), *Inner-City Entrepreneurship Development: The Microcredit Challenge,* Institute for Contemporary Studies, Press.

Blakely, Edward J. and Susan L. Giles (2001), *Fundamentals of Economic Development Finance,* Sage Publications.

Bomstein, O. (1996), *The Price of a Dream: The Story of the Grameen Bank and the Idea that is Helping the Poor to Change their Lives.* New York: Simon and Schustèr.

Bornstein, David (1997), *The Price of a Dream: The Story of the Grameen Bank,* University of Chicago Press.

Branch, Brian and Janette Klaehn (Edited) (2002), *Striking the Balance in Microfinance: A Practical Guide to Mobilizing.* PACT Publishing.

Breth, Steven A. (1999), *Microfinance in Africa, Mexico City:* Sasakawa Africa Association.

Bruce-Radcliffe, Godfrey (1996), *Practical Property Development and Finance,* Sweet & Maxwell Ltd

Brugger, Ernst and Sarath Rajapatirana, (eds.) (1995), *New Perspectives on Financing Small Business in Developing Countries.* San Francisco: ICS Press.

Carr, James H. and Zhong Yi Tong (Edited) (2002), *Replicating Microfinance in the United States,* The Woodrow Wilson Centre Press.

Chambers, R. (1991), Shortcut and participatory methods for gaining social information for projects. In M. Cemea (Ed.) *Putting People First: Sociological Variables in Rural Development* (2nd ed.. New York: Oxford University Press.

Charitonenko, Stephanie (2002), *Commercialization of Microfinance: Bangladesh, Manila*:Asian Development Bank.

Chattopadhya, Kamaladevi (1983), *Indian Women Battle for Freedom* Delhi: Abhinav, p. 98.

Chen, M. (1983), *Quiet Revolution: Women in Transition in Rural Bangladesh*. Rochester, VT: Schenkman Books, Inc.

Chen, Martha Alter (1996), *Quiet Revolution: Women in* Transition in Rural Bangladesh Dhaka: Bangladesh Rural Advancement Committee, p. 80.

Cheung, Steven (1969), *Theory of Tenancy*, Chicago: University of Chicago Press.

Choudhury, Masudul Alam (1997), *Money in Islam: A Study in Islamic Political Economy* (Routledge International Studies in Money and Banking, 3), Routledge.

Clark, Heather (2002), *Microfinance Distance Learning Course*, United Nations Capital Development Fund.

Clark, Peggy and Tracy Huston (1993), *Assisting the Smallest Businesses: Assessing Micro-enterprise Development As a Strategy for Boosting Poor Communities*, Aspen Inst Publications Office.

Cloud, K. (1984), "*Women's Productivity in Agricultural Systems*: Considerations for Project Design", in *Gender Roles in Development Projects*, (Ed.) C. Overholt *et ul.*,West Hartford, CT Kumarain Press.

Coleman, Brett E. (2002), *Microfinance in North-East Thailand: Who Benefits and How Much*? Asian Development Bank.

Conroy, John D. and Robyn Cornford (eds.) (2000), *The Role of Central Banks in Microfinance in Asia and the Pacific* (Vol. 2), The Foundation for Development Cooperation.

Coughlin, Jeanne Halladay and Andrew R. Thomas (2002), *The Rise of Women Entrepreneurs: People,* Processes, and Global Trends, Quorum Books.

Counts, A. (1996), *Give Us Credit: How Muhammed Yunus's Micro-Lending Revolution is Empowering Women from Bangladesh to Chicago.* New York: Times Books.

Cowen, Michael and Robert W. Shenton (1996), *Doctrines of Development,* Routledge.

Cox, Aidan; J. M. Healey; Timo Voipio and Paul Hoebink (2000), *European Development Cooperation and the Poor,* Palgrave Macmillan

Daley-Harris, Sam (2002), *Pathways out of Poverty: Innovations in Microfinance for the Poorest Families,* Kumarian Press.

Daphnis, Franck and Bruce Ferguson (2004), *Housing Microfinance: A Guide to Practice,* Kumarian Press.

Deaton, Angus. (1992), *Understanding Consumption.* Oxford: Clarendon Press.

Diagne, Alinu. (1998, "Default Incentives, Peer Pressure, and Equilibrium Outcomes in Group-Based Lending Programs", IFPRI FCND Working Paper.

Dees, J. Gregory and Jed Emerson (2002), *Strategic Tools for Social Entrepreneurs: Enhancing the Performance of Your Enterprising Nonprofit,* John Willey & Sons.

Desai, Vandana and Robert Potter (Edited) (2002), *The Companion to Development Studies,* Edward Arnold.

Domini, Amy L. (2001), *Socially Responsible Investing: Making A Difference and Making Money,* Dearborn Trade Publishing.

Drake, Deborah (2002), *Commercialization of Microfinance Philippines,* Kumarian Press

Drake, Deborah and Elisabeth Rhyne (Editor) (2002), *The Commercialization of Microfinance: Balancing Business and Development,* Kumarian Press.

Economic and Social Research Foundation (Tanzania) (2000),

Optimal Modalities towards increasing the Access of the Poor to Micro-Credit Facilities, Dar-es-Salaam: ESRF: PACE

Edgcomb, Elaine; Candace Nelson and Julie Redfern (1996), Moving Forward: *Tools for Sustainability and Expansion*, Pact Publications.

Edgcomb, Elaine; Joyce Klein, and Peggy Clark (1996), *The Practice of Microenterprise in the U.S.: Strategies, Costs, and Effectiveness*. Washington, DC: The Aspen Institute.

Eicher, Carl K. and John M. Staatz (Eds.) (1998), *International Agricultural Development*, Johns Hopkins University Press.

Epping, Randy Charles (2001), *A Beginner's Guide to the World Economy: Eighty-One Basic Economic Concepts That Will Change the Way You See the World*, Vintage.

Ester Boserup (1976), *Women's Role in Economic Development*, New York: St. Martin's Press.

Fernandez, A. (1994), *Myrada Experience: Alternative Management Systems for Savings and Credit of the Rural Poor.* Bangalore, India: Myrada.

Fernandez, Aloysius Prakash (1998), *The MYRADA Experience - Alternate Management Systems for Savings and Credit of the Rural Poor*, MYRADA.

Fernandez, Aloysius Prakash (2001), *The MYRADA Experience? Putting Institutions First? Even in Micro Finance*, MYRADA.

Fernando, Nimal A. (2003), *Commercialization of Microfinance: Sri Lanka*, Asian Development Bank.

Fine, Ben (2000), *Social Capital* versus *Social Theory: Political Economy and Social Science at the Turn of the Millennium (Contemporary Political Economy)* Routledge.

Fisher, Thomas and M.S. Sriram (2002), *Beyond Microcredit: Putting Development Back into Microfinance*, Oxfam, Vistaar Publications: New Delhi.

Fitch, Thomas P. (2000), *Dictionary of Banking Terms, Barrons Educational Series*

Forsythe, David P., Roger A. Coate and Thomas George Weiss *(2000), The United Nations and Changing World Politics,* Westview Press.

Freire, Paulo (1968), *Pedagogy of the Oppressed,* New York: Seasbury Press, pp. 32-47.

Friedman, Thomas L. (2000), *The Lexus and The Olive Tree*: Understanding Globalization, Anchor.

Gallardo, Joselito S.; Bikki K. Randhawa and Orlando J. Sacay (1997), *A Commercial Bank's Microfinance Programme: The Case of Hatton National Bank in Sri Lanka* (World Bank Dicussion Papers: 369)

Garnaut, Ross and Ligang Song (2004), *Private Enterprise in China,* Routledge.

Ghosh, H. (1915), *Theory of Cooperative Credit.* Calcutta: S.C. Auddy & Co.

Gilkerson, Linda; Theresia Paauwee, and Theresia Pauwee (1997), *Self-Employment — From Dreams to Reality: Business Planning for Micro-Enterprises,* Jist Works.

Goetz, Anne Marie (2001), *Women Development Workers: Implementing Rural Credit Programmes in Bangladesh,* Sage Publications.

Goodwin-Groen, Ruth (1998), *The Role of Commercial Banks in Microfinance in the Asia-Pacific Region,* The Foundation for Development Cooperation.

Granovetter, M. (1994), Business groups. In N. Smelser and R. Swedberg (Eds.) *Handbook of Economic Sociology. Princeton,* NJ: Princeton University Press.

Gulli, Hege (1998), *Microfinance and Poverty: Questioning Conventional Wisdom,* Bandai Co. Ltd.

Gup, Benton E. (2002), *The Future of Banking,* Quorum Books.

Harper, M. (2002), *Promotion of Self-Help Groups under the SHG Bank Linkage Programme in India's Microcredit Innovations Department,* NABARD, Mumbai.

Harper, Malcolm (2002), *Microfinance: Evolution, Achievement and Challenges*, London: ITDG.

Harper, Malcolm (2003), *Microfinance*, ITDG Publishing.

Harper, Malcolm (2003), *Practical Microfinance*, ITDG Publishing.

Henry, Carla, Cecile Lapenu and Manfred Zeller (2003), *Microfinance Poverty Assessment Tool*, World Bank.

Holloh, Detlev (1999), *Microfinance in Indonesia: Between State, Market and Self-Organization*, Lit Verlag.

Hossain, M. (1988), *Credit for Alleviation of Rural Poverty: The Grameen Bank in Bangladesh*, Washington, DC: International Food Policy Research Institute.

Hulme, D. and Mosley, P. (1996), *Finance Against Poverty.* (Volumes 1 & 2); New York: Routledge.

Hulme, David and Paul Mosley (1996), *Finance Against Poverty, Volume 1*, Routledge, London and New York.

Hulme, David and Paul Mosley, (eds.) (1996), *Finance against Poverty.* London: Routledge.

Hutton, Sandra and Gerry Redmond (2000), *Poverty in Transition Economies*, Routledge

International Fund for Agricultural Development (2002), *Rural Poverty Report 2001— The Challenge of Ending Rural Poverty*, Oxford University Press.

International Monetary Fund (2001), *World Economic Outlook, October 2001, The Information Technology Revolution*, International Monetary Fund.

Ivanceanu, Ina (2000),*The Dynamics of the Husband's TV : Participation and Empowerment in Development Co-operation : the Case of Micro-Credit Programmes in Uganda*, Wien : Afro-P.

Jagger, A. (1983), *Politics and Human Nature, Brighten*: Harvester.

Jayawardana, K. (1988), *Feminism and Nationalism in the Third World*, London: Zed Books.

Johnson, Susan and Ben Rogaly (1997), *Microfinance and Poverty Reduction (Oxfam Development Guidelines)*, Oxfam Academic.

Kabeer, Naila (1994), *Reversed Realities: Gender Hierarchies in Development Thought*, London: Verso.

Karmakar, K.G. (1999), *Rural Credit and Self-Help Groups: Micro-Finance Needs and Concepts in India*, Thousand Oaks: Sage Publications, New Delhi.

Karunaratne, Garvin (1997), *Micro-Enterprise Development: A Strategy for Poverty Alleviation & Employment Creation in the Third World: The Way out of The World Bank & IMF Stranglehold*, Sarasavi Bookshop.

Kashuliza, A.K. (1998), *The Role of Informal and Semi-Formal Finance in Poverty Alleviation in Tanzania : Results of a Field Study in Two Regions*, Dar-es-Salaam : Research on Poverty Alleviation.

Katrak, Homi and Roger Strange (2002), *Small-Scale Enterprises in Developing and Transitional Economies*, Palgrave Macmillan.

Keohane, Robert O. (2002), *Power and Governance in a Partly Globalized World*, Routledge

Khandker, S. and Khan, Z. (1993), *Is Grameen Bank Sustainable?* Washington, DC: World Bank.

Khandker, Shahidur R. (1998), *Fighting Poverty with Micro-Credit: Experience in Bangladesh*, Oxford University Press, New York.

Khandker, Shahidur. (1998), *Fighting Poverty with Microcredit: Experience in Bangladesh*. New York: Oxford University. Press for the World Bank.

Kimenyl, Mwangi S., Robert C. Wieland and J.D. von Pischke (Eds.) (1998), *Strategic Issues in Microfinance (Contemporary Perspectives on Developing Societies)*, Ashgate Publishing Limited

Klobuchar, Jim and Susan Cornell Wilkes (2003), *The Miracles of Barefoot Capitalism: A Compelling Case for Microcredit*, Kirk House Pub.

Koopman, Jeanne (2001), *Micro-Finance Institutions in Kenya: Client Profiles and Institutional Growth*, Boston, MA: African Studies Center, Boston University.

Krahnen, J. and Schmidt, R. (1994), *Development Finance as Institution Building: A New Approach to Poverty-Oriented Banking*. Boulder, CO: Westview Press.

Ledgerwood, Joanna (1999), *Microfinance Handbook: An Institutional and Financial Perspective*, World Bank US.

Ledgerwood, Joanna (2001), *Microfinance Handbook: An Institutional and Financial Perspective (Sustainable Banking with the Poor)*, World Bank Publications.

Levitsky, Jacob (1989), *Micro-Enterprises in Developing Countries: Papers and Proceedings*, Palgrave Macmillan.

Levitsky, Jacob (1989), *Micro-Enterprises in Developing Countries*, Intermediate Technology.

Liddle, J. and Ramma Joshi (1986), *Daughters of Independence: Class, Caste, Gender in India* ,London: Zed Books.

Liedholm, Carl and Donald C. Mead (1999), *Small Enterprises and Economic Development (Routledge Studies in Development Economics)*, Routledge.

Lowell, Stephanie (2000), *The Harvard Business School Guide to Careers in the Nonprofit Sector*, Harvard Business School Press.

Lustig, Nora (2001), *Shielding the Poor: Social Protection in the Developing World*, Washington, D.C.: Brookings Institution Press.

Marcus, Rachel; Beth Porter and Caroline Harper (1999), *Money Matters: Understanding Microfinance*, London: Save the Children.

Matthaus-Maier, Ingrid and J. D. von Pischke (Edited) (2003), *The Development of the Financial Sector in South-East Europe: Innovative Approaches in Volatile Environments*, Springer Verlag.

Mayoux, Linda (2003), *Sustainable Learning for Women's Empowerment: Ways Forward in Microfinance*, ITDG Publishing.

McKinley, Terry (2001), *Macroeconomic Policy, Growth and Poverty Reduction*, Palgrave Macmillan.

Meier, Gerald M., Joseph E. Stiglitz and Nicholas Stern (Edited) (2000), *Frontiers of Development Economies: The Future in Perspective*, World Bank.

Mendelson, Sarah Elizabeth and John K. Glenn (2002), *The Power and Limits of NGOs*, Columbia University Press.

Meyer, Richard L. and Geetha Nagarajan (2001), *Rural Financial Markets in Asia: Policies, Paradigms, and Performance (Study of Rural Asia, V. 3)*, Oxford University Press.

Mibanco, Nimal A. Fernando and Patricia Calcetas (2004), Peru: *Profitable Microfinance Outreach, with Lessons for Asia*, Asian Development Bank.

Microcredit Summit (1999), *Declaration and Plan of Action*. Washington, DC: Results Educational Fund.

Mikdashi, Zuhayr (2001), *Financial Intermediation in the 21st Century: Leaders Dialogues on Global Finance*, Palgrave Macmillan.

Montgomery, R ; D. Bhottacharya and D. Hulme (1996), "Credit for the Poor in Bangladesh, the BRAC Rural Development Programme and the Government Thana Resource Development and Employment Programme", in David Hulme and Paul Mosley (eds.)" *Finance Against Poverty*, Vol. 2, Routledge, London and New York.

Morduch, J. (1998), *Microfinance Revolution*. Cambridge, MA: MIT Press.

Mwenda, Kenneth (2002), K. Banking and Microfinance Regulation and Supervision: Lessons from Zambia, Universal Publishers.

MYRADA (2001), *The MYRADA Experience —A Manual for Capacity Building of Self Help Groups*, MYRADA.

MYRADA (2002), *The MYRADA Experience — A Manual for Finance and Management Systems of Self-Help Groups*, MYRADA.

MYRADA (2002), *The MYRADA Experience? A Manual for Finance and Management Systems of Self-help Affinity Groups with Criteria for a Social Audit, MYRADA.*

MYRADA (2003), The MYRADA Experience? *Why Do Self-Help Groups Sometimes Fail. A short study* of Non—Functioning Self-Help Groups in Three Myrada Project Areas, MYRADA.

Naples, Nancy A. and Manisha Desai (Edited) (2002), *Women's Activism and Globalization: Linking Local Struggles and Transnational Politics*, Routledge.

OECD (1993), *New Directions in Donor Assistance to Micro-Enterprises*, OECD.

Olomola, Ade S. (2001), *The Nature and Determinants of Rural Loan Repayment Performance in Nigeria: The Case of FADU's Micro-Credit Programme*, Ibadan : Nigerian Institute of Social and Economic Research.

Olson, M. (1965), *Logic of Collective Action*, Cambridge, Mass.: Harvard University Press.

Otero, M. and Rhyne, E. (eds.) (1994), *New World of Microenterprise Finance: Building Healthy Financial Institutions for the Poor.* West Hartford, CT: Kumarian Press.

Otero, Maria and Elizabeth Rhyne (1994), *The New World of Microenterprise Finance: Building Healthy Institutions for the Poor*, Kumarian Press, West Hartford, CT.

OXFAM (1995), *Poverty Report*, London: OXFAM,

Panganiban, Andres G. (1998), *Barefoot Banking: Microfinance in the Philippines*, New Pillars Pub.

Parpart, J. (ed.) 1989, *Women and Development in Africa: Comparative Perspectives*, University Press of America, Lanham, MD, USA.

Parzen, J. and Kieschnick, M. (1992), *Credit Where It's Due: Development Banking for Communities*. Philadelphia: Temple University Press.

Patten, R. and Rosengard, J. (1991), *Progress with Profits: The Development of Rural Banking in Indonesia*. San Francisco: ICS Press.

Paxton, J. (1996), *Worldwide Inventory of Microfinance Institutions*, World Bank, Washington D.C.

Potts, David, Patrick Ryan and Anna Toner (2003), *Development Planning and Poverty Reduction*, Palgrave Macmillan.

Rahman, Aminur (2001), *Women and Microcredit in Rural Bangladesh: An Anthropological Study of Grameen Bank Lending*, Westview Press.

Remenyi, J. (1991), *Where Credit is Due: Income-Generating Programs for the Poor in Developing Countries*. London: Intermediate Technology Publications.

Remenyi, Joe (2000), *Microfinance and Poverty Alleviation*, ORCA Book Services.

Remenyi, Joe and Ben Quinones (Edited) Muhammad Yunus (Foreword) (2000), *Microfinance and Poverty Alleviation: Case Studies from Asia and the Pacific (Global Development and the Environment)*, Thomson Learning.

Remenyi, Joe and Benjamin Q. Jr. (2000), *Microfinance and Poverty Alleviation: Case Studies from Asia and the Pacific*, Pinter, New York.

Rhyne, Elisabeth (2001), *Mainstreaming Microfinance*, Kumarian Press.

Rhyne, Elisabeth (2001), *Mainstreaming Microfinance: How Lending to the Poor Began, Grew, and Came of Age in Bolivia*, Bloomfield, Conn : Kumarian Press.

Robinson, Marguerite (2001), *The Microfinance Revolution: Sustainable Finance for the Poor*, World Bank.

Robinson, Marguerite (2002), *The Microfinance Revolution: Lessons from Indonesia*, World Bank

Robinson, Marguerite S. (2001), *The Microfinance Revolution*, World Bank.

Robinson, Marguerite S. (2001), *The Microfinance Revolution: Sustainable Finance* for the World Bank Publications.

Robinson, Marguerite S. (2002), *Microfinance Revolution, Volume 2*: Lessons from Indonesia, World Bank.

Robinson, Marguerite S. (2004), *Microfinance Revolution: The Emerging Industry*, World Bank.

Rodriguez, Cheryl Rene (1995), *Women, Microenterprise, and the Politics of Self-Help (Garland Studies in Entrepreneurship)*, Garland Publications.

Rogaly, Ben (1998), *Learning from South-North Links in Microfinance*, Oxfam.

Rogaly, Ben; Thomas Fisher and Ed Mayo (1999), *Poverty, Social Exclusion and Microfinance in Britain, Oxford:* Oxfam in association with the New Economics.

Rogers, B. (1980), *Domestication of Women: Discrimination in Developing Societies*, London: Kegan Press.

Roy, Kartik C.; Clement A. Tisdell and Hans C. Blomqvist (1999), *Economic Development and Women in the World Community*, Praeger Publishers.

Ruit, Catherine van de, Julian May and Benjamin Roberts (2001), *A Poverty Assessment of the Small Enterprise Foundation on behalf of the Consultative Group to assist the Poorest*, Durban : Poverty and Population Studies Programme, University of Natal.

Rutherford, Stuart (2000), *The Poor and their Money*, Oxford University Press, New Delhi.

Rutherford, Stuart. (1995), ASA: The Biography of an NGO. Dhaka: Association for Social Advancement.

Saez, Lawrence (2004), *Banking Reform in India and China*, Palgrave Macmillan.

Sampson, A. (1989), *Midas Touch: Money, People and Power from West to East*. London: Hodder and Stoughton.

Schmidheiny, Stephan, Chad Holliday and Philip Watts (2002), *Walking the Talk: The Business Case for Sustainable Development*, Berrett-Koehler Pub.

Schneider, Hartmut (1997), *Microfinance for the Poor*, OECD.

Schreiner, Mark (2003), *Performance of Subsidized Microfinance Organizations — Bancosol of Bolivia and the Grameen Bank of Bangladesh* (Millen Studies in Economics), Edwin Millen Press.

Schreiner, Mark (2003), *The Performance of Subsidized Microfinance Organizations*, Edwin Mellen Press.

Sen, A. (1981), *Poverty and Famines*. Oxford: Clarendon Press.

Sen, Amartya and Jean Dreze (1995), *India Economic Development and Social Opportunity*, New York: Oxford University Press.

Sharif, Iffath (2001), *Challenges for Second Generation Microfinance*: Regulation, Supervision, and Resource Mobilization, University Press.

Sheldon, Tony and Charles Waterfield (1998), *Business Planning and Financial Modelling for Microfinance Institutions*: A Handbook, Pact Publications.

Smith, A. 1976 (1776), *Wealth of Nations*. Chicago: University of Chicago Press.

Soto, Hernando De (2000), The Mystery of Capital: Why Capitalism Triumphs in the West and Fails Everywhere Else, Basic Books.

Tinker, I. and M. Branisen (eds.) (1976), *Women and World Development*, New York: St. Martin's Press.

Tschach, Ingo (2002), *The Theory of Development Finance: How Microcredit Programmes Alleviate Credit and Labour Market Segmentation* (Entwicklung Und Finanzierung, Bd. 11.), Peter Lang Pub.

UNDP (1997), Microstart Guide: *A Guide for Planning, Starting and Managing A Microfinance Program*, The UNDP PSDP.

Van Ness, Richard J., Helen Chan and Richard J. Van Ness (1998), *The Book of Profit*, Garborg's, Inc.

Vandersluis, Sarah Owen and Paris Yeros (2000), *Poverty in World Politics*: Whose Global Era? Palgrave Macmillan.

Wahid, A. (1993), *Grameen Bank: Poverty Relief in Bangladesh.* Boulder, CD: Westview Press.

Waterfield, Charles and Nick Ramsing (1998), *Management Information Systems for Microfinance Institutions : A Handbook*, Pact Publications.

Webster, Leila and Peter Fidler (Eds.) (1996), *The Informal Sector and Microfinance Institutions in West Africa*, World Bank.

Weiss, Anita M. and S. Zulfiqar Gilani (2001), *Power and Civil Society in Pakistan, Karachi*: Oxford University Press.

Williamson, O. (1975), *Markets and Hierarchies: Analysis and Antitrust Implications*. New York: Free Press.

Wolff, H. (1910), *People's Banks: A Record of Social and Economic Success* (Third Edition). London: P. S. King & Son.

World Bank (1988), *Targeted Programs for the Poor during Structural Adjustment*, Washington, DC.

World Bank (2001), *World Development Report 2000/2001: Attacking Poverty*, Oxford University Press, New York.

Wright, Graham (2000), *Microfinance Systems: Designing Quality Financial Services for the Poor*, Zed Books.

Wright, Graham A.N. (2000), *Micro-finance systems: Designing Quality, Financial Services for the Poor*, London; New York: Zed Books, Dhaka: University Press.

Yunus, Muhammad (1999), *Toward A Poverty Free World: Story of Muhammad Yunnus and the Grameen Foundation*, Public Affairs, U.S.

Yunus, *Muhammad and Alan Jolis (1998), Banker to the Poor: The Autobiography of Muhammad Yunus, Founder of the Grameen Bank*, Aurum Press, London.

Yunus, Muhammad and Alan Jolis (2001), *Banker to the Poor:*

The Autobiography of Muhammad Yunus, Founder of Grameen Bank, OUP Pakistan.

Zeller, Manfred and Richard L. Meyer (Edited) (2002), *The Triangle of Microfinance: Financial Sustainability, Outreach, and Impact (International Food Policy Research Institute Series),* The Johns Hopkins University Press.

Zeller, Manfred and Richard L. Meyer (Edited) (2002), *The Triangle of Microfinance: Financial Sustainability, Outreach, and Impact (International Food Policy Research Institute Series),* The Johns Hopkins University Press.

Journals and Web Links

ACCION International. (1997), *Credit Lines* 3:1 (An Update of the ACCION U.S. Network), March.

Adams, Dale and J.D. von Pischke. (1992), "Microenterprise Credit Programs: Deja Vu", *World Development,* Vol. 20, No. 10, pp. 1463-70.

Angrist, Joshua; Guido Imbens, and Donald Rubin. (1996), "Identification of Causal Effects Using Instrumental Variables", *J. Amer. Stat. Assoc., Vol.* 91, No. 34, pp. 444-56.

Akelof, George (1984), "The Markets for 'Lemons': Quantitative Uncertainty and Market Mechanisms", *Quarterly Journal of Economics,* pp. 488-500.

Aportela, Fernando (1998), *"Effects of Financial Access on Savings by Low-Income People"*, MIT Econ. Dept., Draft.

Armendariz de Aghion, Beatriz and Christian Collier (1997), *"Peer Group Formation in an Adverse Selection Model"*, Econ. Dept., U. College, London, Draft.

Armendariz de Aghion, Beatriz and Jonathan Morduch. (1998), *"Microfinance Beyond Group Lending"*, Harvard and Princeton, Draft.

Banerjee, Abhijit; Timothy Besley, and Timothy Guinnane

(1994), "Thy Neighbour's Keeper: The Design of a Credit Cooperative with Theory and A Test", *Quart. J. Economic*, Vol. 109, No. 2, pp. 491-515.

Bandarage, A. (1984), "*Women in Development: Liberalism, Marxism and Marxist-Feminism*", *Development and Change*, Vol. 15, No. 3, pp. 495-515.

Batliwala, Srilatha (1994), "Meaning of Empowerment: New Concepts Form Action", in *Population Policies Reconsidered: Health Empowerment and Rights*, (Ed.), Gita Sen, Adrienne Germaine, and Lincoln Chen, Cambridge, Harvard University Press, pp. 129-131.

Benaria, L. and G. Sen (1992), "Class and Gender Inequalities and Women's Role in Economic Development: Theoretical and Practical Implications", *Feminist Studies*, Vol. 8, No. 1, pp. 157-76.

Besley, T. and S. Coate (1995), "Group Lending, Repayment Incentives, and Social Collateral", *Journal of Development Economics*, Vol. 46, No. 1, pp. 1-18.

Besley, T., S. Coate and G. Loury (1993), "The Economics of Rotating Savings and Credit Associations", *American Economic Review* 83, No. 4, pp. 792-810.

Braverman, Avishay and Luis Guasch(1993), "Administrative Failures in Government Credit Programs", in *The Economics of Rural Organization: Theory, Practice, and Policy*, ed., Karla Hoff, Avishay Braverman, and Joseph E. Stiglitz, New York: Oxford University Press, p. 60.

Bencivenga, Valerie and Bruce D. Smith (1991), "*Financial Intermediation and Endogenous Growth*", *Rev. Econ. Stud.*, *Vol.* 58, No. 2, pp. 195-209.

Besley, Timothy (1994), "How Do Market Failures Justify Interventions in Rural Credit Markets?" *World Bonk Res. Observer, Vol.* 9, No.1, pp. 22-47.

Besley, Timothy and Stephen Coate (1995), "*Group Lending, Repayment Incentives, and Social Collateral*", *J. Devel. Econ.*, Vol. 46.

Besley, Timothy; Stepheo Coate, and Glenn Loury (1993), "The Economics of Rotating Savings and Credit Associations", *American Economic Review*, Vol. 83, No. 4, pp. 792-810.

Bolnick, Bruce R. (1988), "Evaluating Loan Collection Performance: An Indonesian Example", *World Development*, Vol. 16, pp.501-10.

Bolton, Patrick and David Sharfstein. (1990), "A Theory of Predation Based on Agency Problems in Financial Contracting", *Amer. Econ. Rev.*, SO, pp. 93-106.

Bose, Pinaki (1998), "*Formal-Informal Sector Interaction in Rural Credit Markets*", *J. Devel. Econ.*, Vol. 56, pp. 256-80.

Brill, Betsy. (1999), "A Little Credit, A Huge Success", San Francisco *Examiner*, May 2.

Burtless, Gary. (1995), "The Case for Randomized Field Trials in Economic and Policy Research", *J. Econ. Perspect, Vol.* 9, No. 2, pp. 63-84.

Campbell, Donald T. (1969), "Reforms as Experiments", *Amer. Psychologist*, Vol. 24, pp. 409-29.

Chu, Michael, (1996), "*The Numbers Begin to Add Up for Microcredit; Poor Entrepreneurs Find Doors Opening*", *World Paper*, April.

Churchill, Craig F. (1995), "*The Impact of Credit on Informal Sector Enterprises in South Africa: A Study of Get Ahead Foundation's Stokvel Lending Programme*". Clark U. MA Thesis, Worcester MA. Christen, Robert Peck; Elizabeth Rhyne, Robert

Cockburn, Cynthia (1977), *The Local State: Management of Cities and People*, London: Pluto Press.

Cohen, Monique (2002), '*Making Micro Finance More Client-led*' in *Journal of International Development*, 14, pp: 335-50.

Connell, R. W. (1990), "The State, Gender and Sexual Politics: Theory and Appraisal", *Theory and Society,* Vol. 19 No. 9, pp. 506-45.

Conning, Jonathan (1997), *"Joint Liability, Peer Monitoring, and the Creation of Social Collateral"*, Econ Dept., Villiams College, Draft.

Consultative Group to Assist the Poorest [CGAP]. (1996), *"Microcredit Interest Rates"*, Occasional Paper No. 1, Washington, DC, August.

Currie, Janet and Duncan Thomas. (1995), "Does Head Start Make a Difference?" *Amer. Econ. Rev., Vol.* 85, No. 3, pp. 341-64.

Das Gupta, Monica and D. Narayana. (1996), *"Bangladesh's Fertility Decline from a Regional Perspective"*, Harvard Center for Population and Development Studies, WP, 96.03.

Devereux, J. and Fishe, R. (1993), "Economic Analysis of Group Lending Programs in Developing Countries". *The Developing Economies,* Vol. 31, No. 1, pp. 102-121.

Devereux, Stephen (1993), "Collection of Production and Income Data: A Commentary" in *Data Needs for Food Policy and Household Surveys,* ed. Joachim Von Braun and Detle Puetz, Washington, DC: International Food Policy Research Institute, pp. 202-7.

Dulfo, Annie (2005), 'ICICI Banks the Poor in India: *Demonstrates that Serving Low-Income Segments Is Possible', Microfinance Matters,* Issue 17, October.

Durham, Brad. (1996), *"A Movement May Face a Battle for its Soul : Microcredit Plays for High Stakes with the World Bank", World Paper,* April.

Edgcomb, Elaine and Laura Barton (1998), *Social Intermediation and Microfinance: A Literature Review,* Microenterprise Best Practices Report, USAID/ Development Alternatives, Inc., Aug. [www.mip.org].

The Economist. (1997), "Microlending: From Sandals to Suits", Feb. 1, p. 75.

Flora, Maria and Debraj Ray. (1997): "Vertical Links Between Formal and Informal Financial Institutions", *Rev. Devel. Econ*. 1:1.

Foster, James; Joel Greer, and Erik Thorbecke (1984), "A Class of Decomposable Poverty Measures", *Econometrica*, 52:3, pp. 761—66.

Faqhunda, E. P. (Year), "The Nuclear Household Model in Nigerian Public and Private Policy: Colonial Legacy and Socio-Political Implications", *Development and Change*, Vol.18, pp. 281- 95.

Fernando, Jude (2001), '*The Perils and Prospects of Micro Credit, Non-Governmental Organisations, Neoliberalism and the Cultural Politics of Empowerment*,' Paper Presented at the International Conference on Livelihood, Savings and Debt in a Changing World, Developing Anthropological and Sociological Perspectives, Wageningen, May 14-16.

Fernando, Jude L. (1997), Non Governmental Organizations, Micro-Credit, and Empowerment of Women, *Annals of the American Academy of Political and Social Science*, Vol. *554*, pp. 150-177.

Folber, N. (Year): "Household Production in the Philippines: A Non-Neoclassical Approach", *Economic Development and Cultural Change*, Vol. 32, pp. 303-430.

Fuentes, Gabriel. (1996), *"The Use of Village Agents in Rural Credit Delivery"*, *J. Devel. Stud*., 33:2, pp. 188—209.

Fugelsang, Anareas and Dale Chandler, with Daya Akuretiyagama. (1993), *Participation as Process—Process as Growth: What We* Can *Learn from Grameen Bank*, Bangladesh. Dhaka: Grameen Trust.

Ghatak, Maitreesh. (1999), "Group Lending, Local Information and Peer Selection", *J. Devel. Econ*., forthcoming.

Ghatak, Maitreesh and Timothy Guinnane. (1999), "The Economics of Lending with Joint Liability: Theory and Practice", *J. Devel. Econ.*, forthcoming.

Ghnsh, Parikshit and Debraj Ray. (1996), "Cooperation in Community Interaction without Information Flows", *Rev. Econ. Stud.*, 63, pp. 491-519.

— (1997), *"Information and Repeated Interaction: Application to Informal Credit Markets"*, Texas A&M and Boston University., Draft.

Ghate, Prabhu (2006), *Microfinance in India: A State of the Sector Report 2006.*

Goetz, Ann Marie and Rina Sen Gupta (1996), "Who Takes Credit? Gender, Power, and Control over Loan Use in Rural Credit Programs in Bangladesh", *World Development*, Vol. 24:1, pp. 45-63.

Graham, D.; Cameron Thraen and J. Paxton (2000), "Modelling Group Loan Repayment Behaviour: New Insights from Burkina Faso", *Economic Development and Cultural Change*, Vol. 48, No. 3, pp. 639-55.

Grameen Bank (1995), *"Phase III Project: Project Completion Mission, Final Report"*, Grameen Bank, pp. 1-6.

Guinnane, T. (1994), "A failed Institutional Transplant: Raiffeisen's Credit Cooperatives in Ireland, 1894-1914", *Explorations in Economic History*, Vol. 31, No. 1, pp. 38-61.

Gonzalez-Vega, Claudia; Mark Schreiner, Richard Meyer, Jorge Rodriguex-Meza, and Sergia Navajas (1997): *"BancoSol: The Challenge of Growth for Microfinance"*, in *Microfinance for the Poor?* Hartmut Schneider, ed. Paris: OECD. Grameen Bank (various years), *Annual Report*. Dhaka: Grameen Bank.

Guinnane, Timothy (1994), *"A Failed Institutional Transplant: Raiffeisen's Credit Cooperatives in Ireland, 1894—1914"*, *Explor. Econ. Hist.* 31, pp. 38-61.

————(1997), *"Cooperatives as Information Machines: German Rural Credit Cooperatives, 1883—1914"*, Econ. Dept., Yale University, Draft.

Gurgand, Marc; Glenn Pederson, and Jacob Yaron. (1994), *"Outreach and Sustainability of Six Rural Finance Institutions in Sub-Saharan Africa"*. Washington, DC, World Bank Discuss. Paper 248.

Hashemi, Syed M. and Sidney Schuler, (1997a), *"Sustainable Banking with the Poor: A Case Study of the Grameen Bank"*, WP #10, JSI Research and Training Institute,Washington, DC; 1997b. *"The Influence of Women's Changing Roles and Status in Bangladesh's Fertility Transition: Evidence from a Study of Credit Programs and Contraceptive Use"*, *World Devel.*, 25:4, pp. 563-75.

Hatch, John and Laura Frederick. (1998), *"Poverty Assessment by Microfinance Institutions: A Review of Current Practice"*, Microenterprise Best Practices Report, USAID/ Development Alternatives, Inc., Aug. [www.irnp.urgj.

Heckman, James J. and Jeffrey A. Smith. (1995), "Assessing the Case for Social Experiments," *J. Econ. Perspect.* 9:2, pp. 85-110.

Hoff, *Karla and Joseph Stiglitz. (1998)*, "Moneylenders and Bankers: Price-Increasing Subsidies in a Monopolistically Competitive Market", *J. Devel. Econ.* 55, pp. 485-518.

Hollis, Aidan and Arthur Sweetman. (1997), *"Micro- credit: What Can We Learn from the Past?"* Econ. Depts., University of Calgary and University of Victoria, Draft.

Hoff, K. and J. Stiglitz (1990), *"Introduction: Imperfect Information and Rural Credit Markets—Puzzles and Policy Perspectives"*, World Bank Economic Review, 4(3).

Hoff, Karla; Avishay Braverman and Joseph E. Stiglitz (1993), *The Economics of Rural Organization: Theory, Practice, and Policy*, New York: Oxford University Press.

Hollis, A. and Sweetman, A. (1997a), Microcredit in Pre-famine Ireland. University of Calgary, Department of Economics, Discussion Paper 97-05.

Hollis, A. and Sweetman, A. (1997b), *Complementarity, Competition and Institutional Development: The Irish Loan Funds through Three Centuries*. University of Calgary, Department of Economics, Discussion Paper 97-06.

Hollis, A. and Sweetman, A. (1998), Microcredit: What can we learn from the past? *World Development*.

Hossain, Mahabub. (1988), *"Credit for Alleviation of Rural Poverty: The Grameen Bank in Bangladesh"*, International. Food Policy Research Institute Res. Report 65, Washington, DC.

Huppi, Monica and Gershon Feder (1990), "The Role of Groups and Credit Cooperatives in Rural Lending", *World Bank Research Ohs.*, 5:2, pp. 187-204.

International Monetary Fund. (1996), *Intl. Financial Stat. Yearbook* XLIX. Washington, DC: IMF.

Ito, Sanae. (1998), *"The Grameen Bank and Peer Monitoring: A Sociological Perspective"*, Paper presented at the Workshop on Recent Research on Microfinance, University of Sussex. 13 February.

Iyer, Preeti R. (2006), "ICICI joins Hands with 3 VCs to Fund Microfinance Institutions", *The Economic Times*, June 5.

Jain, Pankaj. (1996), "Managing Credit for Rural Poor: Lessons from the Grameen Bank", *World Devel.*, 24:1, pp. 78-89.

Jain, Pankaj and Mick Moore (2003), 'What Makes Microcredit Programmes Effective? Fashionable Fallacies and Workable Realities', IDS working Paper 177, Institute of Development Studies, Brighton, Sussex, England.

Jauqette, J. S. (1984), "Women and Modernization Theory: A Decade of Feminist Criticism", *World Politics*, Vol. 34, No. 1, pp. 14-26.

Johnson, Susan (1997), "Micro Finance North and South:Contrasting Current Debates", mimeo, Centre for Development Studies, University of Bath.

Jam, Sanjay. (1999), "The Interaction of Formal and Informal Credit Markets in Developing Countries: Symbiosis *versus* Crowding Out", *J. Devel. Econ.*, 59:2, pp. 419-44.

Johnston, Don. (1996), "Notes on Bank Kredit Desa", Bank Rakyat Indonesia/Harvard Institute for Management. Development (Jakarta).

Khalily, MA. and R. Meyer. (1993), "The Political Economy of Loan Recovery", *Saving and Devel.* 17:1, pp. 23-38.

Kalpana, K. (2005), "Shifting Trajectories in Microfinance Discourse", *Economic and Political Weekly*, No. 51, December 17.

Kalpana, K. (2006), "Microcredit Wins Nobel: A Stocktaking", *Economic and Political Weekly* XLI (50), December 16-22, pp : 5110-5113.

Kumar, S. Nagesh (2006), "The Making of Debt Trap in Andhra Pradesh". *The Hindu*, April 20.

Khandker, Shahidur R., Baqui Khalily, and Zahed Kahn (1995), *Grameen Bank: Performance and Sustainability*, World Bank Discuss. Paper 306, Washington DC.

Lalonde, Robert (1995), "The Promise of Public Sector-Sponsored Training Programs", *J. Econ. Perspect.* 9:2, pp. 149-68.

Lakshman Nadini (2006), "India's Banks are Big of Microfinance", *Business Week*, August 22.

Light, Ivan and Michelle Pham. (1998), "Micro-Credit and Informal Credit in the United States: New Strategies for Economic Development", *J. Devel. Entrepreneurship*, 3:1.

Macmnko, J.; R. Rodriguez-Garcia, B. Schwethelm, and Stephen Smith, (1997), "Village Banking, Income Generation and Maternal and Child Health: Design and

Evaluation of a Social Science Experiment in Ecuador and Honduras", George Washington University., Draft.

Madajewicz, Margaret. (1997), "Capital for the Poor: The Role of Monitoring", Harvard University. Econ. Dept., Draft.

Matisi, Irnraii. (1997), "Repayment Performance of Grameen Bank Borrowers: The "Unzipped State", *Savings and Devel.* 4.

McGuire, Paul. (1998), "The Asian Financial Crisis—Some Implications for Microfinance", *Microbanking Bulletin*, Boulder, CO: Economics Institute.

McKernan, Signe-Mary (1996), "The Impact of Micro-Credit Programs on Self-Employment Profits: Do Non-Credit Program Aspects Matter", Brown University. (Draft).

Micro Banking Bulletin. (1998), Boulder, CO: Economics Institute.

Microcredit Summit Report. (1997),Washington, DC: RESULTS Educational Fund.

MkNelly, Barbara and Chatree Watetip. (1993), "Impact Evaluation of Freedom from Hunger's Credit with Education Program in Thailand", Freedom From Hunger Foundation. Davis, CA.

Moffit, Robert (1991), "Program Evaluation with Nonexperimental Data", *Evaluation Rev.* 15:3, June, pp. 291-314.

Molyneux (1992), "Mobilization without Emancipation: Women's Interests, State and Revolution in Nicaragua", *Feminist Studies*, Vol.11, No. 2, pp. 232.

Mark, Susan Gold and Jay Rosengard (1985), *Manual for Evaluating Small-Scale Enterprise Development Projects*, AID Program Design and Evaluation Report No. 6 Washington, DC: Agency for International Development.

Matin, I. (1998), "Mis-Targeting by the Grameen Bank — A Possible Explanation" *IDS Bulletin*, 29(4).

Montgomery, Richar (1995), "Disciplining or Protecting the Poor? Avoiding the Social Costs of Peer Pressure in Microcredit Schemes" International Development No. 12, Centre for Development Studies, University of Wales, Swansea.

Morduch, Jonathan and Stuart Rutherford (2003), "Microfinance:Analytical Issues for India", Background Paper Prepared for the World Bank, Washington DC.

Morduch, Jonathan. (1995), "Income Smoothing and Consumption Smoothing", *J. Econ. Perspect.*, 9:3, pp. 103-14.

—,(1998), "Does Microfinance Really Help the Poor? Evidence from Flagship Programs in Bangladesh", Hoover Institution, Stanford University., July, Draft.

——,(1999), "The Role of Subsidies in Microfinance: Evidence from the Grameen Bank", *J. Devel. Econ.*, Oct.

——,(2000),"The Microfinance Schism", *World Development*.

Mosley, Paul. (1996), "Metamorphosis from NGO to Commercial Bank: The Case of BancoSol in Bolivia", Chapter 10 in *Finance Against Poverty*. David Hulme and Paul Mosley, (eds.), London: Routledge.

Navajas, Sergio; Mark Schremner, Richard Meyer, Carlos Gonzalez-Vega, and Jorge Rodriguez Meza. (1998), "Microcredit and the Poorest of the Poor: Theory and Evidence from Bolivia", Dept. Agricultural, Environmental, and Development Econ., Ohio State University., Draft.

Nelson Eric R. and Bolnick Bruce R. (1986), "Survey Methods for Assessing Small Credit Programs Evaluating the Economic Impact of KIK/KMKP Credits". *J. Devel. Stud.*

Nelson, Candace; Barbara MCNelly, Kathleen Stack, and Lawrence Yanovitch. (1995), *Village Banking: The State of the Practice*. New York: Small Enterprise Education and Promotion (SEEP) Network.

The New York Times. (1997), "Micro-loans for the Very Poor", (editorial), February 16.

O'Brien, Timothy. (1998): "For Banks, A Big Nudge to do More: Communities Fear Lending Drop Off", *New York Times,* July 5, pp. Dl, D9.

Otero, Maria and Elisabeth Rhyne. (1994), *The New World of Microenterprise Finance.* West Hartford, CT: Kumarian Press.

Patten, Richard and Jay Rosengard. (1991), *Progress with Profits: The Development of Rural Banking in Indonesia.* San Francisco: ICS Press.

Patten, Richard H. and Donald R. Snodgrass. (1987), "Monitoring and Evaluating Kupedes (General Rural Credit) in Indonesia", HIID Development Discuss. Paper 249, Harvard University.

Pham, Alex. (1996), "Profile: Michael Chu; A Man of Principles—and Principals", *Boston Globe,* July 21, pp. Dl, D5.

Pitt, Mark and Shahidur Khandker. (1998a), "The Impact of Group-Based Credit Programs on Poor Households in Bangladesh: Does the Gender of Participants Matter?" *J. Polit. Econ.* 106:5, pp. 958—996.; (1998b): "Credit Programs for the Poor and Seasonality in Rural Bangladesh", Brown U. and World Bank, Draft.

Pearl, Daniel and Michael M Phillips (2001), 'Grameen Bank, Which Pioneered Loans for the Poor, Has Hit a Repayment Snag', The Wall Street Journal, *www.wsj.com.*

Pitt, M. and Khandker, S. (1998), "Impact of Group-based Credit Programs on Poor Households in Bangladesh: Does the Gender of Participants Matter?" *Journal of Political Economy,* Vol.106, No. 5, pp. 958-996.

Pitt, Mark; Shahidur Khandker, Signe-Mary McKernan, and M. Abdul Latif. (1999), "Credit Programs for the Poor and Reproductive Behaviour in Low Income Countries:

Are the Reported Causal Relationships the Result of Heterogeneity Bias?" *Demography*, Feb.

Prescott, Edward S. (1997), Group Lending and Financial Intermediation: An Example, *Fed. Reserve Bank of Richmond Econ. Quart.* 83:4, Fall, pp. 23-48.

Pulley, Robert (1989), "Making the Poor Creditworthy: A Case Study of the Integrated Rural Development Program in India", World Bank Discuss. Paper 58, Washington, DC.

Putnam, Robert (1993), *Making Democracy Work.* Princeton, NJ: Princeton University Press.

Rahman, A. (1999), "Microcredit Initiatives for Equitable and Sustainable Development: Who Pays?" *World Development*, Vol. 27, No. 1.

RBI (2005), "Report of the Internal Group to Examine Issues Relating to Rural Credit and Microfinance".

Rathgeber, E. (1990), "WID, WAD, GAD: Trends in Research and Practice", *Journal of Developing Areas*, Vol. 24, No. 4, pp. 489–502.

Reddy, Ravi (2006), 'MFI Suicides:60 Suicide Cases Reported", *The Hindu*, April 17.

Rutherford, Stuart (2006), "Grameen II: The First Five Years 2001-2005: A 'Grounded' view of Grameen's New Initiative", written for MicroSave with Md. Maniruzzaman, SK Sinha and Acnabin & Co, Dhaka, Bangladesh, February.

Rahman, Aminur. (1998), "Microcredit Initiatives for Equitable and Sustainable Development: Who Pays?" *World Devel.* 26:12.

Rashid, Mansoora and Robert M. Townsend (1993) "Targeting Credit and Insurance: Efficiency, Mechanism Design, and Program Evaluation", The World Bank and University of Chicago, Draft.

Robinson, Marguerite (1992), "Rural Financial Intermediation: Lessons from Indonesia", Part One. The

Bank Rakyat Indonesia: Rural Banking, 1970-91, Harvard Institute format. Development Discuss. Paper 434.

——,(1995), "Indonesia: The Role of Savings in Developing Sustainable Commercial Financing of Small and Micro Enterprises", in *New Perspectives on Financing Small Business in Developing Countries.* Ernst A. Brugger and Sarath Rajapatirana, eds. San Francisco: ICS Press.

Sadoulet, LoIc (1997), "The Role of Mutual Insurance in Group Lending", Department of Economics, Princeton University, Manuscript.

Schreiner, Mark (1997), A Framework for the Analysis of the Performance and Sustainability of Subsidised Microfinance Organisations with Application to BancoSol of Bolivia and Grameen Bank of Bangladesh. Unpublished Ph.D. Dissertation, The Ohio State University.

Schuler, Sidney Ruth; Syed M. Hashemi, and Ann P. Riley. (1996), "Rural Credit Programs and Women's Empowerment in Bangladesh", *World Devel.*, 24:4. pp. 635-53.

Sharma, Manohar and Manfred Zeller. (1996), "Repayment Performance in Group-Based Credit Programs in Bangladesh: An Empirical Analysis", FCND Discuss. Paper 15, Management of Food Policy Research Institute, Washington, D.C.

Stiglitz, Joseph. (1990), "Peer Monitoring and Credit Markets", *World Bank Econ. Rev.* 4:3, pp. 351-66.

Stiglitz, Joseph and Andrew Weiss. (1981), "Credit Rationing in Markets with Imperfect Information", *Amer. Econ, Rev.*, 71:3, pp. 393-419.

Standing, G. (1989), Global Feminization Through Flexible Labour. *World Development*, 17(7), 1077–1095.

Sebstad, Jennefer and Monique Cohen (2000), "Microfinance, Risk Management and Poverty" United States Agency for International Development and World Bank, Washington DC.

Snodgrass, Donald R. and J. Sebstad (2002), "Clients in Context: The Impacts of Microfinance in Three Countries", *Synthesis Report*, Assessing the Impact of Microenterprise Services (AIMS), Management Systems International, Office of Microenterprise Development, US Agency for International Development.

Stiglitz, J. (1989), Markets, Market Failures, and Development. *American Economic Review*, Vol. *7, No. 2,* pp. 197-203.

Stiglitz, J. (1990), Peer Monitoring and Credit Markets, *World Bank Economic Review,* Vol. 4, No. 3, pp. 351-66.

Stiglitz, Joseph (1974), "Incentives and Risk in Share Cropping", *Review of Economic Studies,* Vol. 41, pp. 219-55.

Surya, D. (2006), "Did Small Loans Lead to 7 Suicides?" *The Economic Times,* March 17.

Tenenbaum, Shelly (1993), *A Credit to Their Community: Jewish Loan Societies in the United States, 1880-1945.* Detroit: Wayne State University Press.

Tendler, J. (1988), "What Happened to Poverty Alleviation?" Paper delivered at the World Conference on Micro-Enterprises, Washington DC.

Varian, Hal. (1990), "Monitoring Agents with Other Agents", *J. Instit., Theoretical Econ.,* 146, pp. 153-74.

Vengroff, Richard and Lucy Greevey. (1994), "Evaluation of Project Impact: ACEP Component of the Community Enterprise Development Project", Report to USAID/ Dakar. University, Connecticut: Storrs.

Varian, H. R. (1990), "Monitoring Agents with Other Agents", *Journal of Institutional and Theoretical Economics,* Vol.146, pp. 153-74.

Varian, H. R. (1990), Monitoring Agents with Other Agents, *Journal of Institutional and Theoretical Economics*, Vol. 146, No. 1, pp. 153-74.

von Pishke, J. D., *et al.*, (eds.) (1983), *Rural Financial Markets in Developing Countries* Baltimore, MD: Johns Hopkins University Press.

von Pishke, J.D. (1991), *Finance at The Frontier: Debt Capacity and The Role of Credit in the Private Economy*, Washington, DC: The World Bank, EDI Development Studies.

Vogel, and C. McKean (1995), "Maximizing the Outreach of Microenterprise Finance: The Emerging Lessons of Successful Programs", USAID Program and Operations Assessment Report No. 10, Washington, DC.

Wenner, Mark D. (1995), "Group Credit: A Means to Improve Information Transger and Loan Repayment Performance", *J. Devel. Stud.* 32:2, pp. 264-81.

Woller, Gary; Christopher Dunford, and Warner Woodworth. (1999), "Where to Microfinance?" *Management Journal Econ. Devel.* Forthcoming.

Wood, Geoffrey and Iffath Sharif, (eds.), (1997), *Who Needs Credit? Poverty and Finance in Bangladesh*. Dhaka, University Press Ltd.

Woolcock, Michael. (1998), "Social Theory, Development Policy and Poverty Alleviation: A Comparative-Historical Analysis of Group-Based Banking in Developing Economies", Unpubished Ph.D. Dissertation, Dept. Sociology, Brown University.

Wenner, Mark D. (1995), "Group Credit: A Means to Improve Information Transfer and Loan Repayment Performance", *Journal of Development Studies*, Issue 32(2), December.

Williamson, J. (1996), Globalization, Convergence, and History, *Journal of Economic History*, Vol. 56, No. 2, pp. 277-306.

Wilson, E. (1977), *Women and the Welfare State*, London: Tavistock.

Woolcock, M. (1998), Social Capital and Economic Development: Toward A Theoretical Synthesis and Policy Framework, *Theory and Society*,Vol. 27,No. 2, pp. 151-208.

Woolcock, Michael J. M. (1999), Learning from Failures in Microfinance: What Unsuccessful Cases Tell Us about How Group- Based Programs Work, *American Journal of Economics and Sociology*, Vol. 58, No. 1, pp.17-42. http://links.istor.org/sici?sici—0002-9246%28199901%2958%3A1%3C17%3ALFFIMW%3E2.0.CO%3B2-E, accessed on 12.02.2004.

Woolcock, Michael. (1999), "Learning from Failures in Microfinance: What Unsuccessful Cases Tell Us About How Croup-Based Programs Work", *Amer. J. Econ. Sociology*, forthcoming.

Working Capital (1997), "Information Packet,", Winter/ Spring Materials, Cambridge, MA.

Wydick, W. Bruce. (1999), "Can Social Cohesion Be Harnessed to Repair Market Failures? Evidence from Group Lending in Guatemala", *Econ. J.*, 109:457, pp. 463-75.

Yaron, Jacob. (1992), "Successful Rural Finance Institution," World Bank Discuss. Paper 150, Washington, DC.

Yaron, Jacob; McDonald Benjamin, and Stephanie Charitonenko. (1998), "Promoting Efficient Rural Financial Intermediation", *World Bank lies. Observer*, Aug.

—., (1992): Successful rural financial institutions. World Bank Discussion Papers, No. 150 Washington, DC: World Bank.

Yunus, M. (2005), "Eliminating Poverty through Market-based Social Entrepreneurship", *Global Urban Development Magazine*, 1(1).

Yunus, M. (2006), "Grameen Bank At a Glance", *http://www.grameen-info.org/bank/GBGlance.htm.*

Yunus, Muhammad (2002), "Grameen Bank II: Designed to Open New Possibilities", *http://www.grameen-info.org/bank/bank2.html*

Yunus, Muhammad. (1995), [Testimony before the House of Representatives of the U.S.] Committee on Management of Relations, *Fed. News Service*, June 27.

Zaman, H. (2004), "The Scaling-up of Microfinance in Bangladesh: Determinants, Impact and Lessons", World Bank Policy Research Working Paper Series No. 3398, WB, Washington DC.

Zaman, Hassan (1999), "Assessing the Poverty and Vulnerability Impact of Micro-Credit in Bangladesh: A Case Study of BRAC", paper commissioned as background material for the WDR 2000-01, World Bank, Washington DC.

Zander, R. M., J. D. von Pischke and J. Yaron (1998), "Why Credit Project Repayment Performance Declines", *Savings and Development*, Vol. 22, No. 2, pp. 149-80.

Zaman, Hassan. (1997), "Micro-Credit Programmes: Who Participates and What Does it Matter?" *Who Needs Credit? Poverty and Finance in Bangladesh.* Geoffrey Wood and Iffath Sharif (eds.) Dhaka: University Press Ltd.

Zeller, Manfred, Akhter Ahmed, Suresh Babu, Sumiter Broca, Aliou Diagne, and Manohar Sharma. (1996), "Rural Financial Policies for Food Security for the Poor: Methodologies for a Multicountry Research Project", Management of Food Policy Research Inst., FCND Discuss. Paper 11.

Index